D1263928

DATE DUE

The Politics of Precaution

The Politics of Precaution

REGULATING HEALTH, SAFETY, AND ENVIRONMENTAL RISKS IN EUROPE AND THE UNITED STATES

David Vogel

PRINCETON UNIVERSITY PRESS

PRINCETON AND OXFORD

Copyright © 2012 by Princeton University Press
Published by Princeton University Press, 41 William Street, Princeton, New Jersey 08540
In the United Kingdom: Princeton University Press, 6 Oxford Street, Woodstock, Oxford-
shire OX20 1TW

press.princeton.edu

ISBN 978-0-691-12416-2

Library of Congress Cataloging-in-Publication Data

Vogel, David, 1947–
The politics of precaution : regulating health, safety, and environmental risks in Europe
and the United States / David Vogel.
    p. cm.
  Includes bibliographical references and index. ISBN 978-0-691-12416-2 (hardcover :
alk. paper)
  1. Consumer protection—Europe.   2. Consumer protection—United States.   3. Safety
regulations—Europe.   4. Safety regulations—United States.   5. Public health laws—
Europe.   6. Public health laws—United States.   7. Environmental policy—Europe.
8. Environmental policy—United States.   I. Title.
  HC110.C63V616   2012
  363.10094—dc23
                                                                    2011031843

British Library Cataloging-in-Publication Data is available

This book has been composed in Sabon

Printed on acid-free paper. ∞

Printed in the United States of America

10 9 8 7 6 5 4 3 2 1

To
Maximilien and Alexandre Girerd,
the future of transatlantic relations

Contents

Preface

THE IDEA BEHIND THIS book originated during the 2000–2001 academic year, which I spent on sabbatical in France. The almost daily media accounts of new food safety scares and the haste with which French politicians were competing with one another to propose ever more risk-averse regulations to address them made me feel as if I was in a time warp. I felt I was back in the United States during 1970, when President Richard Nixon and Democratic presidential aspirant Senator Edward Muskie of Maine had competed with each other over who was a stronger supporter of stringent emissions standards for motor vehicles. Living in Europe for a year made me more aware of the extent to which the salience of health, safety, and environmental risks had declined in the United States during the previous decade. This was in marked contrast to France, where Parisians, faced with renewed outbreaks of mad-cow and foot and mouth disease, were now asking each other, "what did your dinner have for dinner?" rather than asking, "what did you have for dinner?"

In 2003, I published an article in the *British Journal of Political Science* and a lengthier essay in the *Yearbook of European Environmental Law* that described how and explained why the politics of consumer and environmental risk regulation had changed on both sides of the Atlantic.[1] In the fall of 2004, Chuck Myers, the political science editor at Princeton University Press, invited me to expand these essays into a book. Its completion has been considerably delayed by three other projects: a book and several essays and articles on corporate social responsibility, a co-edited volume on food safety regulation in Europe, and a co-edited volume on transatlantic regulatory cooperation. But this delay has proved fortuitous. It has enabled me to draw on a considerable body of research published in the interval as well as more recent political and policy developments.

---

[1] "The Hare and the Tortoise Revisited: The New Politics of Consumer and Environmental Regulation in Europe," *British Journal of Political Science* 33, part 4 (October 2003): 557–80. Reprinted in *Environmental Risk*, vol. 2, ed. John Applegate (Burlington, VT: Ashgate, 2004) 481–504; Andrew Jordan, ed., *Environmental Policy in the European Union*, 2d ed. (London and Sterling, VA: Earthscan, 2005), 225–52; Cary Coglianese and Robert Kagan, eds., *Regulation and Regulatory Processes* (Burlington, VT: Ashgate, 2007), 101–26; Martin Levin and Martin Shapiro, eds., *Transtlantic Policymaking in an Age of Austerity* (Washington, DC: Georgetown University Press, 2004), 177–20. "Risk Regulation in Europe and the US," in *The Yearbook of European Environmental Law*, vol. 3, ed. H. Somsen (Oxford: Oxford University Press, 2003), 1–42.

The subject of risk regulation is highly contentious. Reasonable people can and do disagree about which health, safety, and environmental risks are credible and which risks governments should try to prevent or ameliorate. But this book is a work of analysis, not advocacy. Like any informed citizen, I have my own views, but this book does not attempt to argue or demonstrate which or whose risk regulations are "better" or "ill-informed." More stringent regulations may or may not be welfare-enhancing, and governments can err by regulating too little as well as too much. I have tried to describe and explain each of the risk regulations adopted—or not adopted—on either side of the Atlantic as fairly and objectively as possible. I leave it up to the reader to decide which particular risk regulations he or she considers salutary or unwarranted.

I am pleased to acknowledge a debt to several colleagues and friends, both at Berkeley and elsewhere, who took the time to read all or significant portions of various drafts of this manuscript and offer me the benefits of their comments and criticisms. The suggestions of Bob Kagan, Graham Wilson, Dan Kelemen, Tim Büthe, Sean Gailmard, Robert Falkner, Brendon Swedlow, Jonathan Wiener, Robert Van Houweling, Mark Pollack, Paul Pierson, Henrik Selin, Albert Alemanno, and Jonathan Zeitlin, along with the anonymous reviewers for Princeton University Press, and my editor at Princeton University Press, Chuck Myers, have made this a much better book than I could have written without their assistance. Needless to say, none of these individuals bears any responsibility for the final product.

Sections of this book draw on my previous research on consumer and environmental regulation, including *National Styles of Regulation: Environmental Policy in Great Britain and the United States*; *Fluctuating Fortunes: The Political Power of Business in America*; *Trading Up: Consumer and Environmental Regulation in A Global Economy*; "The Globalization of Pharmaceutical Regulation"; and "Trade and Environment in the Global Economy: Contrasting European and American Perspectives."[2] I also have used material from essays and articles I co-authored with Dan Kelemen, Michael Toffel, Diahanna Post, Nazli Uldere Aargon, Jabril

[2] *National Styles of Regulation: Environmental Policy in Great Britain and the United States* (Ithaca, NY: Cornell University Press, 1986); *Fluctuating Fortunes: The Political Power of Business in America* (New York: Basic Books, 1989); *Trading Up: Consumer and Environmental Regulation in a Global Economy* (Cambridge, MA: Harvard University Press, 1995); "The Globalization of Pharmaceutical Regulation," *Governance* 11, 1 (January 1998): 1–22; *Barriers or Benefits? Regulation in Transaltantic Trade* (Washington, DC: Brookings Institution Press, 1997); "Trade and Environment in the Global Economy: Contrasting European and American Perspectives," in *Green Giants? Environmental Policy of the United States and the European Union*, ed. Norman Vig and Michael Fauve (Cambridge, MA: MIT Press, 2004), 231–52.

Bensedrine, Ragner Lofstedt, and Olivier Cadot, as well as from two books I co-edited: *What's The Beef? The Contested Governance of Food Safety*, with Chris Ansell, and *Transatlantic Regulatory Cooperation: The Shifting Roles of the EU, the US, and California*, with Johan Swinnen.[3]

I benefited from the opportunity to present my analysis to seminars at the Haas School of Business and the Department of Political Science at the University of California, Berkeley, Boston University, the London School of Economics, the University of Michigan, Duke University, and Kings College, London.

In discussing the findings of this book to students and policy makers on both sides of the Atlantic, I was often struck by how many were unaware that during the three decades prior to around 1990, it was the United States that was more likely to adopt more stringent, innovative, and comprehensive regulations for addressing a wide range of national and global health, safety, and environmental risks than were most European governments and the European Community. I hope that this book contributes to a more informed understanding of regulatory policymaking on both sides of the Atlantic during the previous five decades.

Financial support for this project was generously provided by the Solomon P. Lee Chair at the Haas School of Business and the Committee on Research of the University of California, Berkeley. I have been privileged to spend my career at a university that has been so supportive of my research.

This book could not have been completed without the extraordinary research assistance of Victoria Kinsley. In addition to helping me collect research materials and put my references in order, she edited several drafts of each chapter. Karin Edwards prepared a number of research memos at the inception of this project, and Sanaz Mobasseri provided important research assistance. Peter Ryan ably assisted me in editing, and

---

[3] "Trading Places: The Role of the US and the EU in International Environmental Treaties" (with R. Dan Keleman), *Comparative Political Studies* 43, 4 (April 2010): 427–56; "Environmental Federalism in the European Union and the United States" (with Michael Toffel, Diahanna Post, and Naxli Z. Uludere Aragon), *A Handbook of Globalization and Environmental Policy: National Government Interventions in a Global Arena*, ed. Frank Wiken, Kees Zoeteman, and Joan Peters (Cheltenham, UK: Edward Elgar, 2011); "Comparing Risk Regulation in the United States and France: Asbestos, AIDS and Genetically Modified Agriculture" (with Jabril Bensedrine), *French Politics, Culture & Society* 20 (Spring 2002): 13–32; "The Changing Character of Regulation: A Comparison of Europe and the United States" (with Ragnar Lofstedt), *Risk Analysis* 21, no. 3 (2001): 399–416; "France, the United States, and the Biotechnology Dispute" (with Oliver Cadot), *Foreign Policy Studies*, Brookings Institution (January 2001); *What's the Beef? The Contested Governance of European Food Safety* (co-editor Chris Ansell) (Cambridge, MA: MIT Press, 2006); and *Transatlantic Regulatory Cooperation: The Shifting Roles of the EU, the US and California* (co-editor Johan Swinnen) (Cheltenham, UK: Edward Elgar, 2011).

substantially improving, the manuscript, and Karen Verde did an out-standing job editing the final draft.

As always, my greatest debt is to my wife Virginia, whose patience and encouragement provided me with the time and emotional support that made the writing of this book possible. Both of us are relieved by its completion.

I am delighted to dedicate this book to my twin grandsons, Max and Alex Girerd, who, because they were smart enough to be born to an American mother and a French father, enjoy citizenship on both sides of the Atlantic. One of my goals was to finish this book before they were able to read it, an objective which I have achieved. But I suspect it will be several years before they find it of interest, because, like Grandpa's other books, it has no pictures of trucks or animals—though it does discuss regulations that affect both.

In closing, my most heartfelt thoughts and deepest appreciation are for the tireless support and encouragement of my beloved son, Philip. I miss him more than words can ever say.

Berkeley, California
June 2011

The Politics of Precaution

CHAPTER ONE

The Transatlantic Shift in Regulatory Stringency

In 1962, the united states[1] enacted regulations for the approval of drugs that were more stringent than those of Great Britain and Germany.

In 1969, the United States banned the artificial sweetener cyclamate, which remains permitted in each member state of the European Union.[2]

In 1975, catalytic converters were required for all new cars sold in the United States; they were required for all new cars sold in the EU beginning in 1992.

In 1979, the plant-growth regulator Alar was banned in the United States; all but one European country as well as the EU permits its use.

In 1985, the EU prohibited the administration of growth hormones to beef cattle; the United States allows them.

In 1989, the United States eliminated the use of lead in gasoline/petrol. The EU ended its use of this fuel additive in 2005.

Since 1992, the United States has approved more than one hundred genetically modified (GM) varieties for planting, feed, or food; the EU has approved twenty-eight, most of which are not in commercial use. Virtually all processed food in the United States contains GM ingredients, while virtually none sold in the EU does.

In 1997, the EU ratified the Kyoto Protocol, which committed its member states to reduce their emissions of six greenhouse gases (GHG); the United States has not done so.

In 1999, the EU banned the use of six phthalates in children's products; the United States adopted a similar restriction in 2008.

In 2003, the EU banned the use of six hazardous materials in electrical and electronic products beginning in 2006; the United States still permits their use.

---

[1]Unless otherwise noted, the "United States" or the "U.S." refers to the American federal government.

[2]The term "European Union" did not formally come into use until 1993, when it was adopted as part of the Treaty on European Union or "Maastricht" Treaty signed in 1992; prior to that date, the EU was called the European Economic Community or EEC. However, for purposes of clarity, I have chosen to use the current name throughout the text, though some quotations refer to the "Community" or the "European Community."

In 2006, the EU significantly strengthened and broadened its health and environmental regulations for chemicals; the last comprehensive statutory reform of American chemical regulation took place in 1976.

These and other comparisons among health, safety, and environmental regulations in the United States and Europe are the subject of this book. It describes and explains why, during the last half century, citizens in Europe and the United States have frequently perceived, and policy makers have often responded differently to, many similar consumer and environmental risks—in some cases temporarily and in other cases over an extended period of time.

Within political systems, there are important linkages among many health, safety, and environmental risk regulations. Their public issue life cycles overlap and they often follow parallel or convergent political trajectories.[3] This means that if a government is adopting more stringent regulations toward some consumer or environmental risks caused by business, then it is also more likely to address other risks with similarly strong measures. Alternatively, if it is not stringently regulating a specific health, safety, or environmental risk, then it is also less likely to adopt more risk-averse regulations for others. In short, risk regulations are both interdependent and shaped by similar political developments. These can be stable for long periods of time, but the policy equilibriums that underlie them can also change significantly.

A noteworthy discontinuity in the politics of regulatory stringency took place on both sides of the Atlantic in about 1990. If a new risk regulation was enacted on either side of the Atlantic during the three decades prior to 1990, then it is *more likely* that the American standard was initially, and in some cases has remained, more risk averse. However, if it was adopted on either side of the Atlantic after 1990, then it is *more likely* that the regulation adopted by the European Union was initially, and has often remained, more risk averse.

Why, then, since 1990, has the EU more stringently regulated a number of health, safety, and environmental risks caused by business than the United States, including in several areas that were previously regulated more stringently by the United States? What affects changes in the public's demand for protective regulations and the willingness of policy makers to respond to them? What happened to disrupt the previous pattern of policymaking on both sides of the Atlantic? These important shifts in the stringency of new risk regulations in both the United States and the EU raise a broader question: what explains significant shifts in policy-linked issue life cycles?

---

[3] For an influential case study of a public issue life cycle in the United States, see Christopher Bosso, *Pesticides & Politics: The Life Cycle of a Public Issue* (Pittsburgh: University of Pittsburgh Press, 1987).

These are important and challenging questions. Each regulatory decision or non-decision has distinctive and multiple causes, and no parsimonious explanation or single theory can adequately account for all the policy outcomes that have taken place in both Europe and the United States since 1960. I have developed a "big picture" explanatory framework that focuses on the role and interaction of three factors: the extent and intensity of public pressures for more stringent or protective regulations, the policy preferences of influential government officials, and the criteria by which policy makers assess and manage risks. Since around 1990, each has changed significantly in both the United States and the EU.

Prolonged periods of relative regulatory stringency, such as that which occurred in the United States between roughly 1960 and 1990 and in Europe beginning around 1990, are typically characterized by strong public demands for more stringent regulations, by the influence of policy makers who are more supportive of stringent regulatory controls over business, and by decision-making criteria that promote or permit the adoption of highly risk-averse regulations. Alternatively, prolonged periods when relatively few stringent regulations are adopted, such as has occurred in the United States since around 1990, are typically characterized by weaker public demands for more stringent risk regulations, by the increased influence of policy makers opposed to expanding the scope or stringency of health, safety, and environmental risk regulation, and by decision-making criteria that make it more difficult for highly risk-averse regulations to be adopted.

THE TRANSATLANTIC SHIFT IN REGULATORY STRINGENCY

The Regulatory Leadership of the United States

For approximately three decades, the United States was typically one of the first countries to identify new health, safety, and environmental risks and to enact a wide range of stringent and often precautionary standards to prevent or ameliorate them. Several important American consumer safety and environmental regulations, including rules for the approval of new drugs; many pesticide, food safety, and chemical standards; controls on automobile emissions, including lead in gasoline/petrol; and restrictions on ozone-depleting chemicals, were among the most risk-averse in the world. "The United States was the clear global leader in environmental policy in this era, and many other countries copied its policy initiatives."[4]

---

[4]John Dryzek et al., *Green States and Social Movements: Environmentalism in the United States, United Kingdom, Germany, and Norway* (Oxford: Oxford University Press, 2003), 160.

The Policy Shift

Around 1990, the locus of transatlantic regulatory policy innovation and global regulatory leadership began to shift. While American policy makers previously had been "quicker to respond to new risks, more aggressive in pursuing old ones," more recently it is European policy makers who have been more likely to identify new risks and been more active in attempting to ameliorate existing ones.[5] Europe has not simply "caught up" to the United States; rather, many of the risk regulations adopted by the EU since 1990 are now more stringent and comprehensive than those of the American federal government. In "many policy areas [the EU] has taken over the role of world leader,"[6] a role formerly played by the United States.

The rate at which the federal government has adopted new stringent and comprehensive regulatory statutes and rules markedly declined after 1990. "Further building of the green state—at least at the national level—essentially stopped around 1990."[7] By contrast, "[the] EU surged forward," issuing a steady stream of "higher and tougher standards."[8] To borrow Lennart Lundqvist's influential formulation, which he used to contrast American and Swedish air pollution control standards during the 1970s, since around 1990 the American federal regulatory policy "hare" has been moving like a "tortoise," while the pace of the European "tortoise" resembles a "hare."[9] "It has become almost a constant trend to see more and more legislation being planned or adopted in Europe that sets higher standards to protect health or the environment than in the United States."[10]

Not all American risk regulations enacted between around 1960 and 1990 were more stringent than those adopted by any European country or the EU. For example, the EU's ban on beef hormones was adopted

[5]Sheila Jasanoff, " American Exceptionalism and the Political Acknowledgement of Risk," in *Risk*, ed. Edward Burger (Ann Arbor: University of Michigan Press, 1993), 63.

[6]Quoted in Jonathan Wiener, "Whose Precaution After All? A Comment on the Comparison and Evolution of Risk Regulatory Systems," *Journal of Comparative and International Law* 13 (2007): 214.

[7]Christopher Klyza and David Sousa, *American Environmental Policy, 1990–2006: Beyond Gridlock* (Cambridge, MA: MIT Press, 2008), 43.

[8]Quoted in Robert Donkers, "US Changed Course, and the EU Surged Forward," *Environmental Forum* (March/April 2006): 49. The second quotation is from Alasdair Young and Helen Wallace, *Regulatory Politics in the Enlarging European Union: Weighing Civic and Producer Interests* (Manchester and New York: Manchester University Press, 2000), 9.

[9]Lennart Lundqvist, *The Hare and the Tortoise: Clean Air Policies in the United States and Sweden* (Ann Arbor: University of Michigan Press, 1980).

[10]Theofanis Christoforou, "The Precautionary Principle, Risk Assessment, and the Comparative Role of Science in the European Community and the US Legal System," in *Green Giants? Environmental Policies of the United States and the European Union*, ed. Norman Vig and Michael Faure (Cambridge: MIT Press, 2004), 25.

in 1985, while during the 1970s and 1980s some European countries adopted restrictions on chemicals that were either comparable to or more risk-averse than those of the United States. Nor has every consumer safety or environmental regulation enacted by the EU or any of its member states since 1990 been more stringent than those adopted by the United States during the last two decades. For example, American mobile source or vehicular emission standards for health-related (criteria) pollutants have been steadily strengthened and remain stricter than those of the EU.

There has also been increased transatlantic convergence in some policy fields. Following changes in the regulatory policies of the Food and Drug Administration (FDA) that began in the late 1980s, but accelerated during the early 1990s, and the centralization of drug approval policies by the EU during the first half of the 1990s, the "drug lag" has disappeared: a new drug is now as likely to be first approved for use in the United States as in the EU. Both the EU and the United States have now imposed similar bans on lead and phthalates in children's products, with the United States acting a few months earlier in the former case and the EU nine years earlier with respect to the latter.

Some differences in European and American risk perceptions and regulations are long-standing. For example, the health risks of traditional or natural food preparations have been accepted in Europe since medieval times. In 1949, the American FDA banned the sale of any milk product unless all of its dairy ingredients had been pasteurized, while the production and sale of cheeses made from unpasteurized milk is permitted in the European Union.[11]

While not *every* European and American consumer or environmental risk regulation is consistent with a transatlantic shift in regulatory stringency since 1990, a *disproportionate number* of the consumer and environmental regulations adopted, or not adopted, on either side of the Atlantic during the last five decades do fit this pattern. For roughly three decades, *relatively few important* risk regulations adopted by either individual European countries or the EU were more stringent than those of the American federal government. But since 1990, a *significant number of important* risk regulations adopted by the EU fall into this category.

In some cases, such as chemical regulation and restrictions on ozone-depleting substances, there has been a literal "flip flop," with the United States and the EU switching places with respect to the adoption of more stringent and comprehensive regulations. But more commonly, the more

[11] Marsha Echols, "Food Safety Regulation in the European Union and the United States: Different Culture, Different Laws," *Columbia Journal of International Law* 4 (Summer 1998): 525–43.

stringent regulations adopted by the EU since around 1990 address risks that were not previously regulated on either side of the Atlantic. Recent European regulations are likely to be more stringent and often more precautionary than those of the United States for those health, safety, and environmental risks that have emerged or become more salient since around 1990, such as global climate change, genetically modified food and agriculture, antibiotics in animal feed, hazardous materials in e-waste, and chemicals in cosmetics.

INTERNATIONAL ENVIRONMENTAL AGREEMENTS

The transatlantic shift in regulatory stringency and global leadership is reflected in changes in the pattern of support for international environmental treaties.[12] Beginning in the 1970s, the United States and the member states of the EU closely cooperated in the establishment of numerous environmental agreements, with the United States often playing a leadership role. At the 1972 Stockholm United Nations international conference on the environment, the United States was "a strong proponent of international action to protect the environment."[13] The United States played a critical role in the negotiations that led to the adoption of the London Convention on Dumping at Sea (1972), the Convention on International Trade in Endangered Species and Fauna (1973), the decision of the International Whaling Commission to ban commercial whaling (1984), and the Montreal Protocol on Ozone Depleting Chemicals (1987).

The 1992 Rio "Earth Summit" marks a shift in global regulatory leadership from the United States to the EU. While every major environmental agreement supported by the United States has been ratified by the member states of the EU and/or the EU itself, since the early 1990s the United States has not ratified twelve important international environmental agreements ratified by the EU and/or its member states.[14] These include the 1992 Convention on Biological Diversity, the 1997 Kyoto Protocol on climate change, the 2000 Cartagena Protocol on Biosafety, and the 2001 Stockholm Convention on Persistent Organic Pollutants.[15]

---

[12]For a complete list of international environmental agreements since 1959 and their legal status in both the United States and Europe, see Miranda Schreurs, Henrik Selin, and Stacy VanDeveer, "Expanding Transatlantic Relations: Implications for Policy and Energy Policies," in *Transatlantic Environment and Energy Politics: Comparative and International Perspective*, ed. Schreurs, Selin, and VanDeveer (Burlington, VT: Ashgate, 2009), 8–9.

[13]Donkers, "US Changed Course, and the EU Surged Forward," 49.

[14]Schreurs, Selin, and VanDeever, "Expanding Transatlantic Relations," 8, 9.

[15]Robert Falkner, "American Hegemony and the Global Environment," *International Studies Review* 7 (2005): 585.

THE SHIFTING PATTERN OF TRANSATLANTIC TRADE DISPUTES

The shift in transatlantic regulatory stringency is also evident in the changing pattern of European-American trade disputes.[16] The earlier wave of disputes over the use of protective regulations as non-tariff trade barriers (NTBs) between Europe and the United States primarily involved European challenges to, or complaints about, the barriers to transatlantic commerce created by more stringent American regulatory standards. The EU and/or various European governments filed formal complaints with the General Agreement on Tariffs and Trade (GATT) over the excise tax provisions of the 1986 Superfund reauthorization, the American secondary boycott of tuna imports from Spain and Italy (which was based on the Marine Mammal Protection Amendments of 1984 and 1988), and American corporate fuel economy standards (CAFE), which were adopted in 1975 and amended in 1980. European officials were also highly critical of the testing requirements for new chemicals adopted by the United States in 1976.

However, more recent transatlantic regulatory-related trade disputes have revolved primarily around American complaints about the trade barriers posed by more stringent European regulations. In 1996, the United States filed a formal complaint with the World Trade Organization (WTO) that challenged the legality of the EU's ban on the sale of beef from cattle to whom growth hormones had been administered, which was applied to American beef imports in 1989. In 2003, the United States filed a complaint with the WTO challenging the EU's procedures for the approval of genetically modified organisms (GMOs), as well as the unwillingness of some member states to permit GMO varieties approved by the European Commission. In 2009, the American government filed a complaint with the WTO over the EU's refusal to permit imports of processed poultry treated with anti-bacterial chemicals such as chlorine dioxide, a processing method that differed from the method required by the EU in 1997.

American officials and firms have also complained to the EU about the obstacles to transatlantic commerce posed by a wide range of other European consumer and environmental regulations, including its ban

---

[16]For a summary and analysis of several trade disputes stemming from more stringent European standards, see Sebastiaan Princen, *EU Regulation and Transatlantic Trade* (Hague: Kluwer Law International, 2002). For case studies of EU-U.S. trade disputes over risk regulations, see David Vogel, *Benefits or Barriers? Regulation in Transatlantic Trade* (Washington, DC: Brookings Institution Press, 1998). For a more general discussion, which includes case studies of transatlantic risk-related disputes, see Ernst-Ulrich Petersmann and Mark Pollack, eds., *Transatlantic Economic Disputes: The EU, the US, and the WTO* (New York: Oxford University Press, 2003).

on the milk hormone rBST, its ban on human-use antibiotics as growth promoters in livestock feed, its electronic recycling requirements and bans on hazardous toxic substances in electronics, and the Registration, Evaluation, Authorization and Restriction of Chemicals (REACH), the EU's stricter and more comprehensive chemical approval and testing regulation adopted in 2006.[17] The latter statute was strongly opposed by American government officials and American-based chemical firms. American-based airlines have also objected to the 2008 decision of the EU to regulate the greenhouse gas emissions of foreign airlines that take off and land in Europe.

While previously it was the United States that had sought to protect its more stringent regulations from legal challenges by other countries, more recently the EU has become the primary advocate of changes in WTO rules in order to make them more compatible with the protective regulations it has adopted.[18] The EU has supported new trade rules that would clarify the relationship between the WTO and multilateral environmental agreements—many of which have been signed by the EU and several other countries but not the United States. It also has requested that the WTO accord legal recognition to the precautionary principle in order to "help ensure that measures based on a legitimate resort to the precautionary principle, including those that are necessary to promote sustainable development, can be taken without the risk of trade disputes."[19] The latter proposal has been strongly opposed by the United States on the grounds that it would become a "guise for protectionist measures."[20]

---

[17] For an extensive list of American business criticisms of EU regulatory policies, their lack of scientific basis, and the harm they pose to American firms, see *Looking Behind the Curtain: The Growth of Trade Barriers that Ignore Sound Science* (Washington, DC: National Foreign Trade Council, 2003); Lawrence Kogan, *Unscientific "Precaution": Europe's Campaign to Erect New Foreign Trade Barriers* (Washington, DC: Washington Legal Foundation, 2003); *EU Regulation, Standardization and the Precautionary Principle: The Art of Crafting a Three-Dimensional Trade Strategy That Ignores Sound Science* (Washington, DC: American Foreign Trade Council, 2003); Lawrence Kogan, *Precautionary Preference: How Europe's New Regulatory Protectionism Imperils American Free Enterprise* (Princeton, NJ: Institute for Trade, Standards and Sustainable Development, 2005).

[18] For a more detailed discussion of the shifts in European and American positions on the trade rules governing consumer and environmental regulations as non-tariff trade barriers, see David Vogel, "Trade and the Environment in the Global Economy: Contrasting European and American Perspectives," in *Green Giants? Environmental Policies of the United States and the European Union,* ed. Norman Vig and Michael Faure (Cambridge, MA: MIT Press, 2004), 231–52. See also *EU's Environmental Agenda* (Cuts Centre for International Trade, Economics & Environment, 2001), and Dirk De Bievre, "The EU Regulatory Trade Agenda and the quest for WTO Enforcement," *Journal of European Public Policy* 13, 6 (September 2006): 851–966.

[19] Quoted in Vogel, "Trade and the Environment in the Global Economy," 252.

[20] Quoted in ibid.

THE PRECAUTIONARY PRINCIPLE

The EU's adoption of the precautionary principle has become a major focus of transatlantic tension in other forums as well. It reflects and has reinforced an important difference between the EU and the United States about the appropriate criteria for regulating risks. The precautionary principle has increased the discretion of Europeans policy makers by enabling them to impose restrictions on commercial activities whose risks are uncertain, unproven, or disputed. The application of this principle underlies many of the more stringent risk regulations adopted by the EU. The precautionary principle has in turn been strongly criticized by American-based firms and American government officials. They have argued that it undermines the importance of scientific risk assessments as a guide to risk management decisions and is likely to lead to regulations based on public fears or "phantom risks" rather than on "sound science."[21]

These transatlantic differences in risk assessment criteria have become highly contentious. As Jonathan Wiener notes:

> Some observers see a civilized, careful Europe confronting a risky, reckless and violent America. To this group, the precautionary principle is an antidote to industrialization, globalization, and Americanization. On the other hand, other observers see a statist, technophobic, protectionist Europe trying to rise to challenge a market-based, scientific, entrepreneurial America. To this group, the precautionary principle is an obstacle to science, trade, and progress.[22]

According to Alan Larson, the former U.S. Under Secretary of State:

> For some in Europe, the "precautionary principle" appears to mean that when it suits European authorities, they may withhold approval until the risk assessment process has convinced even the most irrational consumer of the absence of even the most hypothetical risk of the most remote theoretical uncertainty.[23]

---

[21] For defenses of its approach to risk assessment and management, see, for example, Carolyn Raffensperger and Joel Tickner, eds., *Protecting Public Health and the Environment: Implementing the Precautionary Principle* (Washington, DC: Island Press, 2003); Joel Tickner, ed., *Environmental Science and Public Policy* (Washington, DC: Island Press, 2003); and Nancy Myers and Carolyn Raffensperger, eds., *Precautionary Tools for Reshaping Environmental Policy* (Cambridge, MA: MIT Press, 2006). For criticism, see, for example, Frank Ross, "Paradoxical Perils of the Precautionary Principle," *Washington and Lee Law Review*, 21 (1996): 851–925; Julian Morris, ed., *Rethinking Risk and the Precautionary Principle* (Oxford: Butterworth-Heinemann, 2000); and Cass Sunstein, *Laws of Fear: Beyond the Precautionary Principle* (Cambridge: Cambridge University Press, 2005).

[22] Jonathan Wiener, "Whose Precaution After All? A Comment on the Comparison and Evolution of Risk Regulatory Systems, *Journal of Comparative and International Law* 13 (2007): 214–15.

[23] Quoted in M. Eli, "The Precautionary Principle—What the US Thinks," *European Affairs* 1, no. 2 (1987): 85.

But Pascal Lamy, the former EU trade commissioner, counters that, "in the U.S. they believe that if no risks have been proven about a product, it should be allowed. In the EU it is believed that something should not be authorized if there is a chance of risk."[24]

In many respects, we have come full circle: many of the criticisms by American officials of the more stringent risk regulations recently adopted by the European Union echo those made earlier by European officials about many American ones. Formerly, it was Europeans who often accused Americans of acting too hastily to impose highly stringent risk regulations that lacked adequate scientific justification. More recently, American officials and firms have criticized many of the more stringent risk regulations adopted by the EU in identical terms.

HISTORICAL PARALLELS AND DISCONTINUITIES

Parallels

There are a number of parallels between the periods of relative regulatory stringency on both sides of the Atlantic. During the 1970s and 1980s, American regulatory policies often served as a benchmark for European consumer and environmental activists: they often criticized the EU for its unwillingness to adopt regulatory standards as stringent as those of the United States, most notably for automotive emissions, the lead content of fuel, and chemicals that harmed the ozone layer. More recently, many American consumer and environmental activists have urged the United States to follow Europe's regulatory lead.[25] They have criticized American policy makers for not giving Americans the same level of environmental, health, and safety protection now enjoyed by citizens of the EU.[26] At the same time, many of the criticisms previously made about many American protective regulations, namely that they were often unnecessarily strict, too burdensome, and diminished rather than enhanced public welfare, have also been made about many European ones. [27]

[24] Wiener, "Whose Precaution After All?" 213–14.

[25] See, for example, Myers and Raffensperger, eds., *Precautionary Tools for Reshaping Environmental Policy*.

[26] See, for example, Mark Shapiro, *Exposed: The Toxic Chemistry of Everyday Products: Who's at Risk and What's at Stake for American Power* (White River Junction, VT: Chelsea Green Publishing, 2007).

[27] For American criticisms of American risk regulations, see, for example, Harvey Sapolsky, ed., *Consuming Fears: The Products of Product Risks* (New York: Basic Books, 1986); Edith Efron, *The Apocalyptics: Cancer and the Big Lie* (New York: Simon & Schuster, 1984); and Michael Fumento, *Science Under Siege: Balancing Technology and the Environment* (New York: William Morrow, 1993). For European criticisms of European ones, see Frank Furedi, *Culture of Fear: Risk Taking and the Morality of Low Expectation* (London:

During both periods of relative regulatory stringency, regulatory policymaking became more centralized, moving from states to the federal government in the United States and from member states to the EU, though both American states and national governments in Europe continue to play important policy roles.[28] This centralization of regulatory policymaking played an important role in the strengthening of many regulatory standards in the United States and the EU. However, while the regulatory policy regime established by the federal government during the late 1960s and early 1970s remains in place, the policies it produced changed substantially after 1990.

Discontinuities

There is, however, an important difference between the two periods. Many of the relatively stringent American regulations enacted during the 1970s and 1980s either directly or indirectly influenced European regulatory policies. "European states were heavily influenced by U.S. environmental policy developments in the 1960s and 1970s. Many policy ideas and programs diffused across the Atlantic."[29] During the 1970s, Sweden's automotive emission standards were modeled on those of the United States, while the National Environmental Policy Act (NEPA) of 1969 shaped the development of environmental policy in Germany. America's more stringent automobile emissions standards contributed to the EU's decision to progressively strengthen its own emissions standards, including for restrictions on lead in motor fuels. The EU's Sixth Amendment, enacted in 1979, which tightened controls over the approval of new chemicals, was a direct response to the more stringent regulatory standards of the Toxic Substances Control Act (TSCA), enacted by the United States three years earlier. America's restrictions on ozone-depleting chemicals also shaped subsequent policy developments in Europe. In fact, during the 1980s some European policy makers argued:

Cassell, 1997); Christopher Booker and Richard North, *Scared to Death: From BSE to Global Warming: Why Scares Are Costing Us the Earth* (London: Continuum, 2007); and Morris, ed., *Rethinking Risk and the Precautionary Principle.*

[28] For an analysis of the legal and policy implications of this development, see R. Daniel Keleman, "Environmental Federalism in the United States and the European Union," in *Green Giants? Environmental Policies of the United States and the European Union,* ed. Norman Vig and Michael Faure (Cambridge, MA: MIT Press, 2004), 113–34. For a more extensive analysis of European regulatory federalism that demonstrates its similarities to the United States, see R. Daniel Kelemen, *The Rules of Federalism: Institutions and Regulatory Politics in the EU and Beyond* (Cambridge, MA: Harvard University Press, 2004).

[29] Schreurs, Selin, and VanDeever, "Expanding Transatlantic Relations," 7.

With the advent of global markets, the standard of product acceptability for international consumers would be increasingly set by the country with the most stringent pollution control standards. Thus . . . Europe would only be able to take full advantage of economies of scale in globally competitive markets provided that it legislated *for high environmental standards on a par with those found . . . in the USA.*[30]

More recently, the EU's decision to employ a cap-and-trade scheme for regulating greenhouse gas emissions from stationary sources drew upon the successful emissions trading schemes established by the Clean Air Act Amendments of 1990. The EU's "Better Regulation" initiatives have also been influenced by American administrative practices.

By contrast, there has been much less regulatory policy diffusion *from* the EU *to* the American federal government. The United States has affected European regulatory policies over the past five decades far more than it has been affected by them. With the notable exception of American drug approval policies—which have drawn on and been influenced by European policy approaches—European regulatory policies and politics have had much less national policy impact in the United States than American regulatory policies previously had in Europe. Rather, as before around 1990, federal regulatory policies remain relatively autonomous: they are shaped primarily by domestic politics.

The EU's Global Regulatory Impact

The response—or lack thereof—of Washington to Brussels is atypical. For the EU has been highly successful in "exporting" many of its regulations to other countries. The European Commission has repeatedly urged other countries to adopt its more stringent consumer and environmental standards and has put considerable efforts into encouraging them to do so. As Rockwell Schnabel, the former U.S. ambassador to Brussels, observes, "Europe is increasingly seeking to act as the world's economic regulator."[31]

The EU's active efforts to "globalize" its protective regulations stem from several motives. One is economic. Just as the harmonization of national regulatory requirements creates a level playing field for firms within the EU, so does the adoption of European regulations by other

---

[30]Emphasis added. Quoted in Albert Weale, "Environmental Rules and Rule-Making in the European Union," in *Environmental Policy in the European Union: Actors, Institutions and Processes*, ed. Andrew Jordan (London: Earthscan, 2002), 204.

[31]Tobias Buck and George Parker, "Washington Bridles at EU's Urge to Regulate," *Financial Times*, May 12, 2006.

countries mean that the global competitors of European firms will be forced to meet similar requirements in their home markets. Another is defensive: the more countries that adopt its regulations, the greater is their legitimacy. It is "a lot harder to argue that a risk management regime is unnecessary, disproportionate or unfair if it is endorsed by a significant proportion of the world's population."[32]

The EU's efforts to export its regulations are "an attempt to reel other regions into the European sphere of influence." They are a key component of its

> ... strategy to increase stability in the regions surrounding the EU through the regularization of public administration along a familiar format, and a way of creating kinship and interdependence by opening scope for cooperation and exchange, in which the EU, as the original architect of the regulatory format, is poised to take a central role.[33]

They represent a form of "empire building" through the exercise of "soft" power.[34] The EU's "global [regulatory] project has ... given Europe's elites a new mission."[35] It has enabled the EU "to carve out an identity and a profile for itself as a 'normative' or 'civilian' power on the world stage."[36]

The significant expansion of the EU's membership itself has directly expanded the geographic scope of Brussels' regulatory impact, as its twelve accession states are brought into compliance with the *acquis communautaire*, the body of EU regulations and directives which are legally binding on all member states. Because of their extensive commercial ties with the EU, many of the risk regulations of Norway and Switzerland are similar to those of the EU, and many Russian regulations have been based on those adopted by Brussels.

But the geographic impact of EU regulations extends beyond Europe. As a report to the European Commission observed, "frequently the world looks to Europe and adopts the standards that are set here."[37] Many countries have adopted EU regulations in order to retain access to its large internal market. For global firms, adopting EU rules confers an important advantage: because they are typically the world's most stringent, if their

---

[32] Veerle Heyvaert, "Globalizing Regulation: Reaching Beyond the Borders of Chemical Safety," *Journal of Law and Society* 36, no. 1 (March 2009): 116.

[33] Ibid., 116–17.

[34] Ibid., 116.

[35] J. Zielonka, "Europe as a Global Actor: Empire by Example," *International Affairs* 84, no. 3 (2008): 479.

[36] R. Daniel Kelemen, "Globalizing European Union Environmental Policy," *Journal of European Public Policy* 17, no. 3 (2010): 338.

[37] Tobias Buck, "Standard Bearer: How the European Union Exports its Laws," *Financial Times*, July 10, 2007.

products comply with EU standards, they can be marketed anywhere in the world.

The EU's strong support for multilateral environmental agreements has been a critical component of its efforts to "manage globalization" and assert a leadership role in global regulatory governance.[38] "The EU has been the chief *demander* of every major environment agreement since the early 1990s."[39] It has played an active role in promoting global agreements that are based on its own regulatory policies, including for biodiversity and biosafety, hazardous waste exports, global climate change, and persistent organic pollutants. A number of these treaties explicitly reference the precautionary principle, which the EU has sought to make an international legal norm. This principle is now incorporated in more than fifty international agreements.

Government regulation of business represents one of the EU's most successful "exports." "Over the last decade, [the EU] has proven that it has the capacity to shape international economic governance across a host of regulatory domains."[40] The marked increase in Europe's global regulatory influence, which extends beyond health, safety, and environmental regulations and includes, for example, anti-trust policy, data policy, data privacy, and technical standards for automobiles and mobile telephones, is obviously linked to the large size of the EU's internal market, especially following the EU's expansion to central Europe.

But this is only part of the explanation. For "a sizeable market must be coupled with powerful and capable regulatory institutions."[41] The growth in the EU's regulatory capacities has also been critical. The institutional capacities and legal principles that have been developed to create and govern a single market among the EU's member states have given EU officials the technical and administrative expertise to promote global regulatory policy coordination.[42] European officials have taken many of

---

[38]Kelemen, "Globalizing EU Environmental Policy," 336; see also Wade Jacoby and Sophie Meunier, "Europe and the Management of Globalization," *Journal of European Public Policy* 17, no. 3 (2010): 299–317.

[39]Emphasis in original Kelemen, "Globalizing," 337.

[40]Abraham Newman, *Protectors of Privacy: Regulating Personal Data in the Global Economy* (Ithaca, NY: Cornell University Press, 2008), 121.

[41]David Bach and Abraham Newman, "The European Regulatory State and Global Public Policy: Micro-institutions, Macro-influence," *Journal of European Public Policy* 14, no. 6 (September 2007): 82.

[42]For an analysis of the EU's regulatory architecture, and why it readily lends itself to adoption by other countries, see Charles Sabel and Jonathan Zeitlin, "Learning from Difference: The New Architecture of Experimentalist Governance in the EU," *European Law Journal* 14, no. 3 (May 2008): 27–327; and Charles Sabel and Jonathan Zeitlin, eds., *Experimentalist Governance in the European Union: Towards a New Architecture* (Oxford University Press, 2010).

the principles and practices that underlie "vertical" regulatory integration within Europe and extended them "horizontally" outside its borders.

As a result of the EU's economic importance—with its expansion to twenty-seven countries the EU's GDP is now roughly 30 percent larger than that of the United States and its population is twice as large—the growth of its regulatory capacity, *and* the relative stringency of its regulatory standards, global business regulations are increasingly being "made in Brussels."[43] As the *Wall Street Journal* observes, "Americans may not realize it, but the rules governing the food they eat, the software they use and the cars they drive increasingly are set in Brussels."[44] European regulations have forced "changes in how industries around the world make plastics, electronics, toys, cosmetics and furniture."[45]

According to an American corporate lobbyist based in Brussels, "Twenty years ago, if you designed something to U.S. standards you could pretty much sell it all over the world. Now the shoe is on the other foot."[46] Jeffrey Immelt, the chairman and CEO of General Electric, observes that "Europe in many ways is the world's global superpower. It can speak with one voice and a degree of certainty."[47] For many of GE's businesses, ranging from light bulbs to plastic, "almost 99% of new regulations will, over time, come from the EU."[48] The successful global diffusion of many European regulatory policies also means that many important American environmental, health, and safety standards are not only less stringent and comprehensive than those of the EU, but that some are now weaker than those of many developed and developing countries, including China.

Alternative Mechanisms of Policy Diffusion

As a response to a perceived regulatory vacuum at the national level, a number of American states have adopted protective regulations that are similar to and often modeled on those of the EU. Several American states have imposed restrictions on greenhouse gas emissions, banned some heavy metals from landfills, required manufacturers to take back electronic equipment for recycling, and banned various hazardous substances and chemicals restricted by the EU but not by the federal government. The EU's regulatory influence has been felt most strongly in California,

[43] "Charlemagne: Brussels Rules OK," *The Economist*, September 22, 2007.

[44] Brandon Mitchener, "Increasingly, Rules of Global Economy Are Set in Brussels," *Wall Street Journal*, April 23, 2002.

[45] Marla Cone, "Europe's Rules Forcing US Firms to Clean Up," *Los Angeles Times*, May 16, 2005.

[46] Mitchener, "Increasingly, Rules of Global Economy Are Set in Brussels."

[47] Marc Gunther, "Cops of the Global Village," *Fortune*, June 27, 2005.

[48] Mitchener, "Increasingly, Rules of Global Economy Are Set in Brussels."

historically America's "greenest" state, which has adopted a wide range of risk regulations similar to and often modeled on those of the EU.[49]

The dynamics of "trading up" or the ratcheting of regulatory standards upward thus continues, but the nature and mechanisms of global regulatory emulation and policy diffusion have shifted.[50] Now it is the EU, rather than the American federal government, whose regulatory policies are playing an important role in strengthening the risk regulations of many of its trading partners. The "California effect," a term that describes the process by which a government's more stringent regulatory standards are diffused to other political jurisdictions, has become the "EU effect." While California formerly served as a vehicle for the "export" of more stringent American environmental standards *to* Europe, more recently it has become an "importer" of several more risk-averse and comprehensive regulations *from* Europe.

In addition to changing what products they produce or how they produce them in order to retain access to the EU's large internal market, many global firms have also chosen to comply with some, or all, EU regulations for many of the products they sell outside Europe, including in the United States. They have done so both to protect their global brands and reputations and because it is often more efficient for them to market similar products globally. Many American food processors and retailers also produce and sell food products that conform to European health, safety, and environmental standards. These private, market-based forms of "trading up" have reduced the gap between some European standards and American business practices.

Clarifying the Argument

The fact that many European protective regulations are now more stringent than American ones does *not* mean that European consumer and environmental regulations are "better." Whose regulations are "better" or "worse" depends on one's policy preferences and values. If one considers more stringent or precautionary regulations to be welfare-enhancing, then the United States was formerly "ahead" of Europe, but now "lags behind" the EU. However, if one is more skeptical of the benefits of more stringent regulations, then the recent pattern of American regulatory policymaking would be considered salutatory. Supporters of more stringent

---

[49] Jim Wasserman, "California Becoming Nation's New Gateway for European Environmental Laws," *SF Environment*, July 24, 2003.

[50] David Vogel, *Trading Up: Consumer and Environmental Regulation in a Global Economy* (Cambridge, MA: Harvard University Press, 1995).

regulations would like the United States to "catch up" to Europe by adopting its precautionary approach to many health, safety, and environmental risks, while critics of European regulatory policies hope that the EU will emulate the United States by relying more on scientific-based risk assessments and cost-benefit analyses.

Since around 1990, in part as a response to many widely publicized examples of "over-regulation," American policy makers have placed more emphasis on avoiding false positives, i.e., unnecessarily stringent regulations (Type I policy errors), while their European counterparts, responding to a wide range of policy failures attributed to "under-regulation," have placed greater priority on reducing false negatives, i.e., insufficient stringent regulations (Type II policy errors). Defenders of more stringent regulations tend to emphasize the risks of false negatives, while critics of protective regulations focus on the shortcomings of false positives.

But both kinds of policy errors can be harmful. The harms of false negatives include exposing both citizens and the natural environment to preventable, and possibly irreparable, risks, while the harms of false positives include imposing unnecessary costs on both producers and consumers, reducing technological innovation, and needlessly exacerbating public anxieties. Moreover, there are often risk-risk tradeoffs: reducing some risks can increase others. For example, making it more difficult to approve new drugs may deprive patients of helpful medicines. The use of diesel engines promotes fuel economy but adversely affects ambient air pollution, while restrictions on diesel engines improves local air quality but also increases emissions of greenhouse gases.

Citizens, policy makers, managers, and scientists in both Europe and the United States can and do disagree about which specific regulations adopted, or not adopted, on either side of the Atlantic during the last five decades are in the public interest. While the science of risk assessment has become highly sophisticated, risk assessments can be interpreted differently or based on different data, assumptions, questions, or values, and scientists themselves may not always agree. In the face of scientific uncertainty and public pressures, policy makers may choose to be more or less risk-averse. As Mary Douglas and Aaron Wildavsky observe, "Acceptable risk is a matter of judgment and . . . judgments differ."[51] As I note in the preface, the purpose of this book is not to demonstrate or determine whose or which risk regulations are "better." It is rather to describe and explain many of the often different regulatory choices made by the United States and Europe during the previous five decades.

[51] Mary Douglas and Aaron Wildavsky, *Risk and Culture* (Berkeley: University of California Press, 1982), 194.

An exhaustive statistical comparison of risk assessment and regulation in the United States and the EU concludes, "by far the most common pattern we identified . . . is that the United States and Europe are equally precautionary over a thirty-five-year period."[52] This research also finds that, according to one measure, "the United States exhibited greater precaution than Europe from 1970 through the late 1980s, including increasing relative U.S. precaution during 1980–89, and that Europe became relatively more precautionary during the 1990s, and early 2000s."[53] While the latter finding is broadly consistent with my analysis, the relevance of this research to my study is limited by the fact that it also includes risks such as crime and violence, war, security, and terrorism. The claim that there has been a temporal change in European and American regulatory stringency is explicitly challenged by Jonathan Weiner,[54] but his analysis also includes a number of policies that fall outside the scope of my analysis, including speed limits, teenage consumption of alcohol and tobacco, choking hazards embedded in food, gun ownership, restraints on potentially violent persons, and terrorism.

I do not describe or attempt to explain risk regulations in general, or compare policy responses to very different kinds of risks. Rather, my focus is on a subset of risks, namely those that involve health, safety, and environmental risks caused by business. Public policies toward them follow similar political dynamics that do not necessarily hold for public policies toward other kinds of risks.

The list of other risks to which the public may be exposed, and which governments may or may not address, is substantial: it includes different kinds of crime, guns, sexually transmitted diseases, other communicable diseases, the consumption of drugs and alcohol, vaccines, financial fraud and excessive financial risk-taking, lack of access to medical care, unemployment, inflation, natural disasters, poverty, energy dependence, and domestic and international terrorism—to name but a few.[55]

But European and American approaches toward health, safety, and environmental risks caused by business *cannot* be extrapolated to their policies toward the many other kinds of risks citizens may face. For example, American and European policy responses to the risks posed by

---

[52]Brendon Swedlow et al., "Theorizing and Generalizing about Risk Assessment and Regulation through Comparative Nested Analysis of Representative Cases," *Law & Policy* 31, no. 2 (April 2009): 252. For an earlier and broader version of their analysis, see James Hammitt et al., "Precautionary Regulation in Europe and the United States: A Quantitative Comparison," *Risk Analysis* 25, no. 5 (2005): 1215–28.

[53]Brendon Swedlow et al., "Theorizing and Generalizing about Risk Assessment," 251.

[54] See Jonathan Wiener, "Whose Precaution After All?" 225–43.

[55]For a broader analysis of the role of government in responding to the risks faced by their citizens, see David Moss, *When All Else Fails: Government as the Ultimate Risk Manager* (Cambridge, MA: Harvard University Press, 2002).

genetically modified crops and food on one hand, and international terrorism on the other, represent mirror images of each other.[56] The American case for the invasion of Iraq was in part based on precisely the same precautionary principle that the EU has invoked to justify its restrictions on genetically modified agriculture, namely that the lack of clear evidence of harm is not evidence of the absence of harm. As President George W. Bush put it, "if we wait for threats to fully materialize, we will have waited too long."[57] His position precisely echoes the support for precautionary consumer and environmental regulations by Robert Coleman, the European Commission's director general for health and consumer protection, who argues, "those in public office have a duty not to wait until their worst fears are realized."[58]

As one journalist observed: "President Bush argued that the risk of WMDs [Weapons of Mass Destruction] was great enough to warrant an attack, without absolute proof that Iraq was hiding such weapons . . . That's the PP [precautionary principle], American style."[59] In the case of the war in Iraq, many European critics of American policy argued that an invasion was not justified because there was insufficient evidence that Iraq had WMDs. Likewise, many Americans have criticized European policies toward GMOs on the grounds that agricultural biotechnology should not be restricted because there is insufficient evidence that it threatens consumer safety or biodiversity. Thus, while policy makers on both sides of the Atlantic may believe that "it is better to be safe than sorry," they have applied this precautionary principle to different kinds of risks. (In light of the fact that no weapons of mass destruction were found in Iraq, the United States arguably made an important risk management decision based on a false positive policy error.)

In brief, my argument is not that the EU has become more risk-averse than the United States, but rather that it has become more risk-averse

---

[56]This analysis is developed in more detail in Diego Fossati, *Theoretical Perspectives on Risk Regulation: A Transatlantic Comparative Analysis in Two Policy Areas* (Raleigh, NC: Lulu.com, 2006). For a similar comparison of European and American approaches to regulatory and non-regulatory risks, see Cass Sunstein, "On the Divergent American Reactions to Terrorism and Climate Change," *AEI-Brookings Joint Center for Regulatory Studies*, Working Paper 06-13 (May 2006).

[57]Wiener, "Whose Precaution After All?" 229.

[58]Samuel Loewenberg, "Old Europe's New Ideas," *Sierra Magazine*, January/February 2004, available at http://www.samloewenberg.com/articles/sierraeuenvironmental.html, accessed 11/20/2010.

[59]Samuel Loewenberg, "Precaution is for Europeans," *New York Times*, May 29, 2003, 4, 14. For a more extensive analysis of the adoption of the European-style precautionary principle in U.S. national security policy, see Jessica Stern and Jonathan Wiener, "Precaution Against Terrorism," in *Managing Strategic Surprises: Lessons from Risk Management and Risk Assessment*, ed. Paul Bracken, Ian Bremmer, and David Gordon (Cambridge: Cambridge University Press, 2008), 110–83.

toward a broad range of health, safety, and environmental risks caused by business activities.

THE SCOPE OF THE BOOK

The next chapter discusses several alternative explanations for the divergence in transatlantic risk regulation and then further develops my own explanation for the policy shifts that have taken place on both sides of the Atlantic since around 1990. Chapters three through six contain several case studies which compare a wide range of regulatory policies. Chapter three focuses on European and American policies toward the risks of food safety and agricultural production methods, chapter four compares regulations that address the risks of air pollution, chapter five compares policies toward the risks of chemicals and hazardous substances, and chapter six examines European and American policies toward a range of consumer safety risks—other than for food—including drugs, children's products, and cosmetics. I compare and explain both regulatory statutes and specific regulatory decisions, including judicial ones.

The cases discussed in chapters three through six present a selective comparison of consumer and environmental risk regulations on either or both sides of the Atlantic during the last five decades. Thus, they do not by themselves "prove" a historical transatlantic shift in regulatory stringency with respect to consumer and environmental risks caused by business.[60] However, I believe the cases I have chosen to discuss *are* representative of the politics and policies of risk regulation on both sides of the Atlantic between 1960 and 2010. They are also sufficiently important in their own right to warrant an explanation for them. I also discuss and explain important cases that do not confirm to this overall pattern: some demonstrate increased policy convergence and others, continued American regulatory stringency.

Much of my analysis focuses on regulatory decisions and non-decisions made on either side of the idea of the Atlantic since 1990, since my primary objective is to compare and explain the changes in risk regulations that have occurred since then. As I am interested in how governments

[60] For other comparative case studies of European and American consumer and environmental regulations some of which overlap mine, see Miranda Schreurs, Henrik Selin, and Stacy VanDeveer, eds., *Transatlantic Environment and Energy Policies: Comparative and International Perspectives* (Burlington, VT: Ashgate, 2009); and Jonathan Wiener, Michael Rogers, James Hammitt, and Peter Sand, eds., *The Reality of Precaution: Comparing Risk Regulation in the United States and Europe* (Washington, DC: Resources for the Future, 2011), chapters 2–12.

address risks, other dimensions of consumer and environmental regulation, such as conservation or land-use planning, fall outside my analysis.

While the American constitutional system has remained stable, comparing America to "Europe" is more complex. Prior to the passage of the Single European Act of 1986, European risk regulations were primarily made at the national level. Accordingly, in discussing European regulatory policies before the mid-1980s, I often compare the United States to selected European countries. As the authority to make regulatory policies has increasingly shifted to the EU, much of this study compares the regulations adopted by the EU with those of the American federal government and American states.

My study begins around 1960, and thus includes important early examples of relative American regulatory stringency, namely the 1958 Delaney Amendment to the Federal Food, Drug, and Cosmetic Act, which prohibits the addition of carcinogenic chemicals to food, and the 1962 Kefauver Amendments to the same legislation, which transformed American policies for drug approval. However, the significant expansion of federal environmental regulation began around 1970 and thus much of my analysis of the politics of risk regulation in the United States focuses on developments since then. My study ends in December 2010. As I suggest in the concluding chapter, the divergence in transatlantic regulatory stringency of the last two decades show no signs of diminishing.

Chapters seven and eight place my explanatory framework for changes in the transatlantic politics of risk regulation in historical perspective. Chapter seven explores changes in public opinion and the preferences of influential policy makers, while chapter eight describes how and explains why American regulatory policies have moved away from and European policies moved toward a precautionary approach to assessing and managing risks. In chapter nine, I discuss the broader implications of my study.

CHAPTER TWO

Explaining Regulatory Policy Divergence

A POLICY PUZZLE

The extent to which transatlantic regulatory policy divergence has increased during the last two decades presents a puzzle. When compared to the rest of the world, Europe and the United States have much in common. The United States and the fifteen member states of the EU (as of 2003) are affluent democracies with sophisticated public bureaucracies, substantial scientific capacities, and strong civic cultures. Their regulatory officials have access to much of the same scientific expertise and there is extensive communication among policy makers, scientists, business managers, nongovernment organizations (NGOs), and citizens. Thanks to the spread of global media, many Americans and Europeans are well informed of policy developments on the other side of the Atlantic.

Moreover, their economies have become increasingly interdependent. "The transatlantic trade and investment relationship has become a super highway."[1] Bilateral trade in goods between the EU and the United States totaled $563 billion in 2007; each is the other's second most important trading partner. European investments in the United States total $1.5 trillion, and American firms have investments of approximately $1.7 trillion in the EU.[2]

> The result is a staggering degree of interdependence between the two economies, not least because the fabled US and European multinationals are now so thoroughly intertwined by mergers and cross-fertilization. Something close to a quarter of all US-EU "trade" simply consists of transactions within firms with investments on the other side of the Atlantic.[3]

Divergent risk regulations between the United States and the EU add to the costs of transatlantic commerce and also raise the costs of international trade as some countries adopt European standards and others, American ones. Improving regulatory cooperation and coordination has

[1] Matthew Baldwin, John Peterson, and Bruce Stokes, "Trade and Economic Relations," in *Europe, America, Bush: Transatlantic Relations in the Twenty-First Century*, ed. John Peterson and Mark Pollack (London: Routledge, 2003), 29.
[2] *EU Focus*, December 2010.
[3] Quoted in Baldwin et al., "Trade and Economic Relations," 31.

accordingly become an important objective of global firms and government officials on both sides of the Atlantic.[4] Why, then, has transatlantic regulatory polarization increased in so many important policy areas?

ALTERNATIVE EXPLANATIONS FOR REGULATORY POLICY DIVERGENCE

There are a number of alternative explanations for why many American and European risk regulations have diverged since 1990, which I want to critically review before presenting my own explanatory framework in more detail.

Differences in Actual Risks

The most obvious explanation for the differences in the stringency of a wide range of European and American regulations is that they represent a response to differences in the actual risks their citizenry faces. However, cross-national differences in environmental quality cannot account for recent differences in the scope and stringency of risk regulations across the Atlantic. According to a careful and detailed quantitative analysis of changes in national environmental performance among seventeen industrial democracies between 1970 and 1995, all but two of the twelve EU member states included in this study had *higher* total performance scores for overall environmental quality than the United States.[5] A narrower study that measured the percentage changes in national SO2 emissions between 1985 and 1995 reported that these emissions declined *less* in the United States than in all but two member states of the EU.[6] A global environmental index published in 2002 found that environmental quality in the member states of the EU and the United States was roughly comparable: environmental quality in the

[4]Wyn Grant and David Coen, "Corporate Political Strategy and Global Policy: A Case Study of the Transatlantic Business Dialogue," Regulatory Initiative Working Paper series, 42 (November 2000); Carl Lankowski, "The Transatlantic Environmental Dialogue," in *Green Giants? Environmental Policies of the U.S. and the European Union*, ed. Norman Vig and Michael Faure (Cambridge, MA: MIT Press, 2004), 329–44. According to a 2009 study released by the European Commission, aligning non-tariff measures (NTM) would increase the U.S. GDP by $53 billion per year and the EU GDP by $158 billion, though only a portion of these NTMs include the risk regulations explored in this study.

[5]Lyle Scruggs, *Sustaining Abundance: Environmental Performance in Industrial Democracies* (Cambridge: Cambridge University Press, 2003), 51. Scruggs' data is based on six indicators: SO2 emissions, NOX emissions, waste, recycling, fertilizer use and water treatment, all of which he found to be highly correlated.

[6]Sonja Walti, "How Multilevel Structures Affect Environmental Policy in Industrialized Countries," *European Journal of Political Research* 43 (2005): 627.

United States ranked poorer than in four member states, better than in five, and similar to seven.[7]

If we accept the data presented in the first two studies, then the United States should have recently enacted more stringent environmental regulations than the EU, as its environmental quality was poorer. If we accept the data presented in the third study, namely, that each had comparable levels of environmental quality, then the stringency of more recently adopted American and European environmental regulations should have been roughly similar. But neither of these outcomes occurred.

Still, it is possible that many of the specific differences in American and European risk regulations might be due to variations in the actual risks their citizens faced. For example, mad-cow disease posed significantly greater risks for Europeans than for Americans; one would therefore have expected European regulations for animal feed and testing linked to BSE to be more stringent and extensive than those of the United States, which they were.

But more commonly there has been little or no relationship between the magnitude of actual harms or risks faced by citizens in either Europe or the United States and the response of policy makers to them. For example, during the early 1960s, substantially more Germans and British than Americans were harmed by the drug thalidomide, which had not even been approved for sale in the United States. But the United States responded by enacting far more stringent regulations for the approval of new medicines than both Germany and Britain.

For the vast majority of American and European regulatory policies described in this study, it is difficult to discern *any* apparent differences in the *actual* risks faced (or not faced) by Europeans and Americans. Lead in petrol/gasoline posed no more or fewer health risks to Americans than to Europeans, yet this fuel additive was phased out much more rapidly in the United States than in Europe. Many American food safety regulations adopted during the 1960s and 1970s were more risk-averse than many European ones, yet the health risks of consuming the substances banned in the United States were the same as for Europeans. The risks to Europeans of ozone-depleting chemicals were not substantially different than those faced by Americans, yet the United States acted much more rapidly to restrict them.

Likewise, the risks to the health and safety of Europeans from beef or milk hormones, antibiotics in animal feed, hazardous substances from e-waste deposited in landfills, phthalates in children's products

---

[7] *Environmental Performance Measurement: The Global Report 2001–2002*, Daniel Esty and Peter Cornelius, eds. (New York: Oxford University Press, 2002), 16.

and cosmetics, chemicals in general, and the consumption and production of genetically modified (GM) foods have been *no different* than those Americans faced. Nor can it be plausibly argued that Europeans face more risks from global climate change than do Americans. In each of these cases, what *was* different was *not* the actual risks themselves, but rather the public's perception of them, which in turn helped shape differences in the extent and intensity of political demands to address them.

"Catching Up"

A second explanation for this divergence has to do with historical differences in the expansion of regulatory authority across the Atlantic. Because many national European regulations were weaker than American ones during the 1970s and 1980s, by around 1990 the EU arguably had to do more to "catch up." This does explain those policy areas in which European regulations have become both more stringent and more similar to those in the United States, such as for lead in gasoline/petrol, automotive emissions, and ozone depletion.

However, this explanation cannot account for the fact that many European regulatory policies adopted since around 1990 are *more* stringent than those earlier adopted by the United States. Chemical regulations are an important example. The 1976 Toxic Substances Control Act (TSCA) imposed more stringent and comprehensive safety and environmental regulations than did the EU's Sixth Amendment. Accordingly, the EU might have been expected to "catch up" to the United States by adopting new chemical regulations roughly similar to the TSCA. But the provisions of REACH went significantly beyond those of the American regulatory statute; indeed, they made EU chemical regulations the most precautionary and comprehensive in the world. Nor can a "catch up" theory explain why the EU has enacted *more* stringent regulations for beef and milk hormones, antibiotics in animal feed, chemicals in cosmetics, GM food, and global climate change.

Since the EU only acquired the authority to harmonize a broad range of environmental and consumer regulations after the mid-1980s, and the American federal government began expanding its consumer regulations around 1960 and its environmental regulations around 1970, one would certainly have expected the EU to have issued *more* regulations or directives than the American federal government since 1990, which it has. But this does not explain why many of the standards that the EU enacted were more stringent and comprehensive than those of the United States.

Economic Performance and Growth Rates

A third set of explanations focuses on variations in rates of economic performance and relative living standards. Public support for more stringent risk regulations arguably is affected by economic conditions: accordingly, higher growth rates are likely to increase the rate at which new environmental regulations are enacted—both by exacerbating many environmental problems and making policy makers more willing to impose additional costs on firms—while slower growth rates are likely to make both the public and policy makers more sensitive to the costs of additional regulations. Regulatory stringency is also affected by differences in per capita income: richer nations are more likely to enact more stringent and extensive regulations than less affluent ones.

In the United States, real GDP growth averaged 5 percent between 1965 and 1969, and after a slight downturn in 1970, grew by roughly 5 percent between 1971 and 1973. Concomitantly, the late 1960s and early 1970s witnessed an historic expansion of federal environmental regulation: Congress enacted eight important regulatory statutes between 1969 and 1973. However, the ambitious automobile emission standards of the 1970 Clean Air Act Amendments were subsequently modified in response to the stagflation of the mid-1970s and fewer new regulations were adopted during the economic downturn of the early 1980s. Similarly, the relatively strong growth rates that resumed around 1984—GDP growth averaged 4.3 percent between 1984 and 1989—contributed to the second major expansion of American environmental regulation which took place around 1990.

But while variations in economic performance are associated with many of the changes in American environmental policy between 1969 and 1990, they cannot satisfactorily account for policy developments between 1990 and 2007. After a slowdown in the early 1990s, a long sustained economic expansion began in 1992, with growth rates averaging 3.8 percent over a period of nine years; American incomes grew by 14 percent between 1993 and 2000. The American economy also continued to perform relatively strongly through 2007, with growth rates averaging 3.2 percent from 1993. Yet beginning in the early 1990s, there was a marked decline in the enactment of more stringent risk regulations in the United States.

Moreover, between 2000 and 2007, a period when many of the more stringent risk regulations described in this book were adopted in Europe, annual GDP growth in the United States averaged 2.6 percent as compared to 2.2 percent in the EU-15. If economic growth rates were a critical determinant of national regulatory policies, then since 1990 the United States should have *continued* to adopt more stringent regulations than the EU, at least prior to the economic downturn that began in 2008. In addition, during the first decade of the twenty-first century, GDP per capita was roughly 40 percent higher in the United States than in the EU-15. Finally, if citizens in more affluent societies are more likely to share "postmodern" values, then *both* the United States and Europe should have steadily increased the scope and stringency of their risk regulation.[8] But the United States did not do so.

The Role of Economic Interests

Another explanation for the differences in European and American regulatory policies has to do with the dynamics of global business competition. More specifically, the EU's more stringent risk policies enacted since around 1990 may reflect, or at least may be consistent with, the competitive interests of European firms. The fact that many European regulations have been criticized as non-tariff trade barriers by the United States and three have been the subject of formal World Trade Organization (WTO) dispute proceedings brought by the United States (and other countries) makes this explanation a plausible one.

But it is important to distinguish between regulatory policies that disadvantaged American producers and those that advantaged European firms. In fact, the first of these disputes, the EU's beef hormone ban, did not reduce beef imports into Europe; rather, it shifted their sources to countries whose farmers made less extensive use of hormones. Moreover, the hormone ban was also strongly opposed by several European countries who were important beef producers. The banned hormones themselves were produced by both European and American firms, all of whom strongly opposed and were adversely affected by the EU's decision to ban their use.

In the case of the second of these disputes, over genetically modified organisms (GMOs), while European imports from the United States of corn/maize and soy measurably declined as a result of EU regulations, they have not declined overall. Europe, which produces virtually no soy, continues to rely on imports of this product, since it is a critical source of animal feed and is used in many processed foods. But its sources of supply have shifted from the United States to countries that produce non-GM soy varieties. The same is true of corn, which is used for both human consumption and animal feed. Very little is grown in Europe, which means that the EU must continue to import it—but it is now more likely to do so from countries whose farmers use GM crops approved by the EU.

Nor does opposition to GMOs in the EU reflect either the political preferences or economic interests of most European farmers. Were it not for consumer preferences and activist pressures, many European farmers

[8]Ronald Inglehart, *Modernization and Post Modernization: Cultural, Economics and Political Change in 43 Societies* (Princeton, NJ: Princeton University Press, 1997).

would have planted GM crops. Moreover, European restrictions on the import of GM varieties for animal feed have raised production costs for European farmers. Revealingly, the European country that was initially the strongest proponent of the introduction of GM crops was France, Europe's largest agricultural producer and traditionally the country most strongly identified with European agricultural protectionism.[9] French policy toward GMOs did change radically, but this was because of pressure from environmentalists, consumers, and activists, some of whom were politically militant small farmers, and not because of any shift in the preferences of the country's large agricultural producers or its seed firms. Significantly, France's initial regulations were more favorable to the sale rather than to the cultivation of GM products, the opposite of the policy pattern one would expect if its policy objectives were protectionist.

What about the interests of agricultural biotechnology firms? While several important agricultural biotechnology companies such as Syngenta and Novartis are based in Europe, the global firms most acutely disadvantaged by EU restrictions on GM varieties are based in the United States, most notably Monsanto, the world's most important agricultural biotechnology company. The fact that the United States already had a highly developed agricultural biotechnology industry when GMOs were first being introduced certainly contributed to the American decision to adopt relatively permissive regulations for the introduction of GM varieties. But the fact that Europe initially had fewer and smaller agricultural biotechnology firms does not explain why the EU chose to adopt regulations that significantly impeded the growth of this sector.

Certainly, no European-based biotechnology firm has supported or benefited from the EU's increasingly stringent regulatory controls. Had the EU adopted regulations in 1990 promoting the use of agricultural biotechnology similar to those adopted by the United States in 1986—as the European Commission had strongly advocated—Europe would doubtless now have a much more flourishing agricultural biotechnology industry.

What about global climate change? Clearly, economic interests did play an important role in shaping business preferences as well as policy outcomes on both sides of the Atlantic. An important reason why the EU was a strong supporter of the Kyoto Protocol and the United States refused to ratify it was because of the fact that its percentage reduction requirements were structured in ways that disadvantaged American-based firms and advantaged their European-based competitors. But the

---

[9] For a more detailed discussion of French policy *toward* GM crops and foods, see Oliver Cadot and David Vogel, "France, the U.S., and the Biotechnology Dispute," *Brookings Foreign Policy Studies* (January 2001).

EU maintained and even strengthened its commitments to reduce GHG emissions even after the United States decided not to ratify the Protocol. While European firms have been more willing to accept regulations for greenhouse gases than have most American ones, this is not because they were economically advantaged by them.

It is certainly true that once the EU has adopted more stringent domestic production or product standards, it then becomes in the interests of European firms to also have them applied to imported products; this is the underlying source of many American complaints about EU regulations that serve as non-tariff barriers to trade. But this begs an important question: why were these regulations adopted in the first place?

For most of the more stringent EU risk regulations described in this study, *there were no important differences in the preferences of European and American firms.* Both American and European firms have lobbied against many of the risk regulations adopted by the EU, and many of the trade associations that opposed or attempted to weaken them were composed of *both* European- and American-based firms. For example, both European and American chemical firms actively challenged the European Commission's proposal to significantly strengthen European chemical regulation, electronics producers from both sides of the Atlantic opposed the EU's ban on hazardous substances in electronic products as well as its mandatory electronics recycling requirements. Both European and American firms opposed and were disadvantaged by the EU's bans on phthalates in children's toys and cosmetics, beef and milk hormones, and antibiotics in animal feed. Many European firms and business associations have been just as critical of the adoption and application of the precautionary principle as their counterparts in the United States.

While there are certainly examples of what an editorial in the *Wall Street Journal* has described as "the EU's regulatory assault on U.S. companies," most European regulations apply equally to all firms doing business in Europe, though it may be more or less difficult for some firms to comply with particular regulations.[10] This is not to suggest that protectionist motivations have played no role in European risk regulation, or to deny that some regulations have disproportionately favored European producers, only that economic interests have not been central to its increased scope and stringency.[11] The politics of protective regulation in

---

[10] "European Imperialism," *Wall Street Journal*, October, 2007. This article specifically cited the fact that foreign cosmetic companies were required to register all the chemicals in their products three *years* earlier than European firms.

[11] An important example of the former are European restrictions on methods for cleaning poultry, which were strongly supported by European farmers and which have eliminated poultry exports to Europe from the United States.

Europe have been no different from that of the United States: firms have typically opposed more stringent consumer and environmental regulations. *The only difference is that, after 1990, producers became more successful in preventing their adoption in the United States than in Europe.* In short, the strengthening of European risk regulations since around 1990 cannot be satisfactorily explained by either the political preferences or the economic interests of European-based firms—any more than the previous strengthening of American consumer and environmental regulations reflected the political preferences or economic interests of most American businesses.[12]

Attitudes toward the Role of Government

Another plausible explanation emphasizes the critical importance of transatlantic differences in the role of the state and the legitimacy of government regulation. Thus, Europeans are said to "have a stronger tradition and are more accepting of government intervention in the market than Americans,"[13] while the latter are "more ideologically averse to regulation."[14] According to Ludwig Kramer, an official of the European Commission (EC) with responsibilities for environmental governance: "*Traditionally*, Europe has had a stronger commitment to social and more recently to environmental concerns than has the U.S. . . . There is . . . a sort of consensus in Europe that public intervention must also ensure a decent state of the environment, and that environmental protection cannot be left to market forces."[15]

As numerous scholars have noted, patterns of business-government relations in the United States and Europe have long diverged. Historically, European governments have been far more interventionist and controlled a much wider scope of business activity than in the United States. The recent expansion of European consumer and environmental regulation *is* consistent with this broad historical trend. But a variable cannot be explained by a constant. Europe's statist traditions and America's long-standing hostility to "big government" and belief in "free

[12] For the previous politics of consumer and environmental regulation in the United States, see David Vogel, *Fluctuating Fortunes:The Political Power of Business in America* (New York: Basic Books, 1989).

[13] David Bodansky, "Transatlantic Environmental Regulation," in *Europe, America, Bush: Transatlantic Relations in the Twenty-First Century*, ed. John Peterson and Mark Pollack (London: Routledge, 2003), 64.

[14] David Levy and Peter Newell, "Oceans Apart? Business Responses to Global Environmental Issues in Europe and the U.S.," *Environment* (November 2000): 10.

[15] Emphasis added. Quoted in Ludwig Kramer, "The Roots of Divergence: A European Perspective," in *Green Giants? Environmental Policies of the U.S. and the European Union*, ed. Norman Vig and Michael Faure (Cambridge, MA: MIT Press, 2004), 66–7.

enterprise" cannot explain why, for three decades, the United States consistently enacted *more* extensive and costly consumer and environmental regulations than did most European countries as well as the EU.

The Role of Political Systems

Yet another explanation for the changes in European and American approaches to risk regulation emphasizes the importance of transatlantic differences in political systems. David Bodansky writes:

> The recent tradition of divided government between the President and Congress in the US has produced a least-common dominator effect. Which branch is the most conservative tends to prevail . . . In contrast the political economy in Europe of coalition governments has produced exactly the opposite effect—what could be called a greenest denominator rather than a least-common denominator. Green parties care more about the environment and demand Green positions as a condition of supporting the government.[16]

The critical role of party systems as an explanation for differences in patterns of environmental regulation between Europe and the United States is also emphasized by Christopher Green-Pedersen and Michelle Wolf, who argue that "the institutionalization of attention to environmental issues is stronger in the European party system than in the U.S., which with its multiple venue system is more likely to resist institutionalization."[17] They further claim that "the institutionalization of attention to environmental issues is stronger in the European party systems than in the U.S. due to the fact that if an issue becomes attached to a European political party, it is more likely to become strongly institutionalized."[18]

The electoral system of proportional representation, which has periodically made possible the participation of Green parties in a number of European governments, including Germany, France, Denmark, Italy, Finland, and Belgium, as well as in the European Parliament, has clearly played an important role in strengthening many national and European consumer and environmental risk regulations. However, the Democratic Party in the United States previously played as important a role in advancing a "green" political agenda as has any Green Party in Europe. Moreover, the national electoral systems in both Europe and the United States have not changed, yet their policy outcomes have (elections to the European Parliament are based on the electoral system of each member state).

[16] Ibid., 65–6.
[17] Christoffer Green-Pedersen and Michelle Wolfe, "The Institutionalization of Attention in the US and Denmark: Multiple vs. Single Venue Systems and the Case of the Environment," *Governance* 22, no. 4 (October 2009): 626.
[18] Ibid.

Nor has divided government in the United States historically been an obstacle to the adoption of more stringent regulations.[19] The two most important periods of American environmental regulatory expansion, namely the late 1960s and early 1970s, and the late 1980s through 1990, took place under Republican Presidents Richard Nixon and George H. W. Bush and a Democratic-controlled Congress. The American constitutional system has arguably made it more difficult for treaties signed by American presidents to be ratified, since the American legislature is more independent of the executive than in Europe's parliamentary systems.[20] But prior to around 1990, international environmental agreements signed by American presidents were routinely ratified by the American Senate. Moreover, the authority to ratify international agreements is also fragmented in the EU: treaties signed by the European Commission must be approved by the Council of Ministers, and more recently, also by the European Parliament.

The Role of Cultural Values

Another alternative explanation emphasizes the role of deeply rooted cultural values. According to this thesis, "Europeans demonstrate their considerable concern about environmental issues in their behavior as voters, consumers, corporate managers, and policy makers," while "people in the U.S. are more individualistic, more concerned about their life-styles than about the environment."[21] Likewise, it has been argued that "Europeans express more concrete concerns about environmental impact on future generations," most notably in the case of global climate change, and therefore are "more likely to invoke caution regarding unforeseen risks."[22] It has also been suggested that the reason the EU has adopted the precautionary principle and the United States has not done so is because "Europeans are more risk averse and suspicious of technology than Americans and therefore more willing to take action even when the scientific evidence is uncertain."[23]

But the United States previously adopted many regulations that highly constrained the "life styles" of "individualistic" Americans, by limiting,

[19] David Mayhew, *Divided We Stand: Party Control, Lawmaking, and Investigations 1946–1990* (New Haven, CT: Yale University Press, 1991).

[20] See Jeffrey Lantis, "The Life and Death of International Treaties: Double-Edged Diplomacy and the Politics of Ratification in Comparative Perspective," *International Politics* 43 (2006): 24–52.

[21] Levy and Newell, "Ocean's Apart?" 10.

[22] Ibid., 11. See also Willett Kempton and Paul Craig, "European Perspectives on Global Climate Change," *Environment* (April 1993): 16–45.

[23] Bodansky, "Transatlantic Environmental Regulation," in Peterson and Pollack, *Europe, America, Bush*, 64.

for example, the drugs they can take, the land they can develop, the products they can use, and the kinds of cars they can purchase. The United States was among the first countries to ban the use of aerosol spray cans because they produced emissions that harmed the ozone layer, which certainly affected American lifestyles. Americans have been no less concerned about protecting environmental quality for future generations. The Endangered Species Act of 1973 represented a precautionary approach to protect species that were threatened as well as possibly endangered in order to preserve them for future generations.

Nor is there any evidence of a deeply rooted or long-standing European mistrust of technology. The applications of biotechnology to pharmaceuticals and stem cell research are strongly supported in Europe; the latter has been far less controversial than in the United States. Moreover, the debate in Europe and America over the funding of supersonic commercial aviation transport during the early 1970s demonstrates precisely the opposite pattern of public concern: in this case, it was Americans rather than the French and British who were "more suspicious" of the possible negative environmental impacts of a new commercial technology.

The recent adoption of many highly precautionary regulations by the EU does not reflect a distinctively or deeply rooted European approach to managing new or uncertain risks. In fact, for roughly three decades, no nation more consistently employed a more precautionary approach to consumer and environmental risk regulation than the United States. "In the U.S. many laws and regulations [enacted or implemented between 1959 and 1978] require that action be taken to anticipate, prevent, or reduce risk *where there is scientific uncertainty or a lack of clear evidence of risk.*"[24]

As studies of risk regulation by scholars such as Aaron Wildavsky, Mary Douglas, and Sheila Jasanoff persuasively argue, "risk cultures" and public attitudes toward nature, technology, and particular risks do play an important role in shaping the public's risk perceptions.[25] Cass Sunstein further suggests that cross-national cultural variables can function as "predispositions," making some risks more salient than others.[26]

---

[24]Emphasis added. Theofanis Christoforou, "The Precautionary Principle, Risk Assessment, and the Comparative Role of Science in the European Community and the US Legal System," in Vig and Faure, *Green Giants?* 18.

[25]Mary Douglas and Aaron Wildavsky, *Risk and Culture: An Essay on the Selection of Technological and Environmental Dangers* (Berkeley: University of California Press, 1983); Aaron Wildavsky, *The Rise of Radical Equalitarianism* (Washington, DC: American University Press, 1991); Sheila Jasanoff, *Risk Management and Political Culture* (New York: Russell Sage Foundation, 1986).

[26]Cass Sunstein, "Precautions Against What? The Availability of Heuristic and Cross-Cultural Risk Perceptions," *Alabama Law Review* 57, no. 1 (2005): 75–106.

Some of these predispositions have clearly affected both public perceptions and public policies. For example, Americans have historically been
more concerned than Europeans about the risks of cancer, while Europeans have consistently displayed strong preferences for "natural" food
production. The former helps explain the relative stringency of American
regulations regarding carcinogens in the food supply, while the latter may
help explain why Europeans have been more opposed to the introduction
of agricultural biotechnology than Americans or have been more willing
to accept the risks of consuming cheese made from unpasteurized milk.

But many other important differences in policy preferences on both
sides of the Atlantic are neither deeply historically rooted nor are they an
expression of national cultures; rather, they are politically constructed,
which means they are subject to change. The claim that deeply rooted
cultural or social attitudes toward risk, technology, or environmental
protection can adequately explain the large number of current differences in consumer and environmental risk regulations in Europe and the
United States rests on a myopic understanding of the historical pattern of
protective regulation across the Atlantic: *many recent European cultural
and social attitudes toward risk and risk regulation were previously more
characteristic of the United States than of Europe.*

Explaining Policy Divergence

In this book, I identify three critical factors that have shaped transatlantic
regulatory policy divergence since 1990. The first part of my explanation
focuses on changes in political salience of consumer and environmental risks and the extent and intensity of public pressures to ameliorate
them. During the last two decades, Europeans have perceived *more*
health, safety, and environmental risks caused by business to be both
credible and politically unacceptable than have Americans. The breadth
and intensity of public demands for more stringent risk regulations has
declined in the United States and increased in Europe.

My second explanatory factor involves changes in the political preferences of influential policy makers. While Democrats have generally supported more stringent risk regulations than Republicans, through around
1990 there was also considerable bipartisan support for stronger consumer and environmental regulation. But beginning in the 1990s, regulatory policymaking, especially in the area of environmental protection,
became increasingly polarized along partisan lines. Republicans, who
were the majority party in both the House of Representatives and the
Senate between 1995 and 2006 (with one brief exception in the U.S. Senate), and Republican President George W. Bush, who held office between

2001 and 2008, were less willing to support more stringent consumer and environmental risk regulations than were many previously elected Republicans, including Presidents Richard Nixon, Ronald Reagan, and George H. W. Bush. This increase in partisan polarization played an important role in slowing down the rate at which new, more stringent risk regulations were adopted, especially through legislation.

By contrast, in 1995, the same year that a more conservative Republican Party became the majority party in Congress, Sweden, Austria, and Finland, three states with strong "green" preferences, joined the EU. In 1997, members of Green parties served in the governments of France, Germany, Belgium, Italy, and Finland, and the party occupied a total of nearly 150 seats in the national legislatures of eleven member states. Between 1994 and 1999, the number of seats held by European Greens in the European Parliament (EP) increased from twenty-three to thirty-eight, making them the fourth largest party group in the EP. Through 2004, the European Commission had a center-left administration and the EP, center-left majorities. Transatlantic differences in the relative political strength of center-left and center-right political parties between 1995 and 2004 as well as changes in the national composition of the EU help explain the differences in regulatory policies adopted in the EU and the United States during this period.

However, by 2004 most EU member states were governed by center-right majorities and the representation of Green parties in European governments had significantly declined. Elections to the EP in 2004 and 2009 resulted in center-right majorities and the EU has been governed by a center-right European Commission since 2004. But, significantly, center-right politicians and political parties in Europe have been more willing to support expansions of risk regulations than national Republicans have been since the early 1990s in the United States. The politics of European risk regulation has been less polarized along ideological and partisan lines than in the United States.

The third key factor influencing changes in regulatory policymaking on both sides of the Atlantic involves the criteria used by policy makers to decide whether or how to respond to particular risks. While previously, many American policies reflected a willingness to impose regulations in the face of scientific uncertainty, beginning in the 1980s, formal risk assessments began to play an increasingly influential role in the making of risk management decisions. This has often increased the level of scientific evidence necessary to justify new risk regulations, most notably by regulatory agencies. By contrast, the EU's inclusion of the precautionary principle in the 1992 Maastricht Treaty on the European Union has strengthened both the ability and willingness of European regulatory officials to enact more stringent regulations in the face of scientific uncertainty about the causes and consequences of the risks being regulated. It has facilitated their ability to ban or restrict existing commercial activities and to withhold approval for new ones. Equally important, in the United States, federal courts have increasingly subjected the rules issued by regulatory agencies to close and careful scrutiny. By contrast, European courts have been more willing to defer to the decisions, directives, and rules of the European Commission and the Council of Ministers—including those based on the precautionary principle.

As relatively few elections in either the United States or in Europe have been fought or decided on the basis of the electorates' regulatory policy preferences, and much regulatory policy is made by appointed officials, policy makers typically enjoy a degree of discretion in making risk management decisions. This is particularly true in the case of the EU, as most European officials are not directly accountable to the European electorate. Accordingly, policy makers may choose to be more or less responsive to public pressures for more stringent regulations.

But when policy makers are more willing to adopt more stringent risk regulations, it becomes easier for activists to mobilize public support for them. Conversely, when policy makers are less willing to do so, the "hurdle" that new risks must surmount to become politically salient increases. Since around 1990, it has become more difficult for new health, safety, and environmental risks to be placed on the policy agenda in Washington than in Brussels. Alternatively, when public pressures for more stringent regulations are extremely strong, policy makers are more likely to be responsive to them. This helps explain, for example, the support of Republican Presidents Richard Nixon and George H. W. Bush for stricter federal controls on air pollution as well as the Barasso Commission's willingness to back stronger climate-change regulations.

The relative importance of each of these three factors in explaining any particular policy decision or non-decision varies from policy domain to policy domain, and for some of the policies discussed in this book, other factors have also played an important role, which I discuss. But both separately and often in relationship with one another, they provide a useful framework for explaining the shifts in public policies toward a wide range of health, safety, and environmental risks that took place in on both sides of the Atlantic beginning around 1990.

PUBLIC RISK PERCEPTIONS

I have suggested that public opinion is one of the three key factors that have shaped regulatory policies and politics on both sides of the Atlantic.

But this, in turn, raises a critical question that merits further discussion: what explains public opinion, or more specifically, what determines the public's risk perceptions and the extent and intensity of its demands for more stringent regulations to address them?

The more risks that are regarded as both credible and unacceptable by politically influential segments of the electorate, the more likely policy makers will find themselves pressured to adopt more stringent risk regulations. Increases in public demands for more stringent risk regulations essentially stem from a gap between the public's perceptions of the risks they consider *both* credible and unacceptable and the existing scope and stringency of government regulation. Both dimensions of public perceptions are critical. For example, while the risks of smoking are widely regarded as credible on both sides of the Atlantic, it would clearly be politically unacceptable for any country to ban cigarettes. Likewise, while the risks of consuming dairy products made from unpasteurized milk are credible, European consumers consider them to be acceptable.

As is true for many public policies, changes in risk regulations typically have their origin in some kind of triggering mechanism, i.e., some event, information, or development that disrupts or "punctuates" the existing political equilibrium and thus "opens the previously constrained decision-making domain to other interests and participants, and [leads to] a 'reframing' of the issue that undermines the previous policy justification."[27] Such triggering mechanisms or focusing events can include a major accident, catastrophe, or highly visible policy failure, new reports or studies, an influential book, stories in the media, and/or a public campaign waged by activists.[28] "The stronger public concerns are, the more effective NGOs [non-government organizations] are likely to be in affecting public opinion."[29] Likewise, the greater the media coverage of a particular risk, the more likely it is to become politically salient.

A succession of such "triggers" can then create what Cass Sunstein describes as a "risk availability cascade," or what David Hirshleifer

---

[27]Robert Repetto, "Introduction," in *Punctuated Equilibrium and the Dynamics of US Environmental Policy*, ed. Robert Repetto (New Haven, CT: Yale University Press, 2006), 13. The concept of punctuated equilibrium as applied to politics was developed by Frank Baumgartner; see Frank Baumgartner, "Punctuated Equilibrium, Theory and Environmental Policy," in ibid., 24–46.

[28]Repetto, "Introduction," in Repetto, *Punctuated Equilibrium*, 11.

[29]Thomas Bernauer and Ladina Caduff, "In Whose Interest? Pressure Group Politics, Economic Competition and Environmental Regulation," *Journal of Public Policy* 24, no. 1 (2004): 105.

characterizes as an "informational cascade."[30] Such a "cascade" changes the way in which *other* risks are perceived. They make influential segments of the public more likely to regard claims, reports, or information about other risks which they learn or hear about—often indirectly or unrelated to the original triggering mechanism or mechanisms—as both credible and unacceptable. Paul Slovic writes:

> An unfortunate event can be thought of as analogous to a stone dropped in a pond. The ripples spread outward, encompassing first the directly affected victims, then the responsible company or agency, and in the extreme, reaching other companies, agencies and industries. . . . Some events make only small ripples; others make larger ones.[31]

A stream of "unfortunate events" or other policy triggers can then produce what has been described as a "precautionary risk culture" or a "risk society," characterized by a continuous stream of both highly credible and politically unacceptable business-related health, safety, and environmental risks, or a succession of "larger ripples."

Such a "precautionary risk political culture" or "risk society" periodically characterized the United States beginning in the 1960s and especially during the 1970s and 1980s. As a British journalist observed in 1972, "We saw the Americans thrashing around from one pollution scare to the next . . . One moment it was cyclamates, mercury the next, the ozone, lead cadmium—there they seem set on working their way in a random manner through the whole periodic table."[32] A British social scientist commented in 1979, "Americans seem to have taken an excessively strict interpretation of risk, reducing 'reasonable risk' to practically 'zero risk.'"[33] Three years later, Mary Douglas and Aaron Wildavsky wrote:

> Try to read a newspaper or news magazine . . . on any day some alarm bells will be ringing. What are Americans afraid of? Nothing much, really, except the food they eat, the water they drink, the air they breathe . . . In the

---

[30] Cass Sunstein, *Laws of Fear: Beyond the Precautionary Principle* (Cambridge: Cambridge University Press, 2005), 97. See also David Hirshleifer, "The Blind Leading the Blind: Social Influences, Fads, and Informational Cascades," in *The New Economics of Human Behavior,* ed. Mariano Tommasi and Kathryn Ierulli (Cambridge: Cambridge University Press, 1995), 1882

[31] Paul Slovic, "Perception of Risk," in *The Perception of Risk,* ed. Paul Slovic (London: Earthscan, 2001), 227. See also the collected essays of Nick Pidgeon, Roger Kasperson, and Paul Slovic, eds., *The Social Amplification of Risk* (Cambridge: Cambridge University Press, 2003).

[32] Quoted in Stanley Johnson, *The Politics of the Environment: The British Experience* (London: Tom Stacy, 1972), 170–71.

[33] Quoted in David Vogel, *National Styles of Regulation: Environmental Policy in Great Britain and the United States* (Ithaca, NY: Cornell University Press, 1986), 182.

amazingly short space of ten to twenty years, confidence about the physical world has turned into doubt. Once the source of safety, science and technology has become the source or risk. . . . America is more passionately involved than any other nation in the debates about risks to nature.[34]

As these observations suggest, from the early 1960s through around 1990, significant segments of the American public heard and found both credible and politically unacceptable a continuous stream of "alarm bells." These included contaminated cranberries, cyclamates, DES in livestock, strawberries, thalidomide, pesticides, unsafe cars, high levels of air pollution, lead, contaminated toxic waste dumps, a nuclear power accident, mercury-contaminated fish, DDT, asbestos, and two major oil spills, one in Santa Barbara in 1969 and a second, much larger one in Alaska in 1989, to name but a few. Many became associated with one other. As Alan Mazur notes in his historical study of the political salience of many risks that have emerged in the United States,

> Public warnings did not arise in isolation. Nearly every one of them is connected to some other warning or public concern, recently or currently in the news. In motivating partisans to support or oppose it, a technology's association with other contentious issues in politics and society may be as important as its intrinsic risk.[35]

Since around 1990, a similar kind of "precautionary risk culture" has emerged in Europe. In 1988, the *Washington Post* reported: "Dead seals in the North Sea, a chemical fire on the Loire, killer algae off the cost of Sweden, contaminated drinking water in Cornwall. A drumbeat of emergencies has intensified the environmental debate this year in Europe, where public concern about pollution has never been higher."[36] In 1992, the protection of the environment and the fight against pollution had become "an immediate and urgent problem" in the view of 85 percent of EU citizens.[37] In 2001, the *Washington Post* observed:

> Wealthy, well-educated Europe is regularly swept by frightening reports of new dangers said to be inherent in contemporary life. . . . Americans have health concerns too, but not on this scale. The year is two months old and already in 2001 public opinion and public officials have been rattled by alarms over

---

[34] Douglas and Wildavsky, *Risk and Culture*, 10, 151.

[35] Alan Mazur, *True Warnings and False Alarms: Evaluating Fears About the Health Risks of Technology, 1948–1971* (Washington, DC: Resources for the Future, 2004), 44.

[36] R. Herman, "An Ecological Epiphany," *Washington Post National Weekly Edition* (December 11, 1988), 19.

[37] Elizabeth Bomberg, *Green Parties and Politics in the European Union* (London: Routledge, 1998), 13.

risk—proven and not—from genetically modified corn, hormone fed beef and pork, "mad-cow" disease, a widely used measles vaccine, narrow airline seats said to cause blood clots and cellular phones said to cause cancer.[38]

Whether or not objectively Europeans have recently had more reasons to be "scared" than in the past, they often perceived themselves as more vulnerable.[39]

What Happened in the United States?

But what, then, subsequently happened in the United States? Why did fewer consumer and environmental risks become salient in the United States? Why did public pressures or demands for more risk-averse regulations diminish?

One plausible explanation is that after around 1990 Americans experienced fewer "unfortunate events"—or at least certainly none that appeared as threatening to the health of so many people as the outbreak of BSE in Britain or which resulted in as many preventable deaths as from HIV-contaminated blood in France. But this can be only a partial explanation. For one of the central findings of this book is that a dramatic or highly visible "unfortunate event" is neither a necessary nor a sufficient condition to trigger intense public dissatisfaction with the regulatory status quo. Risks rarely speak for themselves. Most "alarm bells" are not based on harms or dangers that are visible or self-evident. Rather, they are typically rooted in claims that a particular commercial activity or product poses a credible and politically unacceptable health, safety, or environmental risk—often made by an activist group, private or government scientific report, a book, or article, and then widely disseminated by the media.

The significance and causes of these (alleged) risks are often based on scientific studies which can be subject to conflicting interpretations and whose data or conclusions few citizens are in a position to independently assess. In many cases, the causal links between these "risks" and the harms associated with them are contentious or difficult to prove or verify, especially as many are based on claims about future harms or dangers.

Most of the politically influential "alarm bells" that have rung on either or both sides of the Atlantic, ranging from cyclamates, Alar, and ozone depletion to antibiotics in animal feed, beef and milk hormones,

[38] T. R. Reid, "Be Careful What You Eat, Where You Sit and . . ." *Washington Post National Weekly Edition*, May 12–18, 2001.

[39] For an influential European perspective on the inherent vulnerabilities of citizens in a modern technological society, see Ulrich Beck, *World Risk Society* (Cambridge, MA: Polity, 1999).

GM foods, global climate change, phthalates in children's toys and cosmetics, fall into this category. For each of them, citizens, the media, and opinion leaders must decide who is more credible: those who insist on the need for more stringent regulations or those who question or challenge such claims. In short, *the public must decide what to worry about and how much to worry.*

After around 1990, Americans did not necessarily have fewer health, safety, or environmental risks to worry about.[40] Nor did they hear fewer alarm bells than Europeans. New health, safety, and environmental risks continued to emerge in the United States, many of which were similar to or echod those raised in Europe. Rather, what changed was their political impact: compared to both the United States before 1990 and Europe since then, fewer alarm bells in the United States rang as loudly or for as long. They became less likely to produce the kind of sustained and intense public response that is necessary to turn an "alarm bell" into a "policy trigger." Equally important, the ringing of one "alarm bell" was less likely to set off a cacophony of others.

Rather than a risk "availability cascade," the last two decades in the United States have been characterized by a risk "availability blockade." Widely publicized disagreement about the credibility of many of the alarm bells rung by activists made it more difficult for the influential segments of the public to be persuaded that additional stringent and comprehensive regulations were needed to protect them. For example, in 2010, a record 48 percent of Americans stated that the "seriousness of global warming" is "greatly exaggerated."[41]

Significantly, according to survey data (discussed in detail in chapter 7), after peaking around 1990, the gap between public demands for more risk regulations and the scope and stringency of existing regulations that had helped drive the previous expansions of consumer and environmental regulation *diminished*; the latter finally caught up with the former. After around 1990, large segments of the public became *more* likely to believe that the United States was *now* (finally) making adequate progress in protecting and improving environmental quality. This in turn affected the extent and intensity of public demands for additional regulation; it made it more difficult for new alarm bells to gain sufficient political traction to become policy triggers. By the twenty-fifth anniversary of Earth Day in

[40] For a description of the many things Americans worried about in 2003, few of which, however, include the kinds of risks discussed in this book, see Jane Spencer and Cynthia Crossen, "Why Do Americans Feel that Danger Lurks Everywhere?" *Wall Street Journal*, April 3, 2003.

[41] Gallup poll, "Americans' Global Warming Concerns Continue to Drop," March 11, 2010, available at http://www.gallup.com/poll/126560/Americans-Global-Warming-Concerns-Continue-Drop.aspx, accessed 11/20/2010.

1995, "the public's sense of urgency about the environment had declined considerably." [42]

In short, enough had now been done: the median voter had become more broadly satisfied with the regulatory status quo. These broad trends continued. According to a Gallup public opinion survey conducted in March 2010, Americans were less worried about a wide range of environmental problems than at any time during the past twenty years. Gallup primarily attributed the long and steady decline in concern for environmental issues since 1989 to "a general belief among Americans that environmental conditions in the U.S. are generally improving."[43] Americans did *not* become less committed to or concerned about protecting the environment; what *did* change was the extent and intensity of public support for *additional* regulations necessary for accomplishing this objective.

CONCLUSION

In this chapter I have reviewed several plausible explanations for the post-1990 divergence in risk regulation between Europe and the United States. Although many of these explanations offer important insights, none provides an adequate explanation for the significant discontinuity in risk regulation that occurred on both sides of the Atlantic after around 1990. I have identified three factors that, based on the evidence I present in this book, provide a more consistent and comprehensive explanation for the transatlantic divergence in regulatory stringency. The case studies presented in the next four chapters both document my dependent variable, namely the transatlantic shift in regulatory stringency, and provide empirical support for my explanatory framework.

[42] David Moore, "Public Sense of Urgency about Environment Wanes," *Gallup Poll Monthly* 335 (April 1995): 17.

[43] Gallup poll, "American's concern for Environment at 20 Year Low," March 16, 2010, available at http://ecopolitology.org/2010/03/16/gallup-poll-american-concern-for-environment-at-20-year-low/, accessed 11/20/2010.

CHAPTER THREE

Food Safety and Agriculture

MANY FOOD SAFETY REGULATIONS adopted in the United States between 1960 and 1990, most notably for suspected carcinogens in the food supply, were more risk-averse than those adopted in individual European countries, as well as by the EU. But more recently, the European Union has approved several regulations for food safety and agricultural production that are more stringent than those of the United States. These include: beef hormones—banned in the EU in 1985, but still permitted in the United States; the milk hormone BST—approved for use in the United States in 1993, but permanently banned in Europe in 1999; the introduction of genetically modified (GM) plants, food, and animal feed—permitted in the United States since 1986, but restricted in Europe beginning in 1990; and antibiotics in animal feed—significantly restricted in Europe in 1998 and 2003—but not in the United States. Some more stringent European regulations have restricted the introduction of new agricultural technologies, such as bovine somatotropin (BST) and GM varieties, while others, such as for beef hormones and antibiotics in animal feed, banned agricultural production methods that were previously used extensively on both sides of the Atlantic. Differences in public risk perceptions, differential risk assessment criteria, and the preferences of influential policy makers have each played a role in shaping these divergent policy outcomes.

A number of food safety regulations were affected by a divergence in transatlantic public risk perceptions. During the 1960s, 1970s, and 1980s, public concerns about the risks of carcinogens in the food supply were greater in the United States than in Europe, while during the 1980s, the safety risks of beef hormones became highly salient in Europe, but not in the United States. During the late 1980s, activists in the United States persuaded many Americans that the risks of consuming apples treated with Alar, a plant-growth regulator, were both credible and unacceptable, while Alar's safety risks did not become politically salient in Europe.

The increased stringency of many European regulations after 1990—most notably the EU's ban on BST and the EU's increasingly restrictive policies toward the planting and consumption of GM varieties—was strongly affected by a series of dramatic, highly visible food safety policy failures that began during the mid-1990s. The most important of these was the belated 1996 admission of the British government that BSE or mad-cow disease could be transmitted to humans. This admission—along with nearly two hundred widely reported deaths from BSE—undermined public confidence in the safety of the European food supply. This and other food safety policy failures also heightened public concerns about the potential dangers of food produced with new agricultural technologies and reduced public trust in the capacity of scientific experts to identify important threats to public health. However, in part because no comparable food safety regulatory failures emerged in the United States, public confidence in government regulators and the scientific advice on which they relied was higher than in Europe.

A second key factor influencing the divergence in regulatory stringency was the criteria employed to make risk management decisions. The earlier stringency of many American food safety regulations reflected the application of more conservative scientific standards for assessing risks to public health. American authorities were prepared to draw policy conclusions from the results of animal tests, while Europeans authorities were less willing to extrapolate the risks to humans on the basis of such tests. The Delaney Clause, which prohibited the approval of any food additives that caused cancer in animals, had no counterpart in any European country.

Subsequently, the criteria used by policy makers in both the United States and Europe to assess and manage risks shifted: American regulatory officials placed increased reliance on scientific risk assessments, while European policy makers began to employ a more precautionary approach to food safety risks. While public opposition to the approval of BST was much stronger in the United States than in Europe, this growth hormone was approved for use in the United States because the scientific studies on which the Food and Drug Administration (FDA) relied consistently reported it to be safe. By contrast, influenced in part by the BSE policy failure, European officials did not regard the evidence for the safety of BSE as sufficiently conclusive to justify permitting its use.

Likewise, American officials determined that the health risks of food produced from genetically modified organisms (GMOs) were no different than from food produced from conventional agricultural production methods. Many European policy makers were more cautious: they believed that there was insufficient evidence of their safety to permit their introduction without more careful scrutiny. While there were comparable levels of concern from many scientists and public health advocates about the health risks of antibiotics in animal feed on both sides of the Atlantic, European and American policy responses differed. European authorities chose to ban them on precautionary grounds, while policy makers in the United States did not believe that the evidence of their links to antibiotic resistance in humans was sufficient to justify restricting them.

The preferences of influential policy makers also played an important role in shaping transatlantic differences in risk regulations for GMOs and antibiotics in animal feed. While both the administrative agencies of the American federal government and the European Commission have generally favored the introduction of GMOs, the former's policy preferences were determinative in the United States, while the latter's were not in Europe. Congress has never adopted any legislation for GMOs, and state governments have not played an important policy role. By contrast, the Commission's policy preferences have been strongly and effectively challenged by the Council of Ministers and the European Parliament (EP) as well as by the governments of some member states. The policy preferences of the U.S. Congress and the EU Council of Ministers toward the use of antibiotics in animal feed also differed sharply; the former has strongly supported their continued use, while the latter has not.

This chapter begins by comparing several food safety standards adopted in the United States and Europe before 1990—most of which were more stringent in the United States. It then discusses the crisis in public confidence in food safety in Europe, which significantly changed the political environment in which European food safety standards were made. It then describes and explains three important examples of more stringent European food safety regulations adopted after 1990, namely BST, GMOs, and antibiotics in animal feed. The final section of the chapter examines food safety policies and politics in the United States since 1990. While several food safety scares have emerged in the United States, relatively few American food safety regulations have been strengthened.

CARCINOGENS IN FOOD

The Delaney Clause and Cancer Risks

The 1958 Delaney Amendment to Section 401 of the Food, Drug, and Cosmetic Act represents one of the earliest and best-known examples of a highly risk-averse American regulatory standard. Its implementation played a critical role in subsequent administrative decisions that made several American regulations more stringent than those adopted in Europe.

This amendment was proposed by Democratic Congressman James Delaney of New York, the chair of a special committee formed to investigate the pesticide contamination of food whose wife had died from cancer. Its introduction reflected increased public concern about both rising rates of cancer deaths and scientific uncertainty about their causes, as well as growing public awareness of the health risks of the widely used chemical DDT. Delaney's amendment, which was approved with remarkably little public or congressional debate, states that "no additive shall be deemed to be safe if it is found to induce cancer when ingested by man or animal, or if it is found, after tests which are appropriate for the evaluation of food additives, to induce cancer in man or animals."[1]

The Delaney Clause essentially established a policy of zero tolerance for any residue of carcinogenic pesticides or additives in processed food, no matter how small the risk or how tenuous the relationship between the results of animal testing and human exposure. It both significantly lowered the scientific threshold required for the banning of any food additives suspected of being a carcinogen and adopted a more stringent approach toward the regulation of carcinogens than any other food safety risk.

The priority placed on avoiding the risks of cancer represented a distinctive feature of American regulatory politics and policies. Carcinogens were again singled out for special attention by the 1976 Toxic Substances Control Act (TSCA), while more than twenty-one different laws adopted after the early 1970s singled out carcinogens for special treatment. Federal regulatory agencies and health research institutes have devoted a disproportionate amount of their research efforts to identifying possible carcinogens. By 1981, the animal testing program of the National Cancer Institute had reviewed the carcinogenic effects of more than two hundred substances, and additional chemicals were being reviewed at the rate of thirty to forty-five a year.

The American regulatory focus on potential cancer-causing substances and the stricter standard to which they were subjected had no parallel in any European country.[2] Neither British nor French regulatory agencies accorded carcinogens a prominent or distinctive place in their regulatory policies. Rather, they regarded carcinogenicity as one of among many possible toxic effects. Their assessment of the risks of carcinogens in the food supply underlies the decision of Britain's Heath and Safety Executive not to update its Carcinogenic Substances Regulations of 1967, which had placed strict controls on only four chemicals. For its part, Germany did place carcinogens in a separate category. According to a commission of the German Research Society, no valid numerical exposure threshold can be established for carcinogens—a view essentially similar to that of the Delaney Clause. But this standard only applied to workplace health and safety regulations, not to food.

These different regulatory approaches do not reflect the greater incidence of cancer in the United States than in many European countries.

[1] James Smart, "All the Stars of the Heavens Were in the Right Places: The Passage of the Food Quality Protection Act of 1966," *Stanford Environmental Law Journal* 17 (1998): 277.

[2] Ronald Brickman, Sheila Jasanoff, and Thomas Ilgen, *Controlling Chemicals: The Politics of Regulation in Europe and the U.S.* (Ithaca, NY: Cornell University Press, 1985), 28–39.

During the second half of the 1970s, deaths from cancer for Americans were lower than in Germany, Finland, Italy, Denmark, and Ireland, but higher than in Sweden, Spain, Greece, and Portugal.[3] According to a World Health Organization study, based on 1979 data, the United States ranked twenty-second out of forty-four countries in incidences of cancer.[4] American polices toward carcinogens primarily reflected public perceptions: "Americans fear cancer more than any other disease." A Gallup poll taken during the mid-1970s found that the public overwhelmingly selected cancer "as the worst thing that can happen to you."[5]

The Delaney Clause also established another influential regulatory policy precedent: it established an extremely low threshold for designating a substance as a carcinogen, one that essentially extrapolated the results of tests on laboratory animals to humans. For many American regulatory agencies, "Animal-man extrapolation *is* 'cancer prevention.'"[6] The American reliance on the results of such tests represented another distinctive feature of American risk management policies. By contrast, European regulators tended to interpret the results of such tests more flexibly, often dismissing evidence judged conclusive by American risk assessments as "flawed, inconclusive, or susceptible to other interpretations."[7] Sheila Jasanoff writes,

> U.S. regulators usually opted to draw conservative inferences when confronting imperfect data; that is inferences more likely to overstate than understate the degree of risk. For example, federal risk assessment guidelines for chemical carcinogens treated positive studies involving rodents as more significant than negative human epidemiological studies. Similarly, in interpreting bioassays, regulatory agencies uniformly endorse the principle of high-dose testing despite the risk of false positives, and accepted benign as well as malignant tumors as indicators of a carcinogenic risk to humans.[8]

The former associate director of the American National Cancer Institute observed, "British work on carcinogenesis seems much more conservative than ours in that they seem to be much more reluctant than American researchers to assert cause-effect relationships."[9]

[3] Edith Efron, *The Apocalyptics: Cancer and the Big Lie: How Environmental Politics Control What We Know About Cancer* (New York: Simon & Schuster, 1984), 449–50.

[4] Ibid., 450.

[5] Quoted in Richard Lichter and Stanley Rothman, *Environmental Cancer–A Political Disease* (New Haven, CT: Yale University Press, 1999), 54.

[6] Efron, *The Apocalyptics*, 449–50.

[7] Sheila Jasanoff, "American Exceptionalism and the Political Acknowledgement of Risk" in *Risk*, ed. Edward J. Burger Jr. (Ann Arbor: University of Michigan Press, 1993), 69.

[8] Ibid., 68.

[9] Quoted in Frances B. McCrea and Gerald E. Markle, "The Estrogen Replacement Controversy in the USA and UK: Different Answers to the Same Question?" *Social Studies of Science* 14, no. 1 (1984): 15.

REGULATORY POLICY DIVERGENCE

Differences in transatlantic standards for assessing the risks of carcinogens had important policy impacts: they led the United States to adopt more stringent regulations, or adopt them earlier, for DES, cyclamates, and several pesticides, and also played a role in the administrative decision to ban the plant growth regulator Alar used to treat apples.

DES

In 1972, the steroid growth promoter DES, which was administered as an implant under the skin of an animal as a feed additive, was banned in the United States. on the grounds that it was a carcinogen, and thus violated the Delaney Clause. Its use was temporarily reinstated in 1974, and in 1976, the FDA set the minimum detectable levels at 2 parts per billion. It was completely banned in the United States in 1979 because there was no credible scientific ground for identifying a residue below which a carcinogenic effect would not occur. By contrast, DES was not banned in the EU until 1987, largely due to uncertainty as to whether there was a definable "no effect" dose for its potential tumor-inducing effects in humans. Thus the American regulatory approach was more risk-averse than that of the EU; the latter allowed "uncertainty" to delay a more stringent risk management decision.

Cyclamates

American and European officials also differed in their assessments of health risks of artificial sweeteners. In 1958, the FDA authorized the use of both cyclamate and saccharin. By the late 1960s, cyclamate—typically used in combination with smaller quantities of saccharin—was an ingredient used in more than 250 foods developed for weight-conscious consumers, with total annual consumption of 18.5 million pounds. It was consumed by three-quarters of all Americans.

In 1969, Abbott Laboratories, the primary producer of cyclamate, reported the results of a four-year animal study which found that laboratory animals that had been fed the highest doses of a combination of cyclamate-saccharin—the equivalent of three thousand packets of Sucaryl, a widely used artificial sweetener, per day—had developed a significant number of bladder tumors, half of which were cancerous. Based on this study, as well as an FDA study that had found bladder tumors in a small number of animals fed a calcium cyclamate and saccharin combination, the FDA, acting pursuant to the Delaney Clause, banned cyclamates in soft drinks, general-purpose foods, and non-prescription drugs in 1968. Within a year this chemical was removed from prescription drugs as well. By contrast, only one European country, Britain, banned cyclamates. This ban was enacted about the same time as in the United States, but was rescinded in 1995. The EU continues to permit its use.

Pesticides

Standards for assessing the risks of pesticides were also more risk-averse in the United States. For example, laboratory studies during the 1960s had found that Aldrin and Dieldrin, two closely related organic pesticides widely used in agriculture in both Britain and the United States, had increased the incidence of liver tumors in mice but did not induce cancer in any other organs of this animal, and failed to induce a carcinogenic response in rats, monkeys, or dogs. The British government concluded that this meant there was insufficient evidence that these pesticides caused malignant tumors in humans; British officials "expected the traditional requirements of scientific causality to be established before labeling a chemical carcinogenic."[10]

But in 1974, the U.S. Environmental Protection Agency (EPA), acting on the basis of the same scientific evidence available to the British government, banned both pesticides, except for some limited uses. It based its decision on the 1972 Federal Environmental Pesticide Control Act, another precautionary regulatory statute, which stated that "suspension [of a pesticide] is to be based upon a potential or likely injury and need not be based upon demonstrable injury or certainty of future public harm."[11] All remaining uses were banned in 1987. For its part, France banned Aldrin and Diedrin, acting two years earlier than the United States, while between 1974 and 1979, Germany imposed restrictions on the use of both and established maximum concentration levels. In 1978, the EU adopted restrictions essentially similar to those adopted by the United States four years earlier.[12]

In 1969, TCDD, a toxic dioxin that is a component of the herbicide 2, 4, 5-T, was linked to birth defects in laboratory animals by an American Presidential Advisory Commission. The following year the EPA banned its use on all food crops except rice and in 1979 suspended its use on forests. Its registration was cancelled in 1983. By contrast, British studies of the health impact of the herbicide issued in 1979 and 1980 concluded that there was no risk at very low levels of exposure. Officials of the

---

[10] Brendan Gillespie, Dave Eva, and Roy Johnston, "Carcinogenic Risk Assessment in the U.S. and Great Britain: The Case of Aldrin/Diedrin," *Social Studies of Science* 9, no. 3 (1979): 289.

[11] Ibid., 285.

[12] Brickman, Jasanoff, and Ilgen, *Controlling Chemicals*, 321.

British Ministry of Agriculture subsequently contended that the EPA was panicked into its partial ban by a now discredited study in Oregon which linked spontaneous abortions to 2, 4, 5-T.[13] In 1980, Britain issued maximum concentration levels. The use of this herbicide was partially banned in Germany in 1974, and in 1979 Germany established maximum concentration levels. Between 1975 and 1977, the French government restricted its use, imposed maximum concentration levels, and prohibited its aerial spraying. The chemical was subsequently classified as "harmful" by the EU in 1978, again illustrating that American officials had acted earlier to adopt more stringent regulations.

During the 1970s, American pesticide regulations were stricter than in Britain, France, and Germany. While all four countries established procedures for reexamining previously approved products if new risks were suspected, such reappraisals were typically perfunctory in the European countries and primarily focused on assessing new ingredients and preparations. By contrast, the 1972 Pesticide Control Act required the EPA to reexamine for re-registration the approximately 35,000 pesticides then on the market. To facilitate the EPA's ability to meet this legislative requirement, the Federal Pesticide Act of 1978 allowed the EPA to develop genetic registration standards for active ingredients. "Despite lags in implementation [American regulations] focus[ed] far greater attention on pesticides already in use than [was] customary in the three European countries."[14]

Alar

Developed by the Uniroyal Chemical Company in the early 1960s, the plant-growth regulator Alar was approved by the U.S. Department of Agriculture for use on apples in 1968 in order to increase fruit yields and improve the appearance of harvested fruits.[15] During the 1970s, several studies found that the active ingredient in Alar, as well as one of its breakdown products, produced tumors in test animals. Pursuant to the terms of the Delaney Clause, the EPA tentatively decided to cancel its registration.

However, before doing so, it consulted the Scientific Advisory Panel (SAP) for pesticides—as it was required to do under federal law. Testifying at the SAP hearings, Uniroyal, the chemical's manufacturer, claimed that the results of the cancer studies were not sufficiently conclusive to justify its withdrawal. The SAP concurred and stated that studies

[13] *The Economist*, "Killing What?" June 21, 1980.
[14] Brickman, Jasanoff, and Ilgen, *Controlling Chemicals*, 37.
[15] This paragraph is based on Jasanoff, "American Exceptionalism," 73–4.

demonstrating that Alar posed unacceptable health risks were flawed. The EPA also agreed with this assessment, concluding that "existing studies, singly or in combination, are inadequate to serve as the basis for regulatory action."[16] The agency then withdrew its proposed ban, though it did list Alar as a "possible carcinogen." At the same time, it changed its estimate of potential cancers from one to ten thousand per million, to the much lower estimate of forty-five per million.[17]

The EPA also authorized Uniroyal to conduct more tests. These studies found that one of Alar's breakdown products did indeed cause blood tumors in mice, though not in rats, and only at very high exposure levels. An analysis of these studies by the EPA concluded that although some mice in the high-dose study were dying early and that "the deaths of these mice were due to the tumors, it may nonetheless be argued that the deaths were the result of excessive toxicity, which may compromise the outcome of the study."[18] An independent review of several studies found that "the weight of the evidence clearly favors classification of daminozide (the substance formed when Alar breaks down in processed apples) as *non-carcinogenic*."[19]

Nonetheless on February 1, 1989, the EPA's acting administrator stated that "there is inescapable and direct correlation between exposure to [Alar] and the development of life-threatening tumors" and announced that the EPA would shortly proceed to ban Alar.[20] He also urged farmers to stop using it. However, the EPA delayed the implementation of its ban for eighteen months in order to allow for formal cancellation proceedings. It granted this extension because, according to the agency's calculations, there was a risk of less than one additional cancer per million during this interval.

At this point, Alar's safety risks become highly politically salient. The Natural Resources Defense Council (NRDC), an environmental non-government organization, commissioned its own study of the risks to children posed from several pesticides and chemical products, including Alar. Its study, *Intolerable Risk: Pesticides in Our Children*, concluded that Alar's risks to human health were several hundredfold higher than those stated by the EPA; it went on to predict that some 5,500 to 6,300 individuals would eventually get cancer from exposure to Alar and various other pesticides, many of them children. The NRDC hired a public

[16] Michael Fumento, *Science Under Siege: Balancing Technology and the Environment* (New York: William Morrow, 1993), 22.

[17] Ibid., 23.

[18] Ibid., 27.

[19] Emphasis added. Ibid., 26.

[20] Al Heier, "EPA Accelerates Process to Cancel Damiozide [Alar] Uses on Apples; Extends Tolerance," *EPA Environmental News*, February 1, 1989.

relations firm, Fenton Communications, to publicize its findings, and arranged for them to first be reported on the widely watched television news show *60 Minutes.*

This program, which was broadcast on February 26, 1989, opened with the dramatic statement, "The most potent cancer-causing agent in our food supply is a substance sprayed on apples to keep them on the trees longer and make them look better."[21] It featured an interview with a representative of the NRDC who informed viewers that Alar had caused "an estimated 240 deaths per million population among children who are average consumers of Alar-treated food," adding that children "are at increased risk because they drink 18 times as much apple juice as their mothers."[22]

The result was the "Great Apple Scare of 1989." Sales of apples and applesauce dropped precipitously; mothers fearful for the safety of their children flooded their physicians with anxious phone calls. New York City and Los Angeles removed apples, apple pie, and applesauce from the lunchtime menus of their public schools. One mother had the police stop her child's school bus so that she could remove the apple she had placed in his lunch box. At a special Senate hearing on Alar's safety, one witness testified that the EPA "is turning American parents into the malevolent stepmother in *Snow White,* handing out enticingly red but fatal apples to our children."[23] The Beech-Nut Nutrition Corporation promised to stop using Alar treated apples, while supermarkets began selling "Alar-free" apples, though many of these labels turned out to be inaccurate.

A memo from Fenton Communications, the public relations firm hired by the NRDC, candidly noted, "Usually, it takes a significant natural disaster to create this much sustained news attention for an environmental problem. We believe this experience proves there are other ways to raise public awareness for the purpose of moving the Congress and policymakers."[24] The NRDC's study was, however, sharply criticized by several scientists, who argued that the environmental organization had overstated childhood exposure to pesticide residues and individual pesticide consumption by factors ranging from 389 to 500. A comprehensive report by the National Research Council concluded that "there was no evidence that residues of individual pesticides in our diet contribute significantly to the overall risks of getting cancer."[25] Nonetheless, in May of that year, the apple industry announced that it would stop using Alar by

---

[21] Fumento, *Science Under Siege,* 19.

[22] Ronald Gots, *Toxic Risks: Science, Regulation, and Perception* (Boca Raton, FL: Lewis Publishers, 1993), 250.

[23] Fumento, *Science Under Siege,* 30.

[24] Ibid., 31.

[25] Ibid., 36.

the fall. For its part, Uniroyal halted distribution for spraying on plants in the United States and the EPA subsequently banned the use of Alar on all food products, classifying it as a "probable human carcinogen."

By contrast, the safety risks of Alar did not become politically salient in Europe. A December 1989 report by the British Independent Advisory Committee on Pesticides concluded that "even for infants and children consuming the maximum quantities of apples and apple juice, subjected to the maximum treatment with daminozide [the technical name for Alar], there is no risk."[26] The advisory committee's chair endorsed Uniroyal's claim that laboratory mice had been given too much daminozide to enable its results to be extrapolated to human exposure. He added that "we don't always make the assumption that the animal data are transferable to man, particularly in the absence of pharmacokinetics that make it clear that the compound is handled in the same way at massive doses as it is at low levels."[27] Its advice was accepted by the Ministry of Agriculture, Fisheries and Food. Only one European country, namely Sweden, banned its use. The most recent European review of the chemical, conducted by the EU in 2005, continued to permit its application.

ANALYSIS

The Alar controversy demonstrated the ability of an activist group in the United States during the late 1980s to ring an "alarm bell" that became highly amplified and effectively transformed the terms of public debate. The dramatic nature of the dangers identified by the NRDC and extensively publicized in the media created an effective "policy trigger." Virtually overnight, the risks of consuming apples treated with a chemical product that had been in use for more than two decades become both credible and politically unacceptable. By contrast, public opposition to Alar did not emerge in Europe and thus European policy makers did not find themselves under pressure to ban it. They continued to permit its use because the scientific advice on which they relied considered it to be safe. The Alar controversy also had a longer term political impact in the United States. It did succeed in placing on the political agenda the need for risk assessments that specifically addressed the heightened vulnerabilities of children to various chemicals in food—an issue that Congress addressed six years later in the Food Quality Protection Act of 1995 (discussed below). But widespread criticisms of the scientific basis of the NRDC's allegations also undermined the credibility of future "alarm bells" rung by activist groups, made the media more reluctant

---

[26] Ibid., 38.

[27] Aaron Wildavksy, *But Is It True? A Citizen's Guide to Environmental Health and Safety Issues* (Cambridge, MA: Harvard University Press, 1995), 214.

to uncritically publicize them, and made regulatory authorities less willing to issue stringent standards in response to them. For critics of the response of the EPA to the NRDC's media campaign, the Alar controversy became a potent political symbol of a false positive policy error based on public fears and "junk science."

BEEF HORMONES

The 1980s also witnessed a European counterpart to the Alar controversy, but one whose long-term policy impact was precisely the opposite of that which occurred in the United States. The EU's 1985 hormone ban reveals how the making of risk management decisions in Europe were beginning to become more confrontational, adversarial, and more responsive to pressures from nongovernmental lobbies and public opinion. As in the case of Alar in the United States, policy makers in Europe chose to override the recommendations of their scientific advisory bodies and adopt a more stringent risk regulation in response to consumer pressures. But unlike in the United States, they subsequently became more, rather than less, likely to do so in several other areas of public policy, including for food safety.

A Crisis Emerges

Controversy in Europe over the safety of growth hormones that were given to cattle dates from 1980, when newspaper articles reported that babies in Italy were growing oversized genitals and breasts because they had eaten veal treated with hormones. European public opinion was outraged, and large numbers of consumers began to boycott veal.[28] A boycott of hormone-treated veal organized by the French Consumers Union resulted in a 70 percent decline in veal purchases.[29] In July 1981, the Council of Ministers voted to ban the use of thyrostatics and stilbenes, two hormonal substances that were generally considered to have harmful effects. This ban included DES (dimethyl stilbenes), significant residues of which had been discovered in Italian baby food. As it turned out, the causal connection between DES, which was commonly administered to dairy cows as a growth supplement (and which had been banned by the United States) and the physical deformities suffered by Italian babies was never scientifically

---

[28] Andre Brand and Amanda Ellerton, *Report of Hormone-Treated Meat* (Brussels: Club de Bruxelles, 1989), 2.9.

[29] Mark Hunter, "Francois Lamy: How France's Nader Won Ban on Hormone-Treated Meat," *Washington Post*, December 25, 1988.

established. But the intense publicity surrounding the adverse impact on Italian babies created a "risk availability cascade" that spilled over to public concern about the safety of *all* hormones given to cattle.[30]

Faced with heightened public concern over beef safety, the European Commission established a scientific inquiry to study the safety of three natural and two synthetic hormones that were widely used for cattle in Europe. The Scientific Working Group on Anabolic Agents in Animal Protection concluded that, under appropriate conditions, such as good husbandry practices and limits on maximum doses, the three naturally occurring steroid hormones presented no danger to human health. However, due to lack of adequate scientific data, it was unable to reach a conclusion as to the health effects of the two artificial hormones, Trenbolone and Zeranol. A subsequent, more extensive inquiry, held in 1984 and 1985, concluded that the two artificial hormones were "harmless for consumers."[31]

Pressures on the EU

Notwithstanding these risk assessments, the Commission found itself under growing pressure to ban the use of all growth-promoting hormones. In fact, the European Commission canceled the Working Group's meetings before it could issue its final report. The Commission's willingness to impose a more sweeping hormone ban was in turn linked to its commitment, expressed in its influential 1985 White Paper, to create a single European market by removing non-tariff barriers among its member states. Because regulations governing the use of hormones had not been harmonized, each member state remained free to establish its own rules governing their use. The result was a wide array of barriers to intra-European trade as some European countries forbade the import of beef produced according to the more permissive standards of other member states.

In light of the importance of livestock farming to the EU—half the farms in Europe raised animals—as well as the extensive amount of intra-European trade in beef, the Commission had been attempting to establish a common veterinary policy even before the hormone controversy erupted. Heightened public anxiety about the health risks beef produced with hormones made this task even more urgent.

Throughout the first half of the 1980s, European consumer and environmental groups waged a vigorous campaign to prohibit the use of all

---

[30] John Peterson, "Hormones, Heifers and High Politics: Biotechnology and the Common Agricultural Policy," *Public Administration* 67, no. 4 (Winter 1989): 461.

[31] Brand and Ellerton, *Report of Hormone-Treated Beef*, 3.6.

growth hormones in animal production. Owing to their success in ringing an alarm bell about the health risks of hormones, their safety became increasingly politically salient and their continued use a highly visible and emotional issue. The campaign to ban all hormones was led by the Bureau of European Consumers Unions (BEUC), a coalition of national consumer unions which lobbies the European Commission on issues affecting consumers.

While the BEUC accepted the conclusion of the Commission's first scientific inquiry that some of these problems could be avoided if the hormones were used appropriately, the Bureau contended that it was very difficult to detect their presence in processed meats. Accordingly, it argued that the only way to ensure that public health was adequately protected was to prohibit hormone use entirely. The BEUC's position was buttressed by the growing number of consumers who preferred to consume "natural" foods, many of whom were willing to pay a premium for such products, including for "hormone-free" meat.

The Bureau further argued that permitting the continued use of growth-inducing hormones made little economic sense since the EU had a large surplus of beef. Calculating that half of the EU's 400,000 tons of stored beef was due to hormone-based production, BEUC concluded that "the only economic advantage of using hormones is to make profits for those who produce and use them."[32] This argument was in turn challenged by a member of the EP who pointed out that "It is manifestly stupid to ban growth promoters for use in beef cattle on health risk grounds just because we have a surplus of beef. If we follow that argument, we should ban tractors on smoke-emission grounds because we have a surplus of grain."[33]

However, the EP, where European consumer and environmental groups enjoyed considerable influence, became a focal point of the opposition to continued hormone use within the EU. When the Commission proposed allowing the use of the three natural hormones for fattening purposes under strictly controlled conditions, the EP strongly registered its objection, and the Commission backed down. The EP was also firmly opposed to a compromise that would have permitted nations to maintain their own regulations for at least some of the disputed hormones; they insisted that all standards be harmonized. Finally, in early 1985 the Council of Ministers approved a resolution committing it to harmonize hormone use throughout the EU.

[32] Ibid., 3.4.
[33] Quoted in Carol Kramer, "Food Safety and International Trade: The US-EC Meat and Hormone Controversies," in *The Political Economy of US Agriculture*, ed. Carol Kramer (Washington, DC: Resources for the Future, 1989), 228.

The EU Beef Hormone Ban

As it approached a decision on the five disputed hormones, the Council of Ministers was divided. The Netherlands, Greece, and Italy favored a complete ban. While Germany permitted its farmers to use the three natural hormones, its strong domestic green movement now persuaded it to join the anti-hormone camp. For their part, Britain and Ireland favored the continued use of all five hormones. Britain's powerful farming lobby claimed it needed to use Trenbolone and Zeranol for managing young bulls, while farming interests in Ireland feared that a ban would only lead to the creation of a black market in hormones. France, Europe's major agricultural producer, also opposed a more general hormone ban. However, as anti-hormone sentiment increased in Europe, some of the nations that permitted hormone use began to fear that their continued use of them would place their producers at a competitive disadvantage, since consumers might now begin to shun their "tainted" beef and veal.

By the time the Council of Ministers was ready to vote on a hormone ban, the only important constituency still firmly opposed to it was the European Federation of Animal Health. This federation represents thirty-one pharmaceutical companies, including the subsidiaries of a number of large American firms, as well as European national associations of veterinary medicine manufacturers. It argued that "authorized products which have been guaranteed by scientists all over the world to be safe, effective and of the highest quality cannot be banned for purely subjective reasons," and urged the Council to accept the advice of the EU's scientific advisory bodies, which had concluded that at least some of the five disputed hormones were safe.[34]

However, in December 1985, the Council adopted a directive extending its ban on the use of hormones to include the five controversial substances omitted from its 1981 directive, though it permitted use of the natural hormones for therapeutic purposes. The Council stated that "assessments of [the hormones'] effect on human health vary and this is reflected in the regulations governing their use . . . this divergence . . . is a serious barrier to intra-Community trade." It concluded that banning "the use of all hormonal substances for fattening purposes . . . [would] ensure that all consumers [would be] able to buy the products in question . . . [and would] bring about an increase in consumption."[35] The Council also reasoned that a complete ban on hormone use represented the best way of resolving the distortions in intra-European trade created

---

[34] Brand and Ellerton, *Report on Hormone-Treated Beef,* 4.3.

[35] Janet Shaner, "The Beef Hormone Trade Dispute," *Harvard Business School Case* no. 9-590-035, (Rev. 12/89): 6.

by divergent national regulations. In light of the pressure from consumer activists and the EU's interest in maintaining public support for its single market project, it made more political sense to force some member states to tighten their standards than to require others to lower them.

The ban represented the first important political victory for European consumer organizations; their public campaign and the public anxieties which it both reflected and reinforced, rather than the judgment of the Commission's own scientific advisory bodies, had carried the day. In defending the EU's decision, Franz Andriessen, the EU's agricultural commissioner, explained: "Scientific advice is important, but it is not decisive. In public opinion, this is a very delicate issue that has to be dealt with in political terms." He added: "not all political decisions are based on science."[36] According to another EU official, "no matter what the scientists say, I'm afraid that we Europeans prefer to eat our meat free of hormones."[37] Another official stated that the ban "simply represents the EU bowing to public pressure," adding that while many scientific authorities had judged hormone-treated beef to be harmless, "the public is still opposed to the meat."[38] The Council's decision presaged the increasingly important role that public risk perceptions and activist pressures would play in many subsequent risk management decisions made by the European Union.

The EU's decision was strongly criticized by American officials. According to an official from the U.S. Department of Agriculture, "What has happened in the short space of six years is that Europe has decided to forgo a scientific consensus in the veterinary drug approval process in favor of a subjective plebiscite based solely on emotion."[39]

In November 1990, the European Court of Justice (ECJ) ruled on a challenge to the hormone ban brought by the European Federation of Animal Growth. The Federation claimed that there was no scientific evidence of any harm to consumers from the proper use of hormones. However, the court ruled the Council of Ministers had acted within their authority when they banned the use of the five hormones because of growing consumer concerns about food safety. Although the precautionary principle had yet to become formally adopted by the EU, the ECJ's decision was implicitly informed by it: the Court held that since there was no proof that the hormone substances *were* harmless, banning them *was* justified. In effect, this decision placed the burden of proof on those who supported hormone use to demonstrate their safety, rather than on those who wanted to ban them to prove that they were harmful.

---

[36] Peterson, "Hormones, Heifers and High Politics," 46.

[37] William Sheeline, "What's the Beef?" *Fortune*, January 30, 1989.

[38] "European Officials Emphasize Hormone Ban Is a Consumer Protection Issue, Not a Trade Barrier," *International Trade Reporter*, February 15, 1989.

[39] *Food Chemical News*, October 17, 1986.

Beef Hormones in the United States

The EU's ban on the use of the five hormones contrasted sharply with the United States which, beginning in 1954, had approved the use of several growth hormones for cattle, including the five now banned in Europe. Consequently, growth hormones had become critical to American beef production, with more than 90 percent of cattle receiving them. According to the U.S. Department of Agriculture (USDA), "the increased production efficiency combined with the higher lean meat percentage gave the farmer an economic benefit of $80 per head," or an estimated $650 million per year.[40]

The position of the American government is not that beef hormones are "risk free," but rather that they do not pose a "significant" risk. In the view of the FDA, the federal regulatory agency with primary authority for food safety, the three natural hormones banned by the EU are metabolized by the animal and leave no residue differentiable from internally produced hormones. Their implantation can only be detected by testing for abnormal hormone levels for which the FDA has established tolerance levels.[41] Similar health protection standards were established for the two synthetic hormones, whose use is easier to detect since they do leave residues in meat.

As the United States was the largest exporter of beef to the EU, and less than 10 percent of American beef exports to Europe were produced without hormones, during the year following the 1989 ban's extension to beef imports, American exports of beef to the EU declined by nearly 80 percent. The United States claimed that the EU's hormone ban had no scientific basis, noting even the Commission's own scientific advisory bodies had not found any evidence that the hormones posed a credible health risk. American officials contended that any test of meat for purity should be based on whether it contains residues of harmful chemicals, *not* on whether hormones had earlier been administered to the animals from whom it was derived.[42] According to an FDA official, when used properly the traces of naturally produced hormones are so minuscule that "a pregnant woman would manufacture several million times more estrogen a day than if she ate a pound of meat each day."[43]

European officials in turn countered that they had the authority to enact whatever regulations they deemed necessary to protect consumers,

---

[40] Quoted in Shaner, "The Beef Hormone Trade Dispute," 5.

[41] Ibid.

[42] Walter Mossberg, "Dispute Over Meat Imports Threatens New Snarl in US-EC Trade Links," *Wall Street Journal*, December 23, 1998.

[43] Adrian Rafael Halpern, "The US-EC Hormones Beef Controversy and the Standards Code: Implication for the Application of Health Regulations to Agricultural Trade, *North Carolina Journal of International Law and Commercial Regulation* 14, no. 4 (Winter 1989): 149.

regardless of their impact on trade, since "every country has the right under world trade rules to restrict imports for health reasons."[44] The French Minister of Foreign Affairs Édith Cresson explained, "This isn't a way to avoid the importation of meat; it's a matter of health."[45] According to the EU's agricultural commissioner, the ban was "no more a trade barrier than prohibition."[46] To further illustrate this point, Sir Roy Denman, the EU's ambassador to the United States, repeatedly raised the issue of American restrictions on unpasteurized cheese from Europe. The United States permits the importation of French cheeses such as Brie, but only if they are baked first, which, Denman observed, "makes brie taste as much like real brie as apple juice tastes like a dry martini."[47] Yet the EU had never demanded a scientific inquiry into the dangers of cheese from unpasteurized milk, which Europeans have been consuming for centuries. Rather, "they have accepted that Americans have expressed a democratic preference for hygiene over taste, however eccentric or unnecessary."[48] Accordingly, the United States should similarly respect European consumer preferences and concerns.

An ad placed in an American publication by the Italian-based Association of Italian Food Processors compared the hormone ban to an American food safety regulation, which had been adopted the same year the EU's hormone ban was applied to imported beef. It read:

> There is no established scientific basis that the pesticide Alar is harmful to human health; however, consumer perception has effectively banned its use in the U.S. Is it then the function of the US Trade Representative to discipline European consumers for perceiving that feeding cattle with growth hormones is undesirable and a hazard to health?[49]

In marked contrast to Europe, the risks of consuming meat from hormone-treated animals did not become politically salient in the United States even though they were used much more extensively than in Europe prior to the EU ban.[50] No American consumer organization demanded that the

[44] Ibid.

[45] Quoted in "European Officials Emphasize Hormone Ban Is a Consumer Protection Issue, Not a Trade Barrier," *International Trade Reporter*, February 15, 1989.

[46] *The Economist*, "Brie and Hormones," January 7, 1989.

[47] Quoted in ibid.

[48] Ibid.

[49] Clyde Farnsworth, "Trade Retaliation Readied If Europe Bars Meats of US," *New York Times*, December 27, 1988.

[50] However, in 1986 the House Committee on Government Operations did issue a report criticizing the FDA for "consistently disregarding its responsibility" for protecting the health of American consumers, which had no political impact. See "Hormones in US Beef Linked to Increased Cancer Risk," *World Wire*, October 21, 2009, available at http://world wire.com/news/0910210001.html, accessed October 29, 2009.

United States follow the lead of the EU and ban their use, although some American consumer groups did express support for the EU's right to do so after the United States filed a complaint with the World Trade Organization (WTO). But American consumers who agree with the EU's assessment that the health risks of hormone-treated beef are both credible and unacceptable do have a market-based alternative: they can purchase beef labeled "hormone free."

The Beef Hormone Trade Dispute

In 1996, the United States filed a formal complaint with the WTO. It argued that the EU's ban on hormone-treated beef was illegal under WTO rules because there was no scientific basis for the claim that American production methods resulted in an unsafe product.

The EU countered that since European consumers *were* fearful that consuming hormone-treated beef might endanger their health, "there is some basis for the belief that an absolute ban is better than a low threshold for hormone presence."[51] Why should European consumers tolerate the presence of substances in imported foodstuffs that they regard as harmful, "absent *conclusive* proof of [no] deleterious health effects?"[52] European officials further contended that the evidence that hormone-treated beef *was* safe was not conclusive: the three natural hormones were known to produce cancer risks when used or consumed for purposes other than growth promotion, while under experimental conditions high dosages of each of the five banned hormones had been found to produce cancer in animals.[53] The latter position, in effect, adopted the highly risk-averse standard of the Delaney Clause that the U.S. Congress had approved three decades earlier.

Unable to settle this issue through negotiations, the United States brought its evidence regarding the safety of the hormones to the Codex Alimentarius Commission, an international standards body that had been authorized under the WTO—Sanitary and Phythosanitary Measures (SPS) agreement to establish global food safety standards.[54] By a

[51] Ibid., 149.
[52] Emphasis added. Werner Meng, "The Hormone Conflict between the EEC and the US within the Context of GATT," *Michigan Journal of International Law* 11, no. 3 (Spring 1990): 836.
[53] Trish Kelly, *The Impact of the WTO: The Environment, Public Health and Sovereignty* (Northampton, MA: Edward Elgar, 2007), 71.
[54] For the relationship between the Codex and the WTO, see Tim Büthe, "The Politics of Food Safety in Global Trade: The Codex Alimentarius Commission and the SPS Agreement of the WTO," in *Import Safety: Regulatory Governance in the Global Economy*, ed. Cary Coglianese, Adam Finkel, and David Zaring (Philadelphia: University of Pennsylvania Press, 2009), 88–109.

vote of 33 to 27, the first divided vote in the history of the Codex, the types and dosages of the growth hormones used by American farmers were determined to be safe. Armed with this favorable scientific ruling, the United States then filed a formal complaint with the WTO, and in 1997, a dispute resolution panel ruled in its favor.

The WTO's Appellate Body confirmed this decision the following year, primarily on the basis that the EU had not produced sufficient scientific evidence to support its claim that the proper use of the hormones presented a health hazard. Because the EU refused to comply with the WTO ruling, the United States imposed retaliatory tariffs of approximately $100 million, equivalent to the annual losses suffered by American beef exporters. These tariffs sparked a wave of protests against the United States by French farmers who had been disproportionately affected by the products selected by the United States for its retaliatory tariffs. Several attacked a McDonalds restaurant in France as a symbol of the threat of American food culture to France's culinary traditions. The Obama administration subsequently reached a provisional agreement with the EU under which the American tariffs would be gradually phased out over four years as the EU increased its imports of hormone-free beef from the United States.

ANALYSIS

The EU's decision to ban all growth hormones for livestock represents the first important case of a transatlantic divergence in a health, safety, or environmental risk regulation stemming from a more stringent European-wide regulation. It reflected the growing influence of public pressures within the EU for more stringent and risk-averse food safety regulations—pressures that led the EU to essentially override the recommendations of its scientific advisory bodies. These pressures would become amplified subsequent to the BSE policy failure the following decade. Likewise, the relative lack of public concern in the United States over the safety of meat from hormone-treated cattle prefigured the relative indifference of the American public to the risks of GMOs.

FOOD SAFETY SCARES IN EUROPE

An important factor underlying the increased stringency of European food safety regulations was that, beginning in the mid-1990s, Europe experienced more highly visible and dramatic food safety policy failures than did the United States. These created a series of "policy ripples" or "risk availability cascades" that affected public perceptions of the safety of other food production technologies. They reduced the trust of

European citizens in the officials and regulatory agencies responsible for protecting their health as well as the credibility of the scientific advice given to government officials. This crisis of public confidence made both the European public and European policy makers considerably more risk-averse toward many food safety risks, especially those linked to the introduction of new agricultural technologies.

BSE

The most important European food safety scare was the "mad-cow disease" epidemic.[55] Bovine spongiform encephalopathy (BSE) is a disease spread among cattle, which appears to have been caused by their being fed ruminant-derived meat and bone meal, a cheap source of animal protein. Outbreaks of the disease were first reported in Britain in 1986. By the early 1990s, more than 70,000 British cattle had become infected, and in 1993 roughly one thousand new cases were being reported each week. But through 1988, the meat of infected animals continued to be sold for human consumption. That same year, the British government banned the feeding of bone meal to cattle, though it continued to be fed to pigs and poultry and to be exported. But the British government's regulatory officials and their scientific advisors assured the British public that BSE could not be transmitted to humans—a position that they publicly maintained for eight years, notwithstanding a number of scientific studies that suggested that human transmission was in fact possible. Their messages were consistent: "British beef is 100 per cent safe,"[56] and "there is no scientific evidence of a causal link between BSE in cattle and Creutzfeldt-Jacob Disease (CJD) in humans."[57]

After ten British citizens had become infected with CJD, a painful and fatal disease, in March 1996, Stephen Donnell, the British Secretary of State for Health, dramatically announced that there *was* a possible connection between BSE and the recent incidences of CJD. The BSE crisis has

---

[55]The material on BSE in Britain and Europe primarily draws upon Katherine O'Neill, "Mad Cows and Ailing Hens: The Transatlantic Relationship and Livestock Diseases" (May 17, 2006), *Institute of European Studies*, Paper 060517, available at http://repositories. cdlib.org/ies/060517, accessed 11/22/2010. Reprinted in Miranda Schreurs, Henrik Selin, and Stacy VanDeveer, eds., *Transatlantic Environment and Energy Policies* (Burlington, VT: Ashgate, 2009), 231–50. See also Maxime Schwartz, *How the Cows Turned Mad* (Berkeley: University of California Press, 2003), and Scott Ratzan, ed., *The Mad Cow Crisis: Health and the Public Good* (New York: New York University Press, 1998).

[56]Tim Lang, "BSE and CJD: Recent Developments," in Ratzan, *The Mad Cow Crisis*. For a detailed analysis of how and why the British government concluded that BSE did not present a human health risk, see Elizabeth Fisher, *Risk: Regulation and Administrative Constitutionalism* (Oxford: Hart Publishing, 2004), chap. 2.

[57]Fisher, *Risk Regulation*, 82.

been described as "the biggest failure in UK public policy since the 1956 Suez Crisis."[58] A 1966 poll of British consumers reported that 73 percent believed that "the Government knew there was a risk and tried to hide it."[59] The British government's admission also sparked a major European crisis as consumers, first in Britain and then in the rest of Europe, cut back on their beef consumption. Within two days, seven member states had banned British beef imports in an effort to shore up consumer confidence in the safety of their own beef production.

The European Commissioner for Agriculture, Franz Fischler, termed the BSE issue "the biggest crisis the EU had ever had."[60] It remained highly visible for several years. In March 1996, the European Commission issued a global ban on British beef exports, which was criticized by the British government as an example of heavy-handed European bureaucracy. It also required Britain to undertake a massive slaughter of cattle in order to eradicate the disease. BSE infected cattle were subsequently discovered in Germany and Spain, leading to a further reduction of domestic beef consumption in both countries. In an effort to rebuild consumer confidence in the safety of European beef, the EU established a mandatory testing program for slaughtered cattle in 2001. The following year, acting on the advice of its Scientific Steering Committee, it temporarily banned the use of animal proteins in animal feed for farm animals bred for human consumption as a precautionary measure. By 2008, nearly two hundred deaths in Europe had been linked to CJD, mostly in Britain, but also in other European countries. Each of these "unfortunate events" received extensive media coverage.

BSE was widely perceived as a major policy failure, not only by Britain, but by the EU. The Temporary Committee of Inquiry into BSE, established by the European Parliament in July 1996, reported that although the Commission had acted promptly to ban exports of British beef, European institutions had mismanaged the crisis by giving greater weight to national agricultural and industrial interests rather than protecting human health. Accordingly, the crisis had "severely damaged the credibility of the EU authorities as regulators and risk managers, triggering an unprecedented crisis of confidence among both citizens and national officials in the way beef was produced and regulated at the EU level."[61]

[58] Erik Millstone, "Comment and Analysis," *Financial Times* (October 6, 2000).

[59] Lang, "BSE and CJD," 71.

[60] Catherine Goethals, Scott Ratzan, and Veronica Demko, "The Politics of BSE: Negotiating the Public's Health," in Ratzan, *The Mad Cow Crisis*, 95.

[61] Ellen Vos, "Responding to Catastrophe: Towards a New Architecture for EU Food Safety Regulation," in *Experimentalist Governance in the European Union: Towards a New Architecture*, ed. Charles Sabel and Jonathan Zeitlin (Oxford: Oxford University Press, 2010), 153.

Other European Food Safety Scares

In 1999, the illegal feeding of dioxin-contaminated feed to Belgian farm animals created another "unfortunate event." High levels of dioxin, a cancer-causing chemical, were found in both Belgian meat products and eggs, though there were no immediate reports of human deaths or illnesses. Most European countries, as well as several non-EU countries, banned imports of Belgian agricultural products, including processed foods such as chocolate.

"Poultrygate," as the Belgian press dubbed the scandal (because poultry and eggs were the first products to be infected), not only brought Belgium's trade in agricultural products to a virtual standstill, but led to the resignation of two government ministers, and the subsequent electoral defeat of the government of Prime Minister Jean-Luc Dehaene, which the public held responsible for the food safety regulatory failure. The *Financial Times* observed:

> Three years after its "mad cow" crisis, Europe is in the grip of another food safety scare. The cause this time is Belgian livestock not British beef. But the story is disturbingly similar. Once again, official incompetence, indecision and obfuscation have endangered public health, played havoc with agricultural production and disrupted international trade. . . . The truth is that food safety policy in the EU is a shambles.[62]

"Poultrygate" was shortly followed by another European food safety scare linked to the injection of carbon dioxide contaminated with traces of chemicals into Coca-Cola at a Belgian bottling facility. The Belgian government banned the sale of Coca-Cola products after more than one hundred people reported becoming ill from consuming the soft drink. The bottling company subsequently admitted that its bottling practices had been flawed and initiated the largest product recall in its history, withdrawing its beverages from throughout Europe. Subsequent studies by Belgian and Dutch scientists reported that the amount of contamination was too small to produce any health effects, suggesting that the reported illnesses may well have been caused by anxiety over food safety associated with the dioxin crisis, rather than the consumption of the contaminated soft drink. Still, the scare resonated with the public. The *Financial Times* noted:

> First, it was mad cow disease. Next came the discovery of dioxin, a carcinogen, in animal feed. And now the scare is contaminated Coca-Cola. Is anything in Europe safe to eat or drink any more? After recent scares, many consumers must be asking that question. So far the answers are not reassuring.[63]

[62] *Financial Times*, "Food: The Pattern of EU Food Scares," *FT.com*, June 14, 1999.
[63] *Financial Times*, "Coca-Cola: Food Scares," *FT.com*, June 21, 1999.

A columnist in the *New York Times* observed:

> The frenzy over Bad Coke is rapidly turning into a Foodborne Toxic Event . . . .
> [or] a new kind of comedic horror, one combining panic, paranoia, ignorance
> and the possibility of genuine danger." . . . Americans who may be tempted to
> see European food scares as comic or trivial should bear in mind that [BSE and
> dioxin in poultry and pork] have shaken people's confidence in Government
> nearly as much as Watergate did in the States.[64]

A senior European official confirmed this assessment: "The past years
have seen a big dip in consumer confidence in the safety of the food supply and, in consequence, in Member States authorities tasked with the job
of overseeing the food industry. There seems to be an endless supply of
[food scares]."[65] Moreover, "the mismanagement of the BSE crisis which
unfolded publicly in 1996, compounded by a series of food safety and
health scares in other areas, undermined the regulatory credentials of
scientists, national governments, and EU institutions . . . [and] the idea of
scientists as 'objective" and 'independent'."[66] This string of unfortunate
events created a policy "ripple" with important policy consequences for
other food safety policies.

Examples of Increased Transatlantic Policy Divergence

Beginning in 1990, the EU adopted several food safety and agricultural
production standards that were more stringent than those of the United
States. These included its policies toward the approval of a growth hormone for dairy cows, the planting of GM crops and the food derived
from them, and the use of antibiotics in animal feed.

Milk Hormones

While the EU's beef hormone ban sought to reduce the risks of an already
widely used agricultural production method, the policy debate over BST
on both sides of the Altantic focused ed on whether to approve a new
agricultural technology.

BST is a growth hormone naturally produced by cows. When a dairy
cow is given extra doses of this hormone, her feed is more efficiently
converted into milk and her milk yield rises; the cows also produce less

[64] John Lanchester, "Mad Coke Disease," *New York Times Magazine*, July 4, 1999, 7–8.
[65] "Back to the Future," *Consumer Voice*, Special Edition, 2000.
[66] Grace Skogstad, "Legitimacy and/or policy effectiveness? Network governance and
GMO regulation in the European Union," *Journal of European Public Policy* 10, no. 3 (June
2003): 329–30.

waste. While the potential of giving additional quantities of BST to cows had long been recognized, it was not until the application of genetic engineering during the 1970s that it became possible to inexpensively produce this hormone. This was accomplished in 1982 by harvesting the hormone from bacteria that had been genetically induced to produce it.[67]

THE APPROVAL OF BST IN THE UNITED STATES

In the early 1980s, four drug companies, including Monsanto and Eli Lilly, applied to the FDA for permission to market BST.[68] The federal government responded by conducting extensive testing on the safety of milk produced through the use of BST. In 1985, the FDA, backed by the National Institutes of Health and the Congressional Office of Technology Assessment, concluded that the milk produced from cows who had been administered BST was indistinguishable in every important respect from the milk from cows who had not received additional quantities of the growth hormone.

While in some cases this milk could contain minute quantities of BST (one part per billion), they concluded that the hormone is both inactive in people and is completely destroyed by pasteurization. Milk from cows treated with BST does contain additional amounts of another substance, namely IGF-1, an insulin-like growth factor. While IGF-1 is not destroyed by pasteurization, it is dismantled by digestive elements in the body. According to the American Academy of Pediatrics, milk from BST-treated cows was safe for infants as well as adults. The American Dietetic Association also gave BST-treated milk a clean bill of health.

Opposition to final FDA approval was led by Jeremy Rifken, a prominent critic of biotechnology, who established an organization called the Pure Food Campaign. Rifkin argued, among other things, that extra antibiotics often had to be given to BST-injected cows, as many became more prone to infection after receiving the hormone. These antibiotics then posed an additional risk to public health.[69] Another prominent opponent of BST, Samuel Epstein, an occupational and environmental medical specialist, expressed his "grave concern about the risks of breast cancer from consumption of rBGH milk."[70] The Consumer Policy

---

[67]The latter substance is technically known as rBST or rBHG (the r stands for recombinant), but BST is often used to refer to both the natural and laboratory produced versions of the hormone.

[68]Robert Collier, "Regulation of rBST in the US," *AgBioForum* 3, no. 2 and 3 (2000): 156–63.

[69]Christopher Culp, "Small Farmers Have Regulators Cowed," *Wall Street Journal,* September 1, 1992. See also Henry Gilgoff, "He's having a Cow—Hormone Is Biotech Critic's Latest Target," *New York Newsday,* February 9, 1994.

[70]Samuel Epstein, Letter to the Food and Drug Administration, February 14, 1994, available at http://www.prwatch.org/node/6334, accessed 11/01/2010.

Institute, the research arm of Consumers Union and the publisher of *Consumer Reports*, also expressed reservations about the health effects of the hormones. Echoing the public response to learning of health risks caused by the spraying of Alar on apples, an opinion piece in the *Washington Post* argued:

> The word [milk] is synonymous with the best and purest we have, things like babies and white teeth. If our milk, which is supposed to be nourishing and comforting, is riddled with still more drugs—pumped out of sick and diseased cows—what is left? . . . What person in their right mind would chose to ingest a bioengineered hormone—whose long-term effects have not been studied—so cows can produce more milk that we don't need?[71]

Various surveys reported that between 20 and 50 percent of consumers had reservations about using milk from BST-treated cows, and that 60 percent considered this milk to be unsafe.[72] For their part, the nation's 140,000 dairy producers were divided. Many large producers were attracted by the hormone's ability to improve the efficiency of milk production since, when injected with BST, a typical cow produced about 1,800 additional pounds of milk each year. However, many smaller dairy producers feared that the resulting increase in milk supply would further depress dairy prices. Some dairy producers feared a decline in milk consumption if the hormone was approved.

However, in November 1993, the FDA gave final regulatory approval for BST. FDA Commissioner David Kessler stated, "This has been one of the most extensively studied animal drug products . . . the public can be confident that milk . . . from BST-treated cows . . . is safe," adding that "there is virtually no difference in milk from treated and untreated cows. In fact, it is not possible using current scientific techniques to tell them apart."[73] The Agency also concluded that additional antibiotics in milk and milk products posed no health risks, since its regulations required the testing of all milk products and those that exceeded FDA safety standards for antibiotic content could not be sold. Following the lifting of a ninety-day moratorium requested by Congress to assess the economic impact of the growth hormone on dairy producers, Monsanto began to market the product to farmers in February 1994 under the trade name Posilac. The company also launched an extensive media campaign to correct what it viewed as the misinformation being circulated by critics of BST.

---

[71] Margaret Mason, "A Furor Over Hormones, Labeling & Health," *Washington Post*, March 7, 1994.

[72] Jane Brody, "Of Luddites, Cows and Biotechnology Miracles," *New York Times*, November 17, 1993.

[73] Food and Drug Administration, Press Release (November 11, 1993), available at http://www.fda.gov/bbs/topics/NEWS/NEW00443.html, accessed October 2008.

Several of the nation's dairy co-ops immediately announced that they would not use the hormones, and a number of supermarket chains stated that they would only purchase milk if they were assured it came from dairies that did not use BST. One milk and cream producer promised that "we're not going to buy any milk from herds that are injected with BST."[74] Nevertheless, following initial reluctance to purchase it by many dairy producers, within six years more than a third of U.S. dairy herds were using Posilac.

CONTROVERSY OVER LABELING

What particularly outraged opponents of BST was a subsequent decision of the FDA not to require the labeling of milk products produced from cows that had been administered additional quantities of BST. The agency's position was that such information was misleading since *all* cows produce BST. FDA Commission Kessler rhetorically asked: "where do you draw the line? Do you label all biotech products? Do you list all the fertilizers? All the pesticides?"[75] The Grocery Manufacturers Association stated that mandatory labeling was "misleading and deceptive" because it implied that there was a material difference between milk and milk products from cows that had been administered the supplement and those that had not received it."[76]

But critics of the FDA's decision countered that the agency was depriving consumers of freedom of choice. While a coalition of food producers successfully sued the state of Vermont, which had required the mandatory labeling of rBST milk, the FDA did decide to permit the voluntary labeling of milk "from cows not treated with rBST"—provided the description was accurate and did not imply that dairy products from cows that have been so treated was harmful or in any way different from the products produced by cows who have not received the hormone supplement.

Under rules issued by the Department of Agriculture, dairy products labeled "organic" cannot be derived from cows to which BST had been administered. Both these labels were important politically: they enabled consumers who preferred not to consume dairy products from BST-treated cows to do so and played an important role in diffusing political opposition to the approval of BST. In effect, they enabled BST to be "regulated" by producers and consumers rather than the government. The FDA's approval of BST did not affect levels of milk consumption as some had feared—it actually increased between 1995 and 1996—and

---

[74] Ibid.

[75] Philip Elmer-Dewitt, "Udder Insanity!" *Time Magazine*, May 17, 1993.

[76] *Chemicals Market Reporter*, "FDA Approves Monsanto's Milk Producing Hormone," November 15, 1993.

studies conducted in 1996 revealed that its use was no longer of concern to American consumers. However, over time the proportion of milk labeled "from cows not treated with rBST" has steadily increased. By 2008, only 17 percent of American dairy cows were still receiving the growth hormone, thus effectively narrowing the gap between European standards and American production and consumption patterns.[77]

THE BANNING OF rBST IN EUROPE

In accordance with the procedures established by a 1987 Council directive requiring the approval of all medicinal products, including veterinary ones, Monsanto and Elanco (a division of Eli Lilly) requested marketing approval for rBST in Europe in 1987.[78] Their request was referred to the Committee on Voluntary Medicinal Products (CVMP) for an assessment of the hormone's quality, safety, and efficacy. In April 1990, the Council, acting on a proposal from the European Commission, introduced a moratorium on the marketing of rBST until December 1990, in order to give the Commission more time to examine all its effects on the grounds that notwithstanding the progress that had been made on examining its health impacts by the CVMP, further time was required to complete all scientific studies.

The Council subsequently voted twice to extend this moratorium, first until December 1991 and subsequently until December 31, 1993, on the grounds that still more time was required to complete all scientific studies. In addition, the Council raised a second concern, namely the impact of rBST on the well-being of dairy cows. But in January 1993, the CVMP issued a report on the impact of rBST on both human and animal health and welfare. It concluded that dairy products from cows treated with rBST did not present any health or safety risk to consumers. Nor did its administration to dairy cattle pose any undue risk to the health or welfare of treated animals. Following the scientific clean bill of health by the CVMP, the European Commission informed the two companies that their rBST products would be approved.

However, when rBST had still not been formally approved a year later, the two companies sued the Commission in the ECJ. In its pleading before the Court, the Commission agreed with the two companies and the CVMP that rBST was safe, but it now explained that its refusal to grant final regulatory approval was because of consumer concerns about its safety.

[77] Andrew Martin and Andrew Pollack, "Monsanto to Sell Line That Makes Hormone," *New York Times*, August 7, 2008.

[78] This section is substantially drawn from David Vogel, *Trading Up: Consumer and Environmental Regulation in a Global Economy* (Cambridge, MA: Harvard University Press, 1996), 171–4.

Monsanto and Elanco then undertook further court action. In its brief to the Court, the Commission now noted a possible link between IGF-1 and cancer rates in humans. Subsequently, two separate scientific advisory bodies addressed the impact of rBST on both animal welfare and human health. The Scientific Committee on Animal Health and Welfare concluded that because the use of rBST caused a substantial increase in painful and debilitating levels of foot problems and mastitis for treated cattle, it should not be administered to cows. Another scientific advisory body addressed the hormone's impacts on human health: it stated that while there was no evidence to date that the use of rBST increased rates of breast and prostate cancer, the available scientific evidence was insufficient to permit a definitive conclusion.

In April 1999, the FDA issued a critical analysis of the latter report, arguing that its findings, or to be more precise, its outstanding concerns with respect to IGF-1 levels, were inconsistent with the current state of scientific knowledge. It noted that numerous independent researchers and scientific committees had examined the date of dietary exposure to proteins and milk from rBST and that they had unanimously concluded that the amount of IGF-1 excreted in milk following the administration of rBST was safe for all consumers, including infants. Accordingly, the FDA informed the EU that the scientific evidence for its safety *was* conclusive and that no additional studies were needed. However, a majority of the Council still declined to authorize the marketing of rBST.

With the moratorium on rBST about to expire, in October 1999, the Commission announced that it had decided to convert the moratorium to an outright ban. The subsequent decision of the Council of Ministers not to establish a maximum residue limit for rBST was based explicitly on the precautionary principle, which held that scientific uncertainty—in this case about the possible risks of BST to human health—justified a decision to deny regulatory approval. Moreover, while consumer organizations had not campaigned as extensively against the approval of milk hormone as they had against beef hormones, European officials also feared a public/consumer backlash. As one official stated, "It's not easy to explain to consumers that everything is all right when you are injecting drugs into cows."[79]

The EU's decision was strongly criticized across the Atlantic. U.S. Trade Representative Carla Hills said that she was "troubled by a growing attitude in Europe and elsewhere that technological developments which encourage greater efficiency in agricultural production are socially undesirable."[80] U.S. Agricultural Secretary Clayton Yeutter (correctly)

[79] Quoted in Rockwell, "US Says EC Milk Ban," 6A.
[80] Quoted in ibid.

predicted that it "would also add fuel to the fires of those who wish to have public policy decisions made on the basis of emotion and political pressure."[81] Another American official warned that the Commission's decision to review a new biotechnology product on the basis of its "social and economic implications . . . could set a very dangerous precedent," a prediction that was also prescient.[82]

ANALYSIS

Public opposition to BST was stronger in the United States than in Europe. Why, then, did European officials ban BST while their American counterparts approved its use? One important reason for the European Commission's 1999 decision to convert its 1990 moratorium into an outright ban was the BSE crisis, which surfaced roughly midway between the time the initial application for BST was filed and the decision to convert its earlier moratorium into a ban. This policy failure had made European decision-makers more risk-averse. This case of transatlantic regulatory policy divergence also stemmed from differential criteria in how risks should be assessed. The EU's ban both illustrated and reflected the growing importance and influence of the precautionary principle, which had been incorporated into European law in 1992. The application of this principle both encouraged and permitted European policy makers to impose restrictions on both products and production methods if there were uncertainties about their safety; hence the EU's demand for additional research on the possible negative health impact of BST and its decision to convert its moratorium into a ban. Equally important, it effectively broadened the basis on which risk management decisions could be made by including both social impact and public preferences.

In the United States, however, regulatory policymaking was moving in the opposite direction: it was becoming more technocratic and politically insulated. "In approving the product [rBST], the FDA adhered to its narrow statutory remit. . . . The public controversy and legislative scrutiny that surrounded rBST did not affect American . . . regulators' decision . . . [It] was based only on the evaluation of scientific evidence regarding rBST's safety."[83]

---

[81] Clayton Yeutter, U.S. Secretary of Agriculture, Letter to Ray MacSharry, EC Agriculture Commissioner, July 8, 1989.

[82] "Pressure on Negotiations Stepped Up As July Set for Securing Profile for Final Package," WTO-GATT, NUR-035 (April 19, 1990), available at http://www.wto.org/gatt_docs/English/SULPDF/91490260.pdf, accessed March 2009.

[83] Grace Skogstad, "Regulating Food Safety Risks in the European Union," in *What's the Beef? The Contest Governance of European Food Safety*, ed. Christopher Ansell and David Vogel (Cambridge, MA: MIT Press: 2006), 225–7.

Every scientific study gave BST a clean bill of health. Accordingly, the FDA was empowered, if not required, to base its regulatory decisions on the conclusions and recommendations of these studies, rather than have it influenced by "ill informed" public fears, as the EPA had done in the case of Alar only four years earlier.

Genetically Modified Organisms

Policies toward GM foods, crops, and seeds represent the most economically significant—and undoubtedly the most contentious—divergence between European and American food and agricultural regulations and policies. The regulatory policy frameworks developed by the United States in 1986 and the EU in 1990 differed at the outset; the United States initially acted to facilitate the rapid commercial introduction of GM crops and the foods grown from them, while the EU initially subjected them to greater scrutiny. Subsequently, the divergence between American and European regulations steadily increased as the EU imposed progressively more stringent regulatory requirements, including mandatory labeling, and approved far fewer GM varieties than the United States. Moreover, many GM varieties approved by the European Union have not been commercialized due to both consumer pressures and the refusal of some member states to permit them to be grown.

INITIAL AMERICAN REGULATIONS

During the 1970s, biologists in the United States began to make fundamental advances in recombinant DNA, making possible the genetic modification of seeds. As GM seeds moved closer to commercialization, the Reagan administration began to develop regulations for them. Its primary policy objective was to promote the development of a domestic agricultural biotechnology industry. In 1986, the Office of Science and Technology Policy issued a "Coordinated Framework for the Regulation of Biotechnology." The Framework divided responsibility for regulating biotechnology among three agencies: the FDA would regulate the safety of GM foods, the USDA, the planting of GM crops, and the EPA would be responsible for assessing the environmental and food safety impacts of GM crops with pesticide characteristics.

Substantively, the USDA emerged as the primary American agency governing the introduction of GM plant varieties into the environment either for field trials or for commercial production. The USDA's position was that only GM plant varieties classified as plant pests would be subject to extensive regulatory review. For its part, the FDA issued a policy statement in 1992, reaffirmed in 2001, that GM foods are "substantially equivalent" to conventional foods and thus should be "generally recognized as safe"—a position that was endorsed by the National Academy of Sciences. Pre-market approval would only be required for food products when the genetic manipulation of the seeds used to produce them had altered their substance or safety, in which case they would be regulated as food additives.

Likewise, labeling would only be required if a GM food was not "substantially equivalent" to the corresponding conventional food in terms of composition, nutrition, or safety. In essence, the Coordinated Framework held that the techniques of agricultural biotechnology were neither sufficiently risky nor novel that they could not be regulated under the same laws used to regulate conventionally produced agricultural products with similar composition and intended uses.

Congress has never enacted any legislation governing GMOs, while congressional hearings on GMOs have been primarily conducted "in committees with narrow jurisdictions friendly to the concerns of the biotechnology industry."[84] American policies toward GM varieties have essentially been formulated and implemented by regulatory and administrative agencies that have consistently supported their commercial application. The Coordinated Framework developed by the Reagan administration thus created a pattern of regulatory path dependency. More than two decades later, the Framework remains the basic administrative and legal structure for the regulation of agricultural biotechnology in the United States. It has enabled American agricultural biotechnology firms to retain a privileged position in the policy process and effectively relegated non-business constituencies to a marginal role in this policy area.

INITIAL EUROPEAN REGULATIONS

Unlike the American federal government, during the 1980s the EU had no authority to regulate the introduction of GM varieties. As a result, each member state was free to develop its own regulations. With the notable exception of Denmark and Germany, these were relatively permissive. The agricultural biotechnology industry enjoyed strong political support throughout much of Europe, and its interests were championed by the European Commission's DG Science. The Commission was, however, concerned that the lack of harmonized regulations would make it more difficult for European firms to catch up with the United States, which had already developed a commanding presence in this new and potentially important business sector.

[84] Ibid., 243–68.

In 1990, the EU, as part of its ongoing effort to further the development of the single European market, succeeded in gaining regulatory authority for agricultural biotechnology. But it came at a price: the European Council's 1990 "deliberate release" directive established a European system of risk regulation for the approval, planting, and marketing of GM foods and crops, that "reversed the previous trend toward a business-friendly biotechnology policy in Europe."[85] Its passage reflected both the political weakness of Europe's relatively small and fragmented biotechnology sector, as well as increased concern on the part of some member states about the safety and environmental impact of GMOs.

TRANSATLANTIC POLICY DIFFERENCES

The EU's 1990 Directive differed from the Coordinated Framework adopted four years earlier by the United States in several important respects. Most important, it adopted a distinctive regulatory policy for GMOs, rather than regulating them in terms of existing regulatory policies. Second, unlike the United States, the EU decided to regulate GM foods on the basis of the process by which they were grown, rather than the characteristics of the food product itself. The directive also contained a safeguard clause that allowed member states to temporarily restrict the introduction of GMOs that had been approved by the Commission; however, American policy did not provide for more stringent state regulations.

Unlike in the United States, where the primary regulatory responsibility for GMOs was given to the business-friendly Department of Agriculture, in Europe regulatory authority was placed in hands of the recently created DG Environment, whose officials had successfully argued for an integrated system of regulation that addressed the environmental risks of GMO releases. This directive thus laid the groundwork for "a more precautionary socially oriented biotechnology policy than that obtaining on the other side of the Atlantic."[86]

THE GROWTH OF EUROPEAN OPPOSITION TO GMOS

While the mad-cow crisis in Europe affected other European risk regulations, nowhere was its policy impact greater than for GMOs. Although there was no link between GMOs and the BSE crisis, European consumers connected the two. "BSE . . . made people in Europe very sensitive to new technologies in the food supply industry, and very wary of scientists

---

[85] Robert Falkner, "The Political Economy of 'Normative Power' Europe: EU Environmental Leadership in International Biotechnology Regulation," *Journal of European Public Policy* 14, no. 4 (June 2007): 515.

[86] Sheila Jasanoff, *Designs on Nature: Science and Democracy in Europe and the US* (Princeton, NJ: Princeton University Press, 2005), 92.

and government attempts to reassure them."[87] Following the BSE scandal, only 12 percent of Europeans expressed trust in national regulators. By contrast, around 90 percent of American citizens believed the USDA's views on biotechnology.[88] American consumers also trusted the FDA more than European consumers trusted their food safety authorities to regulate the safety of biotechnology.[89] These differences in public trust both facilitated the political mobilization and effectiveness of anti-GMO political constituencies in Europe and made it more difficult for their counterparts in the United States to gain political traction.

In 1996, only a month after the European Commission had banned the export of British beef, the Commission overrode member state objections and approved the sale of a GM soy product. In the fall of 1996, Europe received its first shipment of GM crops from the United States. The timing was consequential: "Widespread media coverage and public debate about GM food began just as the BSE food crisis struck, which helped link the two issues before the European public."[90] An official from Monsanto, whose firm had developed GM soy, and which bore the brunt of European opposition to the introduction of GMOs, observed, "You have this low burn level of anxiety about food safety and in the midst of all this you have a product introduction of genetically modified soybeans."[91] As a result, "When news of the commercial availability of the genetically modified soybeans spread, the average shopper assumed that authorities were either ignorant or willfully concealing troubling information about GM food."[92] The fact that the soy product was made by an American company further exacerbated public hostility to its introduction in Europe.

A broad coalition of environmentalists, consumer groups, anti-globalization activists, along with small and organic farmers, organized an extensive media and lobbying campaign against the introduction of

[87] C. Cookson and V. Houlder, "An Uncontrolled Experiment," *Financial Times*, February 13/14, 1999.

[88] Mark Pollack and Gregory Shaffer, *When Cooperation Fails: The International Law and Politics of Genetically Modified Foods* (Oxford: Oxford University Press, 2009), 65.

[89] Mark Pollack and Gregory Shaffer, "The Challenges of Reconciling Regulatory Differences: Food Safety and GMOs in the Transatlantic Relationship," in. *Transatlantic Governance in the Global Economy*, ed. Mark Pollack and Gregory Shaffer (Lanham: Rowman & Littlefield Publishers, 2001), 165.

[90] Pollack and Shaffer, *When Cooperation Fails*, 65.

[91] Rich Weiss, "No Appetite for Gene Cuisine," *Washington Post National Weekly Edition*, May 3, 1999.

[92] Paulette Kurzer, "European Citizens Against Globalization: Public Health and Risk Perceptions," Working Paper Lehigh University, (April 2004): 19, available at http://www.lehigh.edu/~incntr/publications/documents/kurzer.pdf [accessed 11/10/2010].

GMOs into Europe. They were able to capitalize on the decline of public trust in national and European food safety policies to create a highly effective European-wide political movement.[93]

Opposition to GMOs was particularly pronounced in Britain, which was still reeling from the government's BSE policy failure. Unfavorable press coverage of agricultural biotechnology increased substantially following the BSE crisis: the British media dramatically labeled GM products "Frankenstein foods," while Prince Charles opined that the production of GM foods "takes mankind into realms that belong to God and God alone."[94] But public opposition to GMOs throughout Europe also became more negative.[95] The percentage of French citizens opposed to GMOs increased from 46 percent in 1996, to 65 percent in 1999 and to 75 percent in 2002. In 1998, more than 80 percent of Germans expressed negative opinions about GMOs.[96] A 2001 Eurobarometer poll reported that nearly 71 percent of those surveyed stated that "I do not want this kind of food," while more than 56 percent believed that "GMO-based food is dangerous."[97,98] In sum, "in the minds of the European public, GM food [became] associated with a high probability of exposure to harm and danger."[97]

THE INCREASED STRINGENCY OF EUROPEAN REGULATION

In 1997, the European Commission approved another GM food crop, a corn variety developed by the Swiss company Novartis. But several member states invoked the safeguard clause of the 1990 directive and refused to accept it. By 2004, nine member state "safeguards" were in place, thus effectively undermining the Commission's effort to create a single market for GM varieties. Threatened by consumer boycotts, and fearful of undermining consumer confidence in the safety of their products, many large European food producers and retailers also refused to use or sell GM foods and several European firms stopped buying GM soybeans from the United States. British retailers issued their own stringent labeling requirements.[98] By 2005, twenty-seven of the thirty largest European food

[93] Quoted in Christopher Ansell, Rahsaan Maxwell, and Daniela Sircuerelli, "Protesting Food: NGOS and Political Mobilization in Europe," in Ansell and Vogel, *What's the Beef?* 97–122.

[94] Pollack and Shaffer, "The Challenges," 165.

[95] Quoted in Ansell, Maxwell, and Sircuerelli, "Protesting Food," 103.

[96] Pollack and Shaffer, *When Cooperation Fails*, 66.

[97] See Kurzer, "European Citizens Against Globalization."

[98] Robert Falkner, "The Troubled Birth of the 'Biotech Century' Corporate Power and its Limits," in *Corporate Power in Global Agrifood Governance*, ed. Jennifer Clapp and Doris Fuchs (Cambridge, MA: MIT Press 2009), 235–38.

retailers had adopted a policy of excluding GM ingredients from products sold in Europe.[99] The decisions of European food retailers created a divergence between their interests and those of European biotechnology firms and played a critical role in the demise of GM-produced food sales in Europe. These private regulatory policies increased the transatlantic divergence in food consumption of GMOs since they meant that many GMO varieties approved by the EU would not be marketed in Europe.

While the EU's Scientific Committee on Plants issued sixteen favorable opinions for various GM varieties of soy and maize, and each was legally authorized for marketing throughout Europe, five were subject to member state bans and thus were not introduced. The switch in French policies toward the cultivation of GM crops was especially significant.[100] The French Ministry of Agriculture initially had been the strongest proponent of GM crops, which large-scale French farmers had been eager to adopt. Through 1997, more GM field experiments were conducted in France than in any other European country. But faced with growing public opposition, by the end of the decade France had joined the anti-GM camp. The number of French field experiments declined from 1,100 in 1998 to below 50 in 2002, and many of these were destroyed by anti-GM activists.

Six member states, including France, Europe's largest agricultural producer, now requested that the EU impose a moratorium on all approvals of GM products until a new and more stringent system of regulation was put in place. By voting in the Council of Ministers to block all new approvals, these countries were able to prevent any new GM varieties from being authorized for sale between 1998 and 2004; the only exceptions were foods judged "substantially equivalent" to those produced by conventional seeds.

After extensive and often heated discussions, in 2001 a new directive regulating GMOs was adopted by co-decision between the Council and the European Parliament. The terms of this directive explicitly drew on the precautionary principle, on which the Commission had issued a communication the previous year. Reflecting a more risk-averse and politicized approach to regulating health, safety, and environmental risks, this communication noted that "judging what is an acceptable risk for society is an eminently political responsibility."[101]

---

[99]Robert Falkner, *Business Power and Conflict in International Environmental Politics* (Hampshire: Palgrave, 2008), 182.

[100]For a detailed discussion and analysis of how GMOs in France became politically and legally redefined from a promising new agricultural technology to an unacceptable risk, see Kyoto Sato, "Politics and Meanings of Genetically Modified Food: The Case of Policy Change in France," unpublished paper .

[101]Pollack and Shaffer, *When Cooperation Fails*, 238.

The Commission's communication had stated that the precautionary principle could be invoked whenever politically negative effects had been identified, but scientific evaluations were unable to determine "with sufficient certainty" the seriousness of those risks. For a number of policy makers at both the national and European levels, GMOs clearly fell into both categories: the negative effects of agricultural biotechnology on the environment had been "identified" and the seriousness of the food safety risks associated with the consumption of food derived from them remained "uncertain." Accordingly, the 2001 directive required that more extensive risk assessments be conducted before GMOs could either be released into the environment or sold as food.

While described by the Parliament's rapporteur as "the toughest laws on GMOs in the world," this directive still failed to satisfy the six member states that insisted on continuing the de facto moratorium as well as their right to maintain regulations more stringent than those of the Commission.[102] In an effort to establish a legal framework for GMOs that would make possible a single market for GM food and feed, the Commission now proposed a new set of regulations. Adopted in 2003 after extensive bargaining among the Commission, the Council, and the Parliament, they further strengthened European regulations governing the approval and marketing of both GM food and feed by extending the criteria for their approval to include an undefined "consumer interest." The directive also ended the simplified approval system for "substantially equivalent" foods that had been approved in 1997; now any foods whose ingredients were grown from GM seeds would require specific regulatory approval.

The EU's 2003 directive also established the world's most stringent and comprehensive labeling requirements. Food products were required to be labeled as "containing GMOs" if they contained material consisting of, or produced from, GMOs greater than 0.9 percent of their ingredients. If they contained material that had not yet been approved for environmental release, the threshold level requiring labeling was reduced to 0.5 percent. Moreover, after three years, no residues of non-approved GMOs would be permitted in food or feed products until new regulations had been enacted to assess their safety. The directive also required the Commission to establish a system of specific identifiers to enable GMOs, and all products produced from them, to be traced throughout their production, processing, and distribution.

Following the adoption of these new regulations, in May 2004 the EU's moratorium finally ended. The Commission approved its first new GM variety in almost six years and a second was approved the following

[102]Ibid., 240.

month. In both cases, however, the vote in the Council was sharply divided, revealing that the EU's new, more stringent and comprehensive regulatory requirements had failed to satisfy an important block of member states who consistently voted against all approvals. This impasse continued for the next several years. The EU's expert advisory bodies, whose members were drawn from each member state, repeatedly failed to reach a qualified majority either for or against the approval of new varieties. This meant that the decision on new approvals was referred to the Council, which was similarly divided, thus placing the Commission in the politically awkward position of overriding both bodies if it decided to approve any of the applications submitted to it.

Eight member states enacted temporary bans on eight different varieties approved by the Commission which they claimed were too unsafe to be placed on the market—notwithstanding the opinion of the recently established European Food Safety Authority (EFSA) which found none of these bans to be scientifically justified. The Commission's difficulties were compounded in 2005 when its proposal to overturn the national bans was rejected by the Council of Ministers. This meant that those member states that had exercised their "safeguard" prerogatives would no longer be required to provide any scientific justification for their decisions. A majority of member states also expressed dissatisfaction with the risk assessment procedures of the EFSA on the grounds that the regulatory agency had ignored input from member state governments and was biased in favor of industry.

On balance, the Commission and the EFSA have been consistently more favorable toward the introduction of GMOs into Europe than have the Council, the EP, and several member states. While political and public opposition to GMOs in Europe has largely focused on their food safety risks, "over eighty scientific studies sponsored by the EU over fifteen years found no scientific evidence of added harm to consumers from the consumption of GMOs"—a finding similar to that of the American National Academy of Sciences.[103] But concerns about their impact on biodiversity have led several countries, including Austria, Luxembourg, Greece, Denmark, Italy, and Portugal, to oppose their planting on biodiversity grounds. These countries contain many niche farmers, many of whom are organic, who feared that the introduction of GM crops into neighboring fields would "contaminate" their own production.[104]

---

[103] Daniel Drezner, *All Politics Is Global: Explaining International Regulatory Regimes* (Princeton, NJ: Princeton University Press, 2007), 151.

[104] Paulette Kurzer and Alice Cooper, "What's for Dinner? European Farming and Food Traditions Confront American Biotechnology," *Comparative Political Studies* 40, no. 9 (September 2007): 1037.

While public support for GMOs has been relatively more favorable in Sweden, Finland, the Netherlands, Ireland, Germany, Britain, Spain, and Belgium, than it has been in other member states, "a majority of Europeans do not support GM foods. They are judged not to be useful and to be risky for society."[105] The contrast between European and American public attitudes is marked: a 1999 survey on attitudes toward the use of biotechnology to grow pest-resistant crops found 78 percent of Americans in favor, as contrasted with 54 percent of Germans, 52 percent of French, 36 percent of Britons, and 29 percent of Spanish.[106]

Since May 2004, the EU has approved several new GM varieties for food or feed, though most are only used for feed. But Austria, Italy, Luxembourg, Greece, Ireland, Hungary, and France have either maintained or strengthened their opposition to GM crops, with both Austria and Ireland declaring their firm intention to remain "GM-free," as have a large number of regional governments in Europe. Thus many member states continue to refuse to accept GM varieties authorized by the Commissions.

Consequently, very few GM crops are grown in Europe: small quantities of GM corn are currently being grown in only six member states, with modest amounts of GM soy are grown in one other.[107] The EU's stringent labeling requirements, combined with fears of boycotts by consumers, have prompted virtually all food producers and retailers to refrain from using or selling any GM foods that would be required to be labeled as such. However, the EU's labeling requirements did exempt products derived from animals that had been raised on GM feed, thus making it possible for European farmers to import animal feed containing GM soy and corn/maize, although many chose to switch to non-GM varieties grown in countries other than the United States. While thousands of products, most importantly cheese, do contain GM organisms or ingredients produced through genetic engineering, their GM content is sufficiently low so as to exempt them from the EU's labeling requirements.

THE POLITICS OF GMOS IN THE UNITED STATES

By contrast, the planting of GM crops in the United States represents "the most rapid adoption of a new technology in the history of agriculture."[108] Between 1995 and 2000, 5,136 GMO field trials were conducted.[109]

---

[105] A 2002 Eurobarometer report quoted in Drezner, *All Politics Is Global*, 156.

[106] Aseem Prakash and Kelly Kollman, "Biopolitics in the EU and the U.S.: A Race to the Bottom or Convergence to the Top," *International Studies Journal* 47 (2003): 627.

[107] Brian Hindo, "Monsanto: Winning the Ground War," *Business Week*, December 17, 2007.

[108] Pollack and Shaffer, *When Cooperation Fails*, 1.

[109] By contrast, only 162 were conducted in Britain and 123 in Germany; see Jasanoff, *Designs on Nature*, 31.

By 1999, 60 percent of processed foods sold in the United States were derived from GM seeds; four years later, the percentage had grown to between 70 and 75 percent, primarily due to the widespread use of soy, corn, and/or cotton by-products in them. As *Business Week* noted in December 2007, "if you have been to a grocery supermarket lately, odds are you've eaten genetically modified foods."[110] Eighty-five to 95 percent of soybeans, cotton, corn, and sugar beets are produced from GM seeds. Smaller quantities of other crops, such as canola, potatoes, tomatoes, papaya, squash, and sunflowers, are also grown from GM seeds. Globally, more than two-thirds of GM crops are grown in the United States and more than fifty GM food crops have been approved for human consumption. Not surprisingly, all the leading agricultural biotechnology firms are based in the United States.

It was not until more than a decade after the adoption of the "Coordinated Framework," and well after GMOs had been widely adopted by both American farmers and food processors, that their safety and environmental impact first became politically salient in the United States. This was in part attributable to political developments in Europe that were reported extensively in the American press. Moreover, a 1999 article in *Nature* reported the results of laboratory tests that had found that the use of a GM corn variety could kill not only the targeted pests, but also the larvae of the monarch butterfly if the corn's pollen traveled to milkweed, the larvae's source of food. The fate of the butterfly became a rallying symbol for opponents of GM crops. While subsequent field trials found the risks to the butterfly to be marginal, the EPA did request farmers cultivating GM corn to plant buffer zones with conventional corn to protect biodiversity.

The following year, public concerns about the impact of GMOs on the safety of the food supply increased following the disclosure that StarLink corn, a GM variety approved for use in animal feed but not for human consumption, had made its way into the food supply and caused allergic reactions among some consumers of Taco Bell taco shells. This policy failure led to a major recall of the corn, and cost Aventis, the firm that had marketed it, hundreds of millions of dollars in legal damages. Under pressure from the FDA, the firm cancelled its marketing license for this GM corn variety.

The StarLink incident did succeed in briefly creating a policy window for opponents of GMOs. Several American consumer and environmental organizations which had previously not been engaged with this issue now demanded that American regulations be strengthened, though few were opposed to GMOs per se. "StarLink" also led to a substantial increase

---

[110] See Hindo, "Monsanto: Winning the Ground War."

in media attention. In 2000, several large-circulation newspapers and magazines published articles on GMOs, highlighting their food safety and environmental risks and questioning whether the United States had acted too hastily in approving GM varieties without adequate regulatory controls and more extensive scientific assessments of their safety. But significantly, rather than being viewed as an indication of the inability of regulatory authorities to effectively manage agricultural biotechnology, the StarLink policy failure led primarily to calls for better monitoring and enforcement of existing regulations.[111] It was politically constructed as a "one-off" event, rather than as symptomatic of a systematic regulatory policy failure, and thus did not weaken public support for agricultural biotechnology.[112]

CONTROVERSY OVER LABELING

As in the case of BST, the issue of labeling has been the most controversial dimension of GM regulation in the United States. Americans overwhelmingly favor the labeling of GM foods, though the intensity of this preference remains unclear.[113] In 1999, forty-nine members of Congress sent a letter to the FDA requesting that it be required, and more than fifty bills to require labeling were subsequently introduced in the American Congress, though none were adopted. In addition, NGOs filed several lawsuits against the FDA in an unsuccessful attempt to force the agency to require labeling. When the FDA held public hearings on product labeling, it received more than 50,000 written submissions, the majority of which supported the labeling of foods containing GM ingredients. However, as in the case of BST, the agency has held firm; it has rejected mandatory labeling on the grounds that it was not required by the Federal Food, Drug, and Cosmetic Act. The agency also specifically warned food processors not to use the term "GMO-free" since it was misleading because all food is likely to contain some bioengineered materials.

But the Department of Agriculture did make an important policy decision which directly affected the labeling of GM-derived foods. The 1990 Farm Bill included the Organic Food Production Act, whose purpose was to create a consistent national standard for the certification of organic foods. In 1997, in the midst of some of the controversy surrounding the introduction of GM varieties into the food supply, the USDA issued a

[111] Jasanoff, *Designs on Nature*, 136.

[112] Thomas Bernauer, *Genes, Trade, and Regulation*, 93.

[113] Ibid., 58. See also William Hallman et al., "Public Perceptions of Genetically Modified Foods: A National Study of American Knowledge and Opinion," Food Policy Institute. Rutgers University, publication RR-103-004 (October 2003): 15, available at http://foodpolicy .rutgers.edu/docs/pubs/2004_Public_Perceptions_and_Responses_to_Mad_Cow_Disease .pdf, accessed 11/01/2010.

proposed rule that, among its other provisions, permitted foods produced through the use of biotechnology to be labeled "organic," since pesticides had not been applied to their production.

The public response was overwhelmingly negative. The agency received an estimated 300,000 public comments—twenty times higher than it had received for any rule it had previously proposed; the majority strongly opposed the proposed rule. At stake was not only the growing number of consumers for whom "buying organic was buying into a mode of production that reinforces basic ethical commitments toward community and nature," but also the business interests of the $6 billion-a-year organic industry whose domestic sales were growing at 20 percent a year.[114] It had also become an important export industry, particularly in markets such as Europe where consumers were unwilling to purchase GM-derived food.

In 2000, the USDA, in what has been characterized as a "resounding political victory for opponents of agricultural biotechnology," redefined "organic" to exclude both foods produced with any GM varieties as well as from any animal that had been fed GM varieties.[115] This decision, like that of the FDA to permit the labeling of milk products that were not produced with BST, enabled American consumers who preferred not to consume GM-derived foods to do so, and essentially took the issue of GM labeling off the political agenda.

PUBLIC ATTITUDES IN THE UNITED STATES

In marked contrast to Europe, public interest in, awareness of, and opposition to GMOs in the United States has been episodic, rather than sustained. A 2006 survey conducted by the Pew Initiative on Food and Biotechnology found little change in either American awareness or support for GM foods and crops during the previous five years. Only 26 percent of those polled believed they had ever eaten GM foods, while 60 percent believed they had not. While support for GM foods has remained relatively stable—increasing from 25 to 26 percent—opposition to them declined from 58 percent in 2001 to 46 percent in 2006.[116]

Another survey reported that while 60 percent of respondents stated they would not buy foods labeled containing GM ingredients, only 33 percent were aware that GM foods were available in supermarkets—even though by this date (2000) they had long been an integral part of the American food supply.[117] The American public's awareness of GM foods did increase marginally in 2001 following the StarLink corn recall, but it

[114] Jasanoff, *Designs on Nature*, 139.
[115] Ibid., 138.
[116] Pollack and Shaffer, *When Cooperation Fails*, 267.
[117] Ibid., 266.

then quickly declined. A 2003 study revealed that 43 percent of Americans had heard "not much" or "nothing" at all about genetic engineering or biotechnology, and almost two-thirds stated that they had never had a conversation about it.[118] Compared to Europe, their introduction in the United States has been much less politically salient and controversial.

"The relatively passive acceptance of GM food in the U.S. is not due a lack of concern about the risks, but instead reflects the trust Americans hold in the food safety regime to accommodate new technologies."[119] The majority of respondents to a 1997 survey agreed that GM foods posed risks for society, while a 2003 survey reported that only 25 percent favored the introduction of GM products into the food supply.[120] But a 2005 study also reported that 63 percent of respondents had "some or a great deal" of trust in what American regulators say about biotechnology, suggesting that "many Americans assume that if genetically modified foods are already on grocery store shelves, they must be safe."[121] In fact, after being informed that most products in grocery stores were produced using some form of genetic modification, the number of respondents who considered GM foods to be safe increased from 27 to 44 percent.[122] In any event, one thing is clear: "U.S. consumers view agricultural biotechnology more favorably than consumers in the EU."[123]

The Strengthening of American Regulation

Nevertheless, as a result of domestic political pressures and as a response to policy developments in Europe, American regulations have been modestly strengthened. In 2000, the FDA entered into an agreement with biotechnology firms under which they agreed to notify the agency 120 days in advance prior to releasing new GMOs intended for food or animal feed and to provide it with research data on the safety of GMOs for human consumption. For its part, the USDA began to require prior

[118] William Hallman, Brian Schilling, and Calum Turvey, "Public Perceptions and Responses to Mad Cow Disease: A National Survey of Americans," Food Policy Institute, Rutgers University (2004): 5-6, available at http://foodpolicy.rutgers.edu/docs/pubs/2004_Public_Perceptions_and_Responses_to_Mad_Cow_Disease.pdf, accessed 11/10/2010.

[119] Adam Sheingate, "Transatlantic Tensions in Food and Agricultural: Coming Together," in *Hard Power, Soft Power and the Future of Transatlantic Relations*, ed. Thomas Ilgen (Ashgate: Ashgate Publishing, 2006), 127.

[120] Ibid., 125.

[121] Ibid., 126.

[122] Adam Sheingate, "Agricultural Biotechnology: Representative Federalism and Regulatory Capacity in the U.S. and the European Union," in *Comparative Federalism: The European Union and the U.S. in Comparative Perspective*, ed. Anand Menon and Martin Schain (Oxford: Oxford University Press, 2006), 324.

[123] Thomas Bernauer, *Genes, Trade, and Regulation*, 92.

notification or permits for the field trials of GM plants. In 2000, the Clinton administration, concerned about public uneasiness with agricultural biotechnology, called for additional research on the safety of GM crops and foods. Two years later, the Bush administration required that crops undergo a "voluntary" preliminary safety assessment by the FDA and EPA before they underwent significant field trials. But none of these policies has adversely affected the continual growth in the planting and consumption of GMO varieties in the United States.

BUSINESS SELF-REGULATION

However, in this and in other policy areas, European regulations have affected corporate practices outside Europe. Some global firms have responded to both the strengthening of European regulations and American consumer and activist pressures by reducing or eliminating their use of GM ingredients, including for products sold in the United States. Following the food safety scare raised by the StarLink incident, Gerber and Heinz announced that all their baby foods would be GM-free. McDonalds made a similar commitment for its french fries, as did Frito Lay with regard to its corn chips. The giant global food firms Unilever, Nestle, and Seagram, as well as the Japanese breweries Kirin and Sapporo, have pledged not to use GM ingredients in any of their products. The American "natural food" retailers Whole Foods Market and Wild Oats Market also pledged to make all their products GM-free. The planting of GM sugar beets was delayed for several years due to concerns about consumer resistance by Hershey and Mars, but in 2007, a number of food processors authorized their growers to plant Roundup-resistant beets.[124]

Some export-dependent American farmers have changed their production methods to conform to European regulatory requirements. While the United States has approved far more varieties of GM crops than has the EU, less than 5 percent of American GM corn production employs varieties not approved by the EU, while virtually all GM soybean production employs only the one variety approved for use in the EU. In 1999, several large American grain traders, including Archer Daniels Midland, have requested that farmers segregate their GM-free crops and announced that they would pay a premium for GM-free soybeans and reject GM corn varieties not approved for use in the EU. In 2002, Monsanto submitted applications for the regulatory approval of bioengineered wheat. But two years later it withdrew them in response to the concerns of American farmers that growing GM wheat would adversely affect their global sales.[125]

---

[124] Andrew Pollack, "Round 2 for Biotech Beets," *New York Times*, November 27, 2007.

[125] Robert Falkner, "The Troubled Birth of the 'Biotech Century," in Calpp and Fuchs, *Corporate Power in Global Agrifood Governance*, 235–38.

THE INTERNATIONAL POLITICS OF GMOS

Like the EU's hormone ban, more stringent European regulations for GMOs have reduced American agricultural exports. This is largely because the American commodity-based collection and transportation system makes it difficult to separate out approved varieties not approved by the EU. American corn exports to the EU worth $200 million per year virtually disappeared because American commodity exporters could not guarantee that they contain only varieties approved by the EU. According to one study, it would cost up to $400 million for American farmers to use GM technology and still be able to export non-GM food that would fall under the EU's labeling threshold.[126] American soy exports to the EU dropped by two-thirds between 1996 and 2004, largely because of the decision of European importers to increase their purchases from countries that produced non-GM soy.

European restrictions on GMOs became another major source of transatlantic tension. In 1997, Dan Glickman from the American Secretary of Agriculture responded to European demands for the separation of GM and non-GM food by insisting, "test after rigorous scientific test has proven their products to be safe. Sound science must trump passion."[127] The U.S. Trade Representative subsequently claimed that the EU's labeling requirements were "unnecessary, in the absence of an identified and documented risk to safety or health."[128] American officials also repeatedly complained to the EU about its slow, confusing, and increasingly more rigid approval procedures, as well as the unwillingness of some member states to permit GM products approved by the Commission. An American trade official characterized the EU's *de facto* moratorium as "Luddite."[129]

The United States initially hesitated to file a complaint with the WTO, fearing a popular backlash if it was seen as forcing GM foods onto a public that was not convinced of their safety. American officials also recognized that the extent of public opposition to GMOs in Europe had tied the Commission's hands. However, in 2003, the United States, joined by Argentina and Canada, decided to file a formal complaint with the WTO. The plaintiffs challenged the legality of the EU's de facto moratorium as well as the marketing and import bans issued by a number of member states.

The American decision to file a formal trade dispute complaint was primarily prompted by three factors. First, the refusal of several African

[126] Drezner, *All Politics Is Global*, 165.
[127] Maggie Urry, "Genetic Products Row Worsens," *Financial Times*, June 21, 1997.
[128] Drezner, *All Politics Is Global*, 167.
[129] Ibid., 165.

countries to accept food aid from the United States because some of those foods were made from GM crops prompted American fears that more developing countries would adopt restrictive regulations similar to those of the EU.[130] Second, the United States hoped that a formal WTO complaint might discourage the EU from adopting more stringent risk regulations in other areas, such as electronic recycling and chemical testing—an expectation that proved to be incorrect. (See chapter 5.) Finally, several influential farm-belt members of Congress had actively lobbied the White House to adopt a more aggressive response to the EU's GMO restrictions.

In 2006, a WTO dispute panel rendered what most observers interpreted as a split decision: it found against the EU on procedural rather than on substantive grounds.[131] It did rule that the EU's confusing and complex approval procedures ("undue delay") as well as the failure of some member states to accept its approval decisions ("the safeguard clause") did violate its obligations under the WTO. But it declined to rule on the safety of biotech food products per se. Nor did it address one of the key issues dividing the disputed parties, namely whether biotech products are "like" their conventional counterparts. Both sides claimed "victory" and neither appealed the dispute panel's ruling. The filing of the complaint did, however, prompt the EU to end its moratorium in 2004. The European Commission subsequently approved a number of GM varieties for import, while at the same time giving member states greater authority over the cultivation of GM crops. In 2009, after the Commission approved GM flax that Canada wanted to export to Europe, Canada withdrew the complaint against the EU it had filed with the WTO.

INTERNATIONAL BIODIVERSITY AND BIOSAFETY REGULATION

The EU and the United States have also clashed in another international forum. One of the framework agreements adopted at the 1992 Rio Earth summit was the Convention on Biodiversity. It committed signatories to develop appropriate procedures regarding the transfer and use of "any living modified organism resulting from biotechnology that may have an adverse effect on . . . biodiversity."[132] However, the United States is

---

[130]The refusal of many developing countries to permit the growing of GM crops has been strongly criticized. See, for example, Robert Paalberg, *The Politics of Precaution: Genetically Modified Crops in Developing Countries* Washington, DC: International Food Policy Research Institute, 2001). For a more general criticism of opposition to GMOs, see John Entine, ed., *Let Them Eat Precaution: How Politics Is Undermining the Genetic Revolution in Agriculture* (Washington, DC: AEI Press, 2006).

[131]For a detailed discussion of this trade dispute and the WTO dispute panel's ruling, which came to over 3,500 pages including annexes, see Pollack and Shaffer, *When Cooperation Fails*, chapter 5.

[132]Ibid., 152.

not a party to it. While President Clinton did sign the Convention, the Senate has refused to ratify it. Subsequently, the parties to the Convention, with the United States acting as an observer, began negotiations on an amendment to the Convention, the Cartagena Protocol on Biosafety, which would govern the transfer of living GMOs across international borders. The EU, wanting to protect and also "export" its own stringent biodiversity regulations, pushed to have the precautionary principle included in the Protocol and to have the Protocol exempted from WTO rules. This effort was strongly opposed by the United States and four other major agricultural producers and as a result, no agreement was reached in Cartagena in 1999.

After heated negotiations, the Cartagena Convention on Biodiversity was adopted in Montreal in 2000. The American negotiating position was weakened by its not being a party to the Convention, and its terms reflected the policy preferences of the EU more than those of the United States. While stating that countries should undertake "risk assessments . . . in a scientifically sound manner," it also explicitly incorporated the precautionary principle: Article 10 permits a signatory country to reject the importation of "a living modified organism for international introduction into the environment" where there is "lack of scientific certainty regarding the extent of the potential adverse effects . . . on biological diversity . . . taking into account risks to human health."[133]

This provision granted the EU's regulatory framework "greater regulatory legitimacy" since it "serves to challenge the U.S.' insistence on full scientific proof as the basis for risk assessment."[134] With respect to the equally contentious issue of the relationship of the Protocol to WTO rules, the United States failed to obtain a clear reservation of its rights under the WTO. As a result, the two international agreements are in conflict: the Biosafety Protocol's incorporation of precautionary principle is inconsistent with the WTO's requirement that a country must produce scientific proof of harm in order to justify a food or agricultural regulation that restricts trade.

GLOBAL IMPACT

More stringent European regulations for GMOs have had a considerable global impact. As of 2002, seventeen countries had adopted mandatory GM food labeling requirements, including Japan, China, Brazil, Chile, Indonesia, New Zealand, Australia, Turkey, Korea, Mexico, China, Taipei, and Saudi Arabia, though none are as strict or as comprehensive as those

[133] Ibid., 171.
[134] Robert Falkner, "Regulating Biotech Trade: The Cartagena Protocol on Biosafety," *International Affairs* 76 (April 2000): 315.

of the EU.[135] As the EU expanded into Central and Eastern Europe, those member states have adopted GMO regulations similar to those of Brussels. As a result of both political pressure from the EU and their dependence on agricultural exports to Europe, Thailand, and several countries in sub-Saharan Africa have not authorized the growing of any GM food crops. In developing countries dependent on agricultural exports to the EU, GM cotton is grown more extensively than any other crop, largely because the import of non-food GM products are less restricted by the EU; nor are they subject to its labeling requirements.

The global planting of GM seeds grew by 15 percent in 2003, 20 percent in 2004, 11 percent in 2005, and 13 percent in 2006. In 2005, the billionth acre was planted and growth is expected to remain in double digits.[136] Nonetheless, the majority of commercially grown GM crops are grown in only six countries, namely China, India, Argentina, Brazil, Canada, and the United States, with the latter accounting for more than half of global production. Thus, in these as in many other areas of regulatory policy, more countries have adopted regulations more similar to those in Europe than those of the United States, though American pressures have reduced the stringency of some national regulations. The United States remains distinctive: it produces more GM crops than the rest of the world combined and its product labeling requirements are the world's least stringent.

ANALYSIS

Each of my three explanatory factors has played a critical role in shaping the divergence of European and U.S. regulations for GMOs.

First, notwithstanding the reservations expressed in some American polling data, and the variance in public acceptance of GMOs within the member states of the EU, the extent and the intensity of public opposition to both their planting and the consumption of food produced from them has been substantially greater among Europeans than Americans. Significantly, while a wide variety of consumer and environmental lobbies, as well as other activist constituencies, strongly campaigned against GMOs in Europe, opposition to them did not become an important political priority for American non-governmental organizations; few consumer and environmental lobbies have opposed GMOs per se, though they did strongly support mandatory labeling.

Second, the preferences of policy makers differed substantially. In the United States, food safety regulatory policy has essentially been made by administrative and regulatory officials, who have strongly supported the

---

[135] Bernauer, *Genes, Trade and Regulation*, 62.
[136] Pollack and Shaffer, *When Cooperation Fails*, 182.

commercial introduction of GM varieties. By contrast, regulatory policy-making in Europe has been shaped in multiple political arenas, including in the European Commission, the Council of Ministers, the European Parliament, and most importantly, by many member states. The regulatory governance structure of the EU has provided a wider range of opportunities for those opposed to GMOs to participate in the policy process and has made European regulatory policies more responsive to their preferences.

Third, the policy decisions of American and European officials have reflected differences in their assessments of the risks of GMOs. As in the case of BST, American policy makers consider GMOs to be safe. The European Food Safety Authority's risk assessments are similar to those of the FDA: neither has found that consumption of foods produced from GM seeds poses any health risks. But other scientific advisory bodies at both the European and the national levels have argued that too much is still unknown about both their safety and environmental impact to permit either their cultivation or their introduction into the food supply, and the latter have had an important policy impact. Thus, just as the environmental risks of global climate change have been more contentious in the United States than in Europe, so have the safety risks of GMOs been more contentious in Europe than in the United States.

One of the most critical risk assessment decisions made on both sides of the Atlantic had to do with how foods produced from GMOs would be defined. In the EU they were regarded as a novel technology that required distinctive regulatory rules, while in the United States they were classified as being no different than foods produced by more conventional production methods. These differences in definition were politically constructed (as was the USDA's decision to define organic in a way that restricted the use of GM ingredients), but their policy impact was substantial.

Antibiotics in Animal Feed

Regulations governing the use of antibiotics in animal feed are a third important example of the growing divergence of risk regulations for food safety adopted in the United States and Europe after 1990. Between 30 and 70 percent of all antibiotics used in both the United States and the EU have been administered to animals, primarily to either stimulate their growth or prevent or treat diseases, which in some cases could be transmitted from animals to humans. Global sales of medicinal feed additives for animals totaled $1 billion in 1999. However, since a significant number of identical antibiotics are administered to both food-producing animals and humans, concerns have been raised by consumer and environmental groups and medical professionals on both sides of the

Atlantic that the administration of medicinal products to food animals has increased human resistance to these medicines. According to a joint report by three international health organizations, "the use of antibiotics in humans and animals places individuals at increased risk of infection, higher treatment failures, and increased severity of illnesses," thus also increasing health care costs.[137]

EUROPEAN RESTRICTIONS

In 1986, Sweden, responding to pressures from both farmers and consumers, became the first country to completely ban the use of antibiotics as growth promoters. Twelve years later, a voluntary ban on the use of antibiotics in animal feed was adopted by Denmark, one of the world's major pork exporters. Following the ban, antibiotic use declined by 54 percent, while production costs only increased by 1 percent. Both countries also required a veterinarian's prescription for all remaining applications of antibiotics to livestock.

As part of its broader effort to strengthen its food safety regulations, the EU has progressively tightened its restrictions on the use of animal antibiotics. Notwithstanding the findings of a scientific advisory body that there was insufficient scientific knowledge to properly assess the risk associated with antibiotic use in animals, in 1998, acting on the basis of the precautionary principle, the Council of Ministers voted to ban all antibiotics used in human medicine from being added to animal feed. Following the ban, only four antibiotics that were not used to treat conditions in humans were permitted for use without a veterinarian's prescription. The USTR, which has sought to protect American exports of antibiotics for animal feed, informed the Commission that its ban might be illegal under the SPS Agreement, as the EU had not informed the United States in advance of its decision and that its decision was not based on a "proper risk assessment," but it has not filed a formal complaint.[138]

In 2003, the EU went a step further and banned the use of all antibiotics as growth promoters in animal feed; they were only allowed to be added to animal feed to treat illness in animals. This restriction, which went into effect on January 1, 2006, was based on the advice of the Scientific Steering Committee (SSC), which had explicitly recommended a precautionary approach. While the SSC noted that it "may take years to quantify . . . the potential risks from their use," it concluded that "it would be better to act now by banning the products in the animal sector and then observing

[137]The Pew Charitable Trust, "Human Health and Industrial Farming," available at http://www.saveantibiotics.org/ourwork.html, accessed 11/01/2010.

[138]Bruce Silverglade, "The WTO Agreement on Sanitary and Phytosanitary Measures: Weakening Food Safety Regulations to Facilitate Trade," *Food and Drug Law Journal* 55 (2000): 519.

whether or not the ban had any effect on antibiotic resistance."[139] According to the EU Commission for Health and Human Protection:

> This ban on antibiotics as growth promoters is of great importance, not only as part of the EU's food safety strategy, but also when considering public health. We need to greatly reduce the non-essential use of antibiotics if we are to effectively address the problem of micro-organisms becoming resistant to treatments that we have relied upon for years. Animal feed is the first step in the food chain, and so a good place to take action in trying to meet this objective.[140]

The EU's decision was strongly criticized by Ghislain Follet of the European Federation of Animal Health Industries, who argued that "the EU's recent precipitous ban on products that have been used safely and successfully as digestive enhancers is indicative of a general desire on the part of Europe's politicians to operate in a risk-free environment." Echoing the American position on the EU's ban on beef hormones, BST, and its restrictive policies toward GMOs, he stated: "One can make a case that the European habit of banning antibiotic products is politically motivated rather than scientifically based."[141]

The EU's restrictions on antibiotics in animal feed were challenged in the ECJ by Pfizer, Alpharma, and Solvay, three large global pharmaceutical firms based on both sides of the Atlantic. They argued that the Council's withdrawal of marketing authorization for a wide range of their products was based on incomplete scientific evidence, adding that its decision had not been informed by a risk assessment that specifically connected the use of their products to an identified health threat. In the specific case of the products produced by Pfizer, the business plaintiffs contended that the Council's decision was actually counter to the expert scientific advice that it had received. Moreover, the Council had banned the antibiotics produced by Alpharma before it had received the assessments of its designated scientific advisory body. However, the Court of First Instance (CFI) upheld the Council's decisions, indicating that it was not prepared to "second-guess the Council's assessment of whether sufficient elements are present to warrant precautionary action."[142]

---

[139] Ghislain Follet, "Antibiotic Resistance in the EU—Science, Politics, and Policy," *AgBioForum* 3, no. 2 and 3 (2000): 154.

[140] European Commission, Press Release IP/05/1687 (December 22, 2005), available at http://europa.eu/rapid/pressReleasesAction.do?reference=IP/05/1687&type=HTML&aged=0&language=EN&guiLanguage=en, accessed March 2009.

[141] Follet, "Antibiotic Resistance in the EU," 153.

[142] Veerle Heyvaert, "Guidance Without Constraint: Assessing the Impact of the Precautionary Principle on the European Community's Chemicals Policy," in *European Yearbook of Environmental Law*, ed. Thijs Etty (Oxford: Oxford University Press, 2006), 27–60.

AMERICAN REGULATORY POLICIES

In 1970, the FDA began to investigate the impact of antibiotics on both animals and humans. The FDA was concerned that some antibiotics approved for use in animal feed were not effective and might actually be making the animals resistant to the bacteria that the drugs were intended to cure; it also wanted to examine the impact of their increasing use on human health. The agency also initiated an efficiency review of all antibiotics used in animal feed. The companies marketing them were also required to present evidence that each antibiotic statistically improved animal growth.

In 1977, the FDA proposed to withdraw permission for penicillin and tetracycline antibiotics because of their importance in human medicine. It also stated it planned to restrict the use of all antibiotics in animal medicine to short-term therapeutic uses, unless the drug's sponsor could submit data demonstrating that their use did not adversely affect human health. However, this proposal was withdrawn following vigorous opposition in Congress from agribusiness firms and farm-state legislators. In 1984, a petition to the FDA by the NRDC to ban both categories of antibiotics was denied by the Department of Health and Human Services on the grounds that the NRDC had failed to establish that the use of antibiotics in animal feed constituted an "imminent hazard." As a result, both penicillin and tetracyclines continue to be administered to animals in the United States—making the United States one of the only major agricultural producers to permit both to be used.

In 1995, the FDA and the USDA requested another study of the human health impact of the use of antibiotics in food.[143] This report, issued in 1999, concluded that while the problem of increased resistance of antibiotics in humans was indeed a serious problem, this was primarily due to increased human use of them. Although it did find a "direct link between the use of antibiotics in food animals, microbial resistance to these antibiotics and human disease," it concluded that "the incidence of resistance was very low," adding that the scientific evidence for such a linkage remained "inconclusive."[144] In light of the economic costs to both producers and consumers of banning the administration of antibiotics to animals, the study recommended further research. But it also strongly advised against an outright ban on the therapeutic uses of antibiotics in food-producing animals.

---

[143]For discussion, see James Coffman, "Regulation of Antibiotic Resistance in the US," *AgBioForum* 3, no. 2 and 3 (2000): 141–7, available at http://www.agbioforum.org/v3n23/v3n23a12-coffman.htm, accessed 11/01/2010.

[144]Ibid., 142.

In 1995, notwithstanding vigorous opposition by the Centers for Disease Control, the FDA approved the use of an antibiotic to prevent E. coli infection in poultry and turkeys, though it did impose some restrictions on its use. Four years later, the FDA tightened its guidelines for approving new antibiotics for animals and for monitoring the effects of previously approved ones. But to date it has only withdrawn authorization for one previously approved animal drug, namely an antibiotic administered to poultry. This drug had been initially approved for animal use in 1995—nearly a decade after physicians began prescribing it for humans. It was withdrawn in 2005 after five years of administrative proceedings—a decision based on evidence that its use had led to a measurable increase in antibiotic resistance on the part of both animals and humans. However, between 2002 and 2004, the agency approved four additional antibiotics for use in animal feed.

The use of antibiotics in animal feed has become increasingly controversial in the United States.[145] More than 350 health, consumer, and environmental organizations have called for an end to the routine use of medically important antibiotics as feed additives—all of which can be purchased and administered without a prescription. According to Dr. David Wallinga of the Pew Commission on Industrial Farm Animal Production, "There is solid consensus among medical and public health officials that the profligate use of antibiotics in both human medicine and animal agriculture is eroding the efficacy of our arsenal of antibiotics."[146] This "consensus," however, has been challenged. Other studies have found no reduction in antibiotic resistance in humans following the EU's ban on antibiotics in animal feed, while some have reported a greater increase in food-borne diseases among Europeans following the EU ban. A summary of several scientific studies concludes:

> it is becoming increasingly apparent that the bans on antibiotic feed additives have not resulted in a safer food supply. The USA should learn from the EU experience and proceed with caution and only make decisions supported by scientific and quantitative risk analysis rather than implementing bans that may actually have effects opposite to their intended uses.[147]

[145] Lisa Jarvis, "Antibiotics Feed Additives Under Review by FDA," *Chemical Market Reporter* 259, no. 4 (2001): 9; Patricia B. Lieberman and Margo G. Wootan, "Protecting the Crown Jewels of Medicine," Center for Science in the Public Interest, available at http://www.cspinet.org/reports/abiotic.htm, accessed March 2009; Sabin Russell, "Fight to Curtail Antibiotics in Animal Feed," *Chronicle Medical Writer*, January 28, 2008.

[146] "House Hears Evidence Against Antibiotic Use," *The BeefSite Latest News*, September 2, 2008.

[147] Hector Cervantes, "Assessing the Results of the EU Ban on Antibiotic Feed Additives," available at http://www.thepoultrysite.com/articles/471/assessing-the-results-of-the-eu-ban-on-antibiotic-feed-additives, accessed 11/01/2010.

There have been periodic legislative initiatives to reduce or restrict animal antibiotics, but none have been adopted. The only statutory policy change took place in 2008, when Congress amended the Animal Drug User Fee Act to require drug makers to issue annual reports on the amount, strength, dosage, and intended purpose of antimicrobials used in feed for animals.

In July 2009, the Obama administration announced its support for legislation that would ban many routine uses of antibiotics in farm animals in order to reduce the spread of dangerous bacteria in humans and also prohibit their addition to animal feed without the supervision of a veterinarian. Its proposal was supported by the American Medical Association as well as other medical and consumer organizations, but opposed by the National Pork Producers Council on the grounds that "there are no good studies that show that some of these antibiotic-resistant diseases—and it seems like we're seeing more of them—have any link to antibiotics use in food-animal production."[148] Faced with congressional inaction, the Obama administration has also begun to consider imposing restrictions through administrative rule-making.

Some American producers have, however, voluntarily reduced the use of animal antibiotics. In 2004, McDonalds, responding to pressure from consumer groups, announced that it would phase out its purchases of meat from poultry and livestock that had been fed drugs to promote their growth. Subsequently, two of the largest producers of poultry in the United States—Tyson Foods and Perdue Farms—announced that they would no longer use sub-therapeutic doses of human-use antibiotics for growth promotion. However, they continue to be used extensively by American farmers. Currently, approximately 15 million pounds of sub-therapeutic antibiotics are annually given to livestock in the United States, while in the EU, they can only be used for medicinal purposes as long as the animal is treated rarely, and they must be withdrawn from meat or milk production for twice the length of time the drug remains in the animal in order to prevent them from being consumed by humans.[149]

ANALYSIS

This case provides another example of the importance of the differences in risk assessments in Europe and the United States. Policy makers on both sides of the Atlantic have been aware of and concerned about the impact on human health of the widespread use of antibiotics in animal feed. Yet the risk assessments commissioned by the FDA and the USDA

---

[148] Gardiner Harris, "Administration Seeks to Restrict Antibiotics in Livestock," *New York Times*, July 14, 2009.

[149] Terry Allen, "The Cruel Irony of Organic Standards," *In These Times*, September, 2010.

and a similar study by the EU's Scientific Steering Committee reached very different conclusions: the former concluded that the evidence for banning their use was "inconclusive," while the latter recommended extensive restrictions on all antibiotics in animal feed on precautionary grounds. Moreover, the contrasts in their policy approaches to antibiotics in animal feed have been upheld by their respective judicial systems.

The preferences of policy makers also played a critical role. While the Council of Ministers has strongly supported the restrictions on antibiotics in animal feed, the American Congress, influenced by political pressures from American farmers, has effectively opposed them. In this and in other cases discussed in this chapter, European policy makers have recently proven more responsive to non-business political pressures for the adoption of more stringent risk regulations than their counterparts in the United States. However, American consumers who prefer to avoid consuming food produced with veterinary drugs can do so as USDA regulations prohibit the administration of any antibiotics to animals whose food products are labeled "organic." Some meat sold in the United States is also labeled, "made without antibiotics."

AMERICAN FOOD SAFETY AFTER 1990

BSE in the United States

Concern about BSE also emerged in the United States.[150] The initial American policy response to the BSE crisis in Europe focused on keeping the infected cattle from the United States. In 1989, the United States banned the import of live cattle, feed, and beef products from Britain, acting seven years earlier than the EU, and in 1997, it extended the ban to all beef imports from Europe—a ban that it has maintained. Within only hours of reports that infected cattle had been discovered in Canada, beef and cattle imports were banned from that country as well.

However, American domestic regulations were less stringent and were implemented later than in Britain. While Britain had banned the practice of feeding meat-and-bone meal to cattle in 1988, subsequently extending it to other farm animals, the United States did not ban most mammal-based animal protein, including meat-and-bone meal as cattle feed, until 1997. The United States also continued to allow it to be fed to other farm animals, including pigs and poultry, creating a risk of cross-contamination

---

[150]This section is primarily based on Kate O'Neill, "US Beef Industry Faces New Policies and Testing for Mad Cow Disease," *California Agriculture* 59, no. 4 (October–December 2005): 203–11.

into cattle feed.[151] American testing of the brain tissue of slaughtered cattle was also less extensive than in Britain.

After one domestic cow tested positive for BSE in 2003, the United States began to reassess its vulnerability; testing was significantly increased and a wide range of other control measures were introduced, which imposed heavy costs on the domestic beef industry. These control measures proved effective: only one additional infected domestic cow was found.

Significantly, consumer confidence in the safety of American beef remained both high and undiminished.[152] In 2003, nearly all Americans had both heard of mad-cow disease and were aware that an infected cow had been discovered in the United States. But 68 percent stated that their confidence in the U.S. beef supply had not changed, while 8 percent responded that it had increased; only 22 percent reported that it had diminished. Only 6 percent were "very worried" that they or someone in their family would contract Creutzfeldt-Jacob Disease (CJD), commonly referred to as "mad cow disease" in their lifetimes. Not only was there no decline in American beef consumption, but it actually increased following assurances from the USDA that American regulations were adequate to insure the safety of American beef.

The Demise of the Delaney Clause

In 1987, a report on pesticide regulation that the EPA had commissioned from the National Research Council of the National Academy of Sciences helped place on the political agenda the need for reforming federal food safety standards.[153] Among its most important findings was a phenomenon that became known as the Delaney Paradox. This referred to the fact that the Delaney Clause did not apply to roughly half of pesticide-related carcinogens because they had no processed form. The committee made two recommendations: all pesticide residues in food should be regulated by the same standards, and a negligible risk standard for carcinogens in food should be consistently applied to all pesticides and all forms of food.

In 1993, a government study reported that children were more vulnerable than adults to pesticide residues because of dietary, physiological,

[151] Steve Stecklow, "Despite Assurances, US Could Be at Risk for Mad-Cow Disease," *Wall Street Journal*, November 28, 2001.

[152] William Hallman, Brian Schilling, and Calum Turvey, "Public Perceptions and Responses to Mad Cow Disease: A National Survey of Americans," Food Policy Institute, Rutgers University, available at http://foodpolicy.rutgers.edu/docs/pubs/2004_Public_Perceptions_and_Responses_to_Mad_Cow_Disease.pdf, accessed 11/23/2010. The references in this paragraph are from this study.

[153] Smart, "All the Stars in the Heavens," 273–351.

and developmental factors. This report argued that estimates of expected total exposure of pesticide residues should take into account the unique characteristics of children and infants. "The Alar scare had shown how politically powerful the idea of protecting children from pesticides could be," which in turn forced the food processing industry to accept the need for new standards that specifically evaluated the potential risks to infants and children.[154]

A further factor prompting congressional action was the publication of *Our Stolen Future* in 1996.[155] Modeled on Rachael Carson's influential book, *Silent Spring*, which had helped trigger the American environmental movement some thirty-five years earlier. the book painted a dramatic and chilling depiction of the sexual abnormalities, reproductive failures, and birth defects that it claimed resulted from chemically induced disruption of the endocrine system. The "alarm bells" it rang clearly resonated with the public. The book received extensive media attention and placed the relationship between these chemicals and harm to the body's immune system on the political agenda.

At the same time, food producing and processing firms as well as lobbyists for the agricultural chemistry industry had also become increasingly critical of the Delaney Clause, especially after the EPA had indicated its intention to more rigorously apply it. Moreover, the Republican Party's congressional leadership was concerned that their unpopular—and largely unsuccessful—efforts to weaken the nation's environmental laws (discussed in chapter 7) might hurt them politically in the 1996 congressional midterm elections. This led them to support new food safety legislation—which also had strong business support. In short, as Representative Pat Roberts, the chair of the House Agricultural Committee, observed, "all the stars in the heavens were in the right places."[156]

The core of the compromise that led to passage of the Food Quality Protection Act of 1996 ended the zero tolerance standard of the Delaney Clause—whose strict standard for regulating carcinogens in the food supply had become widely discredited—and eliminated the discrepancy between the treatment of different classes of pesticide residues. All pesticide residues, whether on raw or processed food, would now be subject to the same health standard: administrators were required to determine that "there is a reasonable certainty that no harm will result from aggregate exposure to pesticide residues."[157] This was a less rigorous standard

[154]Ibid., 306.
[155]Theo Colborn, Dianne Dumanoski, and John Myers, *Our Stolen Future: Are We Threatening Our Fertility, Intelligence, and Survival? A Scientific Detective Story* (New York: Plume, 1997). For a critical
[156]Smart, "All the Stars in the Heavens," 333.
[157]Ibid., 336.

than the Delaney Clause, but at the same time, it established similar regulatory standards for all pesticide residues.

This legislation also required the EPA to give special consideration to the effects of residues on infants and children and to develop and implement a screening program requiring registrants to submit data from endocrine testing. It also mandated the EPA to consider aggregative exposure to pesticide chemical residues, including from environmental exposures and drinking water, in contrast to the EPA's previous practice of considering dietary risk alone. "In sum, the basic quid pro quo of industry victories on old issues and environmentalists' victory on the new ones lies at the heart of the compromise."[158]

Food Safety Policy Failures

Since the early 1990s, there have also been several food safety policy failures in the United States. In 1993, hundreds of Americans became sick from consuming Jack-in-the-Box burgers that had been made from inappropriately prepared meat. Since 1995, there have been twenty-one E. coli outbreaks in food, resulting in seven fatalities and more than one thousand serious illnesses. The most dramatic single case involved the contamination of spinach in 2006, which led to three deaths and 150 reported illnesses.

In 2008, the United States experienced the largest food-borne outbreak of salmonella in more than a decade, which was subsequently attributed to hot chili peppers imported from Mexico. The following year, salmonella-tainted peanut products produced by one plant affected thousands of different products manufactured by more than two hundred companies, including candies and cookies marketed to children. Roughly 20,000 Americans, half of them children, contracted salmonella, and nine deaths were attributed to the consumption of the tainted peanuts. In the summer of 2010, about 1,500 cases of salmonella were linked to the production of tainted eggs produced by two farms in Iowa. They led to several reported illness and a widely publicized recall of half a billion eggs.

But, unlike the food safety policy failures and scares in Europe, these outbreaks did not undermine public confidence in the safety of any specific agricultural production technology, such as GMOs. Arguably, this can be attributed in part to the fact that none of them was as dramatic or as threatening as mad-cow disease, which had been initially predicted to cause tens of thousands of deaths and potentially threatened the health of every European who had ever eaten meat. By contrast, the dangers associated with the food safety policy failures in the United States were narrower

---

[158]Ibid., 345.

in scope: the sources of each contamination were both readily identified and limited to specific production facilities. In almost every case, following the recall of the contaminated food, sales of the tainted food products increased relatively rapidly to their former levels, suggesting a continued high degree of public confidence in the safety of the American food supply.

These "unfortunate events" did, however, place on the political agenda the need to improve the ability of the federal government to better monitor and prevent potential food safety risks.[159] According to one study, "food-borne illness kills 5,000 Americans a year [and] sends an additional 325,000 to hospitals."[160] In 2007, Congress, now controlled by the Democratic Party, approved legislation that required the FDA to establish a Reportable Food Registry to develop an early warning system to enable the FDA to identify contaminations in the food supply before they could spread. In July 2009, the House of Representatives passed the Food Safety Enhancement Act by a vote of 283 to 142, largely on partisan lines.

This legislation gave the FDA $1.4 billion over four years to increase its inspections of food production facilities, enhanced its authority to mandate recalls of tainted food, and required large food producers to develop procedures for conducting hazard analysis and institute improved safety controls. After considerable delay, the Senate passed a similar version of this legislation, relabeled the Food Safety Modernization Act, in the "lame-duck" session of Congress following the 2010 midterm elections. The legislation was supported by all fifty-six Democrats and both of the two independent senators, and its passage was made possible by the support of fifteen of forty Republican senators. The following month, the House of Representatives approved the Senate version of the legislation by a vote of 215-144, and the bill was subsequently signed into law by President Obama.

ANALYSIS

The 1996 Food Quality Protection Act represents one of the very few consumer or environmental statutes approved while Republicans were the majority party in one or both houses of Congress between 1995 and 2006. However, this was a relatively modest piece of legislation whose provisions reflected a political compromise between environmental and consumer advocates, and business. Democratic majorities in both houses of Congress between 2007 and 2010 did make possible the passage of a more important food safety statute. But notwithstanding three major and widely reported outbreaks of salmonella in 2008, 2009, and in the summer of 2010—as well as the support of the nation's major food producers for strengthening federal food inspection—nineteen months elapsed

[159] "Food Registry," *Washington Post Weekly Edition*, September 21–27, 2009.
[160] "Got Safe Food?" *San Francisco Chronicle*, November 25, 2010, A23.

between the passage of legislation by the House of Representatives, and the bill's final legislative approval. Moreover, in order to gain sufficient Republican support, the Senate version of the legislation both eliminated some of the fees food processors would be required to pay and reduced the number of required inspections. In addition, Congress has yet to appropriate the funds for its enforcement.

The extent of partisan polarization in Congress has been somewhat less with respect to the policy area of food safety, which in turn has made it possible for three pieces of food safety legislation to be adopted after 1990. But the considerable delay in passing the 2010 legislation, and the extent to which it was weakened in the Senate, reveals how much more difficult it had become for even highly visible policy failures which resulted in actual illnesses and deaths to become "policy triggers" in the United States after 1990.

CONCLUSION

This chapter has described the shifts in transatlantic regulatory stringency for food safety risks. Prior to around 1990, American regulations were typically more stringent than those adopted in Europe. American regulatory authorities adopted more precautionary regulations for suspected carcinogens in the food supply and banned food additives and pesticides which were permitted in Europe. The EU's decision to ban the use of beef hormones prefigured a progressive tightening of European standards vis-à-vis those of the United States. Subsequently, the EU banned and the United States permitted the use of a GM hormone to promote milk production, the EU adopted more stringent standards for the approval of GM varieties than did the United States, and the EU imposed significantly tighter restrictions on the use of antibiotics in animal feed than did the United States.

CHAPTER FOUR

Air Pollution

THIS CHAPTER COMPARES THE POLICIES in the United States and Europe to several health and environmental risks associated with air pollution—one of the most critical dimensions of environmental regulation. It specifically describes and explains each of their policy decisions toward the health and environmental risks of mobile (vehicular) source pollutants, ozone-depleting chemicals, and global climate change.

Beginning in the 1970s, the United States moved earlier and adopted more stringent controls on automotive emissions than did any European country or the European Union. During the 1970s and 1980s, the United States was the first country to identify the risks of ozone-depleting chemicals, and it adopted more extensive restrictions on them than did most European countries as well as the European Union. However, in the case of global climate change—a policy area that became more salient after around 1990—it was the European Union that adopted more stringent and comprehensive risk regulations than the United States. This chapter also discusses one important exception to the shift in transatlantic regulatory stringency that took place around 1990: American regulations for automotive emissions of health-related pollutants were and have remained more stringent than European ones.

Differences in public risk perceptions, one of my explanatory factors, played an important role in affecting these policy decisions. During the 1970s and through the mid-1980s, public pressures to address the risks of air pollution from vehicles were stronger in the United States than in many member states of the European Union. Public concerns about the health risks of ozone depletion were much more widespread in the United States than in Europe, especially during the 1970s. On the other hand, public concern about the risks of global climate change and support for reducing greenhouse gas (GHG) emissions to address them have consistently been stronger in Europe than in the United States.

Public policies toward the risks of air pollution have also been affected by the preferences of policy makers. Through 1990 in the United States there was relatively strong bipartisan support for addressing the risks of both vehicular pollution and ozone depletion. The two most important air pollution statutes were adopted during the administrations of Republican Presidents Richard Nixon and George H. W. Bush, when Democrats were the majority party in both Houses of Congress. An international treaty restricting ozone-depleting chemicals was negotiated by the administration of Republican President Ronald Reagan and approved by a Democratic-controlled Congress.

By contrast, in Europe, the policy preferences of the Council of Ministers toward strengthening controls on pollution from mobile sources were initially divided—primarily among Germany, the Netherlands, and Denmark on one hand, and France, Italy, and Great Britain on the other. These divisions contributed to the relative weakness of European mobile source emission standards throughout much of the 1980s. In the case of ozone-depleting chemicals, member states with large chemical sectors effectively opposed restrictions on them during the 1970s.

The politics of global climate change reveals a very divergent pattern. In this case, the preferences of American policy makers were more polarized than in Europe. American public policies toward the risks of global climate change have been significantly affected by partisan differences, which increased substantially during the 1990s in this and other policy areas. Republican policy makers in Washington have generally opposed federal controls on GHG emissions and Republican legislators have been less likely to regard the scientific evidence for the human causes of global climate change as credible.

By contrast, European policies toward global climate change have been much less affected by differences in the political preferences of center-left and center-right policy makers. Notwithstanding the appointment of a center-right European Commission in 2004, and the election of center-right governments in several European states, the European Union strengthened its commitments to reduce GHG emissions in 2008. There has been relatively strong support for addressing the risks of global climate change, both among the member states and in the European Commission, the Council of Ministers and the European Parliament (EP)—in sharp contrast to the much more polarized policy preferences of American legislators and occupants of the White House.

Differences in risk assessments also affected policy decisions on both sides of the Atlantic. In the important case of lead emissions from vehicles, American policy makers regarded the available scientific evidence for the health risks of airborne lead as sufficiently conclusive to support progressively tighter restrictions on its use as a fuel additive. In fact, the federal court decision which upheld that the Environmental Protection Agency's (EPA) initial lead restrictions specifically cited the *precautionary* language of the Clean Air Act on which the agency's rule-making was based. By contrast, European officials were initially more skeptical of scientific claims that lead posed a credible public health risk; they demanded a *higher* level of certainty than their American counterparts.

Likewise, American policy makers were prepared to act to restrict ozone-depleting chemicals on precautionary grounds; they issued regulations *before* there was conclusive evidence that the ozone layer was in fact thinning. By contrast, European policy makers demanded stronger scientific evidence for the risks of ozone depletion before they were willing to impose regulations on an important industrial sector. In the case of climate change, the scientific evidence that global climate change is occurring, and that if it is, human activity is causing it, has been much more contested in the United States than in Europe.

MOBILE (VEHICULAR) SOURCE EMISSIONS

Initial American Regulations

The world's first automotive emissions regulations were adopted in California, which, faced with the marked deterioration of air quality in the Los Angeles Basin, began to regulate emissions from vehicles in 1965. Around 1970, public concern about environmental quality increased substantially in the United States.[1] Public opinion surveys conducted in 1969 and 1970 reported that alarm about the environment sprang from nowhere, to reach major proportions in a few short years. Between 1969 and 1970, the percentage of those regarding "pollution/ecology as an important national problem" increased from 1 percent to 25 percent. A Louis Harris survey taken in December 1970 revealed that Americans considered pollution to be "the most serious problem" facing their communities. On April 22, 1970, an estimated 20 million Americans participated in Earth Day, and membership in the nation's five largest environmental organizations grew 20 percent between 1970 and 1971. A sense of urgency—even crisis—suddenly dominated public discussion of environmental issues.

Both the White House and Congress now found themselves under substantial political pressure to enact more stringent national environmental regulations. Among the most important sources of pollution were automobiles, which accounted for the majority of air pollution in the United States and were a particularly important source of poor air quality in urban areas. The Nixon administration, which was anxious to prevent the issue of environmental protection from benefiting the Democratic Party, responded by proposing that the Department of Health, Education and Welfare (HEW) be given additional authority to establish emission standards for new vehicles and engines, as well as to regulate fuel and

[1] This paragraph is based on David Vogel, *Fluctuating Fortunes: The Political Power of Business in America* (New York: Basic Books, 1978), 65.

fuel additives. A bill substantially similar to the administration's proposal was approved by the House of Representatives. However, when this legislation reached the Senate, Democratic Senator Edmund Muskie of Maine, a leading contender for the Democratic president nomination, was harshly criticized by consumer advocate Ralph Nader. Muskie now found himself "in the position of having to do something extraordinary in order to recapture his leadership."[2] At the executive (closed) session of the Subcommittee on Air and Water Pollution of the Senate Public Works Committee which he chaired, Muskie persuaded the other members of the subcommittee to support a significantly stronger bill.

The legislation adopted by this subcommittee included, for the first time, a statutory standard for automobile emissions of three health-related (criteria) pollutants, namely hydrocarbons (HC), carbon monoxide (CO), and nitrogen oxide (NO_x). While its requirements were slightly relaxed in the legislation approved by the full Senate Public Works Committee, the final legislation also incorporated a provision strongly opposed by the oil industry and the manufacturers of lead additives, which granted the newly established EPA the authority to "control or prohibit fuels or fuel additives which harm public health or welfare or impair a device or system to control emissions."[3]

The 1970 Clean Air Act Amendments, which were approved by a Democratic-controlled Congress and then signed into law by Republican President Richard Nixon, made federal mobile source emission standards more stringent than those of any other country. Its passage reflected the extent of political demands in the United States for much tighter pollution controls. These pressures were powerful enough to prompt both Democratic Senator Muskie and Republican President Richard Nixon to support far more stringent regulations than they had initially preferred. The passage of this legislation not only reflected strong bipartisan support for more stringent controls on automobile emissions, but a strong scientific and public consensus that the health risks they posed were both credible and unacceptable. For its part, California was permitted to impose more stringent regulations than those of the federal government.

In 1974, acting under the authority of the Clean Air Act Amendments, the EPA required all cars beginning with model year 1975 to be equipped with catalytic converters—an abatement technology whose use the EPA had determined was necessary to produce the mandated pollution reductions. Since vehicles equipped with such converters required unleaded gasoline (as lead would impair their functioning), the EPA also required

[2] Charles Jones, *Clean Air* (Pittsburgh: University of Pittsburg Press, 1975), 191–92.
[3] *Congressional Quarterly Almanac 1970* (Washington, DC: Congressional Quarterly Press, 1970), 485.

gasoline retailers to offer unleaded gasoline and to design special fuel nozzles so that cars equipped with converters could only accept unleaded fuel.

The 1990 Clean Air Act Amendments

In the late 1980s, Congress began another major revision of the Clean Air Act Amendments. As in the case of both the 1970 Clean Air Act Amendments, political conflict over automobile emission requirements was protracted and bitter.[4] But thanks in large measure to the support of President George H. W. Bush, who had pledged to strengthen the nation's air pollution controls during his 1988 presidential campaign, as well as heightened public concern about environmental quality, the Democratic-controlled Congress enacted, and President Bush signed into law, another important regulatory statute. The 1990 amendments to the Clear Air Act significantly strengthened controls on mobile source emissions, as well as tightened controls on ozone-depleting chemicals. What made this legislation historically important was not only its scope and stringency, but also it marked last time there was extensive bipartisan cooperation to address a major environmental risk.

The mobile source provisions of the 1990 Clean Air Act Amendments specified more than ninety emission standards. Among their most important provisions was a further reduction of tailpipe emission of both HC and NOx by 35 percent and 60 percent respectively, for both cars and light-duty trucks. In addition, the statute provided for the EPA to gradually tighten these pollution controls through administrative rule-making. This statute also established additional restrictions on the content of fuel. While previously Congress had permitted only California to maintain or adopt more stringent emission standards, this legislation allowed other states to enact regulations similar to California's, an option which ten other states, primarily in the heavily urbanized Northeast, chose to exercise.

Initial European Regulations

Standards for both automotive emissions and fuel content were first enacted in Europe in 1970. The first nations to do so were France and Germany, though their standards were considerably less stringent than those adopted in the United States. However, the EU was concerned that their regulations could hinder intra-community trade since they would

---

[4]For a detailed discussion of this legislation, see Gary Bryner, *Blue Skies, Green Politics: The Clean Air Act Amendments of 1990* (Washington, DC: Congressional Quarterly Press, 1993).

prevent vehicles produced in other member states from being sold in those two countries. Accordingly, in 1970, the EU approved a framework directive which set limit values for both CO and HC. These limits were strengthened in 1974, NOx was added in 1977, and the limits for all three pollutants were further reduced in 1978.

These directives attracted little political attention in Europe, where there was still much less public demand for reducing automotive emissions than in the United States. Moreover, their primary purpose was to protect the single market, not to improve environmental quality. It is a revealing indication of the relatively low political profile of automobile emissions within the EU and its member states during the 1970s that the EU did not develop its own standards. Rather, they were based on a framework established by the United Nations Economic Commission for Europe; a standards body based in Geneva whose members included several countries outside the EU.

The Intra-European Debate Over Emission Standards

The political environment surrounding EU mobile source emission policies changed significantly during the 1980s. The impetus for this change initially came from Germany, where public concerns about the damage to its forests due to air pollution led to strong public pressures for strengthened pollution controls. Frustrated with the lack of more stringent environmental regulation at the European level, Germany announced that it would enact its own emission standards for motor vehicles. In 1983, the German Minister of the Interior stated that as of January 1, 1989, all cars marketed in Germany would be required to meet the standards on emissions that previously had been adopted in the United States, the so-called "US-83" standards.

The German automobile industry, as a result of its strong presence in the American market, and especially in California where half of German vehicles exported to the United States were sold, had already begun to orient its research and development toward catalytic converters, the abatement technology required to meet both federal and California standards. For firms such as Mercedes and BMW, requiring the establishment of a similar technology on their vehicles sold in Germany presented them with relatively few technical problems. Not only had they already gained valuable experience with this technology, but such devices could also be relatively easily installed on the larger vehicles that these firms produced.

Those nations with strong domestic environmental movements, namely Germany, Denmark, the Netherlands, favored full conformity with American regulations. German environmentalists argued that only the adoption of the American standards could prevent the death of Germany's forests (*Waldsterben*), while a prominent Dutch environmentalist suggested that American standards should simply replace EU ones. But the political strength of domestic environmental pressures was considerably weaker in France, Britain, and Italy, where there was also less consumer demand for "cleaner" vehicles. The automotive firms based in these countries strongly opposed the adoption of American emission standards.

Although Germany did enact legislation requiring that all new cars be equipped with catalytic converters, it agreed to delay its implementation in order to give the EU more time to act. For their part, the manufacturers of small and medium vehicles in Europe were less concerned about the enactment of more stringent standards for large vehicles—which they did not make in any event—than with the possibility of more stringent environmental standards for the smaller classes of vehicles that they did manufacture. In particular, they were opposed to the mandatory use of catalytic converters because installing them in the smaller vehicles they produced presented more formidable technical problems than for the manufacturers of larger ones.

The Luxembourg Compromise

Finally, in 1987, the EU reached an agreement known as the Luxembourg Compromise. The approval of legislation was made possible by the Single European Act of 1986, which permitted some Council directives to be approved by a qualified majority, rather than by unanimity, which had previously been required for all Council legislation.[5] The Luxembourg Compromise also represented the first time the EU had enacted its own auto emission standards, rather than having them modeled on a European-based standards body. Its specific terms were shaped by the conflicting interests of European automobile producers, which in turn were reflected in the policy decisions of the Council of Ministers. The Commission proposed that "US-83" standards be phased in in two stages, with their final adoption by 1995. This goal, however, was subsequently weakened by the Council of Ministers due to pressures from member states which wanted less demanding standards. As a result, the 1987 directive classified motor vehicles into three categories, based on their cylinder capacity, and established different emission standards and deadlines for each.

The Luxembourg Compromise represented a considerable departure from the Commission's original goal of matching American standards— even at a slower pace. Not surprisingly, European environmentalists were

[5] Under the European Council's qualified majority voting rules, the votes of each member state varies, based roughly on their population. Thus, more than a simple majority of member states is necessary for legislation to be approved.

bitterly disappointed by the Luxembourg Compromise; they argued that the interests of small-car manufacturers had effectively undermined the enactment of significantly more stringent pollution control requirements for all vehicles. During the debate in the EP over the directive, one member complained, "This situation is intolerable . . . If we maintain the dates in this compromise, we will wait nine years. A child will have walked nine years ingesting all the dirt that escapes from our cars, with our complicity and connivance."[6] However, European green activists did secure one important concession—the 1987 directive required the EU to adopt new, stricter emissions requirements for small and medium vehicles that would go into effect in 1992 and 1993.

The Small Car Directive

Shortly after the passage of the Luxembourg Compromise, the Commission began work on establishing stricter emission standards for smaller vehicles. By now, European environmentalists had gained considerable political strength in a number of European countries, including in Britain, one of the strongest opponents of more stringent emission standards for smaller vehicles. Their representation and influence in the EP had also grown. Criticizing the Council's initial proposal to subject both small and medium vehicles to the same, but lower standards, one MEP argued, "it is not with limits like these that we can end the defoliation of our forests," while another claimed, "trees are dying, walls are cracking, and people are falling ill."[7] For its part, the European Environmental Bureau, a lobbying group representing European environmental organizations, demanded that the EU require emission standards as strict as those of the United States, beginning in 1993.

At the same time, the opposition of Europe's small-car producers to catalytic converters had diminished. Not only had they now acquired more experience with this technology—both Renault and Fiat had begun to manufacture vehicles equipped with converters for sale in the Netherlands—but the demand for cleaner vehicles had increased throughout Europe. For its part, the French government had become embarrassed that its opposition to catalytic converters for smaller vehicles had created the impression that "cleanliness was a German vice and dirtiness a French virtue."[8]

[6] Jonathan Story and Ethan Schwarz, "Auto Emissions and the European Parliament: A Test of the Single European Act," *INSEAD Case Study* (Paris: INSEAD-CEDEP, 1990), 25.
[7] Ibid., 27.
[8] *Le Monde*, August 4, 1988.

Finally, after prolonged and often heated negotiations within the Council, and among the Council, the Commission, and the EP, in July 1989 the Council approved the Small Car Directive. This legislation established strict new limits for all motor vehicles sold within the EU beginning in 1992. To meet these standards, all new vehicles would be required to be fitted with catalytic converters. These new standards, which aimed at cutting existing emission levels by 73 percent, were even lower than the 1987 emission control requirements for medium and small cars. European Commissioner for the Environment Carlo Ripa described the directive as "a milestone for Europe," and announced that the Commission subsequently planned to put forward new proposals to impose strict limits on medium and large cars that would bring them in closer alignment with those of the United States.[9]

Lead in Gasoline: The United States

Regulations governing the lead content of gasoline/petrol reveal a similar pattern: while European standards became progressively more stringent, they remained weaker than those of the United States.[10] The use of lead as a fuel additive dates from 1922, when General Motors (GM) contracted with Dupont to produce tetraethyl lead in order to prevent engine "knocking" and improve fuel efficiency. In response to an inquiry from the U.S. Surgeon General, a GM executive responded that adding lead to motor fuel did not pose any health risks, though he did admit that the firm had not conducted any studies.

By 1970, 98 percent of the gasoline sold in the United States contained lead and automotive exhausts accounted for 80 percent of airborne lead. The phase-out of lead in gasoline began indirectly when the EPA, acting under the authority of the 1970 legislation, required all new cars beginning in 1975 to be equipped with catalytic converters, which required the use of unleaded gasoline.

Acting in response to a 1973 government report that found that lead from automotive exhaust represented an immediate threat to public health, the EPA issued regulations that reduced the average amount of

[9] Elizabeth Bomberg, "EC Environmental Policy: The Role of the European Parliament," prepared for delivery at the Eighth International Conference of Europeanists, Chicago, IL (March 27–29, 1992): 25.

[10] The material on American policies is based on Richard Newell and Kristian Rogers, "Leaded Gasoline in the U.S.," in *Choosing Environmental Policy*, ed. Winston Harrington, Richard Morgenstern, and Thomas Sterner (Washington, DC: Resources for the Future, 2004), 175–81, and Peter Dauvergne, *The Shadows of Consumption: Consequences for the Global Environment* (Cambridge, MA: MIT Press, 2008), 79–87.

lead permitted in a refinery's total gasoline output; these standards were introduced in 1975 and were made more stringent four years later.

DuPont and the Ethyl Corporation, the main manufacturers of lead additives, promptly challenged the EPA's restrictions on the lead content of gasoline in the federal courts. A panel of the U.S. Court of Appeals for the District of Columbia set aside the EPA's standards, calling them "arbitrary and capricious" and agreeing with the claim of the business plaintiffs that the EPA was required to demonstrate "actual harm, rather than just significant risk."[11] However, in 1976 the full U.S. Court of Appeals reinstated the lead standard, ruling by 5 to 4 that the EPA could act on the basis of "significant risk." The court stated that the Clean Air Act was "*precautionary*" in nature and does not require proof of actual harm before regulation is appropriate."[12]

While leaded gasoline continued to be used in vehicles manufactured before the 1975 model year, in light of new studies that found increased evidence of the adverse effects of atmospheric lead, especially on children, between 1979 and 1986 the EPA steadily reduced the permissible lead content of gasoline. These regulations were important because in 1985, 40 percent of the gasoline sold in the United States still contained lead. Although the EPA had previously permitted refineries to both average and bank their lead reduction levels, in 1988 both provisions were phased out and all refineries were required to meet a standard of 0.1 grams per gallon standard. By 1989, lead had been completely eliminated from gasoline sold in the United States, though by this date, restrictions on the lead content of gasoline had become largely irrelevant as more than 95 percent of the gasoline produced in the United States was now unleaded due to the steady increase in the number of vehicles equipped with catalytic converters.

Lead in Petrol: Europe

The lead content of petrol in Europe was first addressed by Germany, which, in 1972, imposed restrictions on lead in gasoline, requiring that the lead content of petrol sold within its borders be restricted to 0.4 grams per litter (g/l).[13] After learning of Germany's regulation, the European Commission undertook a study of the health and technical aspects of lead pollution from motor vehicles. In marked contrast to the risk assessment on which the lead restrictions adopted by EPA had been

---

[11] Dauvergne, *The Shadows of Consumption*, 81.

[12] Emphasis added. Ibid., 82.

[13] This section is primarily based on Henrik Hammat and Asa Lofgren, "Leaded Gasoline in Europe: Differences in Timing and Taxes," in Harrington, Morgenstern, and Sterner, *Choosing Environmental Policy*, 192–205.

based, the scientific advisory body to the Commission concluded that the use of lead in petrol posed no immediate danger for public health. Accordingly, it stated that there was no urgent need to reduce the amount of lead in motor fuel. However, the report did suggest that it would be appropriate to establish uniform lead levels both to prevent an increase in air pollution due to the growth in car usage, and to prevent the divergence in national standards for lead content from interfering with intra-European trade.

While the Commission was still deliberating, the German government announced that it planned to make a second-stage reduction to 0.15 g/l, effective January 1, 1976. This level was apparently chosen because it was the lowest amount of lead usable in engines not equipped with catalytic converters. In the fall of 1975, the EP voted to recommend that the EU adopt Germany's initial 0.4 g/l limit.

The Commission now agreed that while it was not convinced that it was necessary to go as far as the German government was planning, European lead regulations did need to be strengthened. Accordingly, a directive adopted in 1978 permitted member states to introduce a national limit of 0.15 g/l, but at the same time it set an upper limit of 0.4 g/l, with both standards to go into effect in 1981. The minimum requirement was intended to prevent any member state from requiring lead-free petrol in order to prevent disruption to the single market. The establishment of the upper limit was strongly influenced by developments in the United States. Both European environmentalists and policy makers were well aware that the United States had moved so much earlier and more rapidly to address the health risks of lead from mobile sources, and this in turn placed pressure on the European Union to strengthen its own risk regulations.

The British Policy Shift

The passage of this directive was facilitated by the fact that in 1978, after heated domestic debate, Britain had adopted a phased-in reduction of 0.45 g/l. The change in British policy preferences was critical. In response to evidence that high blood concentrations of lead presented a health hazard, particularly to children, between 1972 and 1981 Britain had progressively reduced the permissible lead content of petrol from 0.84 g/l to 0.4 g/l, which meant that it was now able to comply with the terms of the 1978 European Union directive.

In May 1981, the British government announced its support for lowering the lead content of petrol to the strictest limit allowed by the EU, namely 0.15 g/l. However, the policy change failed to satisfy those who argued that the only responsible course of action was for Britain to ban the use of leaded petrol altogether. In 1981, several environmental, public health, and social welfare groups organized the Campaign for Lead Free Air (CLEAR). Its supporters included both the Labour Party and the Trades Union Congress; its policy recommendations were endorsed by the British Medical Association and supported by 90 percent of the British public. Implicitly endorsing the tenets of what would subsequently be formalized as the precautionary principle, *The Times* editorialized, "We should not have to wait until the very last mathematical correlation has been established to announce proudly that there is final proof that children have continued to be blighted while the research was concluded. The balance of risk is clearly such as to justify the maximum control on the emissions of lead poisons."[14]

But the British government initially refused to go beyond its earlier commitment to reduce lead levels to 0.15 g/l. Its decision was based on several scientific studies which had concluded, in the words of the *British Medical Journal*, "There is, so far as we are aware, no new evidence to justify [the argument] that there is a strong likelihood that lead in petrol is permanently reducing the IQ of many of our children."[15] The *Economist*, while suggesting that perhaps "Britain should play it safe and go for a ban on lead despite the cost and the scientific uncertainty," nevertheless concluded that "it is a disservice to informed debate . . . to pretend that the medical uncertainties have now been banished."[16]

This policy impasse was broken by the 1983 report of the Royal Commission on Environmental Pollution. While observing that the average concentration of lead in the blood of the British population was roughly a quarter of the level needed to produce overt symptoms of lead poisoning, it nevertheless stated that there was no justification for setting arbitrary figures for safe concentrations. Accordingly, it recommended that, beginning in 1990, all cars produced in Britain be required to run on lead-free petrol. Faced with intense public pressure, the British government took the unusual step of accepting the Royal Commission's precautionary recommendation the same day it was issued. But Britain's regulations could not go into effect until the EU changed its rules that prevented any member state from requiring lead levels below 0.15 g/l.

The European Policy Shift

The locus of policymaking then switched to the EU. With the support of both Britain and Germany for more stringent standards, in March 1985

---

[14] Des Wilson, *The Lead Scandal* (London: Heinemann, 1983), 93.
[15] Ibid.
[16] *The Economist*, "The Lead Debate Is Heating Up," March 6, 1982.

the Council required that fuel containing maximum lead levels of 0.13 g/l be made available for sale in all member states by October 1, 1989. Member states were also encouraged to adopt a maximum limit of 0.15 g/1 for lead content as soon as practicable. Two years later, they were permitted, though not required, to ban all lead in motor fuel.

Due to national differences in the number of sales of cars equipped with catalytic converters, the rate at which leaded gasoline consumption was reduced varied within the EU. By 1995, 80 percent of all gasoline sold in Denmark, Germany, and the Netherlands (as well as in Austria and Sweden, which joined the EU in 1995) was unleaded, while only 30 percent of the gasoline sold in Greece and Portugal was lead-free. In 1998, all EU member states, as well several countries from central Europe, agreed to end the sale of all leaded gasoline by 2005—a ban that the United States had adopted in 1989.

However, this comparison minimizes the more important differences between European and American restrictions on lead in gasoline/petrol. Because the United States had required catalytic converters for all new vehicles much earlier than in Europe, by 1990 American lead emissions were 99.75 percent lower than in the mid-1970s and leaded gasoline only accounted for 0.6 percent of total gasoline sales when it was finally banned.[17] By contrast, because catalytic converters were not required for all new vehicles sold in the EU until 1992—twelve years after the United States—European lead emissions from vehicles only began to significantly decrease during the 1990s. Between 1979 and 1987, the total amount of lead emitted by vehicles in the United States declined from 123,865 tons to 3,306 tons, while in 1987, lead emissions from vehicles within the EU still totaled 23,891 tons—or more than seven times American total vehicular emissions.[18]

American and European Vehicle Emission Standards after 1990

Since 1990, both American and European automotive standards have been progressively strengthened.[19] In the United States this has taken place primarily through administrative rules implementing the provisions of the Clean Air Act Amendments of 1990. "Tier 1" standards were issued in 1991 and phased in between 1994 and 1997. In February 2000,

[17] Dauvergne, *The Shadows of Consumption*, 85.

[18] Jonathan Player, "Green Movement Strengthens," *New York Times*, October 2, 1989.

[19] This section is based on *Vehicle Emission Reductions*, European Conference of Ministers of Transport (Paris: OECD, 2001); "Euro-5 Emissions Standards for Cars," *EurActiv.com*, September 4, 2008, available at http://www.euractiv.com/en/transport/euro-5-emissions-standards-cars/article-133325; "Cars and Light Trucks," *DieselNet*, available at http://www.dieselnet.com/standards/eu/ld.php [accessed 11/01/2010].

the EPA issued more stringent "Tier 2 standards" which were phased in between 2004 and 2009. The latter also included two additional components. One addressed the content of gasoline. The EPA had originally proposed a 50 percent reduction in sulfur content, a proposal that was opposed by the oil industry but supported by the automobile industry since without this reduction it would have been difficult for them to meet the other components of the "Tier 2" standards. But thanks to the strong and effective advocacy campaign by a coalition of environmental and public health organizations, and state and local environmental agencies, the EPA agreed to strengthen its proposed standard, and instead required a 90 percent reduction. Second, the EPA required that all light (pick-up) trucks, passenger cars, medium-duty sport utility vehicles, and passenger vans be subject to the same emission standards by the model year 2009.

In 1998, California's Air Resources Board had identified diesel particulate matter as a toxic air pollutant. In 2000, the state launched a Diesel Reduction Plan to reduce diesel particulate emissions by 76 percent in ten years. Shortly after California acted, the federal government issued a similar standard. In January 2001, the EPA issued a rule requiring a more than thirtyfold reduction in the sulfur content of all diesel fuels in order to reduce the pollution emitted by heavy-duty trucks and buses, many of which ran on diesel engines. This fuel, called ultra-low sulfur fuel, was made available throughout the United States beginning in 2006. By 2014, all diesel fuel sold in the United States, including for all non-road, locomotive, and marine engines, must be ultra-low sulfur.

For its part, the EU has also continued to steadily strengthen its mobile source emission standards. It approved directives establishing Euro-1 standards in 1991 and 1993, Euro-2 standards in 1994, 1996, and 1999, and Euro-3/4 standards in 1998 and 2002. Euro-5 standards went into effect in 2009, and Euro-6 will be implemented in 2014 and 2015.

Comparing Transatlantic Automotive Emission Standards

American automotive emission standards for ground-level pollutants emitted by vehicles remain more stringent than European ones. The American Tier 2 car standards, which took full effect in 2009, "are the toughest in the world, as are the . . . truck standards and off-road vehicle standards that the EPA adopted."[20] Moreover, the durability requirements for American vehicles are longer than in Europe: a car must be designed to maintain its original emission levels for 160,000 km in the United States as compared to 100,000 km in Europe. Equally important, American emissions standards for diesel fueled vehicles are similar to

[20] Stuart Brown, "Have Muffler, Will Travel," *Fortune*, October 17, 2005.

those for vehicles powered by gasoline; that is, they are "fuel neutral," while EU standards for the two differ substantially.

While European standards for emissions of carbon monoxide are more stringent for diesel than for gasoline powered vehicles, they are up to four to five times more lax for both NOx and particulate matter. Euro-4 standards are also more lax than American regulations for both heavy sports utility vehicles and large four-wheel drives. But for all three kinds of vehicles, European standards for both NOx and particulates are measurably weaker than those of the United States. For example, while diesel cars sold in Europe from 2008/9 must emit no more than 200 mg/km of NOx, American standards have set a maximum level of 87 mg/km.

What makes these differences especially significant is that diesels have accounted for nearly one-half of new European motor vehicles, but approximately 1 percent of those sold in the United States. The more widespread use of diesels in Europe in part reflects the greater priority European regulations and taxation policies have placed on fuel economy; diesels are much more fuel efficient than gasoline powered vehicles. But they also emit more ground-level pollutants. The relative scarcity of vehicles powered by diesel fuel in the United States stems from the fact that few of them are capable of complying with American pollution control standards.[21] But, ironically, many of the diesel-powered automobiles that do meet American standards are made by European firms. One European environmental activist observed, "Apparently Europe's cleanest, most innovative diesel engine technology is too good for Europeans. We'll have to carry on breathing dirty air until 2015, while the Yanks can stroll down to their local Mercedes dealer today and pick up a clean diesel car."[22]

The Euro-6 standards adopted in 2008 will substantially close the differences in emission standards between gasoline and diesel-powered vehicles. By around 2015, when they are scheduled for full implementation, European standards will be roughly comparable to the national standards for all vehicles already in effect in the United States. However, even after Euro-6 standards are fully adopted, they will still be weaker for emissions from both gasoline- and diesel-powered cars than the more stringent emission standards of California and the ten other states that have adopted similar requirements.

[21] Gina Chron and Stephen Power, "Cleaning up Diesel's Image," *Wall Street Journal*, November 29, 2006.

[22] "Parliament Says Europe Must Wait Until 2005 for Clean Diesels; America Gets Them This Week," European Federation for Transport and Environment, Press Release, October 18, 2006, available at http://www.transportenvironment.org/News/2006/10/Parliament-says-Europe-must-wait-until-2015-for-clean-diesels%3B-America-gets-them-this-week/, accessed February 2009.

The EU's standard for emissions of fine particulates, which will go into effect in 2015, is weaker than the American regulation adopted in 1997. One member of the European Parliament (MEP) observed that "The U.S. is a good decade ahead of us," while another admitted, "We can't simply copy the US. We have totally different conditions in Europe, particularly in terms of the density of population and transport."[23] The laxer European particulate standard is in part due to the large numbers of older automobiles in the ex-communist countries that have joined the European Union since 2004, as well as Europe's larger number of diesel-powered vehicles.

Analysis

Each of my explanatory factors helps clarify these policy differences. First, public demands for more stringent regulations to address the risks of air pollution from vehicles were much stronger in the United States than in much of Europe, especially between 1970 and through the mid-1980s. Second, while there was relatively strong bipartisan support both within the Congress and from the White House for stronger mobile source emission standards between 1970 and 1990, in Europe, until the late 1980s, the preferences of policy makers within the Council of Ministers were much more divided.

Third, the divergence between American and European policies toward the lead content of gasoline was affected by differential risk assessments. In the case of the United States, the EPA adopted its initial restrictions on precautionary grounds—a policy approach affirmed by a 1976 Court of Appeals decision. During the early 1970s, the scientific advice given to the EPA and the European Commission regarding the health risks of lead in fuel differed markedly; the latter did not consider them sufficiently compelling to justify imposing significantly tighter restrictions. It was not until 1983 that Britain's Royal Commission on Environmental Pollution recommended banning lead in petrol.

But what then accounts for the continued relative stringency of American regulations? Why, in this important case, did the United States continue to adopt more stringent regulations for a wide range of mobile source emissions *after* 1990? What explains this unusual case of regulatory policy path dependency in the United States? One important reason was that progressive tightening of American regulations did *not* require any additional legislation. Because they could be issued administratively, they were not affected by the increased partisan polarization and Republican control of Congress after 1994. Thus, the much more stringent "Tier

---

[23] "EU Setting Tougher Clean-Air Limits," *International Herald Tribune*, December 12, 2007.

2" standards could be issued administratively by the EPA under Democratic President Bill Clinton. His administration was also responsive to public pressures to strengthen them—and, in the case of the EPA's 2000 rules on sulfur fuel content—issued a final rule that was considerably more stringent than the environmental agency had initially proposed.

But why did the EPA during the presidency of George W. Bush also issue more stringent controls for mobile source air pollutants? Part of the reason was again the policy path created by the Clean Air Act Amendments of 1990. This legislation required the EPA to continually review both fuel content and other mobile source emissions that affected public health. Thus, just as in 1986, when the Reagan administration created a policy framework for the regulation of GMOs which has endured—notwithstanding shifts in partisan control of both the Congress and the White House—so has the regulatory framework of the Clean Act Amendments of 1990 continued to guide subsequent federal controls over mobile source emissions that affect public health—again notwithstanding subsequent shifts in partisan control of the White House and the Congress.

Equally important, each of the more stringent rules for mobile source pollutants issued by the EPA during the presidencies of both Bill Clinton and George W. Bush *did* meet both a risk assessment and cost-benefit test: they addressed what has remained a major source of air pollution in the United States whose adverse effects on public health, particularly for urban residents, have been widely recognized and accepted since the 1960s. Moreover, because the number of both vehicles and vehicle-miles driven continued to increase steadily in the United States unless standards were tightened, and broadened to include the larger vehicles which accounted for about half of new passenger car sales, the adverse health impacts of mobile source emissions would increase. Thus, at a minimum, more stringent standards were necessary to prevent urban air quality in the United States from deteriorating.

In marked contrast to the intense political controversy and partisan polarization that has surrounded many of the more stringent risk regulations proposed or debated in the United States after 1990, the continued strengthening of automotive emission standards reflects what has been a strong political and scientific consensus that stronger pollution control standards *are* required to protect public health. The support of local governments, including California and many states and cities, was also an important source of pressure on the federal government to continually strengthen its vehicular emission standards.

An important reason why European standards for health-related pollutants from vehicles have continued to lag behind those of the United States has to do with the tradeoffs between their respective policy priorities. For a variety of historical reasons, public policies in European countries, most notably their taxes on motor fuels, have played an important role in promoting the use of more fuel-efficient engines, most notably diesels. But diesels also produce more health-related pollutants. This helps explain why reducing emissions from mobile sources has proven more difficult for the European Union than for the United States. Finally, in contrast to the United States, which has two different automotive emission standards—one for California and other states that have chosen to adopt California's more stringent standards, and a second for vehicles sold in other states—EU standards apply equally to vehicles sold in all twenty-seven member states. Thus, in this case, the EU's commitment to maintain a single market for automobiles has constrained the ability of member states to adopt more stringent mobile source emission standards, as California and other American states have been able to do.

OZONE DEPLETION

The Initial Policy Response of the United States

Chlorofluorocarbons (CFCs) were first developed commercially during the 1930s for use in refrigeration systems.[24] By the 1970s, they were used in a wide range of industrial processes and commercial products. Closely related compounds such as methyl chloroform were used as solvents and halons were employed in fire extinguishing systems. CFCs and related compounds were released into the environment either during their use, such as in aerosols, or through leakage of product disposals, such as refrigeration or close-cell foams. The first study which suggested that the environmental release of CFCs might deplete stratospheric ozone, thus enabling more ultraviolet light to penetrate to ground level, was published in 1974 in the United States by Sherwood Rowland and Mario Molina.

The study's claim of a link between CFCs and ozone depletion was theoretical; at the time it was released there was no evidence that the ozone layer was actually thinning. Dupont, which produced 50 percent of CFCs in the United States and accounted for a quarter of world

---

[24]This section is based primarily on the following sources: Srini Sitaraman, "Evolution of the Ozone Regime: Local, National, and International Influences," in *The Environment, International Relations, and U.S. Foreign Policy*, ed. Paul Harris (Washington, DC: Georgetown University Press, 2001), 111–33; Robert Falkner, *Business Power and Conflict in International Environmental Politics* (New York: Palgrave Macmillan, 2008), 49–93; Peter Morrisette, "The Evolution of Policy Responses to Stratospheric Ozone Depletion," 29 *Natural Resources Journal* (1989): 793–820; James Hammitt, "CFCs: A Look Across Two Continents," in *Choosing Environmental Policy: Comparing Instruments and Outcomes in the U.S. and Europe*, ed. Winston Harrington, Richard Morgenstern and Thomas Sterner (Washington, DC: Resources for the Future, 2004), 158–76; Edward Parsons, *Protecting the Ozone Layer: Science and Strategy* (Oxford: Oxford University Press, 2003).

output, insisted that further data and study were needed. The Rowland-Molina study's conclusions also met with skepticism from the scientific community; Richard Sconer, a British atmospheric scientist, dismissed the ozone theory as "utter nonsense," as did some American scientists.[25] Anticipating the position of some scientists and firms about the impact of greenhouse gases on global temperatures that would be made after 1990, critics of the Rowland-Molina study argued that even if ozone depletion was occurring, there was no evidence that human activity was causing it.

Notwithstanding the tentativeness of its findings, because the report was released when public concerns about environmental problems, including the risks of environmental cancer, were increasing and the strength of environmental lobbies was growing in the United States, both the American public and policy makers took its claims seriously. American environmentalists now urged the government to ban the production of all CFCs, and Congress held several hearings to discuss the policy implications of the study's findings.

As a result of congressional hearings on ozone depletion, and the considerable media attention devoted to the issue, the American public quickly became persuaded that the use of nonessential products such as aerosol hairsprays and deodorants posed serious environmental and health dangers. "The fear of skin cancer from the depletion of stratospheric ozone due to the use of CFCs as aerosol propellants in spray cans personalized the risks for many people. . . . The public came to view the risks of using CFC-based aerosols as unacceptable."[26] Sales of aerosol products fell sharply and legislation to ban them was introduced in Congress as well as in several states.

In 1975, a governmental interagency task force released a study supporting the CFC/ozone depletion theory and its links to skin cancer. It made the precautionary recommendation that ozone-depleting emissions should be regulated unless new scientific evidence clearly refuted the results of the Rowland-Molina study. But the task force also cautioned that any new regulations would need to be adopted slowly in light of the large size of the refrigeration and CFC industry, whose annual sales totaled more than $7 billion. Another government study released the following year by the National Academy of Sciences (NAS) confirmed the task forces' findings, but also noted that it was unable to specify the urgency of the health and environmental risks posed by CFCs.

However, the NAS did recommend new legislation to enable the government to regulate all sources of CFC emissions, should doing so become necessary. Congress proved responsive and in October 1976, the

[25] Sitaraman, "Evolution of the Ozone Regime," 118.
[26] Morrisette, "The Evolution of Policy Responses," 803–4.

federal government enacted the Toxic Substances Control Act (TSCA), which, among other important provisions, granted the EPA the broad regulatory authority over all CFCs that it had previously lacked. A year later, the 1977 amendments to the Clean Air Act granted the EPA the authority to regulate "any substance . . . which in his judgment may reasonably be anticipated to affect the stratosphere, especially ozone in the stratosphere," . . . [or] may reasonably be anticipated to endanger public health or welfare."[27] In March 1978, the EPA, the FDA, and the Consumer Product Safety Commission jointly issued regulations banning all nonessential uses of CFCs. This decision affected nearly $3 billion worth of domestic production and effectively banned half of all CFC production in the United States. However, no further regulations were issued for the remaining sources of CFC emissions.

The Initial Policy Response of Europe

By contrast, "European countries in general were less inclined to take the threat seriously and to regulate CFCs without conclusive scientific evidence linking CFCs to ozone depletion."[28] An additional factor underlying the difference in the European response to the risks posed by CFCs was the fact that public demands to address the risks posed by them emerged in only three European countries: Germany, Britain, and the Netherlands. Significantly, while the American aerosol market for personal hygiene products had significantly declined during the 1970s, demand for personal aerosol products remained high in much of Europe. Only in the Netherlands was there a public boycott against them comparable to that in the United States. In fact, those American firms that had ceased using CFC propellants in their products sold in Europe found their market shares decline as consumers continued to demand personal hygiene products with higher quality CFC propellants, most notably in Great Britain.

Only one EU member state, namely Denmark, along with Norway and Sweden (which were not then members of the EU), adopted aerosol bans about the same time as the United States, but each had little or no chemical production. Those European nations who *were* major producers and/or users of CFCs were unwilling to do so. Germany did reach a voluntary agreement with CFC producers to reduce CFC use in aerosols by 30 percent between 1976 and 1979, while another major chemical-producing country, the Netherlands, required a warning label. But there was no policy change in Europe's three other major chemical producers,

---

[27] Quoted in Miranda Schreurs, *Environmental Politics in Japan, Germany, and the U.S.* (Cambridge: Cambridge University Press, 2002), 119.

[28] Morrisette, "The Evolution of Policy Responses," 806.

namely Britain, France, and Italy. While the United States was not the only country to ban the use of CFCs in aerosols, it was the only major chemical producer to do so.

The policy arena then switched to the EU, which was faced with a conflict between the Netherlands, Denmark, and Germany, who favored a 50 percent reduction in CFC use, and Britain and France, who opposed any further restrictions. In 1980, the Council approved a compromise directive that required member states not to increase their CFC production capacity and to reduce their use of aerosols by 30 percent from 1976 levels by the end of 1981. However, this legislation was largely symbolic, as European production was currently far below capacity.

In May 1983, the EU announced that no further regulatory action was required. According to an official from the German chemical industry:

> [The] popularity of sprays keeps growing. What environmentalists saw as a warning was scientifically disputed from the very beginning and now has proven to be a miscalculation . . . the authorities should avoid over-hasty measures when it comes to handing down administrative regulations.[29]

The German chemical industry's position would be echoed subsequently by critics on both sides of the Atlantic of other "over-hasty measures" based on "disputed" scientific "miscalculations" undertaken by the EU to address a wide range of health, safety, and environmental risks.

Transatlantic Policy Convergence

In 1985, the announcement of Joe Farman, the leader of a British atmospheric study, that his team had discovered a large hole in the ozone layer over Antarctica transformed regulatory politics and policies on both sides of the Atlantic. Even though its cause had yet to be clearly identified, because the hole could be detected and recorded by satellites, its symbolic impact was substantial. As one scientist observed, "now we've got a hole in our atmosphere that you could see from Mars. . . . it is harder to label [it] as just a computer hypothesis."[30] Shortly afterward, NASA released a new study in collaboration with the United Nations Environmental Program (UNEP) that supported the British study's findings, and which was endorsed by more than 150 scientists from around the world. The EPA now announced that stronger government regulation was necessary to prevent ozone depletion and the agency organized a series of international workshops in an effort to create an international consensus for more stringent regulations.

---

[29] Schreurs, *Environmental Politics*, 124.
[30] Quoted in Sitaraman, "The Evolution of the Ozone Regime," 123.

Policies toward ozone depletion now moved to the international level. The UNEP formed an ad hoc working group that drafted a Framework for the Protection of the Ozone Layer. But at a conference of forty-three countries held in Vienna in March 1985, the positions of the United States and the EU remained divergent. The "Toronto Group" of countries— namely the United States, Canada, Norway, Sweden, and Finland, each of whom had banned nonessential CFC aerosol use, favored a 90 percent reduction or a complete ban in nonessential uses of CFCs. The EU, however, was only willing to support a production capacity cap and a 30 percent cut in nonessential aerosol use of CFCs. This production cap, however, would not restrict CFC production, but would actually allow it to increase, as European chemical producers were still operating substantially below capacity.

International negotiations resumed in 1986. The American position called for freezing the production of both CFCs and halons at 1986 levels and then for reducing them both by 95 percent over ten to fourteen years. This position was based on new research which reported that CFCs posed a substantial risk to public health. For example, "using a scenario of no CFC controls and a continued annual growth of 2.5 percent through 2050, EPA estimated over 150 million additional cases of skin cancer, resulting in more than three million deaths for the U.S. population born before 2075."[31]

"The contrast between the U.S. and European approaches could not be sharper. Whereas the EU adopted a modest cutback of CFC aerosol use largely in step with market trends, the EPA signaled that it was aiming at a more comprehensive reduction of CFC production and use."[32] The American support for more stringent international regulations reflected not only continued strong public concern about the risks of ozone depletion, but also a shift in the position of American industry. During the 1970s, both the producers and users of CFCs had fought hard against any government regulation. While they were unable to prevent the ban on aerosols, they had succeeded in preventing the EPA from regulating non-aerosol uses of CFCs. On the latter issue, the position of American, European, and Japanese chemical firms was identical: all argued that no causal link had been established between CFCs and stratospheric ozone levels.

But by 1986, faced with the recognition that the strong support for additional regulation by the American government and the progress of international negotiations meant that additional controls on CFC regulation were now likely, Dupont, the world's largest producer of CFCs,

[31] Morissette, "The Evolution of Policy Responses," 797.
[32] Falkner, Business Power, 63.

dramatically announced its support for a worldwide limit on CFC emissions. "Dupont's decision to support a CFC control regime was based on a political judgment that the time had come for *precautionary* measures given changing public perception of scientific uncertainty."[33] Dupont had also revived its search for CFC substitutes. The firm stated that suitable alternatives could be made available within five years, provided that it had the appropriate regulatory incentives to adopt them.

Dupont's support for a global limit on CFC production capacity led an industry lobbying group, which formerly had led the opposition to all restrictions on CFCs, to now support a "reasonable" global limit on CFC production capacity. The American chemical industry also expressed its support for the international American negotiating position, reasoning that a treaty that would also bind their global competitors was preferable to the possibility of unilateral American regulations. "With this policy shift, the [American] chemical industry implicitly accepted a *precautionary approach* to the ozone problem . . . [which] laid the foundation for closer cooperation between U.S. industry and governmental representatives" in international negotiations."[34]

The Montreal Protocol

The American delegation to the international negotiations in Montreal initially proposed the phased elimination of 95 percent of all CFCs; though faced with European opposition, it stated that it was willing to accept only a 50 percent reduction and a freeze on halons, another ozone-depleting chemical. While the EU was initially reluctant to go beyond supporting a production cap and further study of the problem, as negotiations proceeded its position began to change. This shift was in part due to the influence of new scientific risk assessments as well as domestic environmental pressures. Following the 1986 Chernobyl nuclear accident, the environmental movement had gained considerable political strength in Europe, especially in Germany. In addition, the large and politically influential German chemical firm, Hoechst, which accounted for about half of German CFC production, decided to phase out all CFC propellants by the end of 1989.

Under pressure from Germany, the Netherlands, Denmark, and Belgium, and overcoming opposition from France, Italy, and the UK, European environmental ministers now agreed that a 20 percent reduction in CFC production could be achieved within four years after an international agreement was signed. However, the European position was still

[33] Emphasis added. Ibid., 73.
[34] Emphasis added. Ibid.

substantially weaker than that of the United States, which favored a minimum 50 percent reduction.

Finally, in the fall of 1987, an international agreement, known as the Montreal Protocol, was reached. It required signatory countries to reduce their aggregate CFC emissions by 20 percent in 1993–94 and by an additional 30 percent in 1998–89, using 1986 as the base year. "The U.S. [was] the principal advocate for a strong protocol. The U.S., EPA, and the State Department in particular, deserve much of the credit for the strength of the Montreal Protocol."[35] In 1987, the Protocol was signed by Republican President Ronald Reagan and ratified by the Democratic controlled Senate—again underscoring the extent of bipartisan support for the expansion of environmental regulation in the United States during this period. The Protocol was transposed into the laws of each EU member state in 1988. It was implemented in the United States by Title VI of the Clean Air Act Amendments of 1990, which also committed the United States to a more rapid phase-out of some ozone-depleting chemicals than the Protocol required.

Regulations after the Montreal Protocol

Shortly after the signing of the Montreal Protocol, "Europe moved from a policy of foot-dragging to political leadership by speeding up the CFC phase-out."[36] At the first meeting of the Protocol's signatory nations held in Helsinki in 1989, the EU decided to support a complete phase-out of CFCs by the end of the century. Recently elected American President George H. W. Bush subsequently endorsed this position, though no formal agreement was then reached. At meetings held in London in 1990, the EU for the first time adopted a stronger regulatory stance than the United States; it now proposed 1997 as the final deadline for eliminating CFC use, while the United States preferred 2000, largely because Dupont insisted that it needed more time to develop CFC substitutes. The American position prevailed and the London Protocol adopted the 2000 deadline.

Subsequent meetings of the parties to the Protocol held in 1992 and 1995 primarily focused on the rate at which all ozone-depleting substances would be phased out. The agreements reached at these meetings both advanced these deadlines and expanded the number of substances covered by them. These policy changes reflected the increased ability of both European and American firms to develop CFC substitutes, as well as the results of new scientific studies that revealed that the rate of ozone depletion was larger than had been previously realized. The 1992

[35] Morrisette, "The Evolution of Policy Responses," 797.
[36] Falkner, *Business Power*, 86.

Copenhagen Protocol mandated the phasing-out of most CFCs, in addition to two other ozone-depleting substances, by 1996, with halons to be eliminated two years prior to that. By the time the Copenhagen conference concluded, it was clear that the end had been reached for CFC production on both sides of the Atlantic.

Only weeks after the Copenhagen agreement, the EU's environmental ministers decided to move up their deadline for eliminating CFC production to 1995. Subsequent negotiations of the Protocol in 1997 and 1999 further tightened its terms and scope, with the EU now continuing to press for stronger controls than the United States, particularly with respect to ozone-depleting chemicals other than CFCs. For example, the Montreal Protocol had committed developed countries to eliminate the use of another ozone-depleting chemical, methyl bromide (MBr), by 2005, though signatory governments were permitted exemptions for its continued use when there were no technically or economically feasible alternatives or for health and safety reasons. But 60 percent of all exemption requests under the Montreal Protocol have been made by the United States—far more than from any European country. According to one study, "These exemptions are big enough to drive a truck through. Technically we may be in compliance, but in essence the U.S. just started calling much of its normal use 'critical' and began relying on exemption permits."[37]

Analysis

The contrasts in transatlantic policies toward the risks that the production and use of CFCs and other chemicals posed to the ozone layer cannot be adequately explained by transatlantic differences in relative abatement costs. A study by Detlef Sprinz and Tapani Vaahtoranta found that American abatement costs were substantially higher than for any European country that produced CFCs.[38] Specifically, in 1986, CFC production per capita was 11.3 in the United States, but only 3.6 in Germany, 3.7 in France, 4.5 in Italy, and 4.5 in the United Kingdom.[39] However, when this study compared "ecological vulnerability," as measured by comparative skin cancer rates, it found that American rates *were* significantly higher than in Great Britain, France, and Germany.[40] This finding may

[37] Amy Coombs, "Methyl Bromide Still Finds its Way into U.S. Fields," *SFGATE*, November 24, 2007.

[38] Detlef Sprinz and Tapani Vaahtoranta, "The Interest-based Explanation of International Environmental Policy," *International Organization* 48, no. 1 (Winter 1994): 77–105.

[39] Ibid., 89.

[40] They were 7.2 in the United States as compared to 2.6 in Britain, 2.5 in France, 2.1 in Germany, and 3.0 in Italy per 100,000. However, they were higher in Australia and Norway, which do not belong to the EU.

partially explain the marked differences in public risk perceptions across the Atlantic. Widespread public awareness of the health risks of ozone-depleting chemicals emerged much earlier and were much more widespread in the United States than in most of Europe.

But this explanation is inadequate. For as other case studies throughout this book clearly demonstrate, there is no necessary relationship between the actual extent of "ecological vulnerability" and the public's perception of the risks it considers both credible and unacceptable. Nor is there any evidence that significant segments of the public or opinion leaders on either side of the Atlantic were aware of their different vulnerabilities to skin cancer. Nonetheless, it is clear that during the 1970s, Americans *were* more concerned about the health risks of CFCs than were Europeans—as they were toward other health, safety, and environmental risks caused by business.

The second factor shaping the initial differences in European and American policies toward the risks of ozone depletion was their respective risk assessments. American regulatory authorities were willing to adopt more stringent restrictions even before there was conclusive evidence that the ozone layer was thinning, that CFCs emissions were a cause of this atmospheric change, and that ozone depletion posed a substantial risk to public health—or in other words, they were willing to issue regulations on precautionary grounds. By contrast, European policy makers were initially unwilling to do so; they insisted on a higher level of scientific proof or certainty before they were willing to impose substantial costs on a very important industry—a pattern consistent with their respective approaches to many food safety risks prior to 1990 as well as their initial responses to the risks of lead in motor fuel.

Finally, the initial political preferences of influential policy makers differed substantially. While the member states of the Council were sharply divided as to whether the EU should move to restrict CFCs, the TSCA was passed with bipartisan support. While the Reagan administration's first EPA director opposed additional restrictions on CFCs, the administration subsequently reversed its position and played a critical role in the negotiations that led to the Montreal Protocol. In turn, the 1990 Clean Air Act Amendments were approved by a Democratic-controlled Congress and signed into law by Republican President George H.W. Bush. In short, while there was relatively strong bipartisan support for addressing the risks of ozone depletion, the preferences of European policy makers were much more divided. In part due to pressure from the United States, transatlantic environmental policies converged—among the last times they would do so.

CLIMATE CHANGE

The Early Politics of Climate Change in Europe

Climate change first became politically salient in Europe during the mid-1980s, most notably in Germany, where it became juxtaposed with the issue of ozone depletion.[41] In Germany, the 1985 discovery of the ozone hole also created a sense of urgency about the need to address the problem of greenhouse gas emissions.[42] A 1986 German scientific report, which predicted an apocalyptic climate catastrophe due to both fossil-fuel consumption and deforestation, received considerable media attention. Ironically, the 1986 accident at Chernobyl also focused public attention on the issue, as it was used by the German nuclear power industry to highlight the role that nuclear power could play in reducing carbon emissions.

In a speech before the *Bundestag* in 1987, German Chancellor Helmut Kohl described climate change as the most serious of all environmental problems. The following year, the German Parliament unanimously approved a report that warned of the serious dangers the greenhouse effect posed and recommended an immediate policy response. A 1990 German government sponsored scientific report unequivocally endorsed a link between a rise in global temperatures and increased greenhouse gas emissions. In turn, the German government agreed to a target of a 20–25 percent reduction in its CO_2 emissions from 1987 levels by 2005. In 1994, the German government pushed the German automobile industry to enter into a "voluntary" agreement to reduce CO_2 emissions from new cars by 25 percent—a modified version of which was agreed to four years

[41]This section primarily draws on Falkner, *Business Power*, 94–139; Judith Layzer, "Deep Freeze: How Business Has Shaped the Global Warming Debate in Congress," in *Business and Public Policy: Corporate Interests in the American Political System*, ed. Michael Kraft and Sheldon Kamieniecki (Cambridge, MA: MIT Press, 2007), 93–126; David Levy, "Business and the Evolution of the Climate Regime," in *The Business of Global Environmental Governance*, ed. David Levy and Peter Newell (Cambridge, MA: MIT Press, 2005), 73–104; Miranda Schreurs, "The Climate Change Divide: The EU, the U.S., and the Future of the Kyoto Protocol," in *Green Giants? Environmental Policies in the U.S. and the EU*, ed. Norman Vig and Michael Faure (Cambridge, MA: MIT Press, 2004), 207–30; Miranda Schreurs, Henrik Selin, and Stacy VanDeveer, "Conflict and Cooperation in Transatlantic Climate Politics: Different Stories at Different Levels," in *Enlarging Transatlantic Relations: Environment and Energy Politics across the Atlantic*, ed. Schreurs, Selin, and VanDeveer (Hampshire, UK: Ashgate, 2009), 233–59; Miranda Schreurs and Yves Tiberghein, "Multi-Level Reinforcement: Explaining the EU's Leadership in Climate Change Mitigation," *Global Environmental Politics* 7, no. 4 (November 2007): 19–46.

[42]This material on Germany is based on Jeannine Cavender and Jill Jager, "The History of Germany's Response to Climate Change," *International Environmental Affairs* 5, no. 1 (Winter 1993): 3–18.

later by the European Automobile Industry Association, which included Ford and GM's European subsidiaries.

During the late 1980s and early 1990s, a number of other European governments announced greenhouse gas reduction targets. In 1989, the Netherlands stated that it would stabilize CO_2 emissions for the following year, and in 1990 it went a step further by pledging to cut them to 3–5 percent of their 1990 levels by 2000. Denmark announced plans to reduce its CO_2 emissions by 20 percent relative to 1998 levels by 2005, while Austria established a goal of a 20 percent reduction of its 1998 CO_2 emissions by 2005.

However, the EU's initial policy response to the risks of global climate change was cautious. In its first communication on the subject, issued in 1988, the European Commission stated that the "reduction of greenhouse gas concentrations does not seem at this stage a realistic objective, but could be a very long term goal."[43] But two years later, it adopted a more proactive stance by announcing its support for an international agreement to stabilize the emissions of greenhouse gases from industrial countries at 1990 levels by 2000. The Commission then went on to propose a European tax on carbon-based energy. However, this proposal met with fierce and effective opposition from the European business community, which, while accepting the need for international regulation, was unwilling to have its burdens borne disproportionately by European firms. But the EU did agree to stabilize carbon emissions at 1990 levels by 2000, largely on the basis of the CO_2 reduction commitments that some member states had previously made.

The Early Politics of Climate Change in the United States

The risks of climate change first emerged on the public agenda in the United States during the early 1980s, largely the result of a report in *Science* magazine by James Hansen, a NASA scientist. He had found a long-term warming trend dating back to 1880 and predicted a warming of "almost unprecedented magnitude" during the next century. Subsequent studies by the EPA and the National Academy of Sciences (NAS) reached similar conclusions to Hansen's but came to different policy recommendations: the EPA recommended an immediate policy response, while the NAS did not. Although several congressional hearings on climate change were held between 1981 and 1984, by the mid-1980s the issue had largely disappeared from the American political agenda.

The issue of global climate change was revived in 1986 and 1987 due to its links with the issue of ozone depletion (CFCs are a greenhouse gas)

[43] Falkner, *Business Power*, 105.

as well as the fact that in 1988 the United States experienced its worst drought in fifty years. 1987 was also the warmest year on record worldwide—an "alarm bell" that received considerable media attention. On June 23, 1988, Democratic Senator Timothy Wirth of Colorado scheduled hearings on the greenhouse effect. By coincidence, the temperature in Washington on that day reached 101 degrees, thus guaranteeing that Hansen's testimony would attract wide publicity. However, several scientists disputed Hanson's claim that the "greenhouse effect" had already arrived, while another study reported that global temperatures had actually declined between 1940 and 1970, thus rendering problematic a causal relationship between increased CO_2 concentrations and global warming.

The Rio Earth Summit

The divergence between the American and European positions on climate change first emerged at the international level at the meetings of the International Panel on Climate Change, which had been established by the UN General Assembly in 1990 to produce a draft treaty on climate change at the 1992 Rio Earth Summit. While the EU was the main supporter of a strong convention on climate change on the grounds that there was now sufficient scientific evidence to support an international agreement to address its risks, the United States led the opposition to legally binding targets. In marked contrast to their earlier respective policy responses to the risks of ozone depletion, it was now the United States which argued that more scientific research was needed. The United States also insisted that any international agreement should also require developing countries to reduce their own emissions.

In a speech in Detroit during the 1988 presidential election campaign, Republican candidate George H. W. Bush stated, "those who think we are powerless to do anything about the 'greenhouse effect,' are forgetting about the 'White House Effect.'"[44] But his views subsequently shifted and four years later, the president threatened to boycott the 1992 Rio Earth Summit if the Framework Convention on Climate Change (FCCC) included any specific, binding goals or deadlines for achieving them. As a result of American opposition, the FCCC only committed signatory countries to work to stabilize greenhouse gas concentrations at levels that would "prevent dangerous anthropogenic interference with the climate system."[45] Both the United States and the EU then subsequently signed and ratified the Framework Convention—the first and only time

[44] Layzer, "Deep Freeze," 98.
[45] Falkner, *Business Power*, 108.

an international agreement to address the risks of global climate change was approved by the U.S. Congress.[46]

Toward Kyoto

The EU, which accounted for nearly a quarter of greenhouse gas emissions in 1990, now led the push for a much stronger international agreement. Already committed to stabilizing carbon emissions at 1990 levels by 2000, it now began to consider more ambitious reduction targets. Its willingness to do so was strongly influenced by Germany and Britain, both of whom supported an international agreement requiring a decline in emissions from industrial countries of 10 percent below 1990 levels by 1995 and 15 percent by 2020. Both countries were in part responding to domestic political pressures: in Germany, the Green Party now had parliamentary representatives at both the federal and regional levels, while in Britain Prime Minister Tony Blair, who had taken office in 1997, was a strong supporter of stronger restrictions on GHG emissions. In addition, the collapse of much of the industry of the East German Democratic Republic following unification considerably facilitated Germany's ability to reduce its carbon emissions. For its part, since the 1980s Britain had reduced its reliance on carbon-intensive oil and coal and switched to less carbon-intensive North Sea gas. Both structural changes made it easier for these countries to set and meet the more ambitious carbon reduction targets demanded by domestic environmental constituencies.

Equally important, major business firms and associations in Europe now indicated their willingness to support government restrictions on GHGs. In 1995, Shell and British Petroleum (BP) dramatically broke ranks with American oil and coal firms by stating that the fossil fuel industry needed to begin preparing for a transition to alternative forms of energy. In 1995, seventeen German industry associations announced a voluntary pledge to reduce their carbon emissions by 20 percent by 2005, while industrial sectors in other European countries also indicated that they were prepared to back international efforts to reduce greenhouse gas emissions. A highly publicized 1997 speech by BP's chairman, Lord John Browne, announced his support for regulations to address the risks of global climate change. The willingness of many European firms and industry associations to adopt a more conciliatory approach than their American counterparts to climate-change

---

[46] However, the Senate did ratify the 1994 Convention to Combat Desertification, which arguably was related to the risks of climate change. But this treaty had no effect on American domestic policies.

reductions—as well as the positions of Germany and Britain—played a critical role in shaping the EU's negotiating stance at both the 1995 meetings of the parties to the Framework Convention in Berlin and the Kyoto meetings in 1997.

The Kyoto Negotiations

The Clinton administration, which came into office in 1993, wanted the United States to play a more proactive role in international climate-change negotiations. With the active involvement of Vice President Albert Gore, who was personally concerned about this issue, the administration announced its support for quantifiable emission targets. This brought the position of the United States into closer alignment with the EU. But after the 1993 defeat of the Clinton administration's BTU energy tax proposal by Congress, which would have reduced American carbon emissions, the administration's enthusiasm for mandatory domestic carbon controls diminished. "Clinton's reluctance to take a strong public stand on global warming reflected a shrewd reading of the public, which was hardly clamoring for him to address the issue."[47]

To further undercut the administration's approach to the Kyoto negotiations, the American fossil fuel industry aggressively lobbied Congress, emphasizing the costs to the American economy of any international agreement that included binding targets on carbon emissions. The gap between the administration and Congress widened considerably following the Democratic Party's loss of control of both houses of Congress in the 1994 midterm elections. Congressional hearings convened by the Republican majority now prominently featured testimony that emphasized both the negative impact of binding targets on the American economy and the importance of including developing countries in any international agreement. But opposition to the international agreement on climate change supported by the EU was bipartisan. In 1997, by a vote of 95 to 0, the Senate approved a resolution expressing opposition to any international climate treaty that would harm the American economy and that did not also include binding obligations on rapidly industrializing developing countries.

The bipartisan Senate resolution severely undercut the ability of American negotiators to reach an international agreement that would satisfy both domestic constituencies and the EU. Caught between the strong opposition of the U.S. Senate and much of the American business community, as well as the demands of European and American environmentalists for binding targets and timetables, "the administration's hands

[47] Layzer, "Deep Freeze," 100.

were tied."[48] Nonetheless, the Clinton administration went to Kyoto with "a strong . . . commitment to realistic and binding limits that [would] significantly reduce our greenhouse gas emissions."[49]

The EU supported a compromise that committed it to reduce its GHG emissions by 8 percent below their 1990 levels by 2008–12, though it had come to Kyoto supporting a more ambitious 10 percent reduction target. For its part, the United States agreed to reduce its GHG emission levels by 7 percent below their 1990 levels over the same time period. Just as the United States was the driving force behind the Montreal Protocol, the EU was the driving force behind the 1997 Kyoto Protocol; its domestic policy initiatives on GHG emissions reduction had established the goals, targets, and norms to which other states responded. "The Kyoto targets would not have been as ambitious as they were without the EU."[50]

The American Response to Kyoto

Although public opinion polls reported that nearly three-quarters of Americans would pay five cents a gallon more for gasoline to combat global climate change, the breadth and intensity of public support for an international treaty remained unclear. A Gallup poll conducted just before the conclusion of the Kyoto negotiations reported that "public fears about global warming had declined substantially from 1992 levels."[51] A 1997 poll reported that only 28 percent of respondents believed that there was a scientific consensus that "global warming exists and could do serious damage, while 58 percent believed that scientists were divided."[52] This was linked to the fact that scientific claims about the risks of global climate change had become increasingly contested. More than a dozen conservative think tanks played a critical role in undermining what had formally been a broad scientific and public consensus. By issuing a steady stream of policy reports, sponsoring public forums, public speeches, and press conferences, many of which received extensive media coverage, they sought to "dispel the myths of global warming by exposing flawed economic, scientific, and risk analysis."[53]

[48] Schreurs, "The Climate Change Divide," 213.

[49] Layzer, "Deep Freeze," 100–101.

[50] Joyeeta Gupta and Lasse Ringius, "Climate Leadership: Reconciling Ambition and Reality," *International Environmental Agreements* 1, no. 2 (2001): 294.

[51] Layzer, "Deep Freeze," 104.

[52] Ibid., 101.

[53] Ibid., 106. See also James Hoggan, *Climate Cover-Up: The Crusade to Deny Global Warming* (Vancouver: Greystone Books 2009), and Naomi Oreskes and Erik Conway, *Merchants of Doubt* (New York: Bloomsbury Press, 2010), 169–215.

The control of Congress by Republicans after 1994 provided critics of climate change with an important policy window: it led to a dramatic increase in the number of climate-change skeptics who were asked to testify before Congress and contributed to increased media coverage of their views. The failure of the United States to "enact a significant climate change policy [was] . . . heavily influenced by the success of the conservative movement in challenging the legitimacy of global warming as a social problem."[54] Aided by Republican legislators, "the conservative movement successfully altered the nature of the global warming debate away from the question of 'What do we need to do to address global warming?' toward the more benign question of 'Is global warming really a problem?'"[55]

Accepting that he lacked sufficient legislative and public support— indeed, the day after the agreement was announced, the Republican congressional leadership declared that the Protocol was "dead on arrival"—President Clinton did not submit the treaty to the Senate for ratification.[56] Congress also refused to approve the administration's request for tax breaks and research spending to assist in meeting U.S. targets under Kyoto. Indeed, Republican congressional opposition to the Kyoto Protocol was so strong that for the next three years, riders were attached to several appropriation bills that explicitly prohibited the use of any federal funds "to propose or issue rules, regulations, decrees or orders for the purpose of implementing, or in preparation for the implementation of, the Kyoto Protocol."[57]

An important factor underlying business opposition to Kyoto in the United States— and this concern was shared by many legislators from both political parties—was the fact that its targets imposed a disproportionately greater burden on the American economy. Achievement of the United States' Kyoto target of a 7 percent reduction from a 1990 baseline would have required an actual reduction of GHG emissions of approximately 20 percent by 2012, as opposed to approximately 5 percent for the EU.[58] These differences were in part due to the fact that the American economy was growing more rapidly than that of the EU, which meant that its CO2 emissions were increasing at a higher rate. They also reflected America's greater use of fossil fuels, especially for transportation, as well as its greater reliance on coal. In addition, the choice of 1990

---

[54] Aaron McCright and Riley Dunlap, "Defeating Kyoto: The Conservative Movement's Impact on U.S. Climate Change Policy," *Social Problems* 50, no. 3 (August 2003): 367.

[55] Ibid., 368.

[56] Kathryn Harrison, "The Road Not Taken: Climate Change Policy in Canada and the U.S.," *Global Environmental Politics* 7, no. 4 (November 2007): 103.

[57] Layzer, "Deep Freeze," 107.

[58] John Vogler and Charlotte Bretherton, "The EU as a Protagonist to the U.S. on Climate Change," *International Studies Perspectives* 18 (2006): 16.

as the benchmark year provided the EU with an important advantage as it allowed it to receive credit for the structural and economic changes in GHG emissions from Germany and Britain during the 1990s.

The George W. Bush Administration

During his 2000 presidential campaign against Democratic Vice President Al Gore, Republican presidential candidate George W. Bush promised to support binding GHG emissions from utilities. However, shortly after assuming office his position changed. Much of this shift was due to the continued intensity of business opposition to either domestic or international restrictions on GHG emissions. "Nowhere was business opposition to the climate change agenda as virulent as in the U.S."[59] A broad alliance of companies, led by oil and coal firms, backed by automobile manufacturers, and supported by companies and firms from other sectors dependent on fossil fuels, expressed strong opposition to domestic restrictions on greenhouse gas emissions as well as to any international agreement that would require the United States to adopt them.

In contrast to their counterparts in Europe, many firms and business associations waged an extensive public campaign to challenge the credibility of the claim that carbon emissions were contributing to a long-term global warming trend or indeed that such a trend was occurring. Both during the Kyoto negotiations and immediately following their conclusion, business opponents launched an intense media campaign, which argued that "strict reductions in greenhouse gases would have catastrophic economic consequences, endangering the lifestyle of every American."[60] They claimed that "the crisis [now] appeared to be at least a generation away [and] any effort to reduce greenhouse gas emissions would produce immediate costs while promising distant benefits."[61]

Shortly after assuming office in January 2001, President George W. Bush, rather than continuing to not submit the Protocol for congressional ratification as President Clinton had done, expressed his opposition to the Kyoto Protocol as well as to any domestic restrictions on CO2 emissions. He described the 1997 Kyoto Protocol as "fatally flawed in fundamental ways," on the grounds that "it exempts 80 percent of the world . . . and would cause serious harm to the U.S. economy."[62] The

[59] Falkner, *Business Power*, 102.

[60] Layzer, "Deep Freeze," 103.

[61] Ibid., 100.

[62] The first part of this quotation is from Steven Brechin, "Comparative Public Opinion and Knowledge on Global Climatic Change and the Kyoto Protocol: The U.S. versus the World?" *International Journal of Sociology and Social Policy* 23, no. 10 (2003): 122; the second is from Schreurs and Tiberghein, "Multilevel Enforcement," 170.

president as well as Republicans in Congress also repeatedly argued that there was too much "scientific uncertainty" about the causal link between increased GHG emissions and observed changes in climate, to support either domestic or international restrictions on GHG emissions.

The American decision to unilaterally withdraw from the Protocol without informing any of its other signatories was criticized as "irresponsible and wrong" by the EU.[63] Several European government officials unsuccessfully urged the United States to reconsider its decision, but to no avail. The *Irish Times* reported that "the rest of the world . . . has reacted with justifiable anger and outrage to the announcement."[64]

Differences in Transatlantic Public Opinion

Public reaction to the administration's announcement revealed a significant gap between public opinion in much of Europe and the United States. While 44 percent of Americans disapproved of the president's decision, public disapproval in Britain, Italy, Germany, and France ranged between 83 and 89 percent.[65] Moreover, five to six times more Americans supported the president's decision than did Europeans.[66] Equally significant, when asked in 2003 to evaluate the seriousness of the problem of climate change or global warming, 63 percent of Italian, 54 percent of German, 50 percent of British, and 46 percent of French respondents judged it to be "very serious," while only 31 percent of Americans shared this assessment. Three to ten times as many Americans considered the problem of global climate change to be "not at all serious" as did the respondents in the four European countries polled.[67]

Although a majority of Americans did support ratification of the Kyoto Protocol, 73 percent also backed the position of the Bush administration, namely that "the same energy regulations to reduce global warming should apply to all countries around the world, suggesting that many were not aware of the treaty's provisions."[68] In a revealing indication of the lack of public engagement with the issue, three years after the United States withdrew from the Kyoto Protocol, 42 percent of Americans still

[63] Schreurs, "The Climate Change Divide," 218.

[64] Schreurs and Tiberghein, "Multilevel Enforcement," 29.

[65] Brechin, "Comparative Public Opinion and Knowledge on Global Climatic Change," 123–4.

[66] Ibid., 126.

[67] Kathryn Harrison and Lisa Sundstrom, "The Comparative Politics of Climate Change," *Global Environmental Politics* 7, no. 4 (November 2007): 7.

[68] Michael Lisowski, "Playing the Two Level-Game: U.S. President Bush's Decision to Repudiate the Kyoto Protocol," *Environmental Politics* 11, no. 4 (2002): 101–19, and "Polls on the Environment and Global Warming," *American Enterprise Institute*, April 18, 2008, available at www.aei.org/publicopinion11, accessed 11/01/2010.

believed that President Bush had *supported* the treaty and fewer than half were aware of the president's opposition to it.[69] Moreover, voter approval of the president's environmental record actually increased during the year he announced American withdrawal from Kyoto.[70]

While a 2005 World Opinion Survey did find that the number of Americans who now considered climate change to be a "very serious problem" had increased to 49 percent, this remained significantly lower than in Germany, France, Italy, and Britain, where agreement with this assessment ranged between 68 and 70 percent.[71] Public opinion polls taken the following year reported that more Americans were now convinced that global warming was in fact occurring and they supported government action to address the issue. Nonetheless, this same survey also found that only 2 percent of Americans regarded global warming as among the most important issues facing the United States, while only 23 percent thought its effects would occur in their lifetime, if at all. It also ranked ninth among ten environmental problems that concerned them.[72] "Disinterest in global warming sets the United States apart from other countries."[73]

An American Policy Shift

Around 2007, the Bush administration found itself under increasing pressure to address the risks of global climate change. Media photos of melting glaciers and polar bears, the destruction created by Hurricane Katrina in New Orleans in 2005, and former Vice President Gore's film on climate change, *An Inconvenient Truth*, which became the third most successful documentary of all time, all placed the issue back on the political agenda. In addition, American dependence on foreign oil was now seen as a national security issue, and the American public was faced with rising fuel prices. In his 2006 State of the Union message, the president criticized America's "addiction to oil" and announced a long-term commitment to reduce its dependence on imported oil.

[69] Program on International Policy, "Americans on Climate Change: A PIPA/Knowledge Networks Study," June 24, 2004, http://www.pipa.org/OnlineReports/ClimateChange/ClimateChange04_Jun04/ClimateChange_June04_rpt.pdf, accessed February 2009.

[70] "Polls on the Environment and Global Warming," *American Enterprise Institute*, April 18, 2008.

[71] World Opinion Survey, 2005. See also Ed Crooks, "Europeans Accept the Need to Act Over Global Warming," *Financial Times*, November 20, 2006.

[72] "Yelling 'Fire' On a Hot Planet," *New York Times*, April 22, 2006.

[73] Deborah Lynn Guber and Christopher Bosso," "Past the Tipping Point? Public Discourse and the Role of the Environmental Movement in a Post-Bush Era," in *Environmental Policy: New Directions for the Twenty-First Century*, ed. Norman Vig and Michael Kraft (Washington, DC: Congressional Quarterly Press, 2010), 55.

Moreover, business political preferences had become more divided. In January 2007, the CEOs of ten major corporations urged the president to set a mandatory limit on greenhouse gas emissions, and later that year, the leaders of 150 global firms, including General Electric, Nike, Coca-Cola, and Shell, called for the establishment of a legally binding framework which would enable them to invest in low-carbon technologies without disadvantaging their shareholders. A report by the Conference Board, a business organization, stated that there was increasing scientific consensus that humans were contributing to the warming of the planet, and that "governments and markets are likely to act on their perception of the science. Increasingly, this perception is swinging toward the belief that climate change is an urgent priority that must be addressed through a variety of measures."[74]

Pressures from segments of the business community, the growing number of state regulations, increased public concern, the beginning of discussions within the United Nations about what to do after the expiration of Kyoto in 2012, and the election of a Democratic Congress in 2006, all played a role in shifting President Bush's position. The president now stated that he was persuaded of the scientific case for global climate change; he cited its risks in his 2007 annual State of the Union message for the first time.[75]

Congress responded by enacting the Energy Independence and Security Act of 2007. This legislation strengthened fuel economy standards for the first time since 1975; by 2020, new cars would be required to have an average fuel economy of 35 miles per gallon. It also required substantial increases in biofuels in motor fuel; provided financial incentives for energy-efficient windows, equipment, and building design; and mandated improved energy efficiency for lighting and appliances. (One of its provisions, which phased out the use of incandescent light bulbs beginning in 2012, was actually more stringent than that of the EU. However, in 2009, the European Commission adopted regulations that phased out these light bulbs *by* 2012.)

Due to Republican opposition in the Senate, and the threat of a presidential veto, the bill omitted two provisions strongly favored by Congressional Democrats and included in the version of the legislation passed by the House of Representatives, namely, a $13 billion tax increase on oil firms, and a requirement that utilities produce 15 percent of their electricity from renewable sources. Both of these provisions were strongly

[74]Layzer, "Deep Freeze," 116.

[75]Peter Baker, "A Greener Bush?" *Washington Post National Weekly Edition*, January 7–13, 2008.

and effectively opposed by business associations representing investor-owned energy utilities, and petrochemical, paper, mining, and refining firms. Notwithstanding a 2007 Supreme Court decision in a suit brought by several states that held that the EPA did have the authority to regulate GHG emissions under the Clean Air Act, the agency declined to issue them. EPA also refused the requests of California and several other states to strengthen their fuel economy standards.

The Obama Administration

Democratic President Barack Obama came to office in 2009 having promised to address the risks of global climate change during his presidential campaign. Approximately 10 percent of the $787 billion allocated by Congress in the 2009 American Recovery and Reinvestment Act was directed toward investments in clean energy. That same year, the Democratic-controlled House of Representatives approved a complex piece of legislation that established a cap-and-trade scheme to reduce GHG emissions. It required a 17 percent reduction in GHG emissions by 2020 and 80 percent by 2050, a commitment that President Obama repeated at the international climate change negotiations held in Copenhagen in December 2009. However, faced with strong opposition from Republicans, as well as from some Democrats, the Senate never voted on this legislation.

Following the Gulf oil disaster in April 2010—the worst oil spill in the history of the United States and the most important environmental "unfortunate event" in the United States since the Exxon *Valdez* oil spill of 1989—supporters of climate-change regulation saw a window of opportunity. Democratic Senator John Kerry of Massachusetts and independent Senator Joseph Lieberman of Connecticut proposed legislation that, in addition to tightening government regulations of off-shore oil drilling, established a cap-and-trade scheme for GHG emission controls for utilities, one of the major stationary sources of carbon emissions.

But only three months later, in July 2010, much to the disappointment of supporters of GHG restrictions on both sides of the Atlantic, it was apparent that the policy fallout from the Gulf oil spill would not affect federal policies toward global climate change.[76] Not only were virtually all Republicans in the U.S. Senate strongly opposed to legislation restricting carbon emissions from utilities, but so were some Democrats from

---

[76] For the disappointment of American commentators, see Ross Douthat, "The Right and the Climate," and Paul Krugman, "Who Cooked the Planet?" *New York Times*, July 28, 2010, A21, and for a European commentary, see Clive Crook, "Action on Carbon Is Down the Drain," *Financial Times*, July 28, 2010, 7.

states dependent on coal production. With the United States still only slowly recovering from the 2008–9 recession, many legislators, as well as much of the public, were not enthusiastic about new regulations that would impose additional costs on an important sector of the American economy and increase energy costs. In any event, the Senate Democratic leadership was unable to muster the "super-majority" of sixty votes required to allow the Senate to vote on this legislation.

Faced with congressional inaction, the Obama administration moved to address the risks of global climate change through administrative rule-making. Lisa Jackson, the new administrator of the EPA, reversed the position of her predecessor and officially classified greenhouse gases as hazardous air pollutants, thus permitting them to be regulated under the Clean Air Act. In November 2010, the agency issued the first-ever federal guidelines for states to reduce GHG emission industrial sources. In December 2010, following the settlement of a lawsuit brought by several states and environmental groups, the EPA issued regulations for major stationary sources of GHGs. They will be phased in gradually: the new rules will first be applied only to firms building new facilities or making major modifications in existing plants. But the agency also indicated that it planned to gradually expand them to cover virtually all sources of GHG emissions. However, these policy initiatives came under intense criticism by the Republican-controlled House of Representatives which took office in January 2011, following the midterm elections held in November 2010, and it is unclear whether or to what extent the agency will be able to implement them.

Nor is it clear how much the American public favors more extensive controls on GHGs. Between 2008 and 2009, the number of Americans who believed that there is "solid evidence" that the earth is warming fell from 71 percent to 57 percent, while the proportion of those who attributed it to human activity declined from 47 percent to 36 percent.[77] The *Economist* observed in 2009: "Al Gore may be universally admired in Europe, but in America he remains a divisive figure."[78] According to a Pew Research Center poll conducted in January 2009, "dealing with climate change" ranked last in importance among twenty other domestic policy priorities. Moreover, the priority attached to it had declined by 8 percent during the previous two years.[79] In late 2009, only 35 percent of Americans regarded global climate change as "a very serious problem." A survey taken just a month before the Gulf oil spill reported that the

---

[77] Christopher Hayes, "Climate Fog," *Nation*, December 21/28, 2009, 6.

[78] *The Economist*, "Farmer v. Greens," November 14, 2009, 44.

[79] Matthew Nisbet, "Communicating Climate Change," *Environment* 51, no. 2 (March/April 2009): 15.

number of politically "moderate" Americans who considered the seriousness of global warming to be "generally exaggerated" had increased from
35 percent to 48 percent since 2008.[80]

These public attitudes in part reflected media coverage of the issue,
which, by giving "balanced coverage" to the scientific debate over climate
change, "had encouraged people to see climate change as an unsettled
source of conflict and confusion rather than as a scientific consensus."[81]
But equally important was deepening partisan polarization on the part
of the American electorate. Between 1997 and 2008, the percentage of
Democrats who told Gallup that global warming had "already begun"
increased from 46 to 76 percent, while the number of Republicans who
shared this appraisal fell from 47 to 41 percent.[82] Republican voters
were also more likely to believe that the seriousness of global warming
had been "exaggerated" by the media, and that warming trends are the
result of natural causes, rather than human activity, than Democrats.[83] In
fact, "partisan polarization is more pronounced among those individuals
reporting greater understanding of global warming."[84]

American State Climate-Change Policies

In response to the unwillingness of the American federal government
either to ratify the Kyoto Protocol or to impose restrictions on GHG
emissions from stationary sources, several American state and local governments adopted their own climate-change policies.[85] By 2007, "more
than half of all U.S. states had formulated a climate change action plan."[86]
Twenty-nine states representing more than half the American population
have enacted renewable portfolio standards for electricity generation.
Twelve states and the mayors of 522 cities have enacted GHG emission

---

[80] *The Economist*, "Let it Be," July 31, 2010. Sixty-eight percent of conservatives and 25
percent of liberals agreed with this position.

[81] "Guber and Bosso, "Past the Tipping Point," 58.

[82] Ibid., 59.

[83] See Riley Dunlap and Aaron McCright, "A Widening Gap: Republicans and Demo-
crat Views on Climate Change," *Environment* (September/October 2008): 26–35. See also
Deborah Lynn Guber, "A Cooling Climate for Change? Party Polarization and the Politics
of Global Warming," paper presented at the 2010 Annual Meeting of the American Political
Science Association, Washington, DC (September 2–5, 2010).

[84] Dunlap and McCright, "A Widening Gap," 33.

[85] For state policies, see Barry Rabe, *Statehouse and Greenhouse—The Emerging Politics
of American Climate Change Policy* (Washington, DC: Brookings Institution Press, 2004).
An updated summary of state policy initiatives can be found in Barry Rabe, ed., *Greenhouse
Governance: Addressing Climate Change in America* (Washington, DC: Brookings Insitu-
tion Press, 2010).

[86] Schreurs, Selin, and VanDeveer, "Conflict and Cooperation," in Schreurs, Selin, and
VanDeever, *Enlarging Transatlantic Relations*, 177.

reduction targets that are either consistent with or exceed those of Kyoto.[87] While they have adopted these policies and commitments primarily in response to local political pressures, many of their policies and strategies have been influenced by developments in Europe.

New Jersey has adopted a mixture of voluntary and coercive policies "involving virtually every sector with some impact on greenhouse gas releases," transforming itself into a national leader on climate change.[88] In 1998, the state pledged it would reduce GHG emissions to "3.5 percent below 1990 levels by 2005"—setting New Jersey on a path to meeting the terms of the Kyoto Protocol.[89] New Jersey has also developed partnerships with other countries, such as the Netherlands, in an attempt to build up its expertise and "to collect practical experiences in several ways to gain better insights into the Kyoto Protocol such as emissions trading . . . to reduce gases."[90] In 1999, Texas initiated a deregulation program that included increasing the proportion of renewable energy for power generation. This would be achieved through the use of wind power, which has grown rapidly over the past decade and permitted the state to increase the amount of renewable electricity it produces.[91]

There has also been considerable cooperation among states. After protracted negotiations, ten states in the northeast established a Regional Greenhouse Gas Initiative (RGGI) that established a regional cap-and-trade program to reduce carbon emissions from the electricity sector. Their cap for carbon dioxide emissions, which went into effect in 2009, was set at a level approximately equivalent to their combined 1990 emissions. After 2014, it will decrease by 2.5 percent a year and their long-term goal is for their emissions in 2018 to be 10 percent lower than in 1990. "The RGGI appears well on its way to joining the EU's emissions-trading scheme as the world's second multijurisdictional entity to oversee implementation of a sophisticated emission-trading program to achieve reduction of greenhouse gas emissions."[92]

Some state plans have reached beyond the borders of the United States. In 2008, an alliance of seven western states and four Canadian provinces agreed on a plan for a 15 percent reduction in GHG emissions

---

[87] Barry Rabe, "Beyond Kyoto: Climate Change Policy in Multilevel Governance Systems," *Governance* 20, no. 3 (July 2007): 429.

[88] Rabe, *Statehouse and Greenhouse*, 3.

[89] Ibid.

[90] Ibid., 133.

[91] Ibid., 7.

[92] Barry Rabe, "Regionalism and Global Climate Change Policy," in *Intergovernmental Management for the Twenty-First Century*, ed. Timothy Colan and Paul Posner (Washington, DC: Brookings Institution Press, 2008), 190. See also "U.S. States Set for Obligatory CO2 Trade Scheme," *Financial Times*, September 14, 2008.

by 2020. In contrast to the RGGI, it covers emissions from several industries, not only electric utilities.[93] New England states have established region-wide standards along with Quebec and the four Maritime Provinces of Canada.[94]

California, in keeping with its historic leadership role in addressing the risks of air pollution, has played a particularly prominent role in addressing the risks of climate change.[95] "It has surpassed any other U.S. state in the sheer range of climate policies enacted and the boldness of its overall emissions reduction plan."[96] In July 2002, the state enacted the California Climate Change bill, which mandated the California Air Resources Board (CARB) to establish a plan for achieving "maximal feasible reduction" of carbon dioxide from vehicles, effective 2006. By 2016, it required vehicles sold in California to achieve an average fuel economy of 35.7 mpg, a rate of reduction twice as rapid as the fuel economy standards approved by Congress in 2007.

In 2006, Governor Arnold Schwarzenegger signed AB-32, the Global Warming Solutions Act. Essentially a state ratification of the Kyoto Protocol, it committed California to reduce its greenhouse gas emissions to 1990 levels by 2020—representing a 25 to 30 percent reduction from its "business as usual" emissions. AB-32 required CARB to develop regulations by January 2011 that would meet the state's GHG reduction target, though in order to make the legislation more palatable to the business community, a "safety-valve" was added that would allow the emission cap to be relaxed if it was causing economic harm.

AB-32 represents the most stringent, legally binding state regulation of GHG emissions in the United States.[97] In signing this legislation, Governor Schwarzenegger stated, "When I campaigned for governor three years ago, I said I wanted to make California No. 1 in the fight against global

---

[93] Felicity Barringer, "U.S.-Canadian Group Plans to Curb Emissions," *New York Times*, September 24, 2008.

[94] Rabe, *Statehouse and Greenhouse*, 21.

[95] Alexander Farrell and W. Michael Hanemann, "Field Notes on the Political Economy of California Climate Change," in *Changing Climate in North American Politics: Institutions, Policymaking, and Multilevel Governance,* ed. Henrik Selin and Stacy VanDeveer (Cambridge, MA: MIT Press, 2009), 87–109.

[96] Barry Rabe, "Governing the Climate from Sacramento," in Colan and Posner, *Intergovernmental Management*, 37.

[97] W. Michael Hanemann, "How California Came to Pass AB-32, the Global Warming Solutions Act of 2006," unpublished paper (January 15, 2007): 2. See also Michael Hanemann and Chris Busch, "Climate Change Policy in California:Balancing Markets versus Regulation," in *Transtlantic Regulatory Cooperation: The Shfting Roles of the EU, the US and California*, ed. David Vogel and Johan Swinnen (Cheltenham, UK: Edward Elgar, 2011), 125–57.

warming. This is something we owe our children and grandchildren."[98] During an official visit to California in June 2007, the European Commission's Ambassador to the United States John Burton described California and the EU as "important allies in the fight against climate change."[99] In November 2010, Californians indicated their support for this legislation by rejecting a ballot measure that would have effectively suspended it.[100]

Due to the large number of motor vehicles in California, the state's plans, which required automakers to cut GHG emissions by 30 percent beginning with the 2009 model year, represented a central component of its climate-change policies. But under American law, states require the federal government's permission to establish any automobile emission standards stricter than those of the federal government. California and other states had received permission to do so for other pollutants from cars and light trucks several times since 1967.

In 2005, the Schwarzenegger administration formally requested a waiver from the EPA to allow California to implement its automotive emission standards, which by then had also been adopted by fourteen other states, primarily on the eastern coast of the United States. In December 2007, the EPA denied the fifteen states' waiver request. In January 2009, President Obama directed the EPA to review the states' request for a waiver—a decision that represented the president's first policy initiative to carry out his campaign pledge of addressing the risks of climate change.[101] He stated, "The federal government must work with, not against states, to reduce greenhouse gas emissions," adding that "The days of Washington dragging its heels are over. My administration will not deny facts; we will be guided by them."[102]

In June 2009, the EPA granted the waiver request after the California's Air Resources Board also agreed to modify its regulations in order to bring them into compliance with new federal standards. The new standards issued by the EPA represented an acceleration of the corporate

[98] "Gov. Schwarzenegger Signs Landmark Legislation to Reduce Greenhouse Gas Emissions," press release, Office of the Governor, September 27, 2006, http://gov.ca.gov/press-release/4111/, accessed February 2009.

[99] "Leading the Fight Against Climate Change," *EU Insight*, September 2007.

[100] *New York Times* editorial, "New Energy Outfoxes Old in California," November 3, 2010.

[101] John Broder and Peter Baker, "Obama's Order Likely to Tighten Auto Standards," *New York Times*, January 26, 2009. See also Matthew Yi and Wyatt Buchanan, "California Emission Law to Be Enforced when Waiver Is Granted, Likely this Spring," *San Francisco Chronicle*, January 27, 2009, and Zachary Cole, "Change in Climate: President Backs State's Rules, Begins Reversing Course Set by Bush," *San Francisco Chronicle*, January 27, 2009.

[102] Alex Cohen and Ron Elving, "Automakers React to New Emission Standards," *National Public Radio*, January 26, 2009.

average fuel economy standards that Congress had mandated in 2007. They required cars and light trucks sold in the United States to improve fuel economy by 5 percent a year and to average 35.5 miles per gallon by 2016 rather than 2020. This compromise was also supported by the automobile industry, which strongly preferred one federal standard to divergent state ones.

If seventeen of the states and 284 of the cities with explicit GHG reduction targets were to meet their goals by 2020, this would constitute about half of the reductions needed to reduce U.S. emissions to 1990 levels, though many of these governments, like the member states of the EU, may not be able to meet their targets.[103] In fact, many American states have adopted restrictions that are more ambitious than those of many member states of the European Union, though unlike in Europe, they are not part of a broader regional or national policy commitment.

Global Approval of Kyoto

The March 2001 decision by President Bush to withdraw the United States from the Kyoto agreement confronted the EU with a twofold challenge. First, it meant that whatever financial burdens the Protocol imposed on firms doing business in Europe would not be borne by firms doing business in the United States. Second, the Kyoto agreement could not become legally binding until it was ratified by industrial countries representing 55 percent of global carbon emissions. This meant that the EU, which accounted for 24.2 percent of global carbon emissions, had to convince nations representing another 30.5 percent of the global total to ratify it. (The United States accounted for 36.1 percent of the carbon emissions from industrial countries.) At a minimum, the EU would have to persuade both Japan, responsible for 8.5 percent of 1990 industrialized state emissions, and Russia, responsible for 17.4 percent, to sign the Kyoto Protocol.

The EU accordingly mounted a major international effort to secure the international adoption of the Kyoto Protocol. The EU acted as a global policy leader, strongly identifying with the issue of global climate change, taking the lead in policy innovations to address it, and persuading other nations to recognize its importance. Climate change "became a wedge issue for the EU, a way for the EU to build coalitional strength with other nations and in the process enhance its strength vis-à-vis the U.S."[104] The EU's strong commitment to the Kyoto Protocol was also strengthened by the American decision not to ratify it; for European policy makers the Protocol had

---

[103] Henrik Selin and Stacy D. VanDeever, "Global Climate Change: Kyoto and Beyond," in Vig and Kraft, *Environmental Policy*, 279.

[104] Schreurs and Tiberghein, "Multilevel Enforcement," 41.

become a symbol of Europe's willingness, and American indifference, to act responsibly to address a critical global environmental risk.

The EU's efforts to play a global leadership role in addressing the risks of global climate have met with strong public approval in Europe. A public opinion survey taken in 2001 reported widespread support for the EU's efforts to play a leadership role in bringing the Kyoto agreement into force—even without U.S. participation. According to a senior EU environmental official, "climate change is an issue that has reached . . . a level of social and political acceptability across the EU." The EU's domestic and international climate-change commitments were repeatedly backed by the EP and also reflected the preferences of the majority of member states. "The EU has staked out a position of clear international leadership on climate change reflecting the scale of the Single Market, the development of Union policies, and the particular opportunities that open up in the aftermath of the Cold War. It is also a consequence of U.S. abdication."[105]

The EU's Council of Ministers formally ratified the Kyoto Protocol in April 2002, and the parliaments of the (then) fifteen member states did so the next month. Additional technical details were worked out at a meeting in Marrakech, Morocco held two months later; its results were hailed as an "important victory for European and environmental leaders."[106] By May 2002, sixty-nine countries had ratified the Protocol and with Russia's ratification two years later, the treaty entered into force in February 2005, by which time it had been ratified by 141 countries. According to a senior EU environmental official, "The EU's commitment and success has been an inspiration to our global partners. Without it, it is certain that the Kyoto Protocol would not have entered into force."[107]

Implementing Kyoto

An important key to the political and economic viability of the EU's climate-change commitments was its decision to establish an internal burden-sharing arrangement, called the EU Emissions Trade Scheme (ETS), which established different emissions targets for each member state. In October 2003, the Council of Ministers, responding to the policy research and recommendations of DG Environment, established the world's first international CO_2 trading scheme which was subsequently extended to the twelve member states that had recently joined the EU. It applied to some 11,500 installations.

---

[105] Vogler and Bretherton, "The EU as a Protagonist," 19.
[106] Schreurs, "The Climate Change Divide," 119.
[107] Schreurs and Tiberghein, "Multilevel Enforcement," 23.

While the EU had earlier opposed this flexible regulatory approach when it had been proposed by the United States, Commission officials now recognized that it offered a more politically acceptable alternative to a carbon tax, a policy proposal that the European Commission had officially abandoned at the end of 2001. European policy makers were also influenced by the example of the United States, which, during the 1990s, had developed an effective "cap-and-trade" program to reduce acid rain. The trading scheme made possible an integrated EU-wide approach to climate change, and was strongly favored by many European business firms and associations on the grounds that it would lower the costs of reducing their GHG emissions.

However, the trading scheme got off to an unpromising start when national governments were allocated too many permits, thus significantly depressing their price.[108] Also, in response to pressures from utilities and smokestack industries that feared for their competitiveness, the Commission abandoned its original plan of auctioning them off and instead allowed national governments to give most of them away for free. As a result, GHG emissions from the industries covered by the cap-and-trade system continued to increase, rising by 0.4 percent in 2006 and by 1.1 percent in 2007.[109] Moreover, approximately half of the EU's total CO2 emissions, namely those from cars, planes, buildings, and retail outlets, were outside the cap-and-trade system.

New European Regulations

To address the evident shortcomings of its existing climate-change reduction program, in 2007 the European Commission proposed the "20/20/20 by 2020" plan.[110] This ambitious plan, which sought to maintain and reinforce the EU's global leadership in addressing the risks of climate change, called for emissions cuts of 20 percent below 1990 levels, a 20 percent increase in energy efficiency over forecasted consumption, and 20 percent of energy to be produced by renewable sources—by 2020. The Commission also proposed to address the initial problems of the EU's cap-and-trade plan by now auctioning off pollution rights. In response to the failure of automakers to meet the voluntary caps to which they had previously agreed, firms selling cars in Europe would now be required to meet binding targets.

---

[108] James Kanter and Jad Mouwad, "Pipe Dreams and Politics," *New York Times Business Section*, December 11, 2008; Leila Abboud, "EU Greenhouse-Gas Emissions Rose 1.1% Last Year," *Wall Street Journal*, April 3, 2008.

[109] Kanter and Mouwad, "Pipe Dreams and Politics."

[110] *The Economist*, "Fiddling with Words as the World Melts," December 20, 2008.

Significantly, the Commission's ambitious policy recommendations were strongly supported by the EU's center-right President Barroso. His appointment in 2004 had worried European environmental groups, especially after he had appointed Stavros Dimas, a former Wall Street lawyer from Greece—the only country in Europe without an environmental minister—as EU Commissioner for the Environment, and after Dimas had chosen a fuel-inefficient German SUV as his official car. But notwithstanding Barroso's concern that additional regulations would frustrate his main policy goal of improving European growth rates, he now decided that "the environment [was] . . . a rare political issue on which Europeans feel very strongly and where the European Commission has the ability to act."[111] When former American vice president Gore visited Brussels, Dimas publically bemoaned the fact that Europeans could not vote in American elections. The Commission's commitment to strengthen European restrictions on GHG emissions was also supported by right-of-center German Chancellor Angela Merkel, and France's right-of-center President Jacques Chirac, as well as British Labour Prime Minister Tony Blair.

Summarizing the results of a survey taken in 2006 in Britain, France, Italy, Spain, and Germany, the *Financial Times* concluded, "in Europe, it seems that the debate on global warming is just about over."[112] It reported that 77 percent of British believed that "human activity is contributing to climate change," while in the other four countries, the number of citizens agreeing with this assessment was close to 90 percent. Substantial numbers of citizens in all five countries also viewed global climate change "as a threat to them and their families in their lifetimes."

However, the willingness of the Council and Parliament to approve both plans was threatened by the economic difficulties that confronted European economies beginning in 2008.[113] Following intense lobbying by European car firms, led by German vehicle manufacturers who complained that the CO2 standards were too onerous and that they lacked the technology for meeting them, the Commission's proposal was weakened: its standards would now be phased in and take full effect by 2015, rather than 2012.[114] However, the plan adopted by the EU did require automakers to reduce their CO2 emissions by almost 3 percent during the next six years, a rate nearly double that of the previous decade. By 2020, the average fuel efficiency of vehicles sold in Europe is expected to

[111] George Parker and Fiona Harvey, "Newly Green Barroso pushes Europe to Act on Global Warming," *Financial Times*, November 20, 2006, 2.

[112] E. Crooks, "Europeans Ready to Save the World—On the Cheap," *Financial Times*, November 20, 2006.

[113] *The Economist*, "Climate of Fear," October 15, 2008.

[114] Leila Abboud and Edward Taylor, "EU Seen Weakening Emissions Law for Auto Makers," *Wall Street Journal*, September 24, 2008.

reach the equivalent of approximately 60 miles per gallon. This means that European GHG emission and fuel economy standards will remain significantly more stringent than American ones.[115] However, it is important to note that vehicles in Europe have always been more fuel efficient because of higher energy taxes.

The Commission's broader "20/20/20" plan also encountered strong opposition from the Union's accession states from central Europe, who rely heavily upon coal for power generation. Many European heavy industries predicted that the Commission's plan would raise their costs sufficiently high to force them to relocate their production facilities outside of Europe.

An elaborate and complex compromise was finally reached at the semi-annual meeting of the European Council of Ministers (which comprised the heads of European government) in December 2008.[116] The EU did maintain its "20/20/20" targets, and agreed to cut the number of emission allowances issued each year after 2013, thus helping to support the carbon prices of the ETS. But the compromise also granted a number of concessions to both central European member states and heavy industries facing global competition, primarily by enabling them to receive all or a portion of their carbon allowances for free. In addition, member states will be allowed to receive credits for emissions reductions from outside Europe and count them for as much as 90 percent of their national reduction targets—a flexible compliance mechanism that, like emissions trading, had previously been supported by American international negotiators and strongly opposed by the EU.

According to a report issued by the EU in 2009, thanks in part to the economic downturn as well as the claiming of forests as "sinks" to offset national emissions, the EU-15 was likely to exceed its Kyoto targets: total emissions were projected to decline by more than 13 percent below their 1990 base by 2008–2012. However, the ability of the EU to achieve its more ambitious 2020 targets remains problematic, especially if growth rates in Europe improve. An assessment by the European Environmental Agency published in 2007 predicted that GHG emissions would increase between 2010 and 2020, reaching a level approximately 2 percent higher than in 2005 and only 6 percent below their 1990 levels.[117]

---

[115] Ibid., 30.

[116] *The Economist*, "Fiddling with Words as the World Melts," December 20, 2008. For a more detailed discussion of the December 2008 climate change and energy policy, see Jon Sjaerseth and Jorgen Wettstad, "Fixing the EU Emissions Trading System? Understanding the Post-2012 Changes," *Global Environmental Politics* 10, no. 4 (November 2000): 101–23.

[117] *Greenhouse Gas Emission Trends and Projections in Europe, 2007: Tracking Progress Toward Kyoto Targets* (Luxembourg: Office for Official Publication of the European Communities, 2007), 6.

Analysis

Public preferences played an important role in shaping differences in European and American policy approaches to the risks of global climate change. The survey data cited in this chapter reveal that Europeans regard the scientific evidence that human activity is contributing to global climate change as more conclusive than do many Americans; they also perceive its risks as more threatening. While the salience of the issue, and the extent of public support for addressing it, has waxed and waned in the United States, it has been much stronger in Europe. Public attitudes in the United States have also been shaped by partisan politics, with Democrats more likely to support restrictions on GHG emissions than voters who identify with the Republican Party. Similar ideological or partisan-based divisions among the electorate have not emerged in Europe. While there are skeptics about the human causes of global climate change as well as the significance of its risks on both sides of the Atlantic, they have had a much greater impact on public opinion in the United States than in Europe.[118] This reflects on both the extent of partisan polarization surrounding public risk percpetions and the stronger public campaign against the credibility of the risks of global climate change mounted by important segments of the American business community, a number of scientists, and conservative think tanks. While European firms have opposed specific GHG regulations, unlike their counterparts in the United States, they have not publically challenged their scientific basis.

Moreover, since the early 1990s, the preferences of policy makers have been more divided in the United States than in the EU—precisely the opposite of their pattern of political support for addressing the risks of lead emissions and ozone depletion during the 1970s and 1980s, when the preferences of European policy makers were *more* divided than in the United States. European policy makers, including many prominent center-right heads of state, have supported policies to address the risks of climate change, as has the European Commission, the Council, and the EP.

By contrast, the preferences of policy makers have been highly polarized in the United States along partisan and ideological lines, with all but a handful of Republican national politicians strongly opposed to restrictions on GHG emissions, which have been supported by Democratic

[118]The most prominent European climate change skeptic is Bjørn Lomborg. For his views on this and other environmental risks, see Bjørn Lomborg, *The Skeptical Environmentalist: Measuring the Real State of the World* (Cambridge: Cambridge University Press, 1998). The most prominent European climate change skeptics are in England, where the credibility of the scientific case for global climate change was temporarily adversely affected by the 2009 public disclosure of 1999 e-mails from the Climate Research Unit at the University of East Anglia, which revealed that some scientific data had been misreported.

presidents Bill Clinton and Barack Obama and the majority of Democratic legislators. A 2007 poll of members of Congress found that 95 percent of Democrats agreed and 84 percent of Republican legislators disagreed with the statement that "it's been proven beyond a reasonable doubt that the Earth is warming because of man-made problems."[119] Republican Senator James Inhofe of Oklahoma described man-made global warming as the "greatest hoax ever perpetuated on the American people."[120] This high degree of partisan polarization may well reflect the unusually high visibility of this issue: no environmental policy in the United States since the early 1990s has attracted as much public attention, or as much business or conservative opposition.

CONCLUSION

This chapter has described shifts in the transatlantic regulatory stringency for air pollution. Prior to around 1990, the United States imposed more stringent regulations for automotive emissions, including lead in motor fuels, than did individual European countries or the EU. It also acted earlier than most European countries to impose restrictions on ozone-depleting chemicals. Automotive emission standards have since been progressively tightened on both sides of the Atlantic, but American standards remain stricter. However, the EU has played a much more active role in regulating GHG emissions than has the United States.

[119] "Congressional Insiders Poll," *National Journal*, March 2, 2007, 6, available at http://syndication.nationaljournal.com/images/203Insiderspoll_NJlogo.pdf, accessed February 2009.

[120] "Climate Skeptics Storm the Capitol," *Business Week*, November 29–December 5, 2010.

CHAPTER FIVE

Chemicals and Hazardous Substances

THIS CHAPTER COMPARES European and American regulations for the health, safety, and environmental risks of chemicals and hazardous substances.

The 1976 Toxic Substances Control Act (TSCA) significantly strengthened American chemical regulations and contributed to the 1979 decision of the European Union to both harmonize and strengthen its chemical regulations, though they remained weaker than those of the United States. While there has been no major statutory change in American chemical regulation since then, in 2006 the EU approved REACH—the Registration, Evaluation, Authorization and Restriction of Chemicals, which made European chemical regulations significantly more stringent and comprehensive than those of the United States.

The Commission's decision to revise and strengthen European chemical regulations was in part a response to a substantial increase in public concern about chemical risks in Europe. The provisions of REACH were also influenced by the precautionary principle on which the Commission had issued an important White Paper in 2000. Its enactment was made possible by support for new chemical regulations by a powerful coalition of member states, including Sweden, which had joined the EU in 1995, the backing of DG Environment within the European Commission (EC), and pro-environmental members of the European Parliament (EP). While chemical risks have also been salient in the United States, they have been more narrowly focused, and proposals to strengthen American chemical regulation have not occupied a prominent place on the national political agenda.

Two related directives, WEEE—the Directive on Wastes from Electronics and Electrical Equipment, and RoHS—the Directive on Restrictions of Hazardous Substances, both approved in 2003, impose restrictions on hazardous substances in electronics and electrical equipment, and require the recycling and reuse of e-waste. There are no comparable federal regulations, though some states have adopted regulations that are similar to those of the EU.

The provisions of WEEE and RoHS reflected a broad commitment on the part of the European Commission to address the full life-cycle impacts of products in order to reduce their environmental "footprint" and promote extended producer responsibility. The mandatory recycling and reuse of electrical and electronic equipment and bans on the use of hazardous materials in these products were important components of these efforts. The provisions of RoHS were also informed by a precautionary assessment of the health risks of the increasing volume of e-wastes being deposited in landfills due to the rapid obsolescence of many consumer electronic products. By contrast, risk assessments by the U.S. federal government do not consider the hazardous substances in electronics deposited in landfills as a threat to public health, though some states, notably California, have restricted the use of toxic substances in some electrical and electronic products. Unlike the EU, the federal government has relied primarily on voluntary business efforts to promote electronic recycling.

REGULATION OF CHEMICALS

European and American Chemical Regulations Before 1990

The first European directive on hazardous chemicals was adopted in 1967. Like much European environmental legislation adopted during this period, its primary objective was to remove intra-European trade barriers. The 1967 Framework Directive on Dangerous Substances established a uniform system for listing, classifying, packaging, and labeling dangerous substances. However, this directive did not impose any restrictions on their use; any chemical could still be produced and marketed throughout the EU provided it was appropriately labeled and packaged.

Beginning in the mid-1970s, the United Kingdom, France, and Denmark had approved legislation requiring the chemical industry to test new products before circulating them for commercial use. Concerned that the increased stringency of some national chemical approval requirements was undermining the single market, the EU began deliberations on adopting a Sixth Amendment to the 1967 Directive. This amendment established a new system for regulating the safety of chemicals sold within the EU; new substances would now have to be tested for potential hazards *before* they could be marketed. It also added a new classification, namely "dangerous for the environment." However, opposition from Germany and Great Britain, Europe's two major chemical-producing countries, prevented its adoption. Both countries had long-standing and well-established approaches to chemical regulation that they were unwilling to see changed.

While deliberations in Europe remained stalemated, in 1976 the United States enacted TSCA. Congress had been debating the need for new chemical legislation since the early 1970s, when the Council on Environmental

Quality had urged policy makers to plug the regulatory gap that both allowed hundreds of new chemicals to be marketed each year without adequate testing and provided no way for the federal government to test the safety of chemicals already in use. Like much of the expansion of American risk regulation during the 1970s and 1980s, the policy trigger for this statute was a series of "alarm bells," which in this case linked birth defects and cancer to the billions of pounds of virtually untested and unregulated chemicals. High levels of PCBs, a toxic compound used as an insulator in electric transformers and capacitors, were also discovered in a number of lakes and rivers.

By essentially requiring manufacturers to prove the safety of new chemicals before they were marketed, TSCA adopted a more rigorous approach to chemical regulation. This legislation gave the United States "by far the most fully developed legal framework for discovering and controlling chemical hazards" in the world.[1] Reflecting increased public concern about the environmental causes of cancer, this legislation, like the Delaney Clause discussed in chapter 3, adopted more stringent restrictions for known as well as suspected carcinogens.

European policy makers and industrialists were troubled by the American legislation's broad scope, vague language, the substantial discretion it granted to the Environmental Protection Agency (EPA), and "most alarming of all," its applicability to imported as well as domestically produced substances.[2] European-based chemical firms saw TSCA as a major threat to their continued access to the American market. EU officials were also annoyed that the United States had not consulted them before enacting a regulatory statute with such an important impact on the extensive transatlantic trade in chemicals. Recognizing that the absence of European-wide requirements for the approval of new chemicals had undermined their bargaining power with the United States, European policy makers now renewed their efforts to enact a comprehensive new chemical directive.

In 1979, three years after the passage of TSCA, the EU adopted the Sixth Amendment to the 1967 Framework Directive. This directive harmonized the approval standards for new chemicals sold or marketed throughout the EU, which had previously been regulated by a diverse set of national regulations—all of which were less stringent than TSCA. Like TSCA, it divided chemicals into two classes, namely existing substances that were already on the market and "new" substances. For new

---

[1] Ronald Brickman, Sheila Jasanoff, and Thomas Ilgen, *Controlling Chemicals: The Politics of Regulation in Europe and the U.S.* (Ithaca, NY: Cornell University Press, 1985), 36.
[2] Ibid., 276.

substances, the manufacturer or importer was required to provide basic data about possible health and environmental effects.

Policy Convergence

The EU's directive in turn made possible an international agreement, brokered through the Organization for Economic Cooperation and Development (OECD), which harmonized notification requirements for new chemicals among several developed countries, including the United States and the member states of the EU. Within two and a half years, the OECD's member states had successfully negotiated agreements for test guidelines, standards of laboratory practice, the mutual acceptance of data, as well as a base set of data requirements for notifying authorities about new chemicals. Taken together, "these efforts have resulted in the most fully developed international regime in the area of hazardous chemical control," though it did not include mutual recognition of the chemicals themselves.[3]

While the Sixth Amendment brought European requirements for the approval of new chemicals into closer alignment with that of the United States, American standards remained distinctive in two respects. First, the European regulation exempted more chemicals from its notification requirements than did TSCA. Second, and most important, TSCA, unlike the Sixth Amendment, also required the testing of previously approved chemical substances, though the length of time a chemical was defined as "new" was longer in Europe.

Chemical Regulation in Sweden

There was, however, an important exception to the relative stringency of European and American chemical regulations prior to 1990, one which would subsequently have an important impact on the EU. Sweden, which did not join the EU until 1995, had more stringent chemical regulations than the United States.[4] Sweden's distinctive regulatory policies reflected both politics and economics: there was substantial domestic political support for protecting human health and environmental quality, and the country had a relatively small chemical industry. As early as 1962, Sweden had begun to place the responsibility for classifying poisonous and dangerous substances on producers. Sweden's 1969 Environmental Protection Act formally reversed the burden of proof, requiring industry to demonstrate the

---

[3] Ibid.

[4] This section is based on Ragnar Lofstedt, "Swedish Chemical Regulation: An Overview and Analysis," *Risk Analysis* 23, no. 2 (2003): 411–21.

safety of all environmentally harmful activities. In 1973, the substitution principle—which required the replacement of more hazardous chemicals by less hazardous ones—was formally incorporated into Swedish law.

A decade later, Sweden established a commission to review the impact of chemicals on the environment and public health, and in 1984 the five Nordic countries, namely Iceland, Sweden, Norway, Finland, and Denmark, jointly developed criteria for classifying environmentally hazardous substances. Sweden's 1985 Law on Chemical Products required an evaluation of the likely impact of all chemical products on both the environment and public health, placing the burden for undertaking this assessment on industry. In 1990, a "good living environment" statute called for use of the heavy metals such as mercury, cadmium, and lead to be reduced by 70 percent by 1995. In 1994, the government banned the diffuse spread of mercury as part of its commitment to create a sustainable society—becoming the first country to do so. Thus, by the time it joined the EU in 1995, Sweden had become, in the words of Prime Minister Goran Persson, "an international driving force and a forerunner in the endeavor to create an ecologically sustainable environment."[5]

THE STRENGTHENING OF EUROPEAN CHEMICAL REGULATION

Pressures for Reform

The continued disparity in the regulatory treatment of "old" and "new" chemicals meant that 99 percent of the total volume of chemicals—or roughly one hundred thousand chemicals—sold in Europe had not been subjected to any testing requirements. This meant that relatively little was known about the health, safety, and environmental impact of nearly all of the 400 million tons of chemicals marketed in the European Union.

Beginning in the late 1990s, public and scientific concerns about the harmful effects of the increasing number of chemicals to which Europeans were exposed became politically salient.[6] When specifically asked in 1999, "which of the following factors could affect your future health?" the highest response was "chemicals." Some public health experts identified the proliferation of chemicals as an important cause of the growing incidence of allergies, asthma, certain types of cancer, as well as various reproductive disorders, including declining sperm counts. Some chemicals were also reported to have endocrine-disrupting properties, producing

---

[5] The following two paragraphs are based on ibid., 414.
[6] European Commission, "Environment Fact Sheet: REACH—a New Chemicals Policy for the EU" (February 2006): 2, available at http://ec.europa.eu/environment/pubs/pdf/fact sheets/reach.pdf, accessed February 2009.

infertility and gender changes in animals such as frogs and birds. Dramatic evidence of high levels of toxic substances in polar bears revealed that chemicals could travel long distances. When the World Wildlife Fund subsequently tested government ministers from fifteen member states for 103 chemicals that were believed to negatively affect human health and wildlife, it found an average of thirty-seven of them in the ministers' blood. European trade unions claimed that a third of all occupational diseases in Europe were related to chemical exposure.

An important source of pressure for a major revision of European chemical regulations came from Sweden, which, as part of its negotiations for joining the EU, had been granted a four-year transition period during which it would be allowed to maintain its more stringent standards. But in return, the EU agreed to review its own regulatory requirements for chemicals. As soon as it joined the EU in 1995, Sweden began to pressure the EU to adopt standards similar to its own. This would enable it to maintain many of its more stringent chemical regulations following the end of the four-year transition period.

The campaign to strengthen European chemical regulations was also supported by the environmental ministers of Austria, Denmark, Finland, and the Netherlands, each of whom contended that European chemical regulation was insufficient and outdated. These four countries, as well as Sweden, joined with European nongovernment organizations (NGOs) and trade unions in an "advocacy coalition" that succeeded in placing the need for a major reform of European chemical regulation on the European policy agenda.[7] In 1999, the Council of Environmental Ministers requested that the European Commission conduct a fundamental review of European chemical regulation. Within the European Commission, the Directorate-General for the Environment under the leadership of Commissioners Ritt Bjerregaard of Denmark (1995–1999) and Margot Wallström of Sweden (1999–2004), were also strong advocates of a new approach to chemical regulation.

The Commission Proposes a New Chemical Regulation

In 2001, DG Environment issued a White Paper that proposed a radical overhaul of European chemical regulation.[8] It stated that the EU's current legislative framework for chemical regulation was inadequate to protect

[7]Dieter Pesendorfer, "EU Environmental Policy under Pressure: Chemicals Policy Change between Antagonistic Goals," *Environmental Politics* 15, no. 1 (February 2006): 104.

[8]Commission of the European Communities, "White Paper: Strategy for a Future Chemicals Policy" (February 27, 2001), available at http://www.sfc.fr/LivreBlanc EU-REACH-01-2.pdf, accessed February 2009.

human health and the environment and recommended the adoption of a new chemical regulation. The White Paper proposed a single regulatory framework that would cover all chemical substances, thus placing the EU's more than five hundred pieces of legislation related to chemical safety into one statutory framework. REACH was proposed as a regulation, not a directive. This meant that its provisions would be automatically binding on all member states, unlike a directive which establishes harmonized policy objectives, but leaves their implementation up to each national government.

REACH's two most important provisions reversed the burden of proof—requiring chemical producers to demonstrate that the chemicals they produced or marketed did not adversely affect human health—and eliminated the distinction between new and existing chemicals. It required chemical manufacturers and importers to gather health and safety data on *all* their substances, assess their potential risks, and develop appropriate risk management strategies. According to Margot Wallström, "The new policy introduces a radical paradigm shift. It is high time to place the responsibility (for chemical safety) where it belongs, with industry."[9] The White Paper also recommended the adoption of the "duty of care" principle, which would make manufacturers and importers responsible for communicating safety information to downstream users and consumers. In turn, downstream users would be required to assess the safety of the products they sold or used for their portion of each chemical's life cycle.

The regulation proposed by the Commission also required that approximately 1,400 substances of "very high concern," including those that were judged to cause cancer or to interfere with the body's reproductive function and hormone system, be specifically authorized. Authorization for them would only be granted if the associated risks were adequately controlled or if the socioeconomic benefits of their authorization outweighed their risks and suitable alternatives did not exist. The Commission estimated that under its provisions, between 1 percent and 2 percent of dangerous chemical substances would be prohibited and replaced by safer alternatives. This requirement was strongly endorsed by a broad coalition of 483 NGOs, as well as by a petition signed by more than 23,000 citizens, who had launched a campaign, "Declaration for Toxics-free Future" that called for the phasing out of hazardous chemicals and their substitution by less harmful ones.[10]

The Commission's approach to chemical regulation was strongly influenced by the precautionary principle on which the Commission had issued a communication in 2000. This communication, along with the

[9] Samuel Loewenberg, "E.U. Starts a Chemical Reaction," *Science* (April 18, 2003).
[10] Pesendorfer, 'EU Environmental Policy Under Pressure," 108.

BSE and dioxin food scandals and the intense debate in Europe over the safety and environmental impact of GMOs, had a significant impact on the Commission's policy recommendations. Several national and international experts now "thought it important to introduce the precautionary principle into chemical laws and regulations in a systematic manner."[11]

The White Paper was accepted by the Council of Ministers in April 2001, and following consultations with the EP's Environmental Committee, which also endorsed the Commission's legislative proposal, in May 2003 the Commission formally presented REACH to the Council and the EP.

European Business Opposition to REACH

REACH represented a major challenge to Europe's important and politically powerful chemical industry. The chemical sector is the third largest manufacturing industry in the EU; its thirty-one thousand companies employ 1.9 million people. Internationally, the EU is the world's largest chemical producer, accounting for roughly a third of global sales. Within the EU, Germany is the most important chemical producer, followed by France, Italy, and the United Kingdom.

The complex and sweeping REACH regulation—its text was more than one thousand pages—was the most controversial health, safety, or environmental legislation in the history of the EU. No other Commission legislative proposal became the focus of such intense lobbying—both within and outside Europe. Controversy began as soon as the Commission began the process of converting its White Paper into a formal proposal. While a broad coalition of European environmental, consumer, and public health groups, backed by Green members of the European Parliament, and the environmental ministers of several member states, strongly supported the legislative proposal outlined in the White Paper, Europe's politically powerful chemical industry was highly critical of it.

The industry was not opposed to a new chemical regulation. It strongly preferred harmonized European standards to increasingly divergent national ones and supported the replacement of the EU's complex network of chemical regulations and directives by a single regulatory framework. Moreover, chemical firms had strongly criticized the Sixth Amendment's distinction between new and existing substances on the grounds that it made it more difficult to secure approval for new chemicals even though they might be safer than the ones currently in use.

Nonetheless, REACH attracted more hostility from industry than any EU environmental proposal. The chemical industry argued that REACH's

[11] Ibid., 104.

sweeping registration, evaluation, and authorization requirements for all existing chemicals were too expensive and administratively burdensome. One industry study estimated that REACH's testing requirements would cost at least 7.5 billion euros and that it would "impose a regulatory stranglehold on our industry, weaken its international competitiveness and cause production and employment to leave Europe."[12]

A study funded by the German chemical industry predicted that REACH's passage would reduce employment by 2.35 million jobs and lead to a 6.4 percent reduction in Germany's GDP, while another consulting report claimed that REACH would cost the French chemical industry between 29 billion and 54 billion euros and eliminate 670,00 jobs.[13] The Commission's proposal was also criticized for its "overriding" reliance on the precautionary principle. In addition, industry officials predicted that its extensive testing requirements would "mean the deaths of millions of test animals."[14] In September 2003, the heads of the governments of Germany, France, and Britain wrote to European Commissioner Romano Prodi to request a more industry-friendly version of the chemical directive. They warned him "not to go ahead with proposals for a new chemicals policy if it was going to affect the competitiveness of European industry."[15]

Revising and Debating REACH

The Commission responded by making two important changes. First, it abandoned the White Paper's "no data, no market" requirement scheme for all chemical substances by reducing testing requirements and simplifying registration procedures for chemicals produced in volumes of less than ten tons. Second, it weakened the White Paper's substitution requirement. According to the Commission, these changes would reduce the financial burdens on the chemical industry and chemical users by approximately 80 percent, or 2.3–5.2 billion euros, over eleven years. The Commission then presented its revised proposal as a "streamlined and cost-effective system" that struck "the right balance between maintaining growth and employment in Europe on one hand and improving health and the environment on the other."[16]

But this compromise pleased no one. Chemical producers still claimed the costs of compliance with REACH's registration requirements were too

[12] Loewenberg. "EU Starts a Chemical Reaction."

[13] Quoted in Arthur Daemmrich, "International Lobbying and the Dow Chemical Company (A)," *Harvard Business School*, HBS Case No. 701-027 (March 23, 2010): 9.

[14] Pesendorfer, "EU Environmental Policy Under Pressure," 103.

[15] Ibid., 109.

[16] Ibid., 110.

high, and would disproportionally burden smaller firms, while NGOs, public health groups, and trade unions were disappointed that REACH's provisions would no longer apply equally to all chemicals.

Both sides, as well as the Commission, subsequently produced a steady stream of reports and rebuttals that offered highly divergent assessments of the costs of REACH. Challenging the chemical industry's claim of additional costs of more than 7.5 billion euros, the Commission estimated additional costs of only 2.1 billion euros. Another study predicted compliance costs of 5.25–8 billion euros, or less than 0.1 percent of the chemical industry's annual sales. REACH's supporters, in addition to challenging industry claims about its costs, further argued that any analysis of the impact of legislation should also include an assessment of its environmental and human health benefits as well as the cost savings of not having to clean up contaminated waste sites.[17] They also claimed that the legislation would improve, rather than weaken, the industry's global competitiveness by making chemicals produced in Europe the world's safest.

American Opposition to REACH

Particularly vigorous opposition to REACH came from the United States. While the legislation was still in draft form, the American government, working closely with the American chemical industry, launched a vigorous lobbying effort to derail it.[18] The stakes for the American chemical industry were substantial. European and American chemical markets are closely linked; the United States annually exports $20 billion worth of chemicals to Europe, while American chemical firms had investments of $1.5 trillion in Europe.[19] One-third of the American chemical industry is European owned and the United States is a net importer of chemicals from Europe. This meant that REACH would not only affect American chemical exports to Europe and the chemicals produced by American firms in Europe, but would also restrict the chemicals produced in Europe

[17] Henrik Selin, "Coalition Politics and Chemicals Management in a Regulatory Ambitious Europe," *Global Environmental Politics* 7, no. 3 (August 2007): 83.

[18] House Committee on Government Reform, "A Special Interest Case Study: The Chemical Industry, the Bush Administration, and the European Effort to Regulate Chemicals" (April 1, 2004), available at http://oversight.house.gov/documents/20040817125807-75305 .pdf, accessed February 2009; Joseph DiGangi, "U.S. Intervention in EU Chemical Policy," Environmental Health Fund (September 2003), available at http://www.noharm.org/details .cfm?type=document&ID=823, accessed February 2009; Paul Thacker, "U.S. Companies Get Nervous About EU's REACH," *Environmental Science & Technology* (April 15, 2005).

[19] Paul Thacker, Elizabeth Becker, and Jennifer Lee, "Europe Plan on Chemicals Seen as Threat to U.S. Exports," *New York Times*, May 8, 2003.

which American firms imported, many of which were critical components of commercial products.

The U.S. Department of Commerce brief warned that if REACH was approved, "hundreds of Americans could be thrown out of their jobs, while the American Chemistry Council (ACC) claimed that REACH would cost American firms $8 billion in additional testing costs over the next decade."[20]American officials and chemical industry executives also feared that other countries lacking adequate regulatory capacities would adopt REACH's regulatory policies, thus compounding its global economic impact. According to one EU official, they had an additional concern: "if Americans see that Europe has these protections, they might want them as well."[21]

In January 2002, American government officials met at the offices of the ACC to develop a coordinated political strategy to oppose REACH. According to an unofficial government position paper developed in close consultation with the American industry, "examination of just four commercially important chemicals on the EU's authorization list shows that $8.8 billion worth of downstream products are at risk for ban or severe restriction under the new system." It characterized the provision requiring the substitution of safer chemicals for hazardous ones as a form of "arbitrary discrimination."[22] The position paper also claimed that REACH's adoption of the precautionary principle for chemicals of "very high concern" would "provide cover for politically-motivated bans and other severe restrictions," adding the by now familiar criticism of more stringent European regulations from across the Atlantic, namely that REACH was based on "unsound science."[23]

The U.S. Secretary of State, Colin Powell, responded to the industry's call for political assistance by sending an "action request" cable to the U.S. embassies in each member state, as well to thirty-five other countries. His cable claimed that REACH "would be significantly more burdensome to industry and government than current U.S. and EU regulatory approaches" and predicted that it would cost American chemical producers tens of billions of dollars in lost exports.[24] Powell urged embassy officials to communicate the American chemical industry's criticisms about REACH to European government officials, business firms

<hr />

[20]Mark Shapiro, "Toxic Inaction: Why Poisonous, Unregulated Chemicals End Up in Our Blood," *Harper's Magazine* 315, no. 1889, October 2007, 78–83; Thaddeus Herrick et al., "U.S. Opposes EU Effort to Test Chemicals for Health Hazards," *Wall Street Journal*, September 9, 2003.

[21]Thacker, Becker, and Lee, "Europe Plan on Chemicals."

[22]DiGangi, "U.S. Intervention," 6.

[23]Ibid., 6, 10.

[24]Ibid., 6.

and associations, as well as the media, and to persuade them that the American approach to chemical regulations, which relied on voluntary safety and environmental screening by industry and selective, rather than comprehensive testing requirements, was a better alternative. The American lobbying strategy specifically targeted European countries with large chemical sectors, as well as European businesses that were major end users of chemicals that REACH might ban or restrict.

To mobilize political opposition to REACH, the U.S. government organized meetings between representatives of the ACC and the American ambassadors to Italy, Ireland, Spain, Austria, and Portugal. Officials from the U.S. Commerce Department held several meetings with EU officials to convey their objections to REACH and lobbied the European Parliament as well. The American campaign against REACH also sought to enlist the support of Hungary, Poland, Estonia, and the Czech Republic, who were then candidates for EU membership (they joined the EU in 2004), warning them that the approval of REACH would hurt European firms competing in foreign markets. The State Department also urged countries that were heavily dependent on chemical exports to the EU, such as Brazil, India, Japan, Malaysia, and South Africa to join with the United States in a coordinated lobbying strategy. Subsequently, fourteen countries issued a joint public statement that urged the EU to instead adopt a risk-based authorization process—which would make European regulations more similar to those of the United States.

European and American officials also heatedly debated the legality of REACH at several meetings of the World Trade Organization's (WTO) Committee on Technical Barriers to Trade. A formal comment filed with the WTO by the United States raised questions about REACH's feasibility. The ACC argued that the European regulation violated the WTO rules on technical barriers to trade because its data collection and testing requirements were "disproportionate" and "unnecessarily trade restrictive." But European officials countered that REACH was consistent with WTO rules that permit countries to take human health and environmental protection measures provided that they are "proportionate" and do not create unnecessary trade obstacles.

According to the ACC, intervention by it and the U.S. government "helped to build an aggressive position worldwide, and brought about significant concessions in the draft now being considered by the European parliament."[25] For example, as the American government had advocated, various low-risk types of chemicals such as certain polymers were excluded from REACH's testing requirements.

[25] Quoted in House Committee on Government Reform, "A Special Interest Case Study," 15.

However, the extensive American government lobbying effort was strongly criticized on both sides of the Atlantic. In 2002 and 2003, a broad coalition of public health professionals, labor unions, children's health advocates, environmental organizations, and community groups wrote to President George W. Bush asking him to stop using federal funds "to undermine this important proposed legislation, and seek ways to support progressive reform of chemicals policy that benefit public health."[26] They also expressed strong support for REACH, and expressed the hope that its passage would also prompt the United States to strengthen its chemical regulations. They received no response.

Some European officials also expressed their displeasure at the extensive American lobbying effort to defeat REACH. Bjorn Hansen, deputy head of the unit for chemicals at DG Environment, explained:

> We have a tacit agreement between the EU and the U.S. that we don't mix at that level in each other's internal affairs. . . . What happens when you do power politics is that you force the community instrument to take a position, and that will be defensive. . . . The way it works in the EU is that you start at a lower level with the people who are actually writing the laws and find ways of taking concerns on board. It's very-low key.[27]

In the European Parliament, the American government's extensive lobbying actually backfired. "European Parliamentary Representatives from Germany, previously hesitant to support the legislation, now signaled they would vote for it, in part due to the hard-line position articulated by the Bush Administration."[28]

New Political Obstacles Emerge

Shortly after the Commission's proposed legislation was finalized, the installation of a new EC in 2004 presented REACH with a new political challenge. The new Commission president, former Portuguese Prime Minister José Barroso, headed a Commission whose center of gravity was to the right of his center-left predecessor, former Italian Prime Minister Romano Prodi. Barroso's administration was also committed to the adoption of market-oriented reforms in order to increase the competitiveness of European firms—a goal that REACH was unlikely to promote and might well impede. In the new EC, Environmental Commissioner Margot Wallström was replaced by Stavros Dimas of Greece, who had little experience in environmental regulation, while Günter Verheugen

---

[26]Ibid., 16.
[27]Daemmrich, "International Lobbying," 12.
[28]Ibid., 14.

of Germany, a strong supporter of his country's chemical industry, was appointed to the politically powerful position of Commissioner of DG Enterprise. Verheugen was willing to submit REACH to the EP, but he also "wanted to make sure companies do not collapse under the weight" of new chemical review requirements.[29] For its part, the EP now had a center-right majority.

The policy impact of these political changes in the composition of the European Commission and the EP was reinforced by the deteriorating economic performance of EU member states. REACH had been proposed and drafted during a period of relatively strong European economic growth. But by the time the legislation was officially submitted to the European Council in March 2003, much of Europe was experiencing an economic downturn. This in turn made the chemical industry's concerns about the costs of compliance with REACH and its adverse impact on European economic growth and global competitiveness more credible.

Not surprisingly, the parliamentary deliberations on REACH were prolonged and heated; the EP considered more than one thousand amendments to the chemical regulation. Pro-environmental members, including many from the Nordic countries, attempted to restore provisions of the original legislation that had been modified by the Commission, while many members from states that were important chemical producers or who belonged to center-right parties, attempted to weaken REACH still further.

The outcome of this political wrangling was a compromise. The EP did vote to strengthen the authorization provisions of REACH by requiring that substances of "very high concern" be authorized for a maximum of five years, after which their substitution by safer alternatives would become mandatory. But it also approved amendments favored by the chemical industry that reduced the data requirements for approximately seventeen thousand substances produced or imported in quantities of less than ten tons per year. In November 2005, an amended version of REACH was approved by the EP by a vote of 407 to 155, and the regulation then went back to the Council of Ministers.

The Council, in turn, agreed to soften the more stringent authorization procedure that the EP had approved. It also rejected the EP's mandatory substitution requirement; instead it only "encouraged" the substitution of hazardous chemicals, and required safer alternatives to be "studied." The Council also eliminated the EP's mandatory five-year limit on chemical authorizations as well as a provision that required that consumers be informed about which chemicals were present in products they

---

[29]Hannah Karp and John Miller, "Chemical Rules Face Possibility of Dilution in EU," *Financial Times*, September 8, 2004.

purchased. The agreement reached in the Council was strongly attacked by health and environmental NGOs on the grounds that it had "diluted" the original purpose of REACH, most importantly by not requiring the phasing-out of dangerous and hazardous chemicals and by excluding approximately two-thirds of the chemicals produced or sold in Europe from its testing and authorization requirements.

Approval of REACH

Finally, in December 2006, after three months of further negotiations between the EP and the Council, REACH was formally adopted by both bodies, and entered into force in June 2007. The most important additional change was the adoption of more flexible registration requirements for certain categories of chemicals. With respect to the treatment of substances "of very high concern"—one of the most intensively debated provisions of REACH—the final legislative text made their authorization more difficult by placing the burden of proof on firms to demonstrate their safety, but it did not require mandatory substitutions; rather, firms were only required to present plans for finding substitutes. As *The Economist* noted, "the final deal . . . bears the unmistakable flavor of political fudge."[30]

Nonetheless, the passage of REACH fundamentally transformed European chemical regulation.[31] REACH eliminated the distinction between "existing" and "new" chemicals; chemicals would now be categorized and regulated based on their annual usage and hazardous properties rather than when they were first introduced. Companies were also required to register the thirty thousand most commonly used chemicals and to provide additional information on substances produced or imported in large volumes. With some exceptions, firms were now required to submit basic physical, chemical, and toxicological data for all chemicals either produced in or imported into Europe above a certain volume. This placed the burden on assessing the risks and hazards of chemical substances on the manufacturers and importers of chemicals rather than on regulatory officials—a reversal of the previous burden of proof. REACH also required explicit authorization—or substitution—for 1,500 chemicals that might be linked to reproductive diseases and cancers within three years. REACH's broader

[30] *The Economist*, "Regulatory Over-Reach," December 9, 2006.

[31] For more detailed summaries of REACH, see Beth Sirull, "Prepare Now for REACH Compliance," *Chemical Engineering Progress* 101, no. 3 (2005): 45–8; European Commission Environment Directorate General, "REACH in Brief" (October 2007), available at http://ec.europa.eu/environment/chemicals/reach/pdf/2007_02_reach_in_brief.pdf, accessed February 2009. Andrew Fasey, "REACH Is Here: The Politics Are Over, Now the Hard Work Starts," Lowell Center for Sustainable Production (2007), available at http://www.chemicals policy.org/downloads/REACHisHere220307.pdf, accessed February 2009.

registration requirements will be phased in over a period of eleven years; after that date, no unregistered chemicals can be produced or sold in the EU. By November 2010, the first REACH deadline, 24,000 registration dossiers had been submitted for 4,300 substances.

REACH has come to symbolize the contemporary EU approach to risk regulation. It is a regulatory approach characterized by:

> the privatization of risk identification and assessment functions; centralized decision-making supported by national input via a committee structure; highly formalized procedures for the introduction and treatment of decision-making inputs. . . . and, most importantly, by its *extremely low thresholds for regulatory intervention, which are both justified and facilitated by an outspoken endorsement of the precautionary principle.*[32]

The legislation established a new regulatory body, the European Chemicals Agency (ECHA), headquartered in Helsinki, to manage the collection of chemical information and register chemicals or request additional information from firms.[33] In 2008, the ECHA released a "blacklist" of fifteen chemicals of "very high concern" whose use will be gradually restricted unless firms can provide conclusive evidence that no alternatives are available. In addition, chemical companies were required to inform consumers if such chemicals are present in any products on sale in Europe.[34] The small number of chemicals initially listed by the ECHA concerned European environmentalists, who contended that a considerably larger number of chemicals merited inclusion on the ECHA's "blacklist." But ECHA officials responded that they lacked the administrative capacity to proceed more rapidly. In November 2009, the ECHS requested public consultation on fifteen additional chemical "substances of very high concern," chosen because of their specific hazardous qualities, and in 2010, sixteen substances were added to the list of chemicals requiring more extensive regulatory reviews.

The Global Impact of REACH

Since Europe accounts for more than half the global trade in chemicals, European officials recognized that REACH's impact would extend far

---

[32] Emphasis added. Veerle Hayvaert, "Globalizing Regulation: Reaching Beyond the Borders of Chemical Safety," *Journal of Law and Society* 36, no. 1 (March 2009): 115.

[33] For a detailed description and analysis of how REACH actually will be implemented, see Veerle Heyvaert, "The EU Chemicals Policy: Towards Inclusive Governance?" A paper presented at the CONNEX workshop on European Risk Governance, 2007.

[34] "First REACH List of Dangerous Chemicals Agreed," *EurActiv.com*, October 30, 2008, available at http://www.euractiv.com/en/environment/reach-list-dangerous-chemicals-agreed/article-176244, accessed February 2009.

beyond the borders of the EU. In fact, the White Paper had expressed the hope that REACH would influence international chemical regulatory initiatives, including those of other governments, via the OECD as well as non-state global regulatory regimes such as the chemical industry's "Responsible Care" program.[35] Since REACH covered many chemicals that were widely used throughout the world, the Commission viewed its adoption by other countries as an effective strategy for reducing the global risks of chemical production and use.

REACH has directly affected American business practices.[36] Once a chemical is included on the EU's list of "substances of very high concern," any firm whose products include such a chemical must receive specific authorization to market it in Europe. In addition, many other chemicals produced by American firms for sale in Europe must also be registered. American manufacturers predict that complying with REACH law will "add billions to their costs."[37] DuPont expects to spend tens of millions of dollars to register about five hundred of its chemicals with the EU; between twenty and thirty of these are expected to be on the "very high concern" list.

Dow Chemical has estimated that REACH's testing requirements will cost the firm between $100 million and $250 million, plus equivalent administrative costs, over eleven years. According to the ACC's managing director, 90 percent of its members will be affected by REACH and many smaller firms will not be able to afford the costs of complying with European registration requirements. REACH will ultimately affect which chemicals are used to make literally thousands of consumer goods sold in the United States. According to the ACC, REACH represents "yet another example of the Commission's attempt to establish the de facto international standard, just as it has attempted to do with respect to genetically modified organisms."[38]

Significantly, in 2008 Dow Chemical announced that it would prepare REACH-qualifying dossiers for all its products, not just those sold in Europe. This suggests that REACH may well have a broader impact on

---

[35] Elizabeth Fisher, "The 'Perfect Storm' of REACH: Charting Regulatory Controversy in the Age of Information, Sustainable Development and Globalization," *Journal of Risk Research* 11, no. 1 (June 2008): 554. See also Diana Bowman and Geert Van Calster, "Reflecting on REACH: Global Implications of the European Union's Chemical Regulation," *Nanotechnology Law & Business* (Fall 2007): 375–84.

[36] Lyndsey Layton, "Taking Responsibility: New European Laws for U.S. Industries to Demonstrate their Chemicals in Products Are Safe," *Washington Post National Weekly Edition*, June 16–22, 2008.

[37] Ibid.

[38] Henrik Selin, "Transatlantic Politics of Chemical Management," in *Transatlantic Environment and Energy Politics: Comparative and International Perspective*, ed. Miranda Schreurs, Henrik Selin, and Stacy VanDeveer (Burlington, VT: Ashgate, 2009), 71–2.

the $637 billion U.S. chemical marketplace, and possibly lead to the voluntary withdrawal by both manufacturers and retailers of chemicals classified by REACH as of "very high concern."[39]

Russia, which is the EU's third largest trading partner, and a major global chemical producer, announced that it planned to base its chemical safety standards on REACH. While this will cost Russian firms up to 10 percent of their export earnings, according to the Energy and Industry Ministry, Russia has little choice: "If one of our main strategic economic partners introduces such strict legislation, we will be forced to apply these requirements."[40] Canada, Australia, China, South Korea, and Japan have also revised their chemical regulations to bring them into closer alignment with REACH.

THE CONTEMPORARY POLITICS OF CHEMICAL REGULATION IN THE UNITED STATES

Comparing REACH and TSCA

While TSCA had made American chemical regulations more stringent and comprehensive than in the EU, REACH reversed this pattern. According to a 2007 report to Congress prepared by the General Accountability Office (GAO) that compared American and European approaches to the risks of toxic chemicals, they now differed in several important respects.[41] First, while REACH required chemical companies to develop and share with regulators information on the effects of the chemicals they produce on human health, TSCA generally does not. REACH specifically gives government officials the authority to require firms to provide whatever scientific data are needed to evaluate a chemical's health and environmental risks, while TSCA requires the EPA to demonstrate that such data are needed before it can require chemical firms to provide them.

Second, REACH places the burden of proof on chemical firms to demonstrate that the chemicals they place in the market do not have adverse effects, while TSCA requires the EPA to demonstrate that chemicals pose risks to human health or the environment *prior* to issuing regulations that restrict their product, distribution, or use. Third, while the TCSA

---

[39] Noah Sachs, "Jumping the Pond, Transnational Law and the Future of Chemical Regulation," *Vanderbilt Law Review* 62, no. 6 (November, 2009), 1283.

[40] "Russia 'Forced' to Apply Costly EU Chemical Standards," *EUbusiness*, July 6, 2007, http://www.eubusiness.com/Chemicals/1184590802.0, accessed March 2009.

[41] U.S. Government Accountability Office, *Chemical Regulation: Comparison of U.S. and Recently Enacted EU Approaches to Protect against the Risks of Toxic Chemicals*, GAO-07-825 (2007): 4–5, available at http://www.gao.gov/new.items/d07825.pdf, accessed February 2009.

granted the EPA differential authority to control the risks posed by new or existing chemicals—specifically by making it more difficult to restrict existing chemicals—REACH makes no distinction between existing and new chemicals.

The Shortcomings of TSCA

Not surprisingly, many of the same criticisms of chemical regulation in Europe that prompted REACH have also been voiced about TSCA. According to a 2003 EPA study, 85 percent of new chemical notices submitted by firms since 1979 lack information on their potential health effects and 67 percent lack health or environmental data of any kind.[42] The EPA has also found it difficult to assess the safety of the approximately sixty-two thousand chemicals in commercial use prior to the TSCA's testing requirements. Currently, 92 percent (by volume) of the highest production chemicals in use fall under this category, but through 2006, the EPA had used its authority to require testing of fewer than two hundred of them.[43]

A 1994 GAO report found that since the approval of TSCA, the EPA had imposed restrictions on only five previously approved chemicals. Moreover, one of these restrictions, namely the EPA's proposed ban on virtually all uses of asbestos, was overturned by the Fifth Circuit Court of Appeals on the grounds that the EPA had presented insufficient evidence—including an adequate risk assessment—to justify its ban. This legal ruling had a chilling effect on the EPA's efforts to use its authority to restrict the production or use of existing chemicals.[44] Since the 1989 asbestos decision, the EPA has not proposed restrictions on any previously approved chemical. "The analytic burdens placed by the Fifth Circuit Court of Appeals effectively emasculated the TSCA regulation in the US and, for all intents and purposes, the EPA regard[s] TSCA as a 'dead letter.'"[45] According to one former EPA official, "TSCA currently places

[42] U.S. Environmental Protection Agency, Office of Pollution Prevention and Toxics, *Programs Overview*, Draft Version 2.0 (Washington, DC: GPO, 2003).

[43] U.S. Government Accountability Office. *Chemical Regulation: Actions Are Needed to Improve the Effectiveness of EPA's Chemical Review Program*, GAO-06-1032T (Washington, DC: GPO, 2006), available at http://www.gao.gov/new.items/d061032t.pdf, accessed February 2009.

[44] "The Promise and Limits of the U.S. Toxic Substances Control Act," Lowell Center for Sustainable Production, (October 2003): 3, available at http.chemicalspolicy.org/downloads/Chemicals_Policy_TSCA.doc, accessed February 2009.

[45] Nicholas Ashford, "The Legacy of the Precautionary Principle in U.S. Law: The Rise of Cost-Benefit Analysis and Risk Assessment as Undermining Factors in Health, Safety and Environmental Protection," in *Implementing the Precautionary Principle*, ed. Nicolas de Sadeleer (London: Earthscan, 2007), 366.

too high a bar for the EPA to jump to assure the health of the public and protection of the environment. Under TSCA, existing chemicals are assumed safe until proven guilty, even when found in breast milk and even as toxicological evidence accumulates.[46]

Public Concerns about Chemical Safety in the United States

Public concerns about the safety of chemicals have continued to emerge in the United States. In 1996, the publication of *Our Stolen Future*, which claimed that endocrine or hormone disruptive chemicals posed a serious and too little understood threat to human health, especially to reproductive health, attracted widespread public attention.[47] In 1996 and 1997, Congress responded to these concerns by adopting amendments to the Food Quality Protection Act and the Safe Drinking Water Act that established a program to investigate the effects of synthetic chemicals on the endocrine system. However, this program has been plagued by many of the same procedural problems as TSCA. It took until 2005 for the EPA to finally develop valid screening tests, and in light of the large investment of time and other resources required to test each endocrine-disrupting chemical, very few of the estimated 87,000 such chemicals have been tested to date.[48]

The specific health risks of Bisphonol A (BPA), a widely used chemical compound that is considered an endocrine disruptor and which has been linked to breast and prostate cancer, early-onset puberty, and polycystic ovary syndrome, have become highly visible in the United States.[49] The FDA has conducted numerous studies of its impact and in 2010 issued a report that raised concerns about the exposure of fetuses, infants, and young children to BPA, though it did not recommend or propose any restrictions. However, five American states as well as some local governments, including the city of San Francisco, have banned the chemical from various consumer products and, responding to public pressures, each of the five major producers of children's plastic bottles in the United States has stopped making them with BPA. (After Denmark banned the chemical in packaging for children up to three years of age in March 2010, followed by France two months later, in November 2010 the European Commission banned its use in plastic baby bottles throughout the EU,

---

[46] Quoted in "The Promise and Limits of the U.S. Toxic Substances Control Act," 6.

[47] Theo Colborn, Dianne Dumanoski, and John Myers, *Our Stolen Future: Are We Threatening Our Fertility, Intelligence, and Survival? A Scientific Detective Story* (New York: Dutton, 1996).

[48] Jason Vogel, "Tunnel Vision: The Regulation of Endocrine Disruptors," *Policy Sciences* 37 (2004): 285–6.

[49] See Groopman, "The Plastic Panic," 26–31, and Denise Grady, "In Feast of Data on BPA Plastic, No Final Answer," *New York Times*, September 7, 2010, D1 and D4.

effective 2011—making BPA the most recent example of a divergence in European and American risk regulations.)[50]

Just as American restrictions for vehicular pollution became a benchmark or rallying cry for European activists who then demanded that the EU adopt similar standards, so "the enactment of REACH has increased NGO calls for a systematic overhaul of U.S. chemical policy, shifting the focus from ad hoc bans or restrictions on specific chemicals. . . . REACH has become an influential regulatory model and has emboldened U.S. environmental activists."[51] According to the co-founder of an organization called MomsRising, "It is outrageous more and more parents look for labels that say items meet Europe regulatory standards because American standards are not to be trusted. We want our families protected from chemical exposure."[52]

Pressures to Reform American Chemical Regulation

In part as a response to the passage of REACH, in 2006 the Senate held its first hearing in more than a decade to consider amendments to TSCA.[53] John Stephenson, environmental director of the Government Accounting Office, informed the Senate Committee on Environment and Public Works that the law's high legal standard had "severely inhibited" the EPA's regulatory efforts. Michael Wilson, an occupational and environmental health researcher at the University of California, Berkeley, urged Congress to enact "a modern chemicals policy" similar to Europe's, while Lynn Goldman of the Lowell Center for Sustainable Production testified that an "overhaul of TSCA is long overdue."[54]

At Senate hearings held in 2008, Democratic Senator Barbara Boxer of California explicitly compared REACH to TSCA: "TSCA puts the burden on the government to prove that a toxic chemical is a risk . . . unlike the European program called REACH . . . which places the burden on the chemical industry—where it should be—to show that chemicals are safe."[55] But an industry representative countered that

---

[50]For an analysis of the politics of BPA in Europe, written prior to the EU's decision to ban it, see Alberto Alemanno, "The Fabulous Destiny of Bisphenol A (BPA)," *European Journal of Risk Regulation*, 1, no. 4 (2010): 397–400.

[51]Sachs, "Jumping the Pond," 1861, 1862.

[52]Joanne Scott, "From Brussels with Love: The Transatlantic Travels of European Law and the Chemistry of Regulatory Attraction," *American Journal of Comparative Law* 57 (2009): 927.

[53]Marla Cone, "Senate Panel Weights Toxic Chemicals Law," *Los Angeles Times*, August 3, 2006. Unless otherwise noted, the quotations in this paragraph are from this article.

[54]"The Promise and Limits of the U.S. Toxic Substances Control Act," 6.

[55]Patricia Van Arnum, "Will REACH Reach the US?" *Pharmaceutical Technology Sourcing and Management* (May 9, 2008).

"An 'American REACH' would not only hamper innovation but would reverse the progress made over the course of many years by federal regulators to appropriately manage risks."[56] However, the committee heard testimony from executives from the chemical industry who agreed that TSCA needed to be modernized—especially in light of the advances in environmental and health science since the mid-1970s—although industry officials stressed that any new legislation should only regulate clearly proven chemical risks.[57]

Several laws have been introduced in Congress to strengthen various aspects of American chemical regulation. The "Kid-Safe" chemical bill, which was co-sponsored by Democratic Congressman Henry Waxman of California, and Democratic Senators Barbara Boxer of California and Frank Lautenberg of New Jersey, was explicitly modeled on REACH: it required the Centers for Disease Control to use bio-monitoring studies to identify chemicals present in umbilical cord blood and then decide whether these chemicals should be restricted or banned. It also "promotes alternatives to hazardous chemicals, shifts the burden to industry to demonstrate 'reasonable certainty of no harm' from chemical products, [and] limits confidential business information claims."[58] This legislative proposal was prompted by an Environmental Working Group study that found an average of two hundred industrial chemicals in the blood of newborn babies.

In May 2010, President Obama's cancer panel issued a report deploring the increasing number of carcinogens released into the environment—including Bisphenol A (BPA)—and called for more stringent regulations and wider public awareness of their dangers. The panel's chairman recommended a precautionary approach to assessing chemical risks, stating that, "the increasing number of known or suspected environmental carcinogens compels us to action, even though we may currently lack irrefutable proof of harm."[59] The Obama administration subsequently announced a "framework for reform of chemicals management legislation." It would expand the EPA's authority by requiring chemicals to be reviewed "against safety standards that are based on sound science and reflect risk-based criteria protective of human health and the environment."[60] However, to date, none of these legislative pro-

[56]Testimony of V.M. DeLisi before the US Senate Committee on Environment and Public Works (April 29, 2008), available at http://epw.senate.gov/public/index.cfm?FuseAction=Files.View&FileStore_id=fa066ac5-7f17-48fa-a618-375631c86a6f, accessed February 2009.

[57]Daemmrich, "International Lobbying," 3.

[58]Sachs, "Jumping the Pond," 1861.

[59]Groopman, "The Plastic Panic," 26.

[60]Daemmrich, "International Lobbying," 3.

posals has been adopted. According to Rich Denison, a senior scientist at the Environmental Defense Fund, "We . . . have quite a ways to go in convincing the U.S. Congress that this is a problem that needs fixing."[61]

AMERICAN STATE REGULATIONS

A number of states have strengthened their chemical regulations. In 1989, Massachusetts passed legislation that was in many respects similar to that of REACH. The Toxics Use Reduction Act of 2003 which was described (prior to the passage of REACH) as "one of the most far reaching pieces of chemicals legislation in the world," requires manufacturing firms that use more than a specified number of pounds per year of some 1,200 substances to engage in a full materials accounting exercise—data from which are made public.[62] Every two years, firms are required to undertake a comprehensive plan to identify production and product alternatives that would reduce their reliance on, and waste from, toxic chemicals. Between 1990 and 2003, this law led to an 80 percent reduction in chemical emissions, a 57 percent reduction in chemical waste, and a 40 percent reduction in chemical use.

California's efforts to strengthen its chemical regulations date from the passage of Proposition 65 in 1986. Anticipating the approach of the EU's White Paper, Proposition 65 adopted a precautionary approach for deciding when a chemical presented a hazard. It requires state officials to place on a hazard list any chemical that had a demonstrated *potential* to cause cancer or reproductive toxicity, without requiring a formal risk assessment.[63] Products containing these chemicals must include a warning label and are prohibited from being discharged into sources of drinking water. Legal actions taken under Proposition 65 have resulted in significant reductions of lead, arsenic, and mercury in a wide range of products sold or used in California.[64]

The subsequent passage of REACH directly affected chemical regulation in California. In 2004, two California legislative committees commissioned a report on" Green Chemistry" that explored "the implications

[61] Quoted in Layton. "Taking Responsibility."

[62] "Precautionary Chemicals Policy Initiatives in the U.S.," Lowell Center for Sustainable Production (October 2003): 3, available at http://www.chemicalspolicy.org/down loads/10-03_Chemicals_Policy_Precaution.pdf, accessed February 2009.

[63] Michael Rogers, "Risk Analysis under Uncertainty, the Precautionary Principle, and the New EU Chemical Strategy," *Regulatory Toxicology and Pharmacology* 37 (2003): 379.

[64] Clifford Rechtschaffen and Patrick Williams, "The Continued Success of Proposition 65 in Reducing Toxic Exposures," *Environmental Law Reporter* 35 (2005): 10850–56.

for California of chemical policy developments in Europe."[65] In 2007, at the request of Governor Arnold Schwarzenegger, the Secretary of State for Environmental Protection established a Green Chemistry Initiative under the Department of Toxic Substances Control (DTSC).[66] Rather than making chemical policy through legislation on a case-by-case basis, the goal of this initiative was to draw on a wide range of scientific expertise, both in California and internationally, in order to evaluate the health effects of chemicals and develop policies to reduce and eliminate those chemicals deemed to be hazardous to the health of consumers and the environment.[67] The same year, California approved legislation establishing the first state-based bio-monitoring program to identify and track the presence of synthetic chemicals and pollutants in the population.

In September 2008, two of the California EPA's "Green Chemistry" recommendations were enacted into law. AB-1879 authorized DTSC to identify and prioritize chemicals of concern, evaluate alternatives, and then undertake a range of regulatory responses including restrictions and bans, while SB-309 established an online Toxic Information Clearinghouse to provide public access to information on chemicals. According to Megan Schwartzman and Michael Wilson, two analysts, the "Implementation of the REACH regulation has informed and bolstered California's chemical policy reform . . . it has provided model methods and structures. . . . By controlling access to European markets, REACH sets what may become a de facto gold standard for information disclosure."[68]

The public information provisions of REACH are likely to strengthen California's regulatory efforts by giving state officials access to REACH's public database, which will include data about the composition and health risks of many chemical products sold in California.

[65] Scott, "From Brussels with Love," 910.

[66] "Gov. Schwarzenegger Applauds Plan to Reduce Toxic Chemicals in Products," Office of the Governor, December 16, 2008, http://gov.ca.gov/index.php?/press-release/11263/, accessed February 2009.

[67] For a comprehensive discussion of the rationale for California's "green chemistry" program, see Michael Wilson et al., "Green Chemistry Cornerstone to a Sustainable California," Center for Occupational and Environmental Health, University of California Regents (January 2008), available at http://coeh.berkeley.edu/docs/news/green_chem_brief.pdf, accessed February 2009. Much of the analysis in this report on the health hazards of many new chemicals and the economic benefits of better chemical regulation are similar to that of the EC's White Paper that proposed REACH.

[68] Megan Schwartzman and Michael Wilson, "Reshaping Chemicals Policy on Two Sides of the Atlantic: The Promise of Improved Sustainability Through International Cooperation," *Transatlantic Regulatory Cooperation: The Shifting Roles of the EU, the U.S. and California*, ed. David Vogel and Johan Swinnen (Cheltenham, UK: Edward Elgar, 2011), 115.

Analysis

The passage of REACH by the European Union partially reflects the extent to which public concern about chemical risks increased in Europe, prompted in part by a number of studies that documented a wide range of credible safety risks. Strong pressure for strengthening European chemical regulations also emerged from European trade unions, as well as a broad coalition of consumer and environmental organizations.

But the request of the Council of Ministers that the Commission propose a major revision of EU chemical policy, which set in motion the long political process that led to REACH's adoption seven years later, was primarily initiated by several member states, who wanted European chemical regulations to be significantly strengthened. A critical role was played by Sweden, which had joined the EU in 1995 and whose chemical regulations were considerably more stringent that those of any other member state. Thus, REACH demonstrates the critical role played by influential policy makers from member states with more stringent regulatory policies and preferences in driving the EU's regulatory policy agenda.

REACH incorporates more risk-averse and comprehensive criteria to identify chemical risks and permits chemicals to be restricted for which there was insufficient evidence of their safety. This approach reflected not only the influence of the precautionary principle, but also several highly visible food safety failures in Europe, as well as the ongoing debate over the safety of GMOs. These issues, policy failures, and debates became linked to one another. REACH thus represents another example of the "risk availability cascade" initiated by "mad-cow disease."

In the United States, the health risks of chemicals have been sufficiently salient to prompt California, Massachusetts, and Maine to strengthen their chemical regulations. In part as a response to the EU's passage of REACH in 2006, political and public support for revising TSCA has grown in the United States. Yet notwithstanding a broad consensus that TSCA has become outdated, support by policy makers in Congress for revising what is now a thirty-five year old regulatory statute remains limited. "Alarm bells" about the safety of various chemicals continue to ring, but they have not been sufficiently amplified to place a major reform of American chemical regulation on the congressional agenda.

Part of this may be due to the fact that the congressional agenda is extremely crowded and that strengthening chemical regulation does not appear sufficiently urgent. But congressional inaction may also reflect the political deadlock and partisan divisions that have made it much more difficult for statutory changes in federal risk regulation to be enacted since 1990. Should a reform of TSCA be seriously debated in Congress, it would likely encounter strong opposition from Republican legislators opposed to further expansions of government regulation of business. By contrast, influential policy makers in both the EP and the Council of Ministers have been much more supportive of expanding the scope and stringency of European environmental legislation, including those from the center-right political parties.

HAZARDOUS WASTES AND RECYCLING

The passage of REACH was part of a broader effort on the part of the European Commission to reduce the environmental impact of commercial products by implementing the principles of "polluter pays" and extended producer responsibility. Specifically, the EU has adopted policies to ban hazardous substances in electronics and electrical products and to promote their recycling and reuse.

WEEE and RoHS

European policy makers have become concerned about the impact of the increasing amounts of electronic and electrical waste being deposited into landfills in Europe. In 1998, six million tons of electronic waste were generated in the EU, and in 2000, the European Commission predicted that volume of e-waste would double by 2010, making it the most rapidly growing component of the municipal solid waste. This waste contained several substances that were known to pose human health hazards, including lead, chromium, cadmium, mercury, and brominated flame retardants. "Other than pesticides and paints, electronics are likely the most hazardous products discarded by households in the industrialized world."[69] For example, approximately one-fifth of the annual global consumption of mercury is found in electronic equipment.

In 2003, while the provisions of REACH were being heatedly debated, the EU approved two important directives: the Directive on Waste from Electronics and Electronic Equipment (WEEE) and the Directive on Restrictions on Hazardous Substances (RoHS).[70] Their purposes were to reduce the amount of electronic waste entering landfills, increase the amount of electronic waste that was recycled, reduce public exposure to hazardous electronic waste, and promote resource conservation. Their

---

[69] Noah Sachs, "Planning the Funeral At the Birth: Extended Product Responsibility in the European Union and the U.S.," *Harvard Environmental Law Review* 30 (2006): 59.

[70] For a summary of these directives, see Henrik Selin and Stacy VanDeveer, "Raising Global Standards," *Environment* 48, no. 10 (2006): 7–18.

long-term goal was to provide incentives for producers to redesign electronics and electrical products in a more environmentally friendly manner. By enacting harmonized standards, the EU sought to make member state regulations more uniform, and to strengthen their overall effectiveness.

WEEE's objective is to reduce the amount of e-waste produced by the more than 9 million tons of electrical and electronic products sold annually in the EU. WEEE covers eighty-one products, divided into ten product categories. These categories are extremely comprehensive, ranging from small and large household appliances to information technology and telecommunications equipment, medical devices, and toys—essentially any product that has a plug or uses a battery. For each product category, the directive established recovery targets for each member state, based on their population. To meet these targets, member states are required to establish collection systems that are free of charge to users.

WEEE's most controversial and politically contested provision required producers to organize and finance the treatment, recovery, and disposal of 60–80 percent of their own electronic and electrical waste, which they can accomplish either by establishing their own take-back systems or by participating in collective arrangements, some of which had already been established nationally. WEEE phased in its recovery targets over four years in order to provide manufacturers with the opportunity to incorporate design for environment strategies into their new products. The EU's long-term objective was to establish an "industrial ecosystem" in which discarded, returned, or used products became material inputs for new products.[71] To comply with the terms of the Basel Convention on the Control of Transboundary Movements of Hazardous Wastes and their Disposal, which the EU had ratified in 1989, member states were also restricted from exporting their hazardous waste to developing countries.

The RoHS directive, which went into effect on July 1, 2006, banned six hazardous materials in the manufacture of electrical and electronic products in eight of the ten product categories covered by WEEE. (The directive did not apply to electrical and electronic devices that are part of larger equipment as well as to some medical devices.) The restricted substances are four heavy metals, namely lead, mercury, cadmium, and hexavalent chromium, and two chemicals, polybrominated biphenyls (PBB), and polybrominated diphenyl ethers (BPDE). According to the European Commission, each of these materials has "toxic and/or persistent and bioaccumulative properties that are *potentially* hazardous

[71]J. Halluite et al., "The Challenge of Hazardous Waste Management in a Sustainable Environment: Insights from Electronic Recovery Laws," *Corporate Social Responsibility and Environmental Management* 12, no. 1 (2005): 31–7.

to human health and ecosystems upon release into the environment."[72] This risk assessment reflects recent research in biological toxicology which has found long-term adverse health effects of lower-level chemical exposure, including neurological, developmental, and reproductive changes.

Business Opposition

Both directives were strongly opposed by trade associations representing electronic firms from the European Union, the United States, and Japan. In a joint statement issued in July 2001, they demanded that the European Council "demonstrate how the impending laws will meet any of their stated environmental aims," adding that "it will be impossible for the vast majority of electronics manufacturers that are small and medium-sized companies to comply with the full phase-out of the banned chemicals before 2008."[73] American manufacturers specifically opposed the ban on flame retardants, arguing that it would increase the risks of fire. In the case of WEEE, both European and American-based European electronics firms preferred a voluntary take-back scheme, the former on the grounds that compliance with the EU's legislative proposal was too complex and the latter on the grounds that WEEE's recycling and reuse requirements would discourage entry into the European markets.[74]

The American Electronics Industry Association launched a major challenge to both directives, arguing that they would pose "a straightjacket for product innovation, and disadvantage both the consumer and the environment."[75] Instead of mandatory regulations, it favored voluntary producer responsibility for end of life products. It also contended that the EU's targets were too rigid. But subsequently, some European firms recognized that they would benefit from a system of mandatory producer

---

[72]Emphasis added. A. D. Martin, C. K. Mayers, and C. M. France, "The EU Restriction of Hazardous Substances Directive: Problems Arising from Implementation Differences Between Member States and Proposed Solutions," *RECIEL* 16, no. 2 (2007): 217. This essay presents a detailed discussion and analysis of the directive's provisions and the challenges faced by member states in implementing it.

[73]"Technology Companies Make Last Stand on EU Electronic Waste Laws," *Business and the Environment* 12, no. 1 (January 2002): 11.

[74]Alastair Iles, "Targeting Consumer Product Environmental Impacts across the Atlantic," in Schreurs, Selin, and VanDeveer, eds., *Transatlantic Environment and Energy Politics*, 99.

[75]Thomas Bernauer and Ladina Caduff, "In Whose Interest? Pressure Groups Politics, Economic Competition and Environmental Regulation," *Journal of Public Policy* 24.1 (2004): 116.

responsibility as it would strengthen their relationship with their customers and enable them to control the market for their used or recycled products.[76]

The Challenges of Compliance to WEEE

The EU has found it difficult to promote compliance with WEEE among consumers.[77] As of 2007, virtually no small appliances, only 25 percent of medium-sized household appliances, and 40 percent of larger appliances had been collected for recycling. This failure of implementation reflects both a lack of consumer awareness of the importance of recycling their electronic and electrical products as well as the lack of adequate collection facilities for them to do so. The Commission has been particularly concerned about the low collection rate of old refrigerators containing CFCs, as these chemicals not only threaten the ozone layer but are an important greenhouse gas. Ironically, the estimated 4.3 tons of mercury contained in the 660 million energy-saving light bulbs sold in the EU-27 in 2006 represent an additional source of toxic pollution—unless they are recycled. Overall, it is estimated that only one-third of e-waste in Europe is currently being treated in accordance with the WEEE directive. Notwithstanding the provisions of the 1994 Basel Convention, which prohibits the EU from exporting electronic waste containing hazardous materials to non-OECD countries, enforcement has proven difficult and many of these products continue to be illegally exported from Europe.[78]

Electronic Recycling and Waste Disposal in the United States

In contrast to the EU, as well as ten other countries including Japan, China, and Korea, no American federal regulations require electronic recycling.[79] According to a GAO study, "federal regulatory requirements (which include the Resource Conservation and Recovery Act and the Pollution Prevention Act) provide little incentive for environmentally

[76] For an analysis of firm strategies toward product recovery, see Michael Toffel, "Strategic Management of Product Recovery," *California Management Review* 46, no. 2 (2004): 120–41.

[77] The following two paragraphs are based on "Recycling of Europe's Electronic Waste Needs Improvement, UN Report Urges," *Science Daily*, November 16, 2007.

[78] Aidan Lewis, "Europe Breaking Electronic Waste Export Ban," *BBC News*, August 4, 2010.

[79] RoHS Information Resource, "Global Environmental Legislation," available at http .rohs.compliance.info/pending-environemntal-legislation.htm, accessed February 2009.

preferable management of used electronics."[80] While federal policy does promote alternatives to waste disposal, and regulates the disposal of electronics by businesses and government agencies, no federal laws require e-waste recycling by households, which produce half of the e-waste generated each year in the United States. As a result, nearly all of it is disposed of with common household garbage in municipal solid waste landfills or in incinerators.[81] The United States also generates more e-waste than any other nation.

To fill the regulatory vacuum at the federal level, and influenced by the passage of WEEE, many city and state governments have enacted their own policies. In 2003, California became the first state to require producer responsibility for recycling electronic products. However, the California E-Waste Recycling Act is narrower in scope than the EU Directive: it only covers video display products with a screen greater than four inches diagonally. The California Cell Phone Recycling Act made it unlawful for a retailer to sell a cell phone in the state if the retailer does not offer a take-back program to its customers. By 2007, more than half of all American states had enacted a total of more than fifty different "producer take backs."[82] While their details vary, most are based on the same principle that underlies WEEE, namely, that manufacturers should be responsible for the collection and reuse of their products. Other states have funded voluntary recycling projects.

In addition, a number of American electronics manufacturers and retailers, including Best Buy, Dell, IBM, Compaq, and Hewlett-Packard, as well as Sony, have established their own recycling programs in the United States, thus voluntarily adopting the principle of extended producer responsibility required by WEEE for products sold in Europe.[83]

However, the impact of both state regulations and voluntary business programs has been limited. Of the 2.5 million tons of televisions, cell phones, and computer products ready for end of life management in 2007, 18 percent of computers and televisions and 10 percent of cell phones had

---

[80]U.S. Government Accountability Office, *Electronic Waste: Observation on the Role of the Federal Government in Encouraging Recycling and Reuse*, GAO-05-937T (Washington, DC: GPO, 2005): 3, available at http://www.gao.gov/new.items/d05937t.pdf, accessed February 2009.

[81]Paul Vitello, "Clearing a Path from Desktop to the Recycler," *New York Times*, November 11, 2006.

[82]U.S. Government Accountability Office, *Electronic Waste: Observation on the Role of the Federal Government in Encouraging Recycling and Reuse*.

[83]"Mail-Back Not Seen as Final Solution for Computer Waste in the U.S.," *Business and the Environment*, July 2001, 11. See also Marc Gunther, "Best Buy Wants Your Junk," *Fortune*, December 7, 2009, 96–9.

been collected for recycling.[84] Overall, only 15–20 percent of the 206 million computer products and 140 million phones discarded in the United States each year are recycled and about half are deposited in landfills.[85]

In response to the proliferation of state electronic recycling requirements, several laws have been introduced in Congress to establish a national electronic-waste recycling program. But while Congress has been concerned about the growing patchwork of state laws that appear to both confuse and burden manufacturers, retailers, recyclers, and consumers, it has not been able to agree on the details of a national e-waste recycling program, in part due to disagreement as to whether it should be mandatory or voluntary. The Energy Policy Act of 2005 initially included language that encouraged the EPA to develop a market-based sustainable electronic recycling infrastructure and to work with manufacturers to develop their own product stewardship programs, but this provision was eliminated from the text of the final legislation.

The United States did play a major role in developing the United Nations-sponsored Basel Convention, which by 1998 had been ratified by 121 countries. Although the United States did sign the Convention, Congress has yet to ratify it. The American recycling industry has been concerned about the provisions of the Basel Convention which had specified which recyclable waste would be exempted from its restrictions on waste exports to developing countries. While this issue was subsequently resolved in a way that was satisfactory to American producers, Congress has yet to change a number of domestic laws that would make it possible for the United States to comply with the terms of the Basel Convention.

The 1984 Resource Conservation and Recovery Act does impose some restrictions on the export of hazardous waste from the United States, but its provisions are weaker than those of the Basel Convention, and thus those of the member states of the European Union. Currently, American law only restricts the export of monitors and televisions with cathode-ray tubes. As a result, 60–80 percent of American e-waste collected for recycling is exported, primarily to China, India, and Pakistan, where according to a 2006 report issued by Greenpeace, *Exporting Harm: The High Tech Trashing of Asia*, its valuable components are extracted in very hazardous working conditions. Jim Bluckett of the Basal Action Network, an international NGO, concludes that the United States is "way behind" Europe, when it comes to e-waste disposal.[86]

---

[84] Linda Luther, "Managing Electronic Waste," *Congressional Research Service* (October 7, 2009): 4.

[85] "Gadget Gluttony," *Fortune*, September 27, 2010, 17.

[86] Quoted in Lewis 'Europe Breaking,"

Federal Regulations of Hazardous Substances

While the EPA has requested that manufacturing firms reduce their use of lead and other hazardous materials, there are no federal regulations restricting or banning the use of hazardous substances in electronic products. The lack of such regulations is in part attributable to the absence of scientific data that electronic waste in landfills presents unacceptable health risks. While a GAO study did note that "the volume of used electronics is large and growing and that if improperly managed can harm the environment and human health," neither the GAO nor the EPA was able to cite any evidence that it had actually done so.[87] According to a 2004 peer-reviewed study by the Solid Waste Association of North America, "extensive data . . . show that heavy metal concentration in leach and landfill gases are generally below the limits . . . established to protect human health and the environment."[88] Another study claims that public concern about electronic waste reflects "hype and hysteria."[89] According to Robert Tonetti, a scientist with the EPA Office of Solid Wastes,

> I don't think [the EU's directives] mean anything . . . to the U.S. government. This is definitely of interest to us and gives us a set of ideas to think about, but has more to do with corporations and companies than with government. We're looking for a more cooperative approach rather than the government controlling anything. [America] is a long way from considering RoHS directives.[90]

American State Policies

While the EPA officially considers e-waste disposal in landfills to be "safe," many state and local governments have expressed concern about their cumulative impact on human health, especially as the volume of discarded electronic equipment continues to grow. In 2005, 2.63 million tons of e-waste were deposited in municipal landfills; two years later, this had increased to 3.01 million tons, making these products the fastest growing component of the municipal waste stream in the United States as well as in Europe. Seventy percent of the heavy metals in landfills in the United States, including both lead and mercury, come from discarded electronic products.

[87] Ben Elgin and Brian Grow, "The Dirty Secret of Recycling Electronics," *Business Week*, October 27, 2008, 414.

[88] Quoted in "How Not to Clean Up," *American Enterprise* 16, no. 3 (2005): 59.

[89] Ibid.

[90] Lynn Schenkman, "EU Government to Enforce E-Waste Recycling, *Waste Age*, December 1, 2002.

To compensate for the Resource Conservation and Recovery Act's exemption for household hazardous waste and the increasing volume of obsolete electronics within their boundaries, several states, including Massachusetts, Minnesota, Arkansas, and California, have banned some lead-contaminated electronic components from landfills. But these restrictions provide no incentives for recycling or reuse, which means that the waste can instead be shipped to other states or overseas.[91]

One state has enacted regulations explicitly based on RoHS: a provision of California's 2003 Electronic Waste Recycling Act prohibits electronic products with video displays larger than four inches "if the electronic device is prohibited from being sold or offered for sale in the EU on or after its date of manufacture."[92] Not only does the California statute explicitly reference RoHS, but it also provides that the list of prohibited substances in these products will expand should the EU amend RoHS to ban additional substances. It thus represents the most explicit adoption of a European regulatory standard in the United States. *In effect, California has agreed to be governed by an EU directive*—a striking example of the EU's global regulatory reach. California subsequently enacted legislation that applies RoHS's restrictions to general-purpose lights for both indoor and outdoor use. Seven other states have enacted regulations influenced by and based in part of RoHS, most commonly by restricting the sale of products containing mercury, though most cover fewer hazardous substances than the California statute.

The Global Impact of RoHS

In the fall of 2001, the Netherlands banned the sale of Sony's popular PlayStation consoles because the cadmium in its peripheral cables exceeded Dutch regulatory limits.[93] Sony's lost sales and the costs to rework their product totaled $150 million and prompted the firm to carry out a systematic review of their supply chains. Following the passage of RoHS, which applied not only to products produced in Europe, but to any products sold within the EU, several major global electronic firms, including

---

[91] "Iles, "Targeting Consumer Product Information," in Schreurs, Selin, and VanDeveer, eds., *Transatlantic Environment and Energy Politics*, 102.

[92] Jonathan P. Scoll and Julie M. Duckstad, "Cal RoHS: California Brings European Hazardous Content Regulation 'Home' to U.S. Manufacturers," *Lindquist & Vennum* (May 2008): 2, available at http://lindquistwc.staged.hubbardone.com/files/Publication/17a798d0-b418-4445-bf6c-03d5dc1691cb/Presentation/PublicationAttachment/7be0efc6-b400-463b-9cdc-0bf13366db4f/RoHS%20part%202.pdf, accessed February 2009.

[93] Joel Makower, "RoHS: Getting the PBBs and PBDEs Out of PCs," *World Changing*, October 2, 2005, available at http://www.worldchanging.com/archives//003569.html, accessed February 2009.

Toshiba, Dell, Hitachi, Intel, Panasonic, Hewlett-Packard, and Apple as well as hundreds of their global suppliers, redesigned their electronic products in order to maintain their access to the EU. "Electronics manufacturers in China, Korea, Taiwan and Japan quickly changed product designs and eliminated the six toxic substances to maintain their access to the EU market."[94] Within a few years, many global consumer electronic products were RoHS compliant, including Apple's iPod portable music players, Dell and HP home computers and servers, Nintendo's Wii, Motorola and Nokia's portable phones, and Netgear's routers. Many global electronics companies have "RoHS status pages" on their corporate websites, which indicate their progress in meeting the EU's regulatory requirements for their products. Environmental activists have closely monitored these efforts and have often pressured firms to expedite their reduction of the toxic substances restricted by the EU.

In Japan, a consortium of several major electronics firms has voluntarily adopted a wide range of restrictions on the use of hazardous substances in their products that go beyond RoHS. Korea adopted a voluntary program to phase out the hazardous chemicals covered by the RoHS Directive. In 2007, China adopted its own version of RoHS, known as "China RoHS": more than 1,800 specific materials and components classified as "electronic information products" will be required to include a label stating if they are RoHS compliant. [95] Products which are not labeled as such will be subsequently banned from sale within China, although the Chinese government has yet to announce when this phase will be implemented. But the Chinese regulation has fewer exemptions than RoHS and also requires that Chinese certified laboratories perform all product testing, including the testing for imported products. More than ten other countries have enacted or are considering enacting legislation similar to RoHS.

The six substances whose use is restricted by RoHS are, or were, commonly used in literally hundreds of thousands of items produced and marketed by semiconductor and other electronics manufacturers. Accordingly, RoHS represents "the most significant transformation in the manufacturing sector since the banning of ozone-depleting substances in the late 1970s."[96] An American engineer described RoHS as "probably the biggest change in 50 years" for the U.S. and global electronic business.[97]

---

[94] Sachs, "Jumping the Pond," 1851

[95] Hazmat Alternatives, "U.S. and European Rules-World Wide Regulations," available at http.hazmat-alternatives.com/Regs-World.php, accessed February 2009.

[96] Makower, "RoHs."

[97] Vanesse Houlder, "Reaching Agreement on the Vast Detail," *Financial Times*, September 8, 2004. For a comprehensive assessment of the directive's business impact, see Tobias Lorenz, Baptiste Lebreton, and Luk N. Van Wassenhove, "The REACH Directive and its

"RoHS-like laws governing manufacturing are likely to be a global fact of doing business by electronics firms everywhere."[98]

Analysis

These differences between American and European policy approaches to reducing hazardous substances in electronic and electoral equipment do not stem from a divergence in public pressures: there has been relatively little public awareness or concern about the health risks of the hazardous substances in electronics on either side of the Atlantic. Rather, they reflect an important difference in their assessments of the health risks posed by the presence of these substances in landfills. The official position of the EPA is not that these substances are not toxic—they have clearly been identified as such—but rather that there is no evidence that their disposal in public waste streams has harmed public health. But the EU has adopted a precautionary approach: it considers their *potential* long-term negative impact on human health to be sufficient to justify an extensive effort to reduce their use in electronic products as well as to reduce the amount of e-waste disposed of in landfills.

WEEE and RoHS also reflects a a broader effort on the part of the European Union to fundamentally change the way products are made in order to make them more eco-friendly. While the idea of making industrial production more sustainable by promoting recycling, developing safer chemicals, and reducing the use of toxic substances is certainly not a European idea—the concept of sustainability has also gained wide currency in the United States—the EU has made it into a key component of its environmental risk regulations. By contrast, in the United States, sustainability is more closely identified with corporate environmental management and thus with the voluntary actions of industry. Expanding the scope of "extended produced responsibility" through legislation and regulation has not been an important priority of American policy makers at the federal level.

CONCLUSION

This chapter has compared American and European policies toward chemicals and hazardous substances. These demonstrate a broad pattern

---

Impact on the European Chemical Industry: A Critical Review," *Faculty and Research Working Paper* 53 (Fontainebleau: INSTEAD, April 2008).

[98] Ann Thyft, "Will RoHS Laws Go Global?" *Nikkei Electronics Asia* (May 2007), available at http://techon.nikkeibp.co.jp/article/HONSHI/20070424/131614/, accessed February 2009.

of relative American regulatory stringency before 1990 and more stringent European regulations since then. The latter pattern of policy divergence both reflects and illustrates the critical role of the precautionary principle in shaping European risk regulations: both REACH and RoHS were explicitly based on this approach to risk assessment. By contrast, in the United States, the federal government does not consider hazardous electronic wastes to pose any public health risks, and the criteria used to restrict or ban a chemical under TSCA are much more rigid than under REACH, as the asbestos case illustrates.

The cases in this chapter again highlight the marked contrast in the rate at which new risk regulations have been enacted by the American federal government and the European Union since 1990. The basic legislation governing chemical regulation in the United States has not been revised for more than three decades; nor has the federal government approved legislation banning toxic substances in electronics or established a national recycling program for electronic products. However, the policies of both state governments and global firms have brought American policies and practices more closely into alignment with those of the EU.

Taken together, WEEE, RoHS, and REACH represent an important change in the locus of international standard setting, with the EU replacing the United States "as the de facto setter of global product standards . . . Whereas U.S. chemical policy in the 1970s and the early 1980s often acted as an inspiration for European policymaking, the EU has taken over the role as leader in chemical policy development."[99]

[99] Selin and VanDeveer, "Raising Global Standards," 14.

CHAPTER SIX

Consumer Safety

THIS CHAPTER COMPARES European and American regulatory policies toward several additional non-food-related health and safety product risks, namely those posed by pharmaceuticals, and chemicals in children's toys and cosmetics. In contrast to many of the other policy areas examined in this book, two of the three cases examined in this chapter show that European and American risk regulations have converged, though the dynamics through which this occurred differed substantially.

Pharmaceutical regulation constitutes the most important exception to the broader pattern of increased transatlantic regulatory policy divergence. What makes this area of regulatory policy distinctive is that its political salience—or public pressures on policy makers to change how risk regulations were being made—increased in the United States but not in Europe. The demands of activist groups in the United States led to changes in American regulations in ways that brought them into closer alignment with those of the European Union, whose regulatory policies remained relatively stable even after they were harmonized. Pharmaceutical regulation also represents an important exception to the dominant pattern of transatlantic regulatory policy diffusion. In this unusual case, European regulatory policies *did* affect those of the United States, first by highlighting the transatlantic "drug lag," and more recently by American decisions to adopt some European practices to expedite drug approvals.

The regulation of phthalate softeners in children's products also converged in the EU and the United States, though with a substantial time lag. By contrast, cosmetics safety regulation demonstrates increased transatlantic policy divergence. While there has been no statutory change in American regulations for several decades, the European Union has progressively tightened and strengthened its safety standards for cosmetics. Many substances permitted in cosmetics sold in the United States are now banned in the European Union.

THE REGULATION OF PHARMACEUTICALS

The modern era of drug regulation on both sides of the Atlantic dates from the 1960s and is associated with the political fallout from the sedative thalidomide, which was taken by pregnant women for morning sickness. This drug was first introduced in Germany in 1957, where it was considered so safe that it was sold over the counter, and it was also marketed in forty-five other countries. Awareness of the drug's adverse effects began to emerge in 1961, when it was linked to a dramatic increase in the number of children born with birth defects, nearly half of whom died by their first birthday. By the time it was withdrawn in 1962, ten thousand children, mostly in Europe, and including four thousand in Germany, had been born with flippers instead of arms and legs. Because the drug had not been approved by the American Food and Drug Administration (FDA) and was only distributed on an experimental basis, only forty children were born with thalidomide-related birth defects in the United States. But it was the United States that responded by enacting the world's most comprehensive and stringent drug regulations.

Policy Changes in the United States

The origin of more stringent American drug policies pre-dates public disclosure of the health risks of thalidomide. In 1957, Democratic Senator Este Kefauver of Tennessee became chair of the Anti-trust and Monopoly Subcommittee of the Senate Judiciary Committee. As part of the committee's investigation of administrated prices, the subcommittee turned its attention to the drug industry's pricing policies, which it concluded were "generally unreasonable and excessive."[1] In an effort to encourage price competition, Kefauver proposed legislation restricting the granting of exclusive rights to drug patents to three years. However, as a result of strong opposition from the pharmaceutical industry, the full Judiciary Committee gutted the bill's key provisions. But three days after the much weakened bill had been approved by the Judiciary Committee, Morton Mintz published a front-page story in the *Washington Post* which reported that it was only the persistent efforts of Dr. Frances Kelsey, an FDA medical officer, which had prevented thalidomide the drug from being approved in the United States. He wrote: "This is the story of how the skepticism and stubbornness of a Government physician prevented what could have been an appalling American tragedy, the birth of hundreds or even thousands of armless and legless children."[2]

While it is not clear that Kelsey's role had in fact been critical—it was highly unlikely that the drug would have been approved by the FDA

---

[1] Quoted in Mark Nadel, *The Politics of Consumer Protection* (New York: Bobbs-Merrill, 1971), 123.

[2] Daniel Carpenter, *Reputation and Power: Organizational Image and Pharmaceutical Regulation at the FDA*, (Princeton, NJ: Princeton University Press, 2010), 242.

in any event—Mintz's article attracted national attention. A 1962 poll reported that more than three-quarters of Americans now favored "more strict" federal controls over drug approvals.[3] What was widely framed as a near policy failure dramatically transformed the terms of both public debate and public policy. Only three months after the article's publication, the Kefauver-Harris amendments to the Pure Food and Drug Act were signed into law by President John F. Kennedy.

Although the 1962 Kefauver-Harris amendments did not address Kefauver's original concern, namely the high price of drugs, they did significantly change government regulation of the pharmaceutical industry. The legislation's most important provision required manufacturers to provide "substantial evidence" that a new drug was "effective" before it could be approved. This standard was also applied retroactively to previously approved drugs. The 1962 amendments also involved the FDA in the clinical research process for the first time. Before testing any drug on humans, a firm was required to submit a drug investigational plan that included the results of animal testing as well as its plans for human tests. The FDA could then deny permission for further testing, request additional information, or modify the terms of the firm's proposed drug investigation plan.

Policy Changes in Europe

By contrast, the changes in European drug approval policies were much more modest. Germany was not only the country hardest hit by the thalidomide tragedy, but it was also the home of Chemie Grunenthal, the product's manufacturer. Germany was also the second largest producer of drugs in the world. In 1961, it had enacted legislation requiring federal registration of all new medicines.[4] While this law was strengthened in 1964 by requiring prescriptions for new drugs, Germany did not enact a comprehensive drug law with formal pre-market requirements for drug safety and efficacy until 1976. Moreover, this legislation did not apply to drugs licensed before 1971. The German legislation did strengthen controls over manufacturing practices, clinical investigations, and the protection of human subjects during clinical trials, but its provisions were substantially weaker than those enacted by the United States fourteen years earlier. In sharp contrast to the United States, German authorities preferred to leave improvements in drug testing procedures up to "indus-

---

[3] Ibid., 259.

[4] This paragraph and the following one are based on Philip Lee and Jessica Herzstein, "International Drug Regulation," *Annual Review of Public Health* (1986): 220–21.

try which has itself the liveliest and most direct interest in insuring the safety and effectiveness of its profits."[5]

The policy response in Britain was also more muted than in the United States. In 1963, the British Ministry of Health established a Committee on the Safety of Drugs (CSD), a group of experts responsible for under-taking pre-market safety reviews and approving the marketing of new drugs—nearly three decades after a similar regulatory system had been enacted in the United States. However, unlike in the United States, the CSD's system of controls was voluntary. It was not until 1968 that Brit-ain established a statutory basis for regulating the manufacture, label-ing, and import of all medicines for human use. Britain only began to require formal proof of efficacy in 1971—nine years after the United States. For its part, the EU enacted its first pharmaceutical directive in 1965. It established common criteria for quality, safety, and efficacy for national regulatory authorities to adopt before approving a new drug, though the latter requirement was much weaker than the one in force in the United States. But even this minimal standard was only adopted by seven of the (then) twelve member states. In 1975, the EU established a European regulatory authority for drugs, known as the Committee for Proprietary Medicinal Products (CPMP), as well as an EU-wide system of mutual recognition of drugs licensed by each member state. Under this system, if a country disagreed with another country's drug approval, it could seek arbitration from the CPMP. However, the CPMP's opinions were not binding and many national regulators still failed to recognize the drugs approved by other member states. As a result, through the mid-1980s, drug manufacturers continued to seek approvals at the national level and drug regulation remained unharmonized.

American and European Differences

After 1962, the American drug requirements became "the most strin-gent in the world."[6] "Precaution was the FDA's official watchdog in part because congressional oversight committees habitually announce hear-ings to rake the agency over the coals whenever the media accuses it of failing to protect the public from unsafe drugs and devices."[7]

---

[5] Carpenter, *Reputation and Power*, 264.

[6] Fredrik Andersson, "The Drug Lag Issue: The Debate Seen from an International Per-spective," *International Journal of Health Services* 22, no. 1 (1992): 70.

[7] Emphasis added. Frances Miller, "Medical Errors, New Drug Approval and Patient Safety," in *The Reality of Precaution: Comparing Risk Regulation in the United States and Europe*, ed. Jonathan Wiener, Michael Rogers, James Hammitt, and Peter Sand (Washing-ton, DC: Resources for the Future, 2011), 206.

More fearful of the political consequences of permitting the marketing of a drug that turned out to be unsafe, than in delaying approval of a drug that turned out to be both safe and effective, American regulatory officials regularly demanded extensive pre-market testing.

Both the costs of compliance and the time required for new drug approval increased substantially. Between 1963 and 1972, the development costs for a total new chemical entity (NCE) rose from $1.2 million to $11.5 million.[8] In 1979, the average drug took approximately ten years to get through the FDA's testing process, four times longer than before 1962.[9] As a result of more stringent testing requirements, average drug development times increased from 8.1 years during the 1960s to 14.2 years by the 1980s.[10] During the 1950s, "the attrition rate of drugs undergoing clinical tests was two out of three," but by the late 1970s, less than one out of every ten new compounds entering clinical trials became new products.[11]

German and British authorities continued to employ a more politically insulated or technocratic scientific review process. In Britain, "decisions about whether new drugs would be safe and effective on entering consumers' bodies were based on a model similar to the process in which scientific articles get accepted or rejected for publication in journals."[12] As the head of the British Department of Health's Medicines Division between 1977 and 1984 put it, "The role of regulators is in fact to achieve the release on to the market of those products which have had peer review which has shown them as satisfactory."[13] In 1986, the chairman of the CSD emphasized that "drug regulatory authorities should be immune from political and public pressure." He subsequently described the Committee's work as "concerned strictly with scientific issues," in marked contrast to the more politicized environment, owing to increased public risk awareness and pressures from Congress, in which the FDA now functioned.[14]

One of the most important policy consequences in Europe of the thalidomide disaster was to stimulate the development of systematic adverse

---

[8] Henry Grabowski, John Vernon, and Lacy Thomas, "Estimating the Effects of Regulation on Innovation: An International Comparative Analysis of the Pharmaceutical Industry," *Journal of Law and Economics* 21, no. 1 (1978): 136.

[9] American Enterprise Institute, *Proposals to Reform Drug Regulation Laws* (Washington, DC: American Enterprise Institute, 1979).

[10] Joseph A. DiMasi, "New Drug Development in the U.S. from 1963 to 1999," *Clinical Pharmacology & Therapeutics* 69, no. 5 (2001): 295.

[11] Grabowski, Vernon, and Thomas, "Estimating The Effects," 136.

[12] John Abraham and Graham Lewis, "Citizenship, Medical Expertise and the Capitalist Regulatory State in Europe," *Sociology* 36, no. 1 (2002): 71.

[13] Ibid.

[14] Ibid., 71–2.

drug reaction reporting. Virtually all European nations established formal mechanisms, known as "yellow card schemes," to provide early warning signals of adverse drug effects. These monitoring and reporting mechanisms frequently resulted in the withdrawal of previously approved drugs. In essence, while American drug regulation focused on preventing harmful effects *before* they occurred, European regulatory authorities placed greater emphasis on reducing harms to public health *after* they occurred. The former relied on assessing drug safety based on experimental or scientific data, while the latter was based primarily on actual evidence of harm to humans. Between 1972 and 1994, the percentage of drugs removed from the market in Great Britain was four times higher than in the United States, while several drugs removed from the British market had not been approved for use in the United States.[15]

The American "Drug Lag"

The relative stringency of American registration requirements after 1962 led to a widely publicized and extensively documented "drug lag"—a term first coined by Dr. William Wardell at a 1972 international conference in San Francisco.[16] During the 1960s, nearly four times as many new medicines were introduced in Britain as in the United States, while between 1963 and 1975, the relative drug lag between Britain and the United States averaged 2.1 years.[17] A study by the Government Accounting Office, which tracked the introduction of fourteen significant new drugs, found that thirteen were available in Europe before they were approved for use in the United States. A German study reported that while the United States remained, by a large margin, the leading producer of new drugs, it ranked ninth out of twelve countries in being the first nation to make such drugs available to its citizens.[18] Of the forty-seven major new drugs approved on either side of the Atlantic through 1973, Germany had introduced all forty-seven, France forty-four, Italy forty-three, and Britain forty-one, while the United States had introduced only thirty-one.[19]

The gap between American and European drug approval policies steadily widened through the mid-1980s. In 1985, nearly half of all

[15] Mary Wiktorowicz, "Emergent Patterns in the Regulation of Pharmaceuticals: Institutions and Interests in the U.S., Canada, Britain and France," *Journal of Health Politics, Policy, and Law* 28, no. 4 (2004): 625.

[16] Unless otherwise noted, the data in the following two paragraphs are drawn from Andersson, "The Drug Lag Issue," 53–72. The quotation is from page 70.

[17] Ibid., 56.

[18] American Enterprise Institute, *Proposals to Reform Drug Regulation Laws.*

[19] Andersson, "The Drug Lag Issue," 57.

U.S.-discovered NCEs had not yet been introduced in the United States, and more were being marketed in Germany than in the United States.[20] That same year, the average time required before marketing approval was granted in the United States was more than thirty months, compared to six months in both Great Britain and France.[21] However, the American drug lag was not the same with respect to all European countries. The rate at which new drugs were introduced in the United States was roughly comparable to that of Sweden, Denmark, and Norway, which had the strictest drug approval policies in Europe, but it was significantly slower than in the EU member states of Germany, Britain, France, and Italy. Between 1961 and 1985, Britain had the fastest approval times for drugs within the EU, followed by Germany.[22] From the point of view of British officials, drug regulation in the United States led to "inflexibility, rigidity, polarization and irrationality."[23]

Reforming Drug Regulation in the United States

In 1979, the House Committee on Science and Technology held the first hearings that criticized the FDA for being overly cautious, rather than insufficiently risk-averse, in approving new drugs. The following year, Democratic Representative James Scheurer of New York, accused the FDA of "contributing to needless suffering and death for thousands of Americans because it is denying them the life-enhancing and lifesaving drugs available elsewhere."[24] Two pharmacologists specifically cited the case of nitrazepam, a drug used to treat severe insomnia, which had been approved for use in Great Britain five years earlier than in the United States. They claimed that thousands of American lives might have been saved during those five years: "in view of the clear benefits demonstrable from some of the drugs introduced into Britain, it appears that the United States had lost more than it had gained from adopting a more conservative approach than did Britain in the post-thalidomide era."[25] In early 1981, the editorial page of the *Wall Street Journal* observed, "It is now clear that the FDA bureaucrats will never take any risks they can avoid. They have nothing to gain from approving an effective drug and everything to

---

[20]Ibid., 67.

[21]Wiktorowicz, "Emergent Patterns," 625.

[22]Abraham and Lewis, "Citizenship," 75.

[23]Frances McCrea and Gerald Markle, "The Estrogen Replacement Controversy in the USA and UK: Different Answers to the Same Question," *Social Studies Review of Science* 14, no. 1 (1984): 12.

[24]John Kelly, "Bridging America's Drug Gap," *New York Times*, September 13, 1981.

[25]William Wardell and Louis Lasagna, *Regulation and Drug Development* (Washington, DC: American Enterprise Institute, 1975), 105.

lose from making a mistake. This kind of approach guarantees a high loss of life."[26] The *WSJ* went on to argue that the FDA's delay in approving the beta-blocker propanolol, used to treat hypertension, anxiety, and panic, had resulted in ten thousand additional Americans deaths.

However, such criticisms had little policy impact until the mid-1980s, when the emergence and spread of AIDS initiated a significant transformation in the American approach to drug regulation. AIDS was a fatal disease that infected large numbers of individuals and for which no existing drugs were available to treat. Those who suffered from AIDS were not interested in waiting for new drugs to be adequately tested for safety and efficacy, since by the time the FDA had completed its lengthy review process, they might no longer be alive. Rather, they wanted immediate access to any drugs that might *possibly* help prolong their lives and reduce their suffering. In 1987, in response to vocal pressures from AIDS activists and their supporters, the FDA approved the drug AZT for the treatment of AIDS in only eighteen months. While this approval was faster than any drug in the FDA's history, this decision still failed to placate the agency's critics, who accused it of "prolonging the roll call of death."[27]

In June 1987, the FDA established new rules designed to expedite the availability of breakthrough drugs for very sick patients before their safety and effectiveness had been proven. The following year, the agency went a step further and announced a new drug approval process that it estimated would reduce the time necessary for the approval of promising new drugs designed to treat life-threatening illness by one-third to one-half. While prompted in large measure by the agency's still slow rate of approval for drugs to treat AIDS, this new policy was also designed to speed up the commercial availability of drugs for a number of other illnesses for which there were no effective treatments, including certain cancers, heart diseases, and brain seizures. As a result, the median approval time for new drugs falling within its purview declined from 26.7 months in 1993 to 19 months in 1994.[28]

In 1992, Congress adopted a new approach to reduce the agency's approval times for all drugs. The Prescription Drug User Fee Act (PDUFA) required firms to submit a user fee for each new drug application; these funds would then be given to the FDA's Center for Drug Evaluation and Research in order to enable it to increase the number of reviewers and thus expedite the drug approval process. This had long been the practice in several European countries. As part of the agreement that produced this legislation, the FDA agreed to review 90 percent of

[26] Carpenter, *Reputation and Power*, 368.

[27] Thomas Kiely, "Rushing Drugs to Market," *Technology Review* (August–September 1987): 13.

[28] "FDA Reform and the European Medicines Evaluation Agency," *Harvard Law Review* 108, no. 8 (June 1995): 2015.

all "standard" new molecular entities (NMEs) within twelve months by 1997, and 90 percent of "priority" drugs within six months. This legislation resulted in a further increase in drug approval times. For new pharmaceuticals processed under this legislation, the median approval time fell to 13.5 months, and to only 10.4 months for therapeutically important applications.[29]

The user fee program was renewed in 1997 by the FDA Modernization Act (FMA). This legislation also made a number of additional changes designed to further expedite the drug approval process.[30] One of its important provisions revised the definition of "substantial evidence" of drug effectiveness, safety, and quality. This allowed the FDA to base such evidence on data from only one clinical investigation, rather than from two trials which the agency was currently requiring. This policy change was strongly supported by the pharmaceutical industry, which had argued that replicating the first costly and complex clinical trial had created substantial disincentives for new drug development. For its part, Congress was concerned that maintaining the two-trial requirement would lead firms to seek initial regulatory approval from the recently created European Medicines Evaluation Agency (EMEA), which only required one trial. As a result, drug research, manufacturing, and marketing would move to Europe, and some firms might even forgo FDA approval altogether given the relatively large size of the European market.[31]

This legislation also led to increased industry consultation with the FDA on drugs under development and review, created a streamlined fast-track approval process, and established external advisory committees to help evaluate drug safety. After resisting such an approach for many years, the FDA adopted a further policy change taken from Europe: it began to authorize the use of third-party assessments for drug safety. Both statutes have "been a resounding success. . . . Supporters of the act(s) say regulators have met performance goals that just a decade ago seemed widely aggressive without compromising standards for safety and effectiveness."[32]

However, some public health advocates have expressed concern that user fees, which in 2000 covered half the FDA's costs for reviewing new drug applications, have made the agency too beholden to industry and also contributed to a "sweatshop" environment, where reviewers are under ever-increasing pressure to approve drugs as rapidly as possible. Their concerns were buttressed by the FDA's recall between 1999 and

[29] Ibid.

[30] Wiktorowicz, "Emergent Patterns," 635.

[31] Jennifer Kulynych, "Will the FDA Relinquish the 'Gold Standard' for New Drug Approval? Redefining 'Substantial Evidence' in the FDA Modernization Act of 1997," *Food and Drug Law Journal* 54 (1999): 127–49.

[32] Naomi Aoki, "A Question of Speed and Safety," *Boston Globe*, November 28, 2001.

2001 of nearly one dozen drugs implicated in more than one thousand deaths, though it is unclear how many of these approvals were due to the FDA's expedited review process. Ironically, the reduction in the FDA's time to review new drugs has meant that American regulators were no longer in a position to observe how patients in European countries were responding to a new drug before deciding whether or not to approve it.

Centralizing Drug Regulation in Europe

A major change in drug regulation also took place in Europe. Following approval of the Maastricht Treaty on European Union in 1992, which gave the EU binding authority on some heath care issues, the European Commission undertook a major new initiative to harmonize national drug approval policies.[33] European legislation established a new regulatory institution, the EMEA, and two new regulatory procedures.[34]

A centralized application procedure placed final regulatory approval at the EU level for the first time. It permitted manufacturers to submit applications directly to the European Agency, which then refers them to a scientific advisory committee for evaluation; the latter is required to issue its opinion within 219 days. Final approval rests with the European Commission, which then has ninety days to draft its own opinion. If the Commission grants marketing authorization, it automatically becomes valid throughout the EU for renewable periods of five years. The EMEA centralized approval process was intended to be relatively rapid, with application to final approval to take a maximum of ten months; this was more than twice as fast as many member state drug regulatory agencies.[35] The EU also established a decentralized approval procedure. Beginning on January 1, 1998, any member state that received an application for a product which had been approved by another member of the Union was required to either recognize that approval, or refer the application to the CPMP for binding arbitration. Thus, pharmaceutical products became, for the first time, subject to mutual recognition under the auspices of the EMEA.

Since companies could now submit one application, rather than fifteen, it was predicted that firms would save up to $5 million annually in national clinical staff and testing equipment.[36] While the application fee for submitting a drug to the EMEA is high—a typical filing costs

---

[33]Tessa Richards, "How Should European Health Policy Be Developed?" *British Medical Journal* 309 (1994): 116.

[34]Richard Kingham, Peter Bogaert, and Pamela Eddy, "The New European Medicines Agency," *Food and Drug Law Journal* 49 (1994): 303.

[35]Ibid., 307.

[36]Ibid.

approximately 200,000 euros—this is about half of what it would have cost to pay all fifteen national registration fees. Centralized approval also enables firms to use identical package inserts and make similar promotional claims throughout the EU.

Transatlantic Policy Convergence

Both American and European drug approval authorities are now substantially funded by application fees submitted by the pharmaceutical industry. The EMEA's standards for new drug approvals are roughly comparable to those of the FDA, making this one of the few important examples of increased transatlantic regulatory convergence after 1990. However, the EMEA, consistent with the emphasis member states have placed on monitoring drug performance after approval, does require more extensive post-market regulation than does the FDA. In Europe, drugs are only approved for an initial five-year period, after which their renewal may require additional safety or effectiveness data.

Largely because of the changes made in drug approval procedures in the United States during the 1990s, a new drug is as likely to be first approved in the United States as in Europe. The "drug lag" has essentially disappeared. During the mid-1990s, 40 percent of the world's new drugs were first approved in the United States. According to FDA Commissioner David Kessler, "Americans [now] have access to essentially all clinically important drugs that are available anywhere else in the world."[37]

According to the Tufts Center for the Study of Drug Development, between 1996 and 1998 the median approval times for thirty drugs approved by both the FDA and the EMEA were virtually identical. The FDA approved sixteen products faster than did the EMEA, while the EMEA approved fourteen products more rapidly than the FDA.[38] An updated study issued in 2007 found the mean approval times for seventy-one new medicinal products approved by both regulatory agencies between 2000 and 2005 was 15.8 months in Europe and 15.7 months in the United States.[39]

---

[37] Quoted in David Vogel, "The Globalization of Pharmaceutical Regulation," *Governance* 11, no. 1 (January 1998): 15.

[38] Tufts Center for the Study of Drug Development, "European and U.S. Approval Times for New Drugs Are Virtually Identical," *Impact Report* 1 (November, 1999), available at http://csdd.tufts.edu/InfoServices/ImpactReportsArchive.asp?subsection=1999, accessed March 2009.

[39] Tufts Center for the Study of Drug Development, "EMEA Meets Performance Goals, But Lags U.S. FDA in Drug Approvals," *Impact Report* 9, no. 1 (January/February, 2007), available at http://csdd.tufts.edu/InfoServices/ImpactReportsArchive.asp?subsection=2007, accessed March 2009.

Increased International Cooperation

The development of the EU's regulatory capacity for pharmaceuticals has affected the balance of power between the United States and Europe in this policy area.[40] Formerly, the FDA was the world's most influential regulatory body, and regulatory authorities in other countries, including in Europe, subsequently adopted many of its policies and procedures, though at a slower rate. But with the increase in the EU's regulatory capacity over pharmaceuticals, the FDA and the EMEA have become co-equal voices in shaping global drug approval policies, even though the size of the American pharmaceutical market is substantially larger than that of the EU (the United States accounts for roughly half of all global pharmaceutical sales).

In marked contrast to many other areas of risk regulations, this policy arena has witnessed a significant increase in transatlantic regulatory cooperation. In 1990, the FDA and the European Commission completed a Memorandum of Understanding that standardized good manufacturing and laboratory practices. The following year, they agreed to harmonize the names of health care products. Between 1992 and 1995, the FDA published four rules in the Federal Registrar which progressively eliminated barriers to sharing information with its foreign counterparts.

In 2007, the FDA and the EMEA agreed on a joint approval process for orphan drugs, which are used to treat rare diseases. The FDA has also begun to accept, in some cases, data from clinical trials conducted on foreign subjects or under the supervision of foreign regulators. It has also agreed to international guidelines for adverse drug reacting, carcinogenicity testing, and the duration of toxicity testing, each of which required changes in American standards. After decades of resistance, the FDA has also adopted the European practices of outsourcing part of the review process to private firms. Finally, as noted above, the United States now uses the European practice of charging drug firms for their applications, and these fees pay for additional staff to expedite the drug approval process.

Analysis

The marked differences in the policy responses of the United States on one hand, and Germany and Britain, on the other, to the thalidomide policy failure during the early 1960s, demonstrates that there is not

---

[40]This section is based on Vogel, "The Globalization of Pharmaceutical Regulation," 1–22, and David Bach and Abraham Newman, "Governing Lipitor and Listerine: Capacity, Sequencing, and Power in International Pharmaceutical and Cosmetics Regulation," *Review of International Political Economy*,14, no. 4 (2010): 665–95.

necessarily a causal relationship between an "unfortunate event"—even one as dramatic as a massive increase in birth defects clearly linked to a false negative regulatory policy failure—and the adoption of more stringent risk regulations. Far more Europeans than Americans were injured from thalidomide, yet it was the United States which responding by adopting far more sweeping regulatory changes. By contrast, while more stringent approval policies were introduced in Europe—many of which were modeled on those of the United States—they were adopted more gradually and were much less demanding. In this case, as in many others described in previous chapters, "alarm bells" about insufficiently protective regulations and the risks of false negatives rang much more loudly in the United States than in Europe before 1990.

But transatlantic drug approval politics and policies after around 1990 reveal a very different pattern. Public demands for more stringent risk regulations did *not* increase in Europe and thus European risk management policies did *not* become progressively more stringent: on the contrary, they became *more* flexible. Drug approval policies in Europe have been notably unaffected by the otherwise increasingly important influence of the precautionary principle as a guide to European risk management decisions.

Rather, the Europeanization of drug approval policies and procedures has been entirely shaped by the common interests of the European Commission and the pharmaceutical industry in creating a single market for drugs and thus making the process of having them available throughout the EU less burdensome. In this sense, it represents a throwback to the European environmental directives enacted prior to the mid-1980s, which were also motivated primarily by the goal of reducing intra-European trade barriers. In contrast to the changes in how many other risk management decisions have recently been made in Europe, in the case of pharmaceuticals, "policy decisions about risk, remained, as before, the preserve of experienced bureaucrats and their established advisory networks."[41]

The changes in American drug approval policies also demonstrate continuity both before and after around 1990, though in a very different way. Since the early 1960s, they have continued to be highly politicized and shaped by public demands. What *has* changed is the nature of those demands. Beginning around 1960 and continuing for nearly two decades, the FDA's risk management policies for drugs were largely shaped by the legacy of thalidomide. This meant that the agency's primary policy priority was to avoid the risks of false negatives, i.e., approving drugs that turned out to be unsafe. What happened beginning in the mid-1980s

[41]Sheila Jasanoff, "American Exceptionalism and the Political Acknowledgement of Risk," in *Risk*, ed. Edward Burger (Ann Arbor: University of Michigan Press, 1993), 63, 66.

is that, thanks in part to pressures from AIDS activists, the risks of false positives—i.e., delaying the approval of drugs that turned out to be beneficial—became much more politically salient.

Pressure from AIDS activists was not the only source of public pressure on the FDA; for example, groups involved in cancer treatment also wanted more rapid drug approvals, as did pharmaceutical firms. But the "alarm bells" rung by AIDS activists about the harmful effects of too slow drug approvals did resonate with both the public and policy makers: they created a policy window that brought about a series of policy changes—some incremental and others more substantial—whose cumulative impact was to effectively end the transatlantic "drug lag."

While the broad changes in American drug approval policies beginning in the late 1980s and accelerating during the 1990s were primarily a response to domestic pressures, the widely publicized and increasingly influential claims about a drug lag between American and European drug approvals also underlay the American policy change. The FDA also adopted two long-standing European policy approaches, namely, charging firms for applications and outsourcing assessments for drug safety testing. Significantly, this unusual example of American regulatory emulation stemmed from a European approach to risk regulation that had *not* become more stringent.

Because the FDA's new policy goal of avoiding false positive errors was similar to European regulatory priorities, which have always placed greater emphasis on expediting drug approvals, the result was a rare example of transatlantic policy convergence—and cooperation. Nonetheless, the United States and the EU arrived at comparable policies through very different means, namely public pressures by those who wanted more drugs to be made available more quickly in the case of the former, and an interest in giving pharmaceutical firms more rapid access to a single European market in the latter.

PHTHALATES IN CHILDREN'S PRODUCTS

Phthalates are a group of several colorless, odorless liquids produced by reacting phthalic anydride with alcohols and eliminated water. Because they are a family of existing chemicals, they are not subject to the screening for toxicity that is required for new chemicals. Polyvinyl chloride (PVC) is a rigid material that can be softened by the addition of plasticizers. The most commonly used plasticizers are various kinds of phthalates, which are used to make plastic products more flexible. Phthalates have been in widespread use for nearly fifty years. They are found in a large number of products, including cars, floor tiles, shower curtains, cosmetics, medical devices such as tubing and fluid containers, as well as products for children such as bath toys, books, rattles, teethers, bibs, dolls, and plastic figures.

Because of their loose chemical bond, they can leach into the human body through the mouth or skin, where they can interfere with reproductive hormones, and are thus suspected to be endocrine disrupters. The United States was one of the first countries to address the health hazards of phthalates for children. During the mid-1980s, the EPA classified one phthalate, DEHP, as a potential human carcinogen. In 1986, under a voluntary agreement between the toy industry and the Consumer Product Safety Commission (CPSC), toy manufacturers stopped using DEHP and instead switched to another phthalate, DINP. However, no testing was done for DINP, though it presented similar health risks.

Risk Perceptions in Europe

The potential health hazards of phthalates first emerged as a political issue in Europe in 1997, when Danish authorities informed the European Commission that they had issued emergency warnings for teething rings manufactured in China for an Italian company.[42] According to a study by the Danish Environmental Protection Agency, these products released various phthalates in quantities that posed health hazards to babies. While the teethers did conform to the EU's safety standards, the firm agreed to voluntarily withdraw them, pending its own study. The firm's subsequent research, based on the most recent testing methods to determine the migration of phthalates in items destined for children, concluded that the teething rings posed no health risks. But shortly afterward, regulatory authorities in both the Netherlands and Sweden also expressed concerns about potentially dangerous levels of phthalate migration in products used by children.

During the mid-1990s, Greenpeace began an international campaign to alert the public to the adverse health effects of PVC infant toys, which, according to the organization's own studies, included liver and kidney damage leading to cancer, and reproductive abnormalities. This campaign was highly successful in Europe as it was linked to increased public skepticism about industry and government claims about product safety following the BSE crisis (as discussed in chapter 3). "Europeans have become

---

[42]This section draws upon Bill Durodie, "Plastic Panics: European Risk Regulation in the Aftermath of BSE," in *Rethinking Risk and the Precautionary Principle*, ed. Julian Morris (Oxford: Butterworth Heinemann, 2000), 140–66.

more willing to see risks in products and NGOs can . . . put pressure on governments who may be more receptive to the precautionary principle."[43]

The Greenpeace campaign against the use of phthalates in PVCs was supported by a number of prominent European politicians. The Consumer Affairs Minister of Austria stated that "based on precautionary consumer protection, PVC toys are not desirable," while the Belgian Minister for Public Health urged retailers to "voluntarily discontinue marketing these products."[44] Associations of retailers in Belgium, Germany, and Italy called upon their members to withdraw all soft PVC products designed to be chewed by young children. In February 1998, the European Commission removed all soft PVC teething toys from its own childcare facilities.

This latter decision further strengthened the public campaign against PVCs; after all, if these products were judged unsafe for the children of Commission employees, why should other European children be exposed to them? Prompted by a "naming and shaming" campaign by Greenpeace, many European retailers ordered their stores to remove all soft PVC toys. Responding to growing consumer concern about the safety of toys with phthalate softeners, Mattel, the world's largest toymaker, announced that it would make its plastic toys out of organically based materials, rather than plastics. Other global firms based in Europe, including LEGO, IKEA, and the Body Shop, also pledged to go "PVC-free."

In November 1997, the European Commission requested that the newly established Scientific Committee on Toxicity, Ecotoxicity, and the Environment (CSTEE) review the scientific evidence on the health impact of soft PVC toys containing phthalates that could be placed in the mouths of children. The committee's working group reviewed several existing studies and recommended margin of safety estimates for each of the six phthalates found in infant teething rings. Subsequently, a Dutch group of scientists reported the results of a study based on the oral leaching of phthalates by adult human volunteers. It concluded that the possibility of a baby exceeding the recommended limits was "so rare that the statistical likelihood cannot be estimated," adding that previous estimates as to how much time children spent chewing on soft PVC products had been grossly exaggerated.[45] Its conclusions were collaborated by an Austrian study, as well as a report on the actual levels of phthalate release issued by the U.S. CPSC.

[43] Alastair Lles, "Identifying Environmental Health Risks in Consumer Products: Nongovernment Organizations and Civic Epistemologies," *Public Understanding of Science* 16 (2007): 379.

[44] Durodie, "Plastic Panics," 148.

[45] Ibid., 156.

The European Phthalate Ban

The European toy industry now assumed that their position on the safety of soft PVC products had been vindicated. However, a Commission Risk Evaluation Unit decided to adopt a more stringent margin of safety for phthalate exposure. It accordingly recommended that the Commission "should be looking for a phase out of phthalates as soon as possible."[46] This recommendation reflected not only the growth in public concern about the impact of phthalates on the health of children, but the fact that eight member states had already enacted their own more stringent restrictions. Concerned about impending regulatory action in Europe, Vernon Weaver, the American Ambassador to the EU, warned the European Commission that "sudden bans on products which have been sold for years and which is based on incomplete and perhaps erroneous information could cause a trade misunderstanding between the U.S. and the EU."[47]

In December 1999, the European Commission issued a temporary European-wide ban. Specifically, PVC articles that were intended for placement in the mouths of children under three years of age could not contain more than 0.1 percent by weight of six different types of phthalates. For those soft PVC toys that were not intended to be placed in the mouths of children, but nevertheless might be chewed, it required a warning label indicating the presence of phthalates. This ban was strongly criticized by the European Council for Plasticizers, which blamed Greenpeace's "alarmist and totally misguided stories for creating anxiety on the part of parents." According to a chemist employed by the Confederation of European Chemical Industries, the EU's phthalate ban was prompted by "politicians' desire to appear to be protecting their constituents from scientifically unproven risks."[48]

The emergency ban was initially put in place for three months, but was repeatedly extended, and in 2004, the Commission, European Council, and the European Parliament voted to make it permanent.[49] This legislation also went beyond the scope of the temporary restriction by extending the ban to all toys, not just those intended for very young children. It prohibited the three phthalates deemed to be toxic, namely DEHP, DBP, and BBP, from *all* toys and child-care articles, while the three other phthalates, namely DINP, DOBP, and DNOP, whose risks were still

[46] Ibid., 153.

[47] Ibid., 158.

[48] Mark Schapiro, "Toxic Toys: Why Europe's Children Are Safer Than Ours," *The Nation*, November 5, 2007, 14.

[49] "Six Chemicals in Soft Plastic Toys Banned Across Europe," *Environment News Service*, July 6, 2005, available at http://www.ens-newswire.com/ens/jul2005/2005-07-06-05.asp, accessed February 2009.

unclear, were banned from *any* toys that *could* be placed in the mouths by children, regardless of whether this was their intended use. Markos Kypianou, the European Commissioner for Health and Consumer Protection, applauded the EU's action, stating that "Toxic chemicals have no place in children's toys. Our action on phthalates shows that when a risk is identified, the EU can act effectively to protect the health of its children."[50]

While Greenpeace was pleased that "the forces of good have finally won out," the European Council of Vinyl Manufacturers expressed "serious concern" that "political decisions [have been] taken which are totally opposite to the outcome of the EU's risk assessments." The trade association's executive director stated:

> We would like to state on this occasion that the PVC industry has always put on the market safe products, which have been used for more than 50 years, without any measurable impact on health or the environment. There is absolutely no reason to limit the use of PVC in any application. DINP has undergone an EU Scientific Risk Assessment and the outcome was clearly that children are not at risk for the use of DINP in any toys.

He added, "DINP has also been investigated by the Consumer Protection Safety Commission in the United States and it also confirmed that there is no health risk from its use in toys."[51] According to the European Council for Plasticizers and Intermediates, the EU's decision was "based on a lot of exaggerated and often incorrect claims about alleged adverse health effects from phthalates. Politicians have been misled into believing that children's health is being endangered. . . . Their(s) is an entirely political decision that misuses the precautionary principle."[52]

Several other countries then followed the EU, including Japan, Norway, Argentina, Mexico, and Canada; they either banned various phthalates from most infant toys or specifically from teethers and rattles. By 2007, sixteen countries had adopted some kind of phthalate ban on children's products—although the United States was not one of them.

Phthalate Restrictions in the United States

Greenpeace's campaign against phthalates gained political traction more slowly in the United States. This was partially due to the fact that one phthalate, DEHP, had already been voluntarily withdrawn from the American market following the recommendation of the CPSC. Also,

---

[50] Ibid.
[51] Ibid.
[52] "Permanent Phthalates Ban in Toys Approved," *EurActiv.com*, July 5, 2005, available at http://www.euractiv.com/en/health/permanent-phthalates-ban-toys-approved/article-142028, accessed February 2009.

most pacifiers sold in the United States were made from latex rather than PVC. But in 1998, acting in response to public pressure from Greenpeace, several American toy manufacturers, as well as the retailers Toys 'R' Us and McDonalds, announced that they would phase out soft PVC products intended for children. More than one hundred hospitals subsequently began to remove products containing phthalates from their neonatal nurseries in order to protect the hormonal development of male children.

In December 1998, the CPSC reported the results of a study on DINP (referred to above) that concluded that "the amount ingested does not even come close to a harmful level." Nevertheless, the regulatory agency did request firms, "as a precautionary measure, while more scientific work is done, to stop selling PVC pacifiers, nipples, rattles, and teething toys."[53] This voluntary ban, however, only covered phthalates in products specifically intended for oral use. In early 2003, it decided not to ban DINP based on new scientific studies conducted between 2000 and 2003 which had concluded that children only faced a significant risk if they placed soft toys in their mouth for more than 75 minutes a day—but that few children did so. "The regulatory responses in Europe and the United States . . . diverged, reflecting different views on whether chemicals in products warrant precautionary intervention despite uncertainties in scientific knowledge."[54]

As a result of the voluntary actions of a number of global firms, the number of children's products containing phthalates sold in the United States declined. But the branded products made or sold by multinational firms only accounted for 60 percent of American sales; the remainder were made by generic brands and often sold on the Internet. This meant that many children's products containing phthalates were still being sold in the United States. A chemical analysis of infant playthings conducted by Environment California and the Public Interest Research Group found that fifteen of the eighteen teethers, bath books, and bath toys it tested contained one or another of the six phthalates banned by the EU.[55] In China, where most toy manufacturing takes place, toys continued to be produced with phthalates for the American market, but without them for sale in Europe.

In October 2007, in response to both the EU's phthalate ban and the failure of the federal government to enact its own regulations, California enacted legislation prohibiting the sale of products containing phthalates

[53] Durodie, "Plastic Panics," 58.

[54] Lles, "Ientifying Environmental Health Risks," 381.

[55] Mark Schapiro, *Exposed: The Toxic Chemistry of Everyday Products and What's at Stake for American Power* (White River Junction, VT: Chelsea Green Publishing, 2007), 17.

in any item intended for use by children under the age of three. According to the bill's author, Democratic Assemblywoman Fiona Ma of San Francisco, "California continues to lead the nation in protecting children from dangerous chemicals and in safeguarding our environment." This bill "sends a clear message to the Consumer Product Safety Commission that if the Bush Administration won't act, states will."[56]

However, American business associations, like their counterparts in Europe, continued to insist on the safety of phthalates. According to the president of the American Chemistry Council, "This [California] law is the product of the politics of fear. It is not good science, and it is not good government. Though scientific reviews in this country and in Europe have found these toys safe for children to use, California businesses will be obligated to take products off the shelves that their customers need and want."[57]

Policy Convergence

In August 2008, in response to widespread media attention and public outrage stemming from high levels of lead in toys imported from China as well as other toy safety hazards—which led to the recall of forty-five million toys and other children's products, including thirty million from China—the United States significantly strengthened its consumer safety standards. The Consumer Product Safety Act (CPSA) represents one of the few more stringent risk regulations enacted by Congress after 1990. It banned lead, beyond minute quantities, from products for children twelve years or younger, and reduced the maximum allowable amount of lead in paint. In this case, the American federal government enacted a more risk-averse statute than the EU, which had not yet strengthened its restrictions on lead in children's products.

The CPSA also included a less publicized provision that banned the same six phthalates the EU had restricted since 1999 from children's products. Like the EU, the American legislation divided these phthalates into two categories: the three deemed toxic by the EU were permanently banned in all children's products, while the other three were provisionally banned from child-care products and children's toys that can be put in a child's mouth, pending the results of further research by the CPSC. Democratic Senator Diane Feinstein of California, on whose initiative the phthalate ban had been added to the bill, informed her fellow legislators:

---

[56] Ibid.

[57] Elizabeth Weise, "California First to Ban Phthalates in Baby Products," *USA Today*, October 16, 2007.

I believe this legislation is important as the first national effort to begin to exercise a *precautionary principle* in the use of chemicals as additives to products that affect human health. It is my belief that chemical additives should not be placed in products that can impact health adversely until they are tested and found to be benign. . . . I am confident that when more science comes in, it will prove that all phthalates are harmful to children and should be permanently banned.[58]

Republican Representative Joe Barton of Texas, the ranking minority member of the House Energy and Commerce Committee, initially opposed the phthalate ban, but then reluctantly agreed to support it. While acknowledging that the Senate-House conference committee had "reached a sensible compromise on the use of phthalates," Barton cautioned that "it's also important that we use unbiased, confirmable science to sort out the real dangers from the mythical ones."[59] The White House supported the phthalate ban although Keith Hennessey, director of the White House National Economic Council, cautioned Congress that "banning a product before a conclusive, scientific determination is reached is short-sighted and may result in the introduction of unregulated substitute chemicals that may harm children's health."[60]

However, it was vigorously opposed by ExxonMobil Chemical, the major American manufacturer of DINP, the phthalate most extensively used in children's toys. The company noted that in 2003, the CPSC had determined that soft plastic toys posed no threat to children's health. The firm also cited a 2004 Commission staff report that cautioned against the risks of removing DINP from children's toys as weaker or brittle plastics without DINP may pose a choking hazard to children.[61]

This legislation, which also increased the budget and strengthened the enforcement authority of the CPSC, represented "the most comprehensive overhaul of U.S. consumer-product oversight in a generation" and was hailed as being long overdue by consumer safety and public health advocates.[62] The *Washington Post* noted that the success of Feinstein's amendment was "a rarity—the first time Congress had banned a chemical in decades."[63]

---

[58]Emphasis added. "The Vinyl Countdown," *ICIS Chemical Business*, October 1, 2008, available at http://www.icis.com/Articles/2008/10/06/9160591/us-phthalates-ban-in-childrens-toys-looms.html, accessed February 2009.

[59]Ibid.

[60]Ibid.

[61]Ibid.

[62]Melanie Trottman, "Lawmakers Clinch Deal to Overall Product Safety," *Wall Street Journal*, July 1, 2008.

[63]Lyndsey Layton, "California Scheming," *Washington Post National Weekly Edition*, January 5–11, 2009.

Four months after the passage of the CPSA in the United States, the EU, as part of a broader set of regulations to strengthen its own rules on toy safety, banned or restricted the use of several dangerous chemicals in toys. The immediate impetus for this directive, which had been under discussion in the European Commission since 1998, was similar to that behind the American toy protection statute, namely the 2007 recall of 20 million Chinese-made toys because they contained excessive lead paint and other unsafe parts. This directive prohibited the use of all chemicals that are believed to be linked to cancer, changing genetic information or harming reproduction, in accessible parts of toys. It also specifically banned the intentional use of both lead and mercury in children's toys.[64]

The EU's tolerance levels for lead are now essentially the same as that of the United States; both allow minute quantities of the heavy metals at levels that are not considered dangerous. But Europe's toy protection standard also bans fifty-five allergenic substances. Moreover, while hazardous substances in electronic toys are not covered by any federal regulation in the United States, in Europe they are restricted by the Restriction of Hazardous Substances (RoHS) directive, which applies to all electrical products.

Analysis

The politics and policies informing the European response to the health risks posed to children from contact with phthalates resemble those that occurred more than a decade earlier with respect to the health risks of beef hormones. In both cases, public pressures prompted the EU to adopt a highly stringent risk regulation. For their part, federal regulators did express concern about the safety of phthalates in children's products, but acting on the basis of much of the same scientific evidence available to European policy makers, they did not consider a ban to be warranted. However, in this rather unusual case, thanks to Senator Feinstein's ability to persuade Congress to include a provision in the CPSA imposing restrictions on phthalates in children's products similar to that previously adopted by both the EU and California, the United States also adopted a precautionary approach to the risks posed by the chemical softeners in children's products.

While strong public pressures along with considerable business support made it highly likely that the CPSA would have been enacted even if Republicans had retained their Congressional majorities, the passage of

---

[64] "New EU Rules for Safe Toys for Our Children," Europa Press Release IP/08/2026 (December 18, 2008), available at http://europa.eu/rapid/pressReleasesAction.do?reference =IP/08/2026&format=HTML&aged=0&language=EN&guiLanguage=en, accessed February 2009.

Feinstein's amendment was likely facilitated by the fact that the Democrats had regained control of both houses of Congress in 2007. Had they remained in the minority, the Republican congressional leadership may well have chosen to defer to the risk assessment of the CPSC, which had determined that most of the phthalates in children's products did not pose any safety risks. After all, the "alarm bells" that led to the passage of the CPSA had focused on the safety of toys, not on whether any chemicals currently permitted in the United States should now be banned. Feinstein was able to take advantage of the policy window created by public outrage over unsafe toys from China to have a ban on phthalates included in the CPSC.

COSMETICS SAFETY

By contrast, the safety of the ingredients used in cosmetics and other personal care products demonstrates steadily increasing European regulatory stringency after 1990.[65]

In the United States, the safety of cosmetics products is primarily the responsibility of their manufacturers. The Cosmetics Ingredients Review (CIR) board, established in 1976, is funded by the industry trade association, with support from both the FDA and the Consumer Federation of America. It reviews and assesses the safety of the more commonly used ingredients in cosmetics, primarily basing its assessments on studies in scientific journals. It then classifies them according to their known or probable risks. But the CIR has no legal authority and the FDA is not obligated to act on its findings. This means that "the FDA has in practice no formal authority to control market access and has comparatively little expertise in cosmetics. . . . The U.S. market, in short, has a weak regulatory structure with limited government monitoring and enforcement."[66] Since the 1960s, there have been no statutory changes in federal cosmetics regulation in the United States. The scope of the American CIR expert panel remains limited; only 11 percent of the 10,500 ingredients found in cosmetics products have been assessed for safety by the panel.[67]

[65] For a comprehensive, but in the case of the EU now dated, comparative description of cosmetics regulations, see "A Comparative Study of Cosmetics Legislation in the EU and Other Principal Markets with Special Attention to so-called Borderline Products," Final Report prepared for the European Commission, DG Enterprise (2004), available at http://ec.europa.eu/enterprise/cosmetics/doc/j457_-_final_report_-_cosmetics.pdf, accessed March 2009.

[66] Bach and Newman, "Governing Lipitor and Listerine," 685.

[67] Tim Little, Sanford Lewis, and Pamela Lundquist, "Beneath the Skin: Hidden Liabilities, Market Risk and Drivers of Change in the Cosmetics and Personal Care Industry," *Investor Environmental Health Network*, 2007, 8, available at http://www.iehn.org/publications.reports.php, accessed March 2009.

Cosmetics regulatory action by the FDA is triggered primarily by adverse reaction reports, whose submission by firms is voluntary.[68]

The Strengthening of European Regulations

In contrast to the United States, the process for proscribing or restricting chemical ingredients in the EU has become more formalized, and more risk-averse. In 1997, the EU created the Scientific Committee on Cosmetic Products, subsequently renamed the Scientific Committee on Consumer Products. This committee is comprised of an independent group of scientists with expertise in risk assessment; its members are appointed from each member state by the European Commission. It is responsible for recommending and reviewing both negative lists of substances, whose use is either prohibited or restricted, and positive lists of ingredients that fall into three categories: colorants, preservatives, and ultraviolet filters. New substances that fall into the latter three categories are subject to a scientific evaluation of their risk by the committee's members.

Between 1976 and 2002, the EU Cosmetics Directive was amended seven times. There were thirty-one changes in the composition of its "positive" and "negative" lists known as "Annexes." The latter have been made primarily under successive amendments to the 1976 directive, which have progressively introduced more stringent cosmetics safety standards. By 2002, the list of banned or restricted cosmetics ingredients had grown substantially; more than four hundred substances fell into the positive category and more than ninety into the negative category.

Since 2002, the EU has steadily strengthened its cosmetics safety regulations. The most important statutory change was the Seventh Amendment to the Cosmetics Directive, which was approved in 2003 and became effective in March 2005. The Seventh Amendment prohibited the use of three major classes of toxic ingredients, namely those which pose the risk of cancer, cause hormonal or reproductive disturbances, or can cause genetic damage. (This amendment also included a highly controversial provision phasing out the testing of cosmetics products or their ingredients on laboratory animals within Europe, which applies to both imported products and their ingredients.)[69] This amendment more than doubled the number of prohibited ingredients. As a result, the number of substances banned from use in cosmetics products grew to one thousand.

By contrast, as of 2005, less than two dozen chemicals have been restricted or banned for use in cosmetic products in the United

[68] Ibid.

[69] "U.S. and EU Approaches to Chemical Safety," The Breast Cancer Fund. available at www.SafeCosmetics.org, accessed March 2009.

States.[70] In 2010, a further divergence between European and American labeling requirements emerged: the EU introduced mandatory labeling requirements for nanoscale ingredients used in cosmetics, becoming the first political jurisdiction to do so. However, the FDA has recommended against both permissible and mandatory labeling on the grounds that "the current science does not support a finding that classes of products with nanoscale materials necessarily present greater safety concerns than classes of products without nanoscale materials"—a policy consistent with the FDA's approach toward the labeling of food with genetically modified ingredients.[71]

Thanks to the increase in its regulatory expertise, its control over market access, the stringency of its standards, and the size of its market for cosmetics—the EU accounted for 29 percent of global cosmetics sales in 2006, while the United States accounted for 21 percent—Europe has become the de facto international standard setter for cosmetics regulation. In cosmetics, "Europe is the undisputed international regulatory hegemon."[72] The extraterritorial application of European cosmetics rules has been actively encouraged by the European Commission, which has sent technical experts to several countries to help strengthen their regulatory capacities and invited foreign regulatory officials to attend Commission-sponsored training programs in Europe. The Mercosur countries, namely Argentina, Brazil, Paraguay, and Uruguay, have enacted legislation that authorizes their regulatory agencies to develop negative and positive lists similar to those of the EU.

The ten members of ASEAN have adopted legislation that is essentially based on European regulations: they employ the European Commission's lists of positive and negative ingredients. One of the provisions of the ASEAN directive on cosmetics regulation requires the monitoring of regulatory developments in Europe, which means that as additional ingredients in cosmetics are restricted by the European Union, they are also likely to be adopted by the ASEAN countries. China has increased the number of substances banned from cosmetics from 412 to more than 1,200, thus bringing Chinese regulations into closer alignment with those of the EU.[73]

---

[70] "Citizens Advisers Releases Research Examining EU Rules for the Cosmetics Industry: What They Mean for U.S. Companies, Consumers and Shareholders?" The Campaign for Safe Cosmetics (October 3, 2005), available at http://www.safecosmetics.org/article.php?id=148, accessed March 2009.

[71] Joel D'Silva and Diana Megan Bowman, "To Label or Not to Label?—It's More than a Nano-sized Question," *European Journal of Risk Regulation* 1, no. 4 (2010): 424.

[72] Bach and Newman, "Governing Lipitor and Listerine," 688.

[73] "China to Ban 1,200 Substances from Cosmetics Production," *Xinhua News Agency*, December 19, 2006.

The Politics of Cosmetics Safety in the United States

The issue of cosmetics safety, or the lack thereof, has also emerged in the United States. Between 2001 and 2005, 165 articles appeared in American newspapers and wire services on cosmetics safety; many described the extent to which American users of cosmetics were unwittingly and unnecessarily being exposed to hazardous substances and criticized the failure of the FDA to effectively test and regulate the health effects of cosmetics.[74] In his 2007 book, *Exposed*, Mark Schapiro reported the results of a study conducted by a non-government organization that found that hundreds of varieties of skin and tanning lotions, nail polish, mascara, and other personal care products were being sold in the United States that contained known or possible carcinogens, mutagens, and reproductive toxins.[75]

According to the Campaign for Safe Cosmetics, "the FDA does not review what goes into cosmetics before they are marketed, cannot compel companies to provide data—including health effects data—and cannot recall products."[76] The Environmental Action Working Group claims that of the more than ten thousand ingredients used in cosmetics and personal care products, 80 percent have never been subjected to a safety evaluation by the FDA; the Group has also urged the United States to change its regulatory policies to match those of the EU.[77]

But, according to the testimony of an FDA official at a congressional hearing reviewing the agency's safety requirements, "The FDA's oversight has ensured that the nation's cosmetics are among the safest in the world. Cosmetics firms are responsible for substantiating the safety of their products and ingredients before marketing."[78]

The Regulation of Phthalates

The safety of one ingredient in cosmetics, namely phthalates, has been highly salient on both sides of the Atlantic. Phthalates are a chemical commonly used in nail polishes to make the veneer more flexible, and they are also used in other cosmetics products such as fragrances, lotion, shampoos, and hair spray. In 2002, the EU, acting on the basis of the

---

[74] Ibid.

[75] Schapiro, *Exposed*, 28.

[76] "U.S. and EU Approaches to Chemical Safety."

[77] Mitchell Clute, "EU Regs Make Cosmetic Ingredients Safer," *Natural Foods Merchandiser*, March 1, 2005, available at http://naturalfoodsmerchandiser.com/tabId/109/itemId/1493/European-Union-regs-make-cosmetic-ingredients-safe.aspx, accessed March 2009.

[78] Stephen Sundlof, "FDA Overhaul," testimony before the Committee on House Energy and Commerce Subcommittee on Health (May 14, 2008), available at http://www.access mylibrary.com/coms2/summary_0286-34567184_ITM, accessed March 2009.

Cosmetics Directive which prohibits the use of chemicals that are known or suspected to cause cancer, mutation, or reproductive disorders, prohibited more than two hundred chemicals, including the phthalates, DHEP, and DBP, from being sold in Europe as of September 2004.

Initially, the European Commission and the Council of Ministers had decided to allow the continued use of these chemicals subject to testing for toxicity, because they feared disrupting Europe's large market for body care products. But the EP overwhelmingly voted in favor of immediately banning them and, thanks to its new legislative powers, it was able to force the Commission and the Council to accept its more risk-averse policy preferences. "Politicians in the European Parliament were more receptive to the multiple, cumulative, and low doses exposure arguments that NGOs were making. These suggested that every European was at risk."[79] In celebrating the ban, Alexander de Roo, a Green MEP, stated, "This is not only an appeal to common sense—nobody wants to have cancer-causing substances in their skin cream—it is also fully backed by the relevant scientific committee."[80]

Since 1998, American non-governmental organizations have pressured the FDA to restrict phthalates in cosmetics are hazardous and should be eliminated. In 2002, the Environmental Working Group, a coalition a group of non-governmental organizations, released a report entitled *Not Too Pretty*, which found that fifty-two of seventy-two cosmetics from major cosmetics firms contained phthalates. These included all seventeen fragrances they had tested, as well as fourteen out of eighteen hair sprays they had examined. The study claimed that women between ages twenty and forty were likely to have absorbed a greater amount of phthalates because they were more likely to use multiple cosmetics and health care products.[81]

However, a 2002 report by the CIR expert panel found no evidence that consumer exposure to the three phthalates used in cosmetics and personal care products posed any health risks.[82] This panel of independent toxicologists and dermatologists unanimously concluded that phthalates "are safe for use in cosmetics products in present practices of use and concentration." The American chemical industry applauded the panel's findings as a "triumph for science-based evidence over scare tactics," while an official of the American Chemistry Council's Phthalate Testers

[79] Lles, "Identifying Environmental Health Risks," 396.

[80] Ibid.

[81] Ibid., 384–85.

[82] Glenn Hess, "CIR Panel Finds Phthalates Safe for Cosmetic Applications," *Chemical Marketing Reporter*, November 28, 2002. The quotations in this paragraph are from this article. See also "U.S. & Europe at Odds on Phthalates Issue," *Cosmetics International*, December 15, 2002.

panel characterized it "as an important victory in the effort to stop activists from turning science on its head and needlessly scaring the public, especially pregnant women."[83] The American Cosmetic, Toiletry, and Fragrance Association, which had strongly criticized the European ban on phthalates in cosmetics as "unnecessary" because studies of the chemical's ill effects had only been conducted on animals, also supported the panel's decision. Equally predictably, activists who had been vigorously campaigning against the use of phthalates in cosmetics accused the expert panel of failing "to protect Americans from dangerous chemicals."[84]

The official position of the FDA is that there is no risk from the use of cosmetic products containing phthalates. The Department of Health and Human Services (HHS) considers the risks of phthalate exposure from nail polish and other cosmetics to be "minimal to negligible."[85] According to Dr. Wilma Bergfeld, the head of clinical research in dermatology at the Cleveland Clinic, "I can assure the American public that these chemicals are safe," a point echoed by Dr. Michael Thun, the head of epidemiological research at the American Cancer Society, who cautioned against extrapolating from the results of animal studies to humans—ironically making the same criticism that European regulatory authorities had earlier made about EPA's (mis)use of animal studies to ban various pesticides and food additives (see chapter 3).[86]

State and Voluntary Regulations in the United States

Frustrated by "the FDA's loose control over cosmetic safety," in 2005 the State of California enacted its own regulations.[87] The Safe Cosmetics Act requires manufacturers to report the use of potentially hazardous ingredients to the state HHS—a list based on Proposition 65—and the HHS will then alert consumers. The HHS was also given authority to investigate whether any product contains substances that could be toxic under normal use and to require that manufacturers submit appropriate health data. According to Kevin Donegan of the Breast Cancer Fund, whose organization had promoted the legislation, "ingredients suspected of causing cancer shouldn't be used in cosmetics." But F. Alan Anderson, the director and scientific coordinator of CIR, countered, "It doesn't make sense for

---

[83] Molly M. Ginty, "U.S. Health: Activists Push for Safer Ingredients in Cosmetics," *Inter Press Service English News Wire*, May 7, 2004.

[84] Quoted in Hess, "CIR Panel Finds Phthalates Safe,"

[85] "Suppliers Move to Eliminate BDP," *MMR*, August 22, 2005.

[86] Laurel Naversen Geraghty, "Should You Worry About the Chemicals in Your Makeup?" *New York Times*, July 7, 2005.

[87] Cynthia Washam, "California Enacts Safe Cosmetics Act," *Environmental Health Perspectives*, July 1, 2006. The quotations in this paragraph are taken from this article.

us to apply the precautionary principle. Instead we use a risk assessment approach, and the wide margins of safety that we have found for chemicals such as phthalates using this approach assures us that the actual use of cosmetics is safe."

Faced with their inability to change federal cosmetics regulations, and inspired by the adoption of more stringent regulations by both the EU and California, the Campaign for Safe Cosmetics has attempted to pressure cosmetics firms to voluntarily adopt restrictions on their chemical ingredients similar to those required for cosmetics sold in Europe. Their efforts have been met with considerable success; many firms have been anxious to protect the reputations of their highly visible and valuable brands.[88] Moreover, this industry is highly integrated: 20 percent of the sales of the largest European and American firms are in each other's markets. Several large global firms, including Revlon, Unilever, and L'Oreal, have reformulated all their products to conform to European standards,[89] while Estee Lauder manufactures 95 percent of its products according to one safety standard.[90] Avon announced plans to reformulate all of its products to remove the phthalate DBP, and it also eliminated this phthalate from its nail products sold in the United States, as have three other major nail polish manufacturers.[91]

While Procter & Gamble also agreed to eliminate DBP, a commonly used plasticizer, from all its global products, the firm emphasized that it did not do so because of any safety concerns and indicated that it plans to continue to use other phthalates at "trace levels" in some products.[92] The company stated:

> In the long history of use in consumer products, there has never been any reliable evidence that the phthalates found in nail polish, or in any other cosmetics, have ever caused anyone any harm. Using estimates of the average amount of DBP found in nail polish, if a person were to absorb all the BDP in almost five bottles of nail polish every day, the resultant exposure would still be at a level at which no effect is seen in laboratory animals.[93]

Although many cosmetics firms have voluntarily removed phthalates from nail polish, they continue to be widely used in many other cosmetics

---

[88] For a list of the changes in the composition of cosmetics sold in the United States in response to activist campaigns, as well as a detailed description of these campaigns, see Little, Lewis, and Lundquist, *Beneath the Skin*, 22–25.

[89] Judy Forman, "Face It: Cosmetic Safety in Doubt," *Boston Globe*, April 5, 2008.

[90] Little, Lewis, and Lundquist, *Beneath the Skin*, 24.

[91] Ibid., 22.

[92] Ibid., 25.

[93] "Suppliers Move to Eliminate DBP," *MMR*, August 22, 2005.

products sold in the United States where their presence is not required to be labeled.

Analysis

The increased stringency of European cosmetics safety regulations has in part been driven by public pressures. NGO campaigns have had a substantial impact on European public opinion; they succeeded in increasing public concerns about the safety of the ingredients used in cosmetics. The progressive strengthening of European cosmetics safety standards also reflects the path dependency of the EU's more precautionary and risk-averse approach to chemical safety. This approach has effectively lowered the scientific burden of proof needed to prohibit a wide variety of ingredients in cosmetics and personal care products, including phthalates.

By contrast, the safety of the chemical ingredients used in cosmetics has not been as politically salient in the United States; the "alarm bells" rung by activists and reported in the media have not been widely amplified. In contrast to the EP, which was highly responsive to activist concerns about chemical safety, the American Congress has been indifferent to them. In the specific case of phthalates, as well as more generally, the FDA has based its policies on risk assessments which have not found any credible evidence that the cosmetics ingredients banned in Europe were unsafe.

But activist pressures in the United States, in addition to persuading California to strengthen its cosmetics safety regulations, have affected the practices of many cosmetics firms. While continuing to oppose more stringent regulations at either the federal or state level—and insisting that the ingredients banned by the European Union, included phthalates, were safe—many have voluntarily limited or restricted a number of ingredients banned by the European Union, including phthalates. Thus, many firms have proven more responsive to the "alarm bells" rung by activists than has the American government. As a result, the dynamics of private "trading up" have reduced the divergence between European regulations and some American practices.

CHAPTER SEVEN

Public Risk Perceptions and the Preferences of Policy Makers

THIS CHAPTER AND THE following one further develop my explanatory framework for the discontinuity in health, safety, and environmental risk regulations that took place on both sides of the Atlantic after around 1990. This chapter focuses on changes in public opinion, specifically the public's risk perceptions, and the preferences of influential policy makers. Both separately and by their interaction with one another, they have had a critical impact on shaping the divergence in transatlantic regulatory stringency.

During the second half of the 1980s, the extent and intensity of public concerns about a wide range of health, safety, and environmental risks increased substantially on both sides of the Atlantic. These concerns in turn played a role in a major expansion of consumer and environmental regulation in both the European Union and the United States. The 1988 Republican presidential candidate, George H. W. Bush, campaigned on a strong pro-environmental platform, and two years later, the Democratic-controlled Congress, with the strong support of the White House, passed three important new environmental laws: the Clean Air Act Amendments, the Oil Pollution Act, and the Pollution Prevention Act. Risk regulations were also substantially strengthened in the European Union at around the same time. In 1989, the EU approved the Small Car Directive, which significantly tightened automobile emissions standards, and the following year it imposed a temporary ban on the milk growth hormone rBST and adopted a rigorous regulatory framework for the introduction of genetically modified varieties.

But while these new regulatory policies represented the *last* major expansion of consumer and environmental risk regulation in the United States, they marked the *beginning* of a steady expansion in the adoption of more stringent risk regulations in Europe. Why, then, after around 1990, did the regulatory policy window narrow in the United States but widen in the European Union across a broad range of risk-related policy areas, and why did this shift in the pattern of relative regulatory stringency persist? What happened after 1990 to create such a marked discontinuity in regulatory politics and policies on both sides of the Atlantic?

This chapter returns to these important questions by presenting a broad historical overview of changes in public demands for more stringent risk regulations and the willingness of policy makers to address them. It begins by describing and explaining the relationship between public opinion and national partisan politics in the United States and then turns to the relationship between public pressures and the preferences of policy makers in the European Union. The latter includes the European Commission, member states in the Council of Ministers, and the European Parliament.

The High Tide of Environmentalism in the United States

During the latter part of the 1980s, the level of public dissatisfaction with environmental quality steadily increased in the United States, reaching levels by the end of the decade that were comparable, and in some respects greater, than during the early 1970s. The percentage of those who listed air and water pollution as among the two or three problems about which they were personally most concerned grew from 13 percent in 1986, to 14 percent in 1988, and then to 21 percent in 1990 and a record 23 percent in 1991.[1] Likewise, the percentage of Americans who believed that the "overall quality of their environment had worsened over the last five years" increased from 34 percent in 1983 to 55 percent in 1990, while the percentage of those who regarded "environmental pollution" as a "very serious threat these days to a citizen like yourself" grew from 44 percent in 1984 to 62 percent in 1989.[2]

In 1990, 76 percent of Americans thought that environmental quality in the United States had declined during the last two decades, while only 14 percent believed that the United States had made a "great deal of progress" in dealing with environmental problems since 1970.[3] The Gallup polling organization reported on the twentieth anniversary of Earth Day in April 1990 that "a little more than one-half of Americans . . . agree that 'life on earth will continue without major environmental disruptions only if we take additional, immediate and drastic action concerning the environment.'"[4]

[1] Everett Carl Ladd and Karlyn Bowman, *Attitudes Toward the Environment* (Washington, DC: American Enterprise Institute for Public Policy Research, 1995), 18–19.

[2] Riley Dunlap and Rik Scarce, "Environmental Problems and Protection," *Public Opinion Quarterly* 55 (1991): 659–61.

[3] Riley Dunlap, "Public Opinion and Environmental Policy," in *Environmental Politics and Policy*, ed. James Lester (Durham, NC: Duke University Press, 1995), 96.

[4] George Gallup Jr. and Frank Newport, "Americans Strongly in Tune with the Purpose of Earth Day 1990," *Gallup Poll Monthly* 295 (April 1990): 5.

This marked increase in public concern with environmental problems—and strong support for stricter and more comprehensive regulations to address them—were linked to a broad range of environmental risks that became more politically salient during the latter part of the 1980s:

> Although the controversy at Love Canal first grabbed headlines in 1979, before Reagan came into office, it proved to be just the first installment in a series of widely publicized cases of human exposure to hazardous wastes that continued to emerge throughout the 1980s. Growing concern with the threat to local water supplies posed by waste sites and chemical spills was reinforced by contamination of ocean beaches along the eastern U.S. and major oil spills, most notably the *Exxon Valdez*. Concern with local air pollution merged with awareness of acid rain and ozone depletion. . . . The possibility of global warming was recognized and then—in the eyes of many—verified by abnormally hot weather and draught.[5]

Public attention to and awareness of these problems were reflected and reinforced by substantial media coverage, which both served to confirm and exacerbate the public's perception that environmental problems were worsening.[6] Between 1987 and 1988, the number of cover stories on environmental topics in *Time* and *Newsweek* doubled from three to six and then doubled again in 1989. In 1988, *Time* magazine named the "Endangered Earth" as "Planet of the Year," in place of its "Man of the Year." The top environmental news story in 1989 was the *Exxon Valdez*, the largest oil spill to date in American history, which dumped crude oil on more than one thousand miles of shoreline in Prince William Sound in Alaska. That same year, a report issued by the Natural Resources Defense Council about the health risks to children posed by pesticides and other chemicals, including Alar, received extensive media coverage. Global environmental risks such as the greenhouse effect, ozone depletion, and rainforest destruction were also widely reported.

The public's increasing concern about environmental quality and its strong support for more environmental regulation was reflected in the 1988 presidential election campaign. Concerned that the Reagan administration's poor environmental reputation would be a political liability in his election campaign and anxious for a "hot button" issue that would galvanize voters, Republican presidential candidate George H. W. Bush decided to make his support for environmental protection a central theme of his campaign. Bush declared, "I have been an environmentalist since I first entered Congress in 1966," and pledged to be a "Republican president in the Teddy Roosevelt tradition. A conservationist. An

[5] Dunlap, "Public Opinion and Environmental Policy," 95.
[6] Ibid., 96.

environmentalist."[7] He specifically promised to improve air quality in the nation's cities, a number of which had experienced severe pollution problems during the summer of 1988. Once elected, Bush proceeded to deliver on his campaign promises.

> By his actions as well as his words, Bush has shown not only how powerful the environment is with American voters, but how a presidential voice can alter the political dynamics of an issue in Congress. His introduction of a wide-ranging anti-pollution measure has transformed a 12-year stalemate into a seeming inevitability: passage of a clean-air bill.[8]

The passage of the Clean Air Act Amendments of 1990—a comprehensive statute that strengthened a wide range of federal controls over air pollution, including for motor vehicles, ozone-depleting chemicals, and acid rain, marked the most significant expansion of federal environmental regulation since 1970. The enactment of this law, which had been pending since the early 1980s, was made possible not only by the strong support of a Republican president and the Democratic congressional leadership but also by the growing political influence and skills of environmental organizations who were now "riding the wave of public anxiety."[9]

In 1989, Robert Mitchell reported that "environmental issues are gaining in salience as well as strength." He predicted that "the public's heightened concern about environmental issues may help create a new political climate more favorable to environmental initiatives."[10] According to one contemporary account, "the fading fearsomeness of Cold War and economic apocalypse has left room for environmental anxieties to reassert themselves . . . [the] unmistakable message from the voting public [is] 'Clean it up'."[11]

THE END OF BIPARTISAN COOPERATION

But in 1992, facing substantial opposition for his support for environmental regulation from his own political party and the business community, and confronting an economic downturn that had begun in 1991, President Bush dramatically reversed course. In his 1992 State of

---

[7] George Hager, "The 'White House Effect' Opens a Long-locked Political Door," *Congressional Quarterly*, January 20, 1990, 139.

[8] David Rapp, "Power of the Earth," *Congressional Quarterly*, January 20, 1990, 138.

[9] Ibid.

[10] Robert Cameron Mitchell, "Public Opinion and the Green Lobby," in *Environmental Policy in the 1990s*, ed. Norman Vig and Michael Kraft (Washington, DC: Congressional Quarterly Press, 2010), 84, 96.

[11] Rapp, "Power of the Earth," 138.

the Union address, the president proposed a ninety-day moratorium on new regulations, thus marking "a major shift in direction by an administration that has presided over the biggest regulatory surge in at least a decade."[12] A reinvigorated Council on Competitiveness was charged with monitoring and reducing regulatory compliance costs by business. The White House also successfully opposed legislation to make the Environmental Protection Agency (EPA) into a cabinet agency, and to boost recycling and tighten waste disposal rules.

President Bush threatened to boycott the 1992 UN Conference on Environment and Development until he had been assured that any climate-change agreement it reached would not contain binding targets for reducing greenhouse gas emissions. The president also refused to sign the other major international environmental agreement adopted at the 1992 Rio Earth Summit, namely the Biodiversity Convention. Bush's policy shift marked the effective end of bipartisan support for new environmental initiatives.

Nevertheless, President Bush went into the 1992 election campaign hoping to benefit from his relatively strong environmental record, especially when compared to that of his Democratic challenger, Governor Bill Clinton of Arkansas. According to a book published by the Institute for Southern Studies and widely circulated by the Bush campaign, among the fifty state governors, Clinton's record was "dead last—none worse when it comes to environmental initiatives."[13] While environmental issues did not occupy a prominent position in Clinton's 1992 presidential campaign, Clinton did stake out a "greener" position on several issues than the incumbent president, whose actions at the Rio Earth Summit had antagonized many environmental organizations. Those groups strongly supported the Democratic presidential candidate, which served to further confirm the views of the Bush administration and many Republicans that their political party had little to gain by supporting environmental legislation.

REGULATORY POLITICS AND POLICIES, 1992–2000

Following the 1992 election results, the Democrats controlled the White House and both Houses of Congress for the first time since 1976. But the high expectations of environmental activists were quickly dashed: during

---

[12] Carolyn Lochhead, "Bush's Shift on Regulation," *SF Chronicle*, January 24, 1992. In the previous three years, EPA's spending had risen 31 percent and the 1990 Clean Air Act was expected to add $25 billion a year to the costs of compliance with existing environmental rules.

[13] Margaret Kriz, "The Selling of 'the Green President,'" *National Journal*, September 19, 1992.

the first two years of the Clinton administration, Congress refused to adopt any of the president's environmental legislative agenda. It denied his request to raise livestock grazing fees, impose new royalties and environmental standards on mining companies, or establish an energy tax based on the energy potential of fuels—the so-called BTU tax. It also rejected two of the administration's major environmental legislative priorities, namely the elevation of the EPA to cabinet status and an overhauling of Superfund, which would have continued to fund hazardous waste site cleanup through a tax on oil and chemical companies. Nor did it renew the 1972 Federal Pollution and Water Control Act. The 1993–94 legislative session produced what was arguably one of the weakest environmental records of any Congress in more than two decades.

Public opinion data help explain the shift in the regulatory policy preferences of Democratic legislators. For the early 1990s marked the time when environmental issues finally appeared to have moved into what Anthony Downs describes as the "post-problem stage" of the issue-attention cycle. This is a state of "prolonged limbo—a twilight of lesser attention or spasmodic recurrences of interest," and one in which "no major environmental programs are likely to receive long-sustained public attention or support."[14]

After peaking around the twentieth anniversary of Earth Day in 1990, public concern about environmental problems began to decline steadily. While in 1991, a record 23 percent of those polled had mentioned pollution of air and water as among the two or three issues about which they personally were most concerned, by 1992 this figure had declined to 16 percent; a year later it stood at 15 percent, and by 1994 it was only 12 percent—an almost 50 percent drop in three years.[15] A survey taken in 1994 reported that 78 percent of Americans now rated the "overall health and quality of the air, water, land and wildlife where respondents lived" as either "excellent" or "good"—a dramatic shift from the widespread public dissatisfaction with environmental conditions reported by public opinion surveys only a few years earlier.[16]

Ladd and Bowman conclude their 1995 study of survey data: "The issue is not whether Americans have soured on the environment or esteem a clean environment less as a central value . . . But we are now more inclined to think that for most Americans, *the urgency has been removed, and the battle to protect the environment is being waged satisfactorily.*"[17] These trends continued through the remainder of the decade. According to a 1999 Gallup

---

[14] Anthony Downs, "Up and Down with Ecology—The 'Issue-Attention Cycle'," *Public Interest* 28 (Summer 1972): 40.
[15] Ladd and Bowman, *Attitudes Toward the Environment*, 19.
[16] Ibid., 47.
[17] Emphasis added; ibid., 51.

survey, Americans "have grown increasingly satisfied this decade with the nation's environmental protection efforts."[18] Between 1993 and 1997, the percentage of those who said they were "very" or "somewhat" satisfied with the state of environmental protection in the United States increased from 52 percent to 64 percent; two years later it stood at 69 percent.[19]

During the 1990s, the historical relationship between increased affluence and public support for additional environmental expenditures was severed. Drawing on data between 1973 and 1991, Euel Elliott, James Regens, and Barry Seldon found that "an increase of $100 in real per capita income increases support for environmental spending by nearly two-thirds of a percentage point.[20] Alternatively, "during periods of economic retrenchment . . . citizens are less willing to support the provision of such social goods in lieu of interventions aimed at ameliorating the effects of economic downturns."[21]

Had this pattern continued throughout the 1990s, the long sustained economic expansion that began in 1992, with GDP growth averaging 3.6 percent over a period of nine years, should have *increased* public support for additional environmental expenditures. *But it did not.* The percentage of those who thought that too little was being spent on the environment peaked at 75 percent in 1990, but then remained at between 56 percent and 59 percent between 1993 and 2000—even though per capita income continued to increase steadily throughout this decade.[22]

In short, an important part of the explanation for the marked slow-down in the rate at which new, more stringent risk regulations enacted by Congress after 1990 was that there was less public demand for them. In effect, the gap between the public's perception as to what the government needed to do to adequately protect them and what it was actually doing—or had already done—had diminished: after roughly two decades, public policy had finally caught up with the public's expectations.

Still, it is important not to exaggerate the extent of the public's complacency about health, safety, and environmental risks during this period. During the early 1990s, the FDA's policy deliberations on approval of the dairy hormone BST were highly controversial, while during the latter part of that decade, there was strong public demand both for labeling food containing genetically modified ingredients and for not allowing food to be labeled "organic" if it came from animals that had been fed crops

[18]Lydia Saad, "1999 Earth Day Poll: Environmental Concern Wanes," *Gallup Poll Monthly* 403, April 1999, 38.

[19]Ibid., 39.

[20]Euel Elliott, James Regens, and Barry Seldon, "Exploring Variation in Public Support for Environmental Protection," *Social Science Quarterly* 76, no. 1 (March 1995): 48.

[21]Ibid., 50.

[22]Roper Center for Public Opinion Research, University of Connecticut.

that had been genetically modified. In 2000, the StarLink policy failure increased public concern about the health risks of genetically modified food. Public concerns about chemical safety, and in particular, the health risks of endocrine or hormone disruptors, also became politically salient during the mid-1990s. But compared to the latter half of the 1980s, fewer "alarm bells" rang as loudly, or for as long.

THE REPUBLICAN PARTY IN CONGRESS

The 1994 midterm congressional elections produced Republican majorities in both Houses of Congress for the first time in more than four decades. The four hundred-page "Contract with America" that served as the policy blueprint for the midterm Republican congressional campaign did not mention the word "environment," and just one of its ten planks indirectly addressed environmental issues, namely, the one calling for regulatory reform. Of the grassroots constituencies whose mobilization played a critical role in the Republican Party's 1994 legislative triumph, two of the most important, Christian conservatives and gun owners, were not especially interested in environmental issues. It is a measure of the relatively low salience of environmental issues in the 1994 midterm elections that the index in Dan Balz and Ronald Brownstein's account of the 1994 Republican political revival, *Storming the Gates*, contains only twelve references to environmental protection and the authors do not devote as much as an entire sentence to environmental policy.[23]

However, the Republican Party that triumphed in 1994 did empower interest groups that were hostile to environmental regulation. The most important of these were organizations representing small businessmen, such as the National Alliance of Independent Businessmen, who had long resented the expansion of federal regulation, including environmental regulation. In contrast to the two previous elections, when public attitudes toward environmental regulation benefited Democrats, in 1994 they benefited Republicans, most notably in the Rocky Mountain West, where opposition to federal land-use policies affected some congressional races. More broadly, the election results reflected a change in "the national mood, the climate in the country, [and] changes in public opinion" that had become more critical of government in general and government regulation in particular. Such "changes in mood or climate have important impacts on policy agendas and policy outcomes."[24]

[23] Dan Balz and Ronald Brownstein, *Storming the Gates* (Boston: Little, Brown, 1996).
[24] John Kingdon, *Agendas, Alternatives, and Public Policies* (Boston: Little Brown, 1984), 153.

Increased Partisan Polarization

What made the Republican congressional electoral triumph especially significant was that the regulatory preferences of Democratic and Republican national legislators had become increasingly divergent, with Republican legislators becoming more likely to oppose new environmental legislation and Democratic Representatives and Senators more likely to support it.[25] While during the early 1970s, Democrats on average supported 20 percent more environmental laws than did Republicans, by the mid-1990s this difference had more than tripled: in 1995, Senate Democrats supported 89 percent of environmental laws while Republicans supported only 11 percent. For their part, House Democrats supported 76 percent of environmental statutes, while House Republicans only supported 15 percent.[26]

The increase in partisan polarization on environmental regulation or "gap in green voting" was re-enforced by a shift in the geographic and ideological base of elected Republican legislators toward the South and the Rocky Mountain West, and away from the more liberal Northeast. This in turn reduced the influence and strength of the "Teddy Roosevelt" wing of the Republican Party, a number of whose Senators and Representatives had been strong advocates of environmental regulation during the 1970s. This meant that the Republican Party, which now commanded majorities in both houses of Congress, was on balance more opposed to protective regulation than many of its elected members had been two decades earlier. According to David Brady, John Ferejohn, and Laren Harbridge, environmental protection is a policy area where the ideological distance between the parties has become especially pronounced.[27] The increased polarization of environmental policy along partisan lines had important policy consequences: "The more polarized the two parties, the greater is the incentive for them to distinguish their records and positions, and the lower is the incentive to strike legislative deals."[28]

---

[25] Glen Sussman, Byron Daynes, and Jonathan West, *American Politics and the Environment* (New York: Longman, 2002), 96–7. See also Charles Shipan and William Lowry, "Environmental Policy and Party Divergence in Congress," *Political Research Quarterly* 54 (2001): 245–63.

[26] Riley Dunlap, Chenyang Xiao, and Aaron McCright, "Politics and the Environment in America," *Environmental Politics* 10, no. 4 (2001): 28–30.

[27] David Brady, John Ferejohn, and Laren Harbridge, "Polarization and Public Policy: A General Assessment," in *Red and Blue Nation? Consequences and Correction of American Polarized Politics*, vol. 2, ed. Pietro Nivola and David Brady (Washington, DC: Brookings Institution Press, 2010), 198.

[28] Sarah Binder, "The Dynamics of Legislative Gridlock," *American Political Science Association* 93, no. 3 (1999): 521.

This increase in partisan polarization on the part of policy makers was both reflected and reinforced by shifts in public attitudes among their constituents. In 1990, Republicans and Democrats expressed roughly comparable levels of concern about a wide range of environmental problems including water pollution, air pollution, drinking water pollution, the loss of tropical rainforests, and global warming. But by 2000, Democrats were more likely to be concerned about each of these issues than Republicans. During the following decade, the gap in levels of public concern with environmental problems based on partisan identification increased still further.[29]

These partisan differences in environmental policy preferences are also reflected in patterns of regulatory policymaking at the state level. Barry Rabe has classified the fifty American states into two categories, based on how many policies each has adopted to address climate change and restrict the growth of greenhouse gas emissions. Of the twenty-six states he classifies as having adopted a "high" number of policies, all but four, namely Arizona, Iowa, Utah, and Texas, are typically Democratic states. By contrast, the only state that falls in his "low" classification and does not typically vote Republican is Michigan, an unsurprising finding given that the state's economy is heavily reliant on auto manufacturers.[30] These divisions are also broadly consistent with differences in state policies with respect to the other risk regulations described in this study. Thus, the state that has consistently adopted the most innovative, comprehensive, and stringent risk regulations across a wide range of policy areas is the typically Democratic state of California.

An Abortive Backlash

The Republican congressional leadership (mis)interpreted the results of the 1994 midterm elections as a mandate for substantially "reforming" or weakening many of the environmental laws that had been enacted during the previous quarter-century. According to Thomas Bliley of Virginia, who now chaired the House Commerce Committee, "The American people sent us a message in November, loud and clear: Tame this regulatory beast! Our constituents want to break the Fed's stronghold on our economy and get them out of decisions that are best left to the individual."[31]

---

[29]Deborah Lynn Guber, "A Cooling Climate for Change," paper prepared for delivery at the 2010 Annual Meeting of the American Political Science Association, 19.

[30]Barry Rabe, "Introduction: The Challenges of U.S. Climate Governance," in *Greenhouse Governance: Addressing Climate Change in America*, ed. Barry Rabe (Washington, DC: Brookings Institution Press, 2010), 11.

[31]Christopher Klyza and David Sousa, *American Environmental Policy, 1990–2006* (Cambridge, MA: MIT Press, 2006), 55.

Shortly after becoming Speaker of the House of Representatives, Representative Newt Gingrich of Georgia stated that the environmental laws of the previous two decades had "been absurdly expensive, created far more resistance than was necessary and misallocated resources on emotional and public relations grounds without regard to either scientific, engineering, or economic rationality."[32] House Whip Tom DeLay of Texas compared the EPA to the Gestapo, adding that "he could not think of a single federal regulation he would keep on the books."[33]

The Republican congressional leadership proposed several legislative initiatives designed to roll back much of the previous expansion of environmental regulation. The most important was to weaken the nation's five major environmental laws, namely the Clean Water Act, including its provisions on wetlands and municipal waste; the Endangered Species Act; the Clean Air Act; the Safe Drinking Water Act; and Superfund. On balance, this was a much more radical agenda than that of the Reagan administration, which had proposed no changes in legislation, but only sought to weaken the enforcement of previously adopted laws, most notably Superfund.

However, these efforts met with essentially the same fate as the Reagan administration's efforts to weaken federal regulatory enforcement a little more than a decade earlier. Thanks to intense grassroots pressures on Republican legislators in key "swing districts" by environmentalists, enough Republicans in either the House or the Senate deserted their party leadership. Congress did not approve the Republican leadership's legislative proposals to rewrite federal environmental regulation. House Majority Whip Tom DeLay conceded defeat in the summer of 1995: "We have lost the way on the environment. I can count votes."[34] But even if the Republican Party in Congress had remained more unified, the ability of Democrats in the Senate to filibuster, and the president to exercise his veto, would have been sufficient to prevent any significant rollbacks.[35]

The defeat of virtually all anti-regulatory initiatives proposed by a party that held commanding and highly disciplined majorities in both Houses of Congress reveals the extent to which the American electorate remained strongly committed to existing levels of environmental protection. But as the response of the Congress in 1993–94 to President Clinton's environmental initiatives revealed, there was also now much less political support for *more* stringent or extensive environmental

---

[32] Ibid., 24.

[33] Ibid., 55.

[34] Catalina Camia, "Environment Edges Up in Budget Debate," *Dallas Morning News*, November 25, 1995, 1A.

[35] See Keith Krehbiel, *Pivotal Politics: A Theory of U.S. Lawmaking* (Chicago: University of Chicago Press, 1998).

regulations, even among Congressional Democrats. In short, the median American voter appeared to broadly favor the regulatory status quo: he or she did not want existing risk regulations to be weakened or repealed, but neither was there substantial public pressure on policy makers to strengthen them.

The Significance of Republican Legislative Control

While the legislative gridlock that began to characterize environmental policymaking in the early 1990s may have been broadly consistent with trends in public opinion, it is also important not to overlook the independent significance of the partisan control of Congress after 1994. First, the environmental community now found itself on the political defensive. Rather than being able to devote its limited political resources to bring new risks to the public's attention, it was now forced to employ its political capital to maintain the regulatory status quo. In effect, what it now meant to be "pro-environment" had become redefined. Whereas through around 1990, it had signified support for new regulatory policy initiatives, after 1994 it had come to be redefined as opposition to weakening those already adopted.

Second, congressional hearings have historically served as an important vehicle for bringing new regulatory risks to the public's attention. But as the majority party in Congress, the Republicans controlled the agenda of committee hearings. This meant that they could no longer serve as a vehicle for expanding the regulatory agenda; in fact, as discussed in chapter 4, they frequently provided a public forum for skeptics of the scientific case for global climate change. Third, as the majority party in Congress, the Republicans may have been unable to enact their environmental legislative agenda, but due to the preferences of their congressional leadership and relatively high levels of partisan discipline, they were in a position to effectively veto any expansions of regulation of which they disapproved.[36]

Majority parties in the House of Representatives over the last decade have been very effective in keeping issues off the political agenda on which they did not wish to legislate.[37] Thus, the control of Congress by Republicans beginning in 1995 meant that the "hurdle rate" for new risks to appear on the national political agenda and become effective policy

[36] For a discussion of the Republican Party's legislative discipline and its impact on Congressional decision-making, see Jacob Hacker and Paul Pierson, *Off-Center: The Republican Party and the Erosion of American Democracy* (New Haven, CT: Yale University Press, 2005).

[37] See Gary Cox and Mathew McCubbins, *Setting the Agenda: Responsible Party Government in the U.S. House of Representatives* (Cambridge: Cambridge University Press, 2005, 2006).

triggers had substantially increased. Compared to the EU, the number of regulatory "non-decisions" made by Congress between 1995 and 2006 is substantial. Thus, Congress did not adopt any legislation regulating GMOs or establishing controls on GHG emissions. Nor did it strengthen safety standards for cosmetics, ban any previously approved chemicals, impose restrictions on antibiotics in animal feed, ban the use of hazardous materials in electronic products or reform chemical regulation.

However, concerned about a public backlash from its abortive efforts to roll back federal environmental protection, the Republican Congressional leadership did respond to the "alarm bells" raised about endocrine disputers and the effect of pesticide residues on the health of children by supporting passage of the Food Quality Protection Act of 1966. This legislation also revised the Delaney Clause, a policy change that had strong business support. It also represents one of the few environmental or consumer protection statutes enacted while Republicans controlled one or both houses of Congress between 1995 and 2006.

THE CLINTON ADMINISTRATION

The priorities and policies of the Clinton administration provide further evidence of the extent to which the political center of gravity had shifted away from the adoption of more stringent risk regulations in the United States. Clinton addressed environmental issues in fewer speeches than any American president since Gerald Ford, who was president for only one term.[38] The Clinton administration did not make any significant administrative changes in the rules governing genetically modified agriculture that had been adopted by the Reagan administration in 1986. Moreover, it was the Clinton administration's appointee to head the Food and Drug Administration (FDA) who approved the use of rBST and opposed labeling requirements for dairy products from cows administered the growth supplement—notwithstanding strong public opposition to both decisions.

With Congress highly polarized after 1994, the locus for environmental policy initiatives shifted to the White House. Accordingly, the Clinton administration issued a number of executive orders that either strengthened or expanded various environmental regulations, most notably with respect to air pollution.[39] In 1997, the EPA issued more stringent air quality

---

[38] Sussman, Daynes, and West, *American Politics and the Environment*, 164.

[39] For a discussion of how the use of presidential authority is likely to increase when Congress is deadlocked, see William Howell, *Power Without Persuasion: The Politics of Direct Presidential Action* (Princeton, NJ: Princeton University Press, 2003).

standards for ground level ozone and particulates, though thanks to a judicial challenge to them, they did not become final until 2002. In 2000, the EPA responded to strong pressures from environmental and public health organizations as well as state and local governments by adopting more stringent regulations for the sulfur content of motor fuel than the EPA had originally recommended. It also issued a number of rules strengthening mobile source air pollution standards, acting under the provisions of the 1990 Clean Air Act. The president also signed both the Biodiversity Convention and the Kyoto Protocol, both of which Congress failed to ratify.

REGULATORY POLITICS AND POLICIES, 2000–2006

In a further sign of the declining salience of environmental issues among the American electorate, Democratic Vice President Albert Gore, notwithstanding his long-standing personal support for government to play a more active role in addressing environmental risks, especially global climate change, chose to place little emphasis on environmental concerns in his 2000 presidential campaign. This decision presumably reflected public opinion polls that revealed that while Americans continued to be "environmentally friendly," the enactment of new risk regulations was not an important priority of the electorate.[40] As a result of Gore's reticence to distinguish his environmental record from that of his Republican rival, George W. Bush, 50 percent of the public was unaware of any differences between the two candidates on this issue.[41]

Just as the Republican Party in Congress between 1995 and 2006 was less willing to support new health, safety, or environmental controls over business than were many Republican senators and Congressmen during the 1970s and 1980s, so was President George W. Bush, who held office between 2001 and 2008, less willing to support stronger consumer and environmental risk regulations than his Republican predecessors, Richard Nixon, Ronald Reagan, and George H. W. Bush prior to the last year of his presidency. In this sense, there is an important continuity between the regulatory policy preferences of George H. W. Bush toward the end of his administration and those of George W. Bush throughout much of his presidency.

Moreover, unlike President Clinton, the Bush administration frequently used its executive authority to weaken new rules proposed by regulatory

[40] Lydia Saad and Riley Dunlap, "Americans Are Environmentally Friendly, but Issue Not Seen as Urgent Problem," *Gallup Poll Monthly* 415, April 2000, 12.

[41] Robert Duffy, *The Green Agenda in American Politics: New Strategies for the Twenty-First Century* (Lawrence: University Press of Kansas, 2003), 123.

agencies. The White House, the Executive Office of the President, and the Office of the Vice President closely monitored regulatory agency rule-making. Proposed regulations were exhaustively reviewed and agencies were required to justify all new rules using a relatively stringent cost-benefit analysis. In addition to these formal procedures, many of which had the effect of slowing down or reversing the adoption of more stringent risk regulations proposed by various regulatory agencies and departments, political appointees often intervened directly in agency deliberations.

"The result was a highly politicized form of administration in which the political interests of the president and his supporters frequently overrode the scientific and technical advice of the bureaucracy"—precisely opposite the pattern in the European Union, where the Commission or the Council frequently issued *more* stringent rules than those recommended by their scientific advisory bodies.[42] While the administration did adopt more stringent standards in some areas, most notably for air pollution from both stationary and mobile sources, fewer new risk regulations were strengthened by regulatory agencies than during the presidency of Bill Clinton.

Environmentalists directed a steady barrage of criticism at the administration's environmental record: the League of Conservation Voters described Bush as "the most anti-environmental president in our nation's history.[43] However, "despite their intense displeasure with the policies of the current Bush Administration, environmentalists [were] not able to generate a widespread backlash and significantly increase public activism akin to what they stimulated during the Reagan Administration."[44]

Revealingly, between 2000 and 2004, the percentage of those who reported feeling "good about the quality of the air, water, and environment where [they] worked or lived remained extremely high, ranged between 69 to 71 percent."[45] Between 2003 and 2007, approximately half of Americans questioned stated that they believed the nation's environmental protection policies were being "kept about the same," while only 39–43 percent thought they were being weakened.[46]

[42] Peter Baker, "A Greener Bush?" *Washington Post National Weekly Edition* (January 7–13, 2008): 10–11.

[43] Deborah Guber and Christopher Bosso, "Past the Tipping Point? Public Discourse and the Role of the Environmental Movement in the Post-Bush Era," in *Environmental Policy: New Directions for the Twenty-first Century*, ed. Norman Vig and Michael Kraft (Washington, DC: Congressional Quarterly Press, 2010), 51. See also Robert Kennedy, Jr., *Crimes Against Nature* (New York: HarperCollins, 2004) and Robert Devine, *Bush Versus the Environment* (New York: Anchor Books, 2004).

[44] Riley Dunlap, "The State of Environmentalism in the U.S.," *Gallup Poll News Service*, April 16, 2007.

[45] "Polls on the Environment and Global Warming," *AEI Studies in Public Opinion*, 18.

[46] Gallup Poll, "Gallup's Pulse of Democracy: Environment," *Gallup Poll News Service* (2007), available at www.galluppoll.com/content/default, accessed October 2009.

A Modest Green Resurgence?

Public dissatisfaction with the Bush administration's environmental record did subsequently increase. A 2001 CBS/*New York Times* poll found that 43 percent of Americans approved of the way "George W. Bush is handling the environment" while only 40 percent disapproved, but six years later, in 2007, only 33 percent registered their approval, while 56 percent expressed disapproval.[47] Similarly, the percentage of those who thought that the country "was losing ground" in addressing the problem of environmental pollution increased from 27 percent in 1997 to 37 percent in 2005, rising to 52 percent in 2007, while the percentage of those who thought the United States was "making progress," after peaking at 43 percent in 1995, declined to 20 percent and 21 percent in 2005 and 2007.[48]

But Gallup also reported in 2007: "The environment is a latent concern. The American public does not have a sense of urgency about the environmental issues at this time. It is not a hot political issue and does not appear in any meaningful way on any of the Gallup's open-ended probes of the public's concerns."[49] Accordingly, "It is proving harder to rejuvenate environmentalism in post-9/11 America than it was in the early 1980s."[50] While "Americans are not opposed to policy initiatives aimed at improving the environment . . . they are not pressing for them at this time."[51]

In 2008, for the first time since 1988, an environmental policy was prominently featured in a presidential campaign. Democratic candidate Barack Obama strongly criticized the Bush administration's unwillingness to address the risks of global climate change and promised to do so if elected. After Obama's election in 2008, the Democratic Party controlled the presidency and both Houses of Congress for the first time since 1993. But Congress did not enact legislation restricting greenhouse gas emissions. However, it did enact the Food Modernization Act, and the Obama administration was able to secure congressional approval for substantial increases in funding for the EPA and the FDA, both of whose budgets had been reduced by the Bush administration. It also strengthened a number of risk regulations through administrative rule-making, including federal fuel economy standards.[52]

[47] Ibid., 6.

[48] Ibid., 8.

[49] Gallup Poll, "Gallup's Pulse of Democracy: Environment," *Gallup Poll News Service.*

[50] Dunlap, "The State of Environmentalism."

[51] Christopher DeMuth and Steven Haywood, "Environmental Policy Outlook," *AEI Outlook Series* (July 2002): 1.

[52] For a summary of the Obama administration's administrative initiatives in the policy areas of risk regulation, see John Judas, "The Quiet Revolution," *New Republic*, February 1, 2010.

The contrast in the response of Congress to the 1989 and 2010 oil spills provides a revealing indication of how much more difficult it had become for "unfortunate events" to become legislative "policy triggers." Congress responded to the 1989 oil spill in Alaska by enacting the Oil Pollution Act of 1990, which significantly strengthened federal regulations. But Congress passed no new legislation in response to the much larger Gulf oil spill of 2010—the most dramatic regulatory policy failure in more than a decade. While legislation was introduced that would tighten regulatory standards for offshore drilling and put a higher dollar limit on liability for damages from any future oil spill, strong Republican support for offshore oil drilling prevented its enactment. Republican control of the House of Representatives following 2010 midterm elections has made the passage of more stringent consumer or environmental legislation even less likely during the remainder of Obama's first term.

The Growth of Environmental Concern in Europe

In Europe, as in the United States, public disaffection with environmental quality measurably increased during the latter part of the 1980s and early 1990s. According to surveys conducted by Eurobarometer, which measures public opinion in the EU, the percentage of respondents who considered environmental protection and the fight against pollution to be an "immediate and urgent problem" increased from 72 percent in 1986 to 76 percent in 1988 and then to 85 percent in 1992.[53]

The public's growing unease with environmental conditions in Europe was linked to a steady stream of environmental disasters. These included the Seveso chemical spill in 1983, the nuclear power plant accident at Chernobyl in 1986, which spread radioactive fallout to the European Union, and a massive chemical spill of toxins into the Rhine River that destroyed half a million fish in four countries that same year. A poll taken in 1986 reported that 52 percent of the German electorate regarded environmental quality as the most important issue facing their nation.[54] To this list of European public concerns can be added the "*scandale du sang contaminé*" in France, which emerged in the mid-1980s. Nearly four thousand patients were infected with contaminated blood—more than a thousand of whom died—as a result of the decision of the French government to delay granting approval for an American technology that

---

[53]Wyn Grant, Duncan Matthews, and Peter Newell, *The Effectiveness of European Union Environmental Policy* (New York: St. Martin's Press, 2000), 14.

[54]David Vogel, "The Making of EC Environmental Policy," in *Policy Issues in the European Union*, ed. Mehmet Ugur (Kent: Greenwich University Press, 1995), 127.

could effectively test blood for contamination with the AIDS virus in order to protect the market share of a French Institute that was in the process of developing a similar test.[55]

An official EU publication noted in 1990, "Major disasters [and] global problems like ozone depletion and the greenhouse effect, and quality of life issues such as drinking water and air pollution have all contributed to a 'greening' of European public opinion, to a widening consensus in favor of cleaner and more sustainable economic growth."[56] The end of the Cold War and the unification of Germany in 1989 both decreased the political salience of peace and anti-war issues—thus providing more political space for environmental concerns—and made many Europeans more aware of the deplorable environmental conditions in East Germany, which was now a part of the EU.

During the latter half of the 1990s, the number of highly salient risk-related policy failures increased in Europe. Around the same time that Americans were reporting increased satisfaction with environmental conditions and the progress government was making in addressing them, European public opinion was moving in the opposite direction, due in no small measure to the British government's dramatic 1996 admission that "mad cow" disease could be transmitted to humans. In 2002, the European Environmental Agency observed:

> Public trust in the politicians and scientists who are trying to protect people and the planet from hazards is very low, especially in Europe, where BSE in the UK and elsewhere, dioxins in Belgium, and the human immunodeficiency virus (HIV)–contaminated blood transfusion affair in France have contributed to a general sense of malaise.[57]

In contrast to the United States, public urgency about environmental problems remained high in Europe. The 1999 Eurobarometer survey reported that 69 percent of Europeans considered environmental protection and fighting pollution to be "an immediate and urgent problem," while more than 60 percent of respondents stated that they had become "more worried" about air, water, and ground pollution, the destruction

---

[55] For a more detailed account of this dramatic policy failure, see David Vogel and Jabril Bensedrine, "Comparing Risk Regulation in the United States and France: Asbestos, AIDS and Genetically Modified Agriculture." *French Politics, Culture* 20, no.1 (Spring 2002), and Monika Stefen, "The Nation's Blood: Medicine, Justice and the State in France," in *Blood Feuds: AIDS, Blood, and the Politics of Medical Disaster*, ed. Eric Feldman and Ronald Bayer (New York: Oxford University Press, 1999), 95–126. France accounted for nearly 60 percent of the blood transfusion of AIDS within the EU.

[56] Quoted in Vogel, "The Making of EC Environmental Policy," 127.

[57] "Introduction," in *The Precautionary Principle in the 20th Century*, ed. Poul Harremoes et al. (London: Earthscan Publications, 2002), 9.

of the ozone layer, global warming, the disappearance of tropical forests, and the use of genetically modified organisms in food than they had been five years earlier.[58] In the most recent European public opinion survey, conducted in 2007, 64 percent ranked protecting the environment as "very important."[59]

THE GOVERNANCE OF THE EU

The support of Europeans for better protection of their health, safety, and environment had an important impact on the governance of the EU.

The European Commission's 1985 White Paper on Completing the Internal Market was intended to address the plethora of divergent national regulatory standards which were raising the costs of doing business within the European Union. However, the single market program was greeted with considerable skepticism by many European consumer and environmental activists, as well as by much of the European public, who feared that it would result in weakening consumer and environmental standards. For not only could the single market just as easily be promoted by the adoption of weaker harmonized regulations as more stringent ones, but the Commission would now be in a stronger position to challenge more risk-averse national regulations as non-tariff trade barriers.

It is a revealing measure of the importance of public concerns about the potential negative health, safety, and environmental impacts of the single market program that the 1986 Single European Act (SEA) incorporated a number of provisions designed to reassure the European public that economic integration would not come at the price of weakening consumer and environmental protection. The SEA explicitly recognized the improvement of environmental quality as a legitimate European objective in its own right. This meant that environmental standards no longer had to be justified in terms of their contribution to economic integration; rather, the EU now had a firm constitutional basis for improving environmental quality in Europe. The SEA also stated that in harmonizing environmental regulations, "the Commission . . . will take as a base a high level of protection." These regulatory commitments in the SEA reflected the extent to which enhancing the quality of life for Europeans was viewed by promoters of European integration as critical to

---

[58] "What Do Europeans Think About the Environment?" The main results of the survey carried out in the context of *Eurobarometer 51.1* (Luxembourg: Office for Official Publications of the European Commission, 1999).

[59] "Attitudes of European Citizens Toward the Environment," Special Eurobarometer Report (March 2008).

the legitimacy and public acceptance of their ambitious single market program.

The SEA also made two important changes in the way European regulatory decisions were made. First, while previously all European legislation had to be approved unanimously, various categories of environmental regulations could now be adopted by a "qualified majority" of the Council of Ministers. As a result of this change in voting rules, between 1989 and 1991 the EU enacted more environmental laws than it had during the previous twenty years.

Second, the SEA expanded the authority of the only directly elected European institution, namely the European Parliament (EP). Under a complex "cooperation procedure," the EP was given the authority to propose amendments to various categories of legislation approved by the Council of Ministers or to reject legislation approved by the Council. If the EP chose the latter course of action, then the legislation could require a unanimous vote of the Council before it would be adapted. This new procedure served to increase the influence of non-business interest groups such as consumer and environmental lobbies, which tend to be better represented in the EP than in other EU institutions. In fact, "lobbying groups and Members of the European Parliament argued that this step was essential if the internal market was seen to be credible from the point of view of environmental protection and public health."[60]

The Treaty on European Union (TEU) signed at Maastricht in 1992 included several provisions that affected the making and content of risk regulation. First, it increased the number of policy areas that could be approved by qualified majority voting, essentially extending it to all aspects of environmental policy. Second, it further expanded the authority of the EP vis-à-vis the Council. A new "co-decision" process now permitted the EP to negotiate amendments to legislation in the areas of environmental and consumer protection and public health directly with the Council, as well as to veto Council legislation. Third, the Maastricht Treaty explicitly expanded the EU's authority to adopt global environmental regulations, a provision that laid the legal and political framework for its increasingly active global regulatory role; by 2005, the EU was a signatory to sixty regional and international environmental agreements.[61] Finally, the Maastricht Treaty strengthened the principle of "preventive action" of the SEA by adding the "precaution-

[60] Bomberg, *Green Parties*, 41.

[61] John Vogler, "The European Contribution to Global Environmental Governance," *International Affairs* 81, no. 3 (2005): 839.

ary principle" to the EU's constitution. This had the effect of changing the nature of policy debates in Europe from disputes over "whether" regulatory action should be taken to "which" measures should be taken and "when."[62]

The Treaty of Amsterdam, adopted in 1997, gave the EU a more central role in promoting the interests of consumers by stating that consumer protection should be taken into account in all EU policies and activities. It also further expanded the "co-decision" procedures between the EP and the Council to most regulatory legislation, effectively making the EP a co-legislator with the Council, and thus giving the EU a bicameral legislature in many policy areas, though the primary authority to initiate legislation remained with the European Commission.

Not all of these institutional changes have been driven by pro-regulatory pressures. For example, the SEA's changes in the voting procedures of the Council of Ministers were driven by policy elites who wanted to strengthen the EU's ability to enact legislation to create a single market. But others, such as the strengthening of the legislative authority of the EP, as well as the various treaty commitments to strengthening health, safety, and environmental protection, did reflect public pressures on European policy makers to link economic integration with stronger consumer and environmental standards. In any event, once enacted, these changes in the EU's governance had an independent impact—one of whose consequences was to facilitate the EU's adoption of a wide range of more risk-averse health, safety, and environmental regulations.

THE EUROPEANIZATION OF RISK REGULATION

Since the enactment of the SEA, risk regulations have been primarily debated within, and determined by, European institutions rather than by national governments. While in many critical areas of public policy, such as taxation, welfare-state provisions, and defense policy, the EU exercises far less authority than does the American federal government, consumer and environmental protection is not among them. Brussels' regulatory authority over consumer and environmental protection has become comparable to that of Washington's. The EU has become "the driving force behind environmental policy across the majority of the continent."[63] Its

---

[62] John McCormick, *Environmental Policy in the European Union* (New York: Palgrave, 2001), 85.

[63] Noah Sachs, "Planning the Funeral at the Birth: Extended Producer Responsibility in the European Union and the U.S.," *Harvard Environmental Law Review* 30 (2006): 88.

highly limited fiscal capacities mean that the EU is essentially a "regulatory state."[64]

Whatever the complaints of European citizens and national politicians about the EU and the discussions among academics about the EU's "democratic deficit," its increased role with respect to health, safety, and environmental protection has been strongly supported by most Europeans. Eurobarometer surveys taken in the 1980s and early 1990s reported that up to 91 percent of EU citizens favored a common European policy for protecting the environment. "Questions on the environment evoked stronger and more positive support for unified EU action than did questions concerning any other area of policy."[65] In 2002, 88 percent of Europeans responded that "protecting the environment" should be an EU priority, ranking its importance only slightly below fighting global terrorism.[66]

Stephen Breyer and Veerle Heyvaert write:

> [Regulatory] centralization may be the expression of growing feeling or unity among the citizens of Europe, of a growing desire to protect the common European heritage across national boundaries, and of rising expectations among Europeans that, when they move from country to country, they will benefit from the same high level of health and environmental protection. This also supports the need for regulations to be made at the European level.[67]

Helen Wallace and Alasdair Young insightfully add:

> Given the EU's limited capacity for distributive measures (and the increasing financial constraints on national welfare policies), there is an underlying incentive for EU policy makers to deliver social benefits via regulatory measures . . . all member governments and the Commission are under pressure to mitigate some of the effects of reduced welfarism . . . by acknowledging civic concerns. These are a means of appearing to enhance societal provision without spending public money.[68]

Harmonizing *and* strengthening consumer and environmental risk regulations has thus enabled European policy makers to simultaneously

---

[64] For an analysis of the EU's growth of regulatory competence and authority, see Giandomenico Majone, "The Rise of Statutory Regulation in Europe," and "The European Commission as Regulator," in *Regulating Europe*, ed. Giandomenico Majone (New York: Routledge, 1996), 47–82.

[65] Bomberg, *Green Parties*, 13.

[66] Eurobarometer, Autumn 2002, 58.

[67] Stephen Breyer and Veerle Heyvaert, "Institutions for Managing Risk," in *Environmental Law, the Economy and Sustainable Development—the U.S., the European Union and the International Community*, ed. R. Revesz, P. Sands, and Richard Stewart (Cambridge: Cambridge University Press, 2000), 327.

[68] Alasdair Young and Helen Wallace, *Regulatory Politics in the Enlarging European Union* (Manchester, UK: Manchester University Press, 2000), 25, 26.

accomplish two objectives: deliver more social benefits to European citizens and create a single market for business firms.

An Alternative Scenario

The critical role of the EU in strengthening European risk regulations can be illustrated by the following scenario. Imagine that the EU did not exist, or that its ability to create a single market and adopt uniform regulatory standards was as limited as that of, for example, the North American Free Trade Agreement. What, then, would a comparison of risk regulations in the United States and individual European countries since 1990 look like? Doubtless, some individual European countries would have enacted some risk regulations either comparable to or more stringent than the United States as, for example, Sweden did before it joined the EU and several countries have done since becoming members. Thus, some European countries would have adopted more precautionary chemical regulations, including for phthalates in children's products and cosmetics; some would have reduced greenhouse gas emissions; some would have banned rBST, beef hormones, and/or antibiotics in animal feed, and hazardous substances in electronics and automobiles; and mandated electronic and automobile recycling, and so on. *But few countries would have adopted as many stringent or precautionary regulations across such a broad array of policy areas as has the European Union.*

Without the EU, the risk regulations of European countries such as Spain, Greece, Portugal, and Italy, as well as those of the accession states that joined the EU after 2004, would have remained far weaker than American ones. There also would have been fewer or weaker new international environmental agreements, as no individual or small group of European countries would have been capable of exercising sufficiently strong global regulatory leadership—particularly in the face of opposition to such agreements by the United States. Specifically, there would be no Kyoto Protocol, since European support for its emissions reduction commitments was based on the burden-sharing agreement that the EU developed and implemented.

In addition, fewer nations outside Europe would likely have adopted risk regulations based on or influenced by those of a single or small group of European countries as the latter's much smaller market would have provided them with much less economic incentive to "trade up." Nor would any European country have had the administrative capacity to promote the globalization of European regulatory standards. Accordingly, the United States would have remained the primary setter of regulatory standards in the global economy—which means that after around 1990, far fewer would have been strengthened.

The development of European institutions which have the technical, administrative, and political capacity, and the policy expertise to develop and negotiate common standards has considerably lowered the transactions costs of regulatory cooperation and coordination within Europe. It has enabled ongoing bargaining over particular standards, with some countries supporting stronger standards in some areas in exchange for other member states backing their policy preferences with respect to others. Moreover, because the EU has jurisdiction over policy areas other than consumer and environmental protection, such as for regional subsidies or the Common Agricultural program, its member states are constantly negotiating with one another. This, in turn, makes possible shifting alliances and tradeoffs among different policy areas. Such tradeoffs, many of which have led to the strengthening of various risk regulations in exchange for other policy concessions or compromises, would have been impossible without the growth of the EU's regulatory authority. Moreover, financial support from the EU has played an important role in promoting support for the strengthening of environmental regulation by the EU's succession states.

In short, if the EU did not exist, it is much less likely that a significant transatlantic shift in regulatory stringency would have occurred. The significance of the Europeanization of risk regulations is similar to the federalization of American environmental regulation that took place around 1970. Both institutional shifts reflected public pressures for more stringent standards, and also facilitated their adoption.

This suggests another scenario: imagine what American health, safety, and environmental regulation would now look like if it had continued to be primarily made by American state governments between 1960 and 1990. In such a case, the United States might well resemble Europe prior to the enactment of the SEA, with a handful of states, such as California, enacting more stringent regulations in particular areas, but without any overall strengthening of national environment standards. (This is, of course, precisely what *has* happened in the United States since the early 1990s.)

THE EU POLICY PROCESS

In what specific ways has the EU created an "opportunity structure" that has often led to policy outcomes that "reflect civic interests more than might be anticipated from the literature on regulatory politics and the economic character of European integration?"[69] Why have the "same supranational institutions so often criticized for their 'democratic deficit,' [become] . . . the best advocates for diffuse interests which do not find adequate representation in national political systems?"[70] What has enabled the dynamics of "collective entrepreneurship" within the EU to produce a wide range of relatively stringent regulatory standards, rather than policies based on the lowest common denominator of member state preferences?[71]

The Role and Preferences of the Member States

The preferences of member states have played a critical role in shaping European regulatory policies. The ministers of member states are represented in the Council of Ministers, the body that must approve all European legislation, and this has given them a central policy role. "The significant participation of the member states means that various ideas that circulate at the national level may diffuse into the EU level."[72] In light of their experience and expertise in many regulatory policy areas, national policy experts in the environmental field have often been seconded or loaned to the Commission, where they have played an important role in transmitting national policy preferences and expertise. Not only are civil servants from "green" states disproportionally represented in or are on loan to the Environmental Directorate, but several of the EU's influential environmental commissioners have come from them, including Margot Wallström of Sweden, who played a critical role in the Commission's support for REACH.

There are important incentives for member states which have adopted more stringent standards to also have them adopted by the EU. For regulations that impose additional costs on national producers, harmonizing them prevents the latter from being disadvantaged by-products produced in member states with laxer standards. Harmonization also protects more stringent national product standards from being challenged by the Commission as non-tariff trade barriers. European-wide standards are also more credible as the Commission is often in a better position to demand their enforcement than are some national governments, especially when they adversely affect a powerful domestic producer. Finally, there is an important first-mover

[69] Ibid., 26.
[70] Majone, "The European Commission as Regulator," 78.
[71] Anthony Zito, *Creating Environmental Policy in the European Union* (London: Macmillan, 2000). 23.
[72] Ibid.

advantage: a nation which has adopted a particular set of regulatory procedures or policies often benefits when they are incorporated into European law.

Member states are major sources of European policy innovation: many of the more stringent risk regulations adopted by the EU are based on or influenced by those previously adopted by one or more member states. For example, one or more of the five beef hormones banned by the EU had been prohibited earlier by various member states, Germany and Denmark imposed restrictions on GMOs before the EU did so, Sweden banned antibiotics in animal feed and Denmark initiated a voluntary ban on them before the EU restricted them, Germany enacted more stringent controls on automotive emissions, including for lead, prior to the strengthening of emissions standards by the EU. Germany, the Netherlands, Denmark, and Austria announced GHG reduction targets before the EU agreed to adopt them. France and Denmark's ban on BPA in products for infants preceded Brussels' decision to do so.

During the 1980s, three member states, namely Germany, the Netherlands, and Demark, had markedly more pro-environmental policy preferences than the other nine. As the history of European automotive standards illustrates, the politics of European risk regulation during the 1970s and 1980s often revolved around the conflict between these three "leaders" and other member states, most notably France, Britain, and Italy, who typically favored less stringent standards. However, the expansion of the EU in 1995 added three member states with relatively strong green preferences, namely Sweden, Finland, and Austria. Their accession significantly added to the strength of the EU's "green coalition." Equally important, thanks to domestic political pressures, Great Britain and France, which had previously been "laggards" with respect to many risk regulations, became more active proponents of more stringent ones, for example, Britain with respect to the strengthening of automotive emissions and climate change, and France with respect to restrictions on GMOs. One or more of these eight countries, along with others in particular policy areas, have played a critical role in the strengthening of many European risk regulations.[73]

[73] For a more detailed discussion of their role in EU policymaking, see Duncan Liefferink and Mikael Andersen, "Strategies of the 'Green' Member States in EU Environmental Policy-Making," in *Environmental Policy in the European Union*, ed. Andrew Jordan (London: Earthscan, 2005), 49–66, and Mikael Andersen and Duncan Liefferink, "Introduction: The Impact of the Pioneers on EU Environmental Policy," in *European Environmental Policy: The Pioneers*, ed. Mikael Andersen and Duncan Liefferink (Manchester: Manchester University Press, 1997), 1–39.

The European Commission and Environmental NGOs

Consumer and environmental pressure groups have played an influential policy role in the deliberations of the European Commission.[74] The European Consumers' Organization (BEUC) established a permanent office in Brussels during the 1970s. Europe's seven main environmental organizations—the so-called group of seven comprised of the European Environmental Bureau, Friends of the Earth, Greenpeace International, the World Wildlife Fund for Nature, Climate Network Europe, the European Federation for Transport and the Environment, and Birdlife International—have had offices in Brussels since the late 1980s.

Consisting of associations of national bodies, they frequently work together to coordinate their activities at the European level; they played an active role in shaping the environmental provisions of each of the EU's treaties and have been active proponents for the strengthening of clean air legislation. Both Greenpeace and BEUC have also demonstrated an impressive capacity to mobilize European public opinion in support of more stringent regulations; the former was instrumental in promoting restrictions on GMOs and played a leading role in the EU's decision to ban phthalates from children's products, while the latter's public campaign played a critical role in the EU's ban on growth hormones for cattle.

Much EU lobbying takes place at the European Commission, where most European legislation is drafted before being submitted to the Council of Ministers and the European Parliament. DG Environmental, in which many risk regulations are developed, has typically been more open to the influence of NGOs than have the environmental administrations of many national governments. Because it has a relatively small staff and a limited budget, it has often turned to the expertise of environmental NGOs in formulating and drafting new regulatory proposals. In order to expand its influence within both the Commission and the Council, the Environment Directorate has widely consulted with European NGOs in order to broaden the basis of political support for its policy initiatives. As one British official put it:

---

[74] For the role of consumer and environmental organizations in shaping European regulatory policies, see Alasdair Young, "European Consumer Groups: Multiple Levels of Governance and Multiple Logics of Collective Action," in *Collective Action in the European Union: Interests and the New Politics of Associability*, ed. Justin Greenwood and Mark Aspinwall (London and New York: Routledge, 1998), 149–75; Ruth Webster, "Environmental Collective Action: Stable Patterns of Cooperation and Issue Alliances at the European Level," in Greenwood and Aspinwall, *Collective Action in the European Union*, 176–95; Sonia Mazey and Jeremy Richardson, "Environmental Groups and the European Community," in Jordan, *Environmental Policy in the European Union*, 124.

Green lobbies are extremely influential. You have to remember that the Commission has no formal system for compiling information . . . It listens to [green groups] because they are a source of advice and they provide a foretaste of the sort of debate the Commission should expect when the proposal goes to the European Parliament . . . The Commission does well to keep green organizations on its side.[75]

The agenda-setting role of European NGOs has been particularly critical: their lobbying efforts and scientific reports have often brought new regulatory issues and problems to the attention of the Commission. NGOs "provide the necessary information and 'intelligence': the Commission the necessary access."[76] They are frequently represented on Commission advisory bodies and their working groups and scientific reports have often put new regulatory risks on the EU's policy agenda, such as, for example, the safety of chemicals. The European Environmental Bureau (EEB), an umbrella environmental organization, which was created in 1974, enjoys access to various Commission bodies and exerts constant and continual pressure on the Commission, lobbying on issues that often become EU legislation. The Commission has actively encouraged the development of European-wide consumer and environmental organizations by providing financial support to many of them

The European Parliament and the Influence of Green Parties

Each successive EU treaty has strengthened the authority of the European Parliament (EP), giving this body, which was first elected in 1979, an increasingly influential role in shaping European regulatory legislation.[77] Since 1997, Green Parties have been the fourth largest parliamentary group within the EP. In European elections held in 2009, just a year before the Republicans again became the majority party in the House of Representatives, a record fifty-five members from Green Parties were elected to the EP.[78]

While they have remained a distinct minority within the EP—which has had between 626 and 736 members since 1999—they have been often able to form alliances with other MEPs, including those from

[75] Bomberg, *Green Parties*, 130.

[76] Ibid.

[77] For an extended discussion of the EP's regulatory policy impact, see Charlotte Burns, "The European Union's Environmental Champion," in *Environmental Policy in the European Union*, 87–105.

[78] Data taken from the official European Green Party website, available at http://www .europeangreens.org/cms/default/rubrik/9/9034.htm, accessed October 26, 2009.

both left-of-center political parties, and the MEPs elected from the EU's greener member states. Unlike in national parliaments, party discipline is relatively weak in the EP, which means that policymaking typically involves the building of coalitions and the making of compromises—a dynamic in which Green Parties are able to participate, notwithstanding center-right majorities in the EP since 2004. The work of the EP takes place primarily through its twenty standing committees, the second largest of which is the Committee for the Environment, Public Health and Food Safety. This is among the more powerful committees in the EP as it deals with more co-decision legislation than any other—it has been the primary promoter of environmental and consumer regulation within the EP.

After the EP was given a formal role in enacting EU legislation, it began to work more closely with the Commission.[79] The willingness of the Commission to engage in dialogue with the EP over the initial formulation of European legislation has considerably expanded the latter's policy impact. The DG Environment has developed a particularly close working relationship with the EP's environment committee; this committee has become the Directorate's political ally in its ongoing conflicts with other Commission directorates. Together these two bodies have emerged as the primary champions of environmental legislation within the EU.

While Green MEPs have often been frustrated by the need to compromise with members from other parties who do not share some of their more radical policy objectives, such as opposition to nuclear power, on balance, "the increase in the EP's power has presented a range of opportunities for environmental activists that they otherwise would not enjoy. They have gained access to the decision-making process and to the Parliament in which their natural allies—the "Greens" are increasingly well represented."[80] According to a senior Commission official, "We [in the Commission] automatically have to pay greater attention to the elective representatives of the environmental movement—the elected Greens."[81]

"The Parliament has often strengthened European standards. For example, it successfully pressured the Commission to support a ban on all beef hormones, to strengthen its regulations for the safety of cosmetics products, and to impose stringent regulations on GMOs. In marked contrast to the U.S. Congress since the early 1990s, the EP has been "one of the most left-leaning and environmental conscious legislative bodies in the world."[82]

---

[79] Burns, "The European Union's Environmental Champion," 92.
[80] Ibid.
[81] Bomberg, *Green Parties*, 137.
[82] Sachs, "Planning the Funeral at the Birth," 87.

Political Constraints

It would be misleading to exaggerate the strength of advocates for more stringent regulations within the EU. Business lobbies remain extremely important in Europe; they are well-represented in Brussels, enjoy substantial influence vis-à-vis national governments—which in turn shapes the decisions of the Council of Ministers—and the sections of the Commission that champion industrial and agricultural interests are among the most powerful in the EU. The Commission has also championed the interests of European business firms rather than the preferences of consumer and environmental pressure groups and some member states, such as for the approval of GMOs. The center-right administration of European Commission President José Barroso, which has held office since 2004, has promoted closer scrutiny of Commission regulatory initiatives that raise the costs of doing business in Europe. Some member states have effectively opposed more stringent risk regulations, and support for them has often divided the EP.

My claim is not that pro-regulatory constituencies have dominated regulatory policymaking in the EU. It is rather that during the last two decades, their political impact has been roughly comparable to that of consumer and environmental organizations in the United States during the preceding three decades. This means that their impact has varied from issue to issue as well as over time. It also means that in some cases, proposals for more stringent regulations have been weakened as they worked their way through the policy process, while in other cases, firms or member states have been given additional time to comply with them. As in the United States during the 1970s and 1980s, European policy makers have also been less willing to adopt more stringent standards during periodic economic down-turns. But, *on balance*, since the early 1990s advocates of more risk-averse regulations have exercised more influence over both the political agenda and policy outcomes in Brussels than in Washington.

A COMPARATIVE POLITICAL ANALYSIS

In addition to the factors discussed above, differences in the regulatory policy preferences of influential policy makers in Europe and the United States since 1990 have been shaped by two other factors.

First, the dynamics of the single market and the EU's governing institutions have given national governments which prefer more stringent standards greater opportunities to shape European policymaking than "greener" American states have been able to exercise vis-à-vis the American federal government. Most obviously, unlike in the United States,

"states" are represented in one of the EU's most important decision-making bodies, namely the Council of Ministers, and state officials often work closely with the European Commission.

Moreover, because the European single market is much newer and more fragile than the American one—the former dates from the mid-1980s and is still a work in progress, while the latter has existed since 1789—"state" regulations that interfere with the single market are more threatening to the EU than to the American federal government: they challenge the former's *raison d'être*. Accordingly, when an important member state or a group of member states have adopted more stringent product regulations that interfere with the single market—and they are acting within their legal authority to do so, the Commission is likely to propose that they be harmonized. This effort has not always been successful—witness the inability of the Commission to standardize regulations for GMOs—but it does mean that they are highly likely to appear on the policy agenda in Brussels.

While some more stringent state regulations have been adopted by the federal government, most notably for automotive emissions, fuel economy, and phthalates in children's products, what is more striking is the number of important risk regulations adopted by various American states since 1990 that have *not* been federalized. This list includes mandatory recycling programs for electronics and electrical products, stricter regulations for cosmetic safety, more stringent chemical regulations, bans on hazardous substances in electronic products, and most important, restrictions on greenhouse gas emissions. Indeed, many have not even appeared on the federal policy agenda. By contrast, if a member state as important as California had adopted so many distinctive consumer and environmental regulations, many of which interfered with the American single market—or, in other words, if California was Germany—the European Commission would have attempted to and usually succeeded in harmonizing them. While those harmonized standards may have been less stringent than those preferred by "greener" member states, they would also have strengthened European standards.

In sum, many more European member state regulations have been adopted by the EU than more stringent state regulations have been adopted by the American federal government. *The dynamics of internal "trading up" have been much more important within the EU than in the United States.*

A second factor has to do with electoral outcomes and the differences in the policy preferences of center-right politicians and political parties. As noted above, since the mid-1990s, American regulatory policymaking has become much more polarized along partisan grounds, most notably with respect to environmental regulation, and only marginally less so for consumer health and safety standards. Consequently, between 1995 and 2006, when the Republican Party was the majority party in the American Congress, and between 2000 and 2008, when it controlled the White House, far fewer new federal risk regulations were adopted. After Democrats regained control of Congress between 2007 and 2010, Congress did strengthen regulations for food and product safety. But the de facto "rule of sixty" in the U.S. Senate enabled Republican legislators to prevent the adoption of the most important risk regulation favored by the Democratic majority and President Obama, namely restrictions on greenhouse gas emissions.[83]

Many of the more stringent European risk regulations described in this book were adopted when many European countries had center-left governments in which Green Parties were often represented, and when the European Commission had a center-left administration and the EP had center-left majorities. The fact that after 1994, center-left parties were more politically powerful in Europe than in the United States helps explain many of the differences in the regulatory policies adopted—or not adopted—across the Atlantic.

Subsequently, the political pendulum shifted in Europe. By around 2004, the majority of EU member states had center-right governments in which Green Party members no longer participated, and since 2004 the EP has had a center-right majority and the EU a center-right Commission. This electoral shift to the right has slowed down the rate at which new, more stringent regulations have been adopted by the EU, as center-right parties in Europe—which are generally closer to business—have been less supportive of more stringent health, safety, and nvironmental standards than center-left ones, which includes Green Parties.

But these changes in partisan governance have not changed European regulatory policies as significantly as did the Republican control of Congress after 1994 and the election of a conservative Republican president in 2000. Rather, Europe since 2004 more closely resembles the United States prior to the early 1990s, when center-right politicians such as Richard Nixon, Ronald Reagan, and George H. W. Bush were often willing to support more stringent consumer and environmental regulations, as have, for example, French center-right Presidents Jacques Chirac and Nicholas Sarkozy, center-right German Chancellor Angela Merkel, and center-right EU Commission President José Barasso. In short, regulatory policymaking has been much more politically and ideologically polarized in the United States than in the EU.

---

[83] For the policy significance of this change in Senate procedures, see Jacob Hacker and Paul Pierson, *Winner-Take-All Politics: How Washington Made the Rich Richer—And Turned Its Back on the Middle Class* (New York: Simon & Schuster, 2010), 241–44.

CONCLUSION

This chapter has described two causal factors that affect the likelihood that a government will adopt a wide array of more stringent risk regulations, namely the extent and intensity of public's "demand" for regulation, and the interest of policy makers in "supplying" that demand. Accordingly, the previous active role played by the United States in identifying and addressing a wide range of health, safety, and environmental risks was the result of periodic risk availability cascades and the electoral strength of Democrats, along with the support of influential Republicans, while the decline in the expansion of risk regulation after 1990 was the result of greater public satisfaction with the regulatory status quo and the electoral strength of conservative Republicans and increased partisan polarization. In Europe, the expansion of risk regulation after around 1990 was due to a substantially more risk-averse public and the stronger support for more stringent regulatory standards by policy makers in influential member states, the European Commission, and the European Parliament.

CHAPTER EIGHT

The Law and Politics of Risk Assessment

THIS CHAPTER FURTHER DESCRIBES and explains the trend away from regulatory stringency in the United States and toward it in the European Union. It begins by documenting the precautionary basis of many of the risk regulations adopted by the United States, primarily before 1990, providing further evidence that there is nothing distinctively "European" about a precautionary approach to risk regulation.[1] It then turns to the increasingly important role of regulatory impact analyses in the United States, which include both scientific risk assessments and cost-benefit analyses. These policy tools have contributed to reducing the number of highly stringent risk regulations adopted in the United States, especially by regulatory agencies. The United States also experienced an influential "backlash" that questioned the rationale behind many of the highly risk-averse regulations it had previously adopted, claiming that many were false positive policy errors. This, in turn, weakened the political credibility of new risk claims as well as the willingness of policy makers to enact more stringent regulations in response to them.

However, a very different policy dynamic took place in Europe, where a precautionary approach to risk management became *more* influential. Its impact was linked to several regulatory policy failures attributed to insufficiently rigorous risk regulations, i.e., false negatives. These in turn diminish public confidence in the capacity of scientific risk assessments to adequately identify threats to public health, safety, and environmental quality. Although the precautionary principle has not been applied consistently, and its application remains controversial, it has played an important role in making many European risk regulations more stringent than American ones. It has also made European decision-makers both more able and willing to respond to highly risk-averse public preferences than their American counterparts.

---

[1] See Jonathan Wiener, "Whose Precaution After All? A Comment on the Comparison and Evolution of Risk Regulation Regimes," *Duke Journal of Comparative and International Law* 13, no. 5 (2003): 207–62; and Jonathan Wiener, "The Rhetoric of Precaution," in *The Reality of Precaution: Comparing Risk Regulation in the United States and Europe*, ed. Jonathan Wiener, Michael Rogers, James Hammitt, and Peter Sand (Washington, DC: Resources for the Future, 2011).

Courts on both sides of the Atlantic have also played an important policy role. While in the United States, they have subjected risk regulations to greater scrutiny, European courts have often given EU policy makers considerable discretion to enact precautionary regulations.

The Precautionary Principle in American Law

Although the precautionary principle has no legal status in the United States, and has not played an explicit role in American policy debates, "no country . . . fully adopted the essence of the precautionary principle in domestic law as the U.S."[2] A "focus on serious and irreversible harms, [and] a willingness to regulate under conditions of uncertainty . . ." were "all firmly embedded into U.S. regulatory statutes."[3] For example, the 1958 Delaney Clause was "in essence a precautionary statute."[4] This was not because it prescribed a "zero risk" standard for carcinogenic food additives.

> Rather, the precautionary element of the Delaney provision lay in the fact that gaps in knowledge about human responses to carcinogens were not taken as a cause for inaction. The moral obligation not to place people at risk was triggered in this instance by surrogate markets, such as positive animal tests, not by actual evidence of harm to human beings.[5]

Many of the first wave of environmental statutes enacted in the United States incorporated important precautionary elements. One of their defining characteristics was an unwillingness to wait for clear evidence of harm before permitting, or in some cases, requiring, regulatory action. For example, the 1966 Endangered Species Act institutionalized caution: a finding of *potential* irreversible harm to a threatened, jeopardized, or endangered species could lead to an order to desist all development activities. The first major American environmental law, the National Environmental Policy Act (NEPA), established rigorous procedural requirements for any federal action that *might* negatively affect environmental quality:

---

[2] James Cameron, "The Precautionary Principle," in *Trade, Environment, and the Millennium*, ed. Gary Sampson and W. Bradnee Chambers (New York: United Nations University Press, 1999), 250.

[3] James Applegate, "The Precautionary Preference—Environmental Protection in the Face of Scientific Uncertainty," *Human and Ecological Risk Assessment* 6 (2000): 420.

[4] Sheila Jasanoff, "A Living Legacy: The Precautionary Ideal in American Law," in *Environmental Science and Preventive Public Policy*, ed. Joel Tickner (Washington, DC: Island Press, 2003), 231.

[5] Ibid.

"NEPA is an example . . . of the use of procedural duties in an effort to act in *precaution*."[6] In the critical case of ozone depletion:

> At the time that the U.S. led the global effort to reduce the use of ozone depleting substances, computer programs were rejecting satellite data on the extent of loss in the ozone layer as being too far from the range of expected results to be valid. Nevertheless, given the monumental potential harms at stake, the U.S. accepted significant economic costs in order to eliminate the possibility of an ozone catastrophe and eventually convinced the rest of the industrialized world to follow its *precautionary* lead.[7]

Beginning in the 1970s, American courts often interpreted American regulatory statutes in ways that endorsed a precautionary approach to risk assessments, initially in the area of occupational health and safety and subsequently with respect to environmental standards.

In *Reserve Mining* (1975), the Supreme Court permitted the Environmental Protection Agency (EPA) to regulate asbestos fibers in mine ore effluent on the basis of a "reasonable" or "potential" showing of danger, rather than the more demanding "probable" threshold requested by the industrial plaintiff. The Court stated: "In the context of the [Clean Water Act], we believe Congress used the term 'endangering' in a *precautionary* or preventive sense, and therefore, evidence of potential harm as well as actual harm comes within the purview of the term."[8] While acknowledging that existing scientific studies were unable to demonstrate that ingested asbestos from drinking water could cause cancer, the Court nevertheless concluded that these "negative results do not dispose of the broader issue of whether the ingestion of fibers poses *some danger* to public health."[9]

In a 1976 Court of Appeals decision upholding the EPA's stringent ambient air standards for lead emissions, *Ethyl v. EPA* (discussed in chapter 4), the Court held that: "A statute allowing for regulation in the face of dangers is, necessarily, a *precautionary* statute. . . . The statutes and common sense demand regulatory action to prevent harm, even if the regulator is less than certain that harm is otherwise inevitable."[10] The Court added: "proof [of harm] may be impossible to obtain if the *precautionary* basis of the statute is to be served."[11] In a related case, the DC Circuit Court ruled that forcing the EPA to delay setting health standards

---

[6] Emphasis added. Cameron, "The Precautionary Principle," 250.

[7] Emphasis added. Douglas Kysar, *Regulating from Nowhere: Environmental Law and the Search for Objectivity* (New Haven, CT: Yale University Press, 2010), 46.

[8] Emphasis added. Quoted in Applegate, "The Precautionary Preference," 423.

[9] Emphasis in original. Quoted in ibid., 426.

[10] Emphasis added. Quoted in David Vogel, *Trading Up: Consumer and Environmental Regulation in a Global Economy* (Cambridge, MA: Harvard University Press, 1995), 182.

[11] Emphasis added. Quoted in Applegate, "The Precautionary Preference," 424.

until it can "conclusively demonstrate that public health is threatened is inconsistent with the statute's *precautionary* and preventive nature."[12]

In *Natural Resources Defense Council, Inc. v. Environmental Protection Agency* (1978), which addressed an industry challenge to the EPA's proposed emissions standards for vinyl chloride, the DC Circuit Court opined that "Congress . . . recognized in Section 112 (of the 1970 Clean Air Act) that the determination for what is 'safe' will always be marked by scientific uncertainty," adding that "EPA's standards must protect against *incompletely understood* dangers to public health, in addition to well-known risks."[13] According to *Maine v. Taylor* (1986), "[the state] has a legitimate interest in guarding against *imperfectly understood* environmental risks, despite the possibility that they may ultimately prove to be negligible."

In *Natural Resources v. Administrator, U.S. EPA* (1990), the court addressed the legality of an EPA proposed rule for ozone and particulate matter. The court explicitly characterized the Clean Air Act as "*precautionary*" because it authorized the EPA to act when an air pollutant "may reasonably be anticipated to endanger public health." While acknowledging that the evidence that particular pollutants whose standards EPA had proposed strengthening posed a health threat at low levels of exposure was "*uncertain or conflicting*," it nevertheless concluded that the EPA was entitled to draw conclusions from "suspected but not completely substantiated relationship between facts, from trends among facts, from theoretical projections from imperfect data . . . and the like."[14]

The precautionary approach toward risk regulations employed in these regulatory rules and statutes and in the judicial decisions which affirmed them is similar in many respects to the way the EU has applied the precautionary principle. However, the role of precaution in shaping American consumer and environmental risk regulation is best understood as a preference or an approach, rather than, as it became in the EU, a legal doctrine or principle. "This means that from time to time, precautionary logic is persuasive to legislators, judges, and administrators. It is then

---

[12]Emphasis in first part of quote added. Quoted in G. D. Fullem, "The Precautionary Principle—Environmental Protection in the Face of Scientific Uncertainty," *Willamette Law Review* 31 (Spring 1995): 495.

[13]Emphasis added. Nicholas Ashford, "The Legacy of the Precautionary Principle in U.S. Law: The Rise of Cost-Benefit Analysis and Risk Assessment as Undermining Factors in Health, Safety, and Environmental Protection," in *Implementing the Precautionary Principle: Approaches from the Nordic Countries, EU and the USA*, ed. Nicholas de Sadeler (London: Earthscan, 2007), 364.

[14]Emphasis added. Quoted in M. Shapiro, "The Frontiers of Science Doctrine, " in *Integrating Scientific Expertise into Regulatory Decision-Making*, ed. C. Joerges, K. M. Ladeur. and Kim Voss (Baden-Baden: Nomos Verlagsgesellschaft, 1997), 332–3.

applied on a case-by-case basis, with little concern for consistency in comparable cases and no systematic effort to justify it."[15]

Moreover, many regulatory statutes also permit or even require regulatory agencies to incorporate other considerations, such as technological feasibility or costs, or to provide evidence of a "significant risk" or "unreasonable risks" before issuing regulations. In many cases, the actual implementation of regulatory statutes that were based on a precautionary approach was subsequently modified when compliance with them proved too expensive or technologically infeasible.[16] Equally important, its application has also been challenged by a number of important judicial decisions that have required stronger scientific evidence of harm to justify more stringent risk regulations.

RISK ASSESSMENTS IN AMERICAN LAW

The need for risk regulations to be justified by scientific risk assessments dates from the 1980 Supreme Court decision in *Industrial Union Department v. American Petroleum Institute*. The issue in this case was an industry challenge to an Occupational Safety and Health Administration (OSHA) regulation that set the acceptable exposure for the carcinogen benzene at 1ppm over an eight-hour period. In striking down this regulation, the Supreme Court held that only "significant risks" could be regulated under the toxic substances provision of the relevant statute. The agency was accordingly instructed to review its standard to determine whether benzene exposure at 1ppm was "significant."

This decision rejected the precautionary logic underlying the *Ethyl* decision, which had allowed the EPA to ban leaded gasoline even in the absence of conclusive scientific evidence of its actual risks to human health. While holding that the magnitude of the risk need not be defined precisely, "the decision strongly implied that some form of quantitative risk assessment is necessary as a basis for deciding if a risk is large enough to deserve regulation."[17] More importantly, it placed the burden of proof on regulators to demonstrate that an environmental risk was sufficiently important to justify regulating it.

---

[15] Kerry Whiteside, *Precautionary Politics: Principle and Practice in Confronting Risk* (Cambridge, MA: MIT Press, 2006), 69. For a discussion of the different ways different courts have interpreted the risk requirements of the Clean Air Act, see E. Shep Melnick, *Regulation and the Courts: The Case of the Clean Air Act* (Washington, DC: Brookings Institution, 2003).

[16] See, for example, John Dwyer, "The Pathology of Symbolic Legislation," *Ecology Law Quarterly* 17 (1990): 223–316.

[17] Gail Charnley and E. Donald Elliott, "Risk Versus Precaution: Environmental Law and Public Health Protection," *Environmental Law Report* 32 (March 2002): 10363.

In *Gulf South Insulation Co. v. Consumer Product Safety Commission* (1983), the Fifth Circuit challenged the Consumer Product Safety Commission's justification for a rule protecting consumers from urea formaldehyde insulation, arguing that it was not based on "good science," adding, "to make precise estimates, precise data are required."[18] This requirement was reaffirmed in *Corrosion Proof Fittings v. EPA* (1991) (discussed in chapter 5), in which the Fifth Circuit Court of Appeals overturned the agency's ban on asbestos products under the Toxic Substances Control Act on the grounds that the EPA had not fulfilled its obligation of demonstrating that the products it proposed to ban presented an "unreasonable risk."[19]

While all risk regulations are subject to the same standard of judicial review, namely that they cannot be "arbitrary or capricious," the nature of the scientific evidence demanded by American courts to justify more stringent risk regulations has varied. In some cases, agencies have been permitted to adopt precautionary regulations, while in others, they were precluded from doing so—depending in large measure on the wording of the statutes under which they were issued. But the role of American courts in subjecting risk regulations to more careful scrutiny represents only one dimension of the challenge to the adoption of relatively stringent risk regulations in the United States. Both the executive branch and the Congress have also played an important role in this process.

Moving Away from Precaution and Stringency

Cost-Benefit Analysis

An important challenge to the adoption of highly risk-averse or precautionary risk regulations in the United States is the requirement that risk management decisions incorporate a cost-benefit analysis. The use of cost-benefit analyses has become a critical and controversial component of American risk regulation. In 1981, President Ronald Reagan, who had campaigned on a platform to reduce "burdensome" protective regulations, issued an executive order requiring all new rules issued by regulatory agencies to meet a cost-benefit test before they could be issued.[20]

---

[18] Quoted in Applegate, "The Precautionary Preference," 341.

[19] See Jerry Adler, "Risking Life and Lungs," *Newsweek*, February 3, 1986, for these and other references to the court's ruling. For an extended discussion of this judicial decision, see Linda Stadler, "Corrosion Proof Fittings v. EPA: Asbestos in the Fifth Circuit—A Battle of Unreasonableness," *Tulane Environment Law Journal* 6 (Summer 1993): 423–38.

[20] Marc Allen Eisner, *Regulatory Politics in Transition* (Baltimore: Johns Hopkins University Press, 1993), 189.

While President Bill Clinton explicitly revoked the Reagan executive order in 1993, he subsequently issued a new executive order that incorporated many of its elements. The Clinton executive order required all regulatory agencies to submit detailed information on the anticipated costs and benefits for OMB review before they undertook any "significant regulatory actions," defined as those likely to have an annual effect on the economy of at least $100 million. It also stated that the cost-benefit information submitted to the president be quantified "to the extent feasible, adding that "each agency . . . shall propose or adopt a regulation only upon a reasoned determination that the benefits of the intended regulation exceed its costs."[21] The latter did, however, represent a slight relaxation of the Reagan administration's requirement that regulations should only be adopted if they "outweighed" their costs.

The Office of Management and Budget (OMB) has interpreted this requirement broadly, often imposing the cost-benefit criterion on agency rule-making even when the relevant statute and its interpretation by the courts required that regulations be based on criteria other than a weighing of their costs and benefits. The administration of George W. Bush retained the executive order issued by President Clinton and subsequently issued guidelines calling for greater use of cost-benefit analyses, analyses of risk-risk tradeoffs, as well as probabilistic scenarios of regulatory costs that exceeded $1 billion—a requirement that was slightly relaxed by President Obama.

During the second half of the 1990s, the now Republican-controlled Congress, as part of its broader political effort to reduce the burdens imposed by federal regulations on both businesses and state and local governments, approved the Unfunded Mandates Reform Act of 1995. This legislation required regulatory agencies to prepare a "qualitative and quantitative assessment of the anticipated costs and benefits" of any rule whose aggregative impact is anticipated to be $100 million or more in any year unless such an assessment "is otherwise prohibited by law."[22] While it did not impose a cost-benefit analysis "as a *substantive* decision-making criterion . . . nonetheless by requiring the agency to calculate the costs and benefits of major regulation, and to place this information into the administrative record, Congress has clearly elevated the importance of the cost-benefit criterion."[23]

The following year, Congress passed the Small Business Regulatory Enforcement Fairness Act, which, among its other provisions, required regulatory agencies to provide Congress with information to "identify and

---

[21] Quoted in "The Legacy of the Precautionary Principle," 360.
[22] Ibid., 357.
[23] Emphasis in original. Ibid.

consider a reasonable number of alternatives, and from those alternatives select the least costly, most cost-effective or least burdensome alternative that achieves the objective of the rule" before adopting any new rule that is likely to have a significant economic impact on small firms.[24]

Risk Assessment

The second procedural or administrative challenge to the application of a precautionary or high risk-averse approach to risk management decisions in the United States is the increased importance placed on science-based risk assessments. In the 1996 amendments to the Safe Drinking Water Act, Congress included a provision requiring that risk assessments conducted under its provisions be based "on the best available peer-reviewed science and supporting studies conducted in accordance with sound and objective scientific practices."[25] In 2000, the Information (Data) Quality Act, which was added as an amendment to an appropriations bill, went a step further. It directed the OMB to "issue guidelines . . . that provide policy and procedural assistance to federal agencies for ensuring and maximizing the quality, objectivity, utility and integrity of information (including statistical information and scientific data) disseminated by federal agencies." It also granted interested parties the right to challenge an agency's adherence to these guidelines in federal courts—a provision strongly supported by business groups.[26]

According to Gail Charnley and E. Donald Elliot, "Over the last two decades, quantitative risk assessment has emerged as the dominant paradigm in the U.S. for including science in regulatory decision making as the best way to manage threats to public health and the environment."[27] Since the *Benzene* decision, virtually all risk management decisions made by regulatory agencies must be accompanied by an extensive factual record that includes any relevant scientific data and expert judgments. In sum,

> The risk-based approach is now the central element in environmental and public health decision-making in the U.S. While there are few explicit statutory requirements for agencies to conduct quantitative risk assessments, U.S. government agencies have adopted risk assessment as the methodical way to defend and insulate the decision-making process.[28]

[24] Quoted in ibid.
[25] Quoted in ibid., 358.
[26] Quoted in ibid.
[27] Charnley and Elliott, "Risk Versus Precaution," 10363.
[28] Joel Tickner and Carolyn Raffensperger, "The American View of the Precautionary Principle," in *Reinterpreting the Precautionary Principle*, ed. Timothy O'Riordan, James Cameron, and Andrew Jordan (London: Cameron, 2001), 199.

Significantly, while the efforts of the Congressional Republican leadership after 1994 to weaken the nation's major environmental statutes were defeated, the Unfunded Mandates Reform Act, the Small Business Regulatory Fairness Enforcement Act, the Information Data (Quality) Act, and the amendments to the Safe Water Drinking Act—all of which sought to subject risk regulations to more extensive scientific and economic scrutiny—were each signed into law by President Clinton. The fact that presidents of both political parties have supported rules and statutory requirements requiring agencies to produce regulatory impact assessments and cost-benefit analyses to justify risk management decisions suggests a broad bipartisan consensus on the criteria which risk regulations must be required to meet.

The Policy Impact of Cost-Benefit Analysis and Risk Assessments

In principle, there is nothing about the requirements that regulations meet a cost-benefit test and/or be justified by a risk assessment that precludes the adoption of relatively stringent or highly risk-averse regulations. Many highly stringent regulations do produce more costs than benefits and many of the relatively stringent risk regulations adopted in the United States, such as the steady strengthening of federal rules for health-related emissions from mobile sources, are justified by both risk assessments and cost-benefit analyses. The several health, safety, and environmental risk regulations issued by the Obama administration have each been subject to a cost-benefit assessment.[29] Nonetheless, these two requirements have had an important impact on slowing down the enactment of stringent regulations by federal regulatory agencies.

They have required agencies to invest considerable resources to developing extensive economic and scientific data sufficient to withstand legal challenges to their rule-making, which in turn means fewer resources are available for developing new regulations. It is estimated that 90 percent of the scientific factual data prepared by the EPA are to enable the agency's decisions to withstand judicial review.[30] As the enforcement of the 1976 Toxic Substances Control Act (TSCA) after the asbestos case reveals, it has also made regulatory agencies reluctant to propose new rules in the first place. The requirement that rules issued by regulatory agencies be accompanied by detailed, often quantitatively based risk assessments has also made it more difficult for rules to be adopted for risks whose adverse impacts are uncertain or not yet proven by risk assessments.

[29] "Red Tape Rising," *The Economist*, January 22, 2011.
[30] Charnley and Elliott, "Risk Versus Precaution," 10363.

THE BROADER CHALLENGE TO REGULATORY STRINGENCY

The increased reliance placed on risk assessments by American regulatory agencies, the courts, and Congress in part reflects the increased sophistication of the science of toxicology since the 1970s. The emergence of quantitative risk assessments as a well-recognized academic discipline has increased the level of scientific knowledge about what constitutes a "safe" level of exposure, or to use the legal term, a *de minimis* risk, information that was largely unavailable when many of the earlier, highly stringent regulatory standards were enacted into law.

For example, when the Delaney Clause was adopted, relatively little was known about the precise cause and effect relationship between pesticide residues in food and human health. Thus, given both the lack of scientific knowledge and increased public concern about the health risks of chemical exposures, a "zero risk" or precautionary standard for carcinogenic food additives made sense. But subsequently, much more was learned about the precise level or threshold of harm posed by human exposure to cancer-causing chemicals. This in turn allowed the Delaney Clause to be replaced in 1996 by the Food Quality Protection Act, which established the risk-based standard of "reasonable certainty of no harm. What changed was the nature of the evidence required to trigger the uncontested moral obligation not to endanger human health."[31]

However, the increased importance of both risk assessments and cost-benefit analyses in making risk management decisions in the United States is not simply a response to the increased stringency of judicial or administrative reviews or more sophisticated regulatory science. It also reflects "a more widespread concern about the perceived over-stringency and inefficiency of many precautionary standards."[32]

In 1987, seventy-five senior staff at the EPA published a report which documented a pervasive gap between the risks about which the public was most concerned and those that experts considered substantiated. This report further argued that "serial panics" had undermined the public's ability to understand which risks it should actually be worrying about.[33] A follow-up study released by the EPA in 1990 concluded: "There are heavy costs involved if society fails to set environmental priorities based on risk. If finite resources are expended on lower-priority problems

---

[31] Jasanoff, "A Living Legacy," 232.
[32] D. Bodansky, "The Precautionary Principle in US Environmental Law," in Riordan, Cameron, and Jordan, *Reinterpreting the Precautionary Principle*, 205.
[33] "Unfinished Business: A Comparative Assessment of Environmental Problems—An Overview," U.S. Environmental Protection Agency, Report #2303287025a (February 1987).

at the expense of higher-priority risk, then society will face needlessly high risks."[34]

These reports both reflected and reinforced broader and more extensive criticisms of the way many American risk regulations had or were being made. The magazines *Regulation*, established by the American Enterprise Institute (AEI) in 1997, as well as the *Public Interest*, founded by Irving Kristol during the mid-1960s, featured a steady stream of articles that challenged both the scientific and economic rationale for many of the health, safety, and environmental statutes and regulations being adopted in the United States. Conservative think tanks such as American Enterprise Institute, the Cato Institute, the Heritage Foundation, and the Center for a Competitive Economy published numerous studies that were highly critical of many American risk regulations, arguing that many were based on insignificant risks, imposed unnecessary financial burdens on both local governments and businesses, and had produced few or in some cases no health, safety, or environmental benefits.

Nor were criticisms of the rationale for many consumer and environmental risk regulations confined to conservative or business-funded organizations. They were also voiced by the centrist Brookings Institution, which in 1998 established a Joint Center for Regulatory Policy with AEI. Brookings also published several books and reports that were highly critical of the scientific rationale for and the public benefits of many of the risk regulations adopted in the United States. In fact, "there were few if any major think tanks openly advocating more or strong federal regulation in the 1970s and 1980s"—a description that is even more descriptive of the two decades since then.[35]

A steady stream of influential academic studies, many of which were published during the 1990s, challenged the logic behind many of the highly risk-averse regulations adopted in the United States, arguing that many of them were based on phantom or exaggerated risks, ignored risk-risk tradeoffs, created more costs than benefits, and had often undermined public welfare.[36] According to Robert Hahn, "There is a growing

---

[34] "Reducing Risk: Setting Priorities and Strategies for Environmental Protection," Environmental Protection Agency (September 26, 1990).

[35] Daniel Carpenter, *Reputation and Power* (Princeton, NJ: Princeton University Press, 2010), 395.

[36] See, in addition to the studies summarized below, *In Search of Safety; Chemicals and Cancer Risk*, ed. John Graham, Laura Green, and Marc Roberts (Cambridge, MA: Harvard University Press, 1988); Joseph Rodricks, *Calculated Risks: The Toxicity and Human Health Risks of Chemicals in our Environment* (Cambridge: Cambridge University Press, 1992); *Phantom Risk: Scientific Inference and the Law*, ed. Kenneth Foster, David Bernstein, and Peter Huber (Cambridge, MA: MIT Press, 1993); *Risk vs. Risk: Trade-Offs in Protecting Health and the Environment*, ed. John Graham and Jonathan Wiener (Cambridge, MA: Harvard University Press, 1995). John Graham headed the office of regulatory

sense among U.S. citizens that government regulation has become excessive . . . A growing body of evidence . . . shows that many recent expenditures on risk reduction have done very little to actually reduce risk. Indeed, in some cases, those investments are likely to have increased risks to human health."[37]

Aaron Wildavsky's *Searching for Safety* argued that "current discussions of risk and safety are too one-sided, focusing on the dangers of risk-taking while neglecting . . . opportunity benefits that would be lost by risk aversion.[38] In a subsequent volume, Wildavsky and several of his students systematically reviewed the scientific evidence behind more than a dozen politically influential health, safety, or environmental "scares" including for dieldrin, saccharin, DDT, PCBs, Dioxin, Alar, arsenic in drinking water, abandoned hazardous waste sites, and asbestos in school rooms.[39] They concluded that in virtually every case, the public had been either misinformed or mislead. Accordingly, the regulations that sought to ameliorate these "risks" had wasted substantial resources without making Americans any safer or healthier.

Likewise, *Breaking the Vicious Circle* claimed that policy makers had been *too* responsive to the public's fears and anxieties.[40] Its author, Stephen Breyer, who was subsequently appointed by President Clinton to the U.S. Supreme Court, argued that poorly informed—and media inflamed—public fears about trivial or non-existent risks had led to an expensive misallocation of regulatory resources. He urged policy makers to place much greater trust in the advice of informed experts in deciding which risks to regulate as well as how stringently to regulate them.

Risk and Reason: Safety, Law, and the Environment, by Cass Sunstein, expanded on Breyer's analysis.[41] Sunstein, who was subsequently appointed to head the Office of Information and Regulatory Affairs in

---

review in the Office of Management and Budget during the administration of George W. Bush; Robert Candall and Lester Lave, eds., *The Scientific Basis of Health and Safety Regulation* (Washington, DC: Brookings Institution, 1981); Ronald Gots, *Toxic Risks: Science, Regulation, and Perception* (Boca Raton, FL: Lewis Publishers, 1993).

[37] Robert Hahn, "Preface," in *Risks, Cost, and Lives Saved: Getting Better Results from Regulation*, ed. Robert Hahn (New York: Oxford University Press, 1996), vii.

[38] Aaron Wildavksy, *Searching for Safety* (New Brunswick, NJ: Transaction Books, 1988), 228.

[39] Aaron Wildavsky, *But Is It True? A Citizen's Guide to Environmental Health and Safety Issues* (Cambridge, MA: Harvard University Press, 1995).

[40] Stephen Breyer, *Breaking the Vicious Circle: Toward Effective Risk Regulation* (Cambridge, MA: Harvard University Press, 1993).

[41] Cass Sunstein, *Risk and Reason: Safety, Law, and the Environment* (Cambridge: Cambridge University Press, 2002). See also Cass Sunstein, *Laws of Fear: Beyond the Precautionary Principle* (Cambridge: Cambridge University Press, 2005) and *Worst-Case Scenarios* (Cambridge, MA: Harvard University Press, 2007).

the OMB by President Barack Obama, criticized the role of "information cascade effects" driven by dramatic news coverage of a "scare" in distorting public perceptions of the actual risks to which they were exposed. "Insofar as people lack their own means for judging a claim's validity, there is a danger that the beliefs generated by a cascade will be factually incorrect."[42] Like Breyer, Sunstein recommended that regulators make greater use of risk assessments as a way of insuring that risk regulations would be "grounded, first, and foremost in an understanding of scientific facts."[43]

As the changes in media coverage of global climate change discussed in chapter 3 reveals, many media outlets became more willing to feature experts, reports, and studies that challenged the credibility of many of the new health, safety, and environmental risks from which activists were now demanding the government protect them, and the planet, most notably global climate change. This chorus of criticism reflected and reinforced a growing ideological polarization toward risk regulation in the United States: each claim about a new risk became increasingly likely to be challenged by a counter-narrative contending that it was misinformed. During the 1990s, five times as many books were published that were skeptical of various environmental risks, most commonly climate change, as during the preceding decade.[44]

THE POLITICAL IMPACT OF REGULATORY SKEPTICISM

The "regulatory skepticism" of influential policy analysts across the political spectrum, as well as of business-funded think tanks and studies, had an important policy impact. If critics of the scientific rationale and effectiveness of many of the highly salient risks that the government had previously acted to protect the public from were to be believed, then how seriously should the media, policy elites, and policy makers now take the new "alarm bells" rung by activists? Might the scientific claims underlying these new risks also turn out to be misinformed or exaggerated? Might devoting considerable resources to preventing them also prove to be ill-advised? Should not the media, the public, and policy makers be more discerning in deciding which "alarm bells" to listen to and respond to?

Few risks speak for themselves. Rather, risk perceptions are politically constructed. One important reason why, since the early 1990s, fewer

[42] Sunstein, *Risk and Reason*, 86.
[43] Ibid., 108.
[44] Naomi Oreskes and Erik Conway, *Merchants of Doubt: How a Handful of Scientists Obscured the Truth on Issues from Tobacco Smoke to Global Warming* (New York: Bloomsbury Press, 2010), 253.

"alarm bells" became amplified in the United States is that the public also heard an equally loud if not more amplified "counter cascade" of "anti-alarm bells" contending that many of the alarms that they had previously found credible were unacceptable, and to which policy makers had often been pressured to respond, were in fact "false alarms." These alternative narratives often served to undermine, or at least confuse, significant segments of the public about the credibility of new "alarm bells," making it more difficult for them to gain political traction and become policy triggers. As a result, what was formerly often a "risk availability *cascade*" became more akin to a "risk availability *blockade*."

In December 2009, the *New York Times* published a chart "Picturing the Last Ten Years."[45] For each year, it listed, among other items, "fears." *But significantly, not one of these fears was a business-related health, safety, or environmental risk.* One suspects that had similar charts been published at the end of the previous three decades, they would have included many of the kinds of risks described in this book.

In short, policy elite, business, and media criticisms of many of the risk regulations adopted in the United States helped weaken public pressures, support, and demands for more stringent risk regulations. Opponents of more stringent regulations became more effective in challenging the claims of pro-regulatory activists in the court of public opinion, while policy makers at the federal level became less responsive to what they perceived as "ill-informed alarm bells"—as reflected, for example, in the Food and Drug Administration's decision to approve BST in 1991 and its decision not to ban phthalates in cosmetics, as well as the strong support by federal agencies and departments for genetically modified (GM) food and agriculture and their opposition to mandatory labeling for both BST and GM food. A recent, critical, study of developments in American environmental law concludes: "By now, the story of modern American environmental law has been redacted into a familiar script, one in which the excesses of our early attempts to regulate the human impact on the environment came to be disciplined by the insight of sound science and economic reasoning, warding off in the process alarmism, inefficiency, and government overreaching."[46] Political and policy developments in Europe, however, have moved in a very different direction.

[45] Phillip Niemeyer, "Picturing the Past 10 Years," *New York Times*, December 26, 2009, A26.

[46] Kysar, *Regulating from Nowhere*, 1. For other criticisms of the (mis)use of cost-benefit analyses and scientific risk assessments in preventing much needed regulation, see Liza Heinzerling and Frnak Ackerman, *Priceless: How to Know the Price of Everything and the Value of Nothing* (Washington, DC: Georgetown Law and Policy Institute, 2002), and Wendy Wagnar and Rena Steinzor, eds., *Rescuing Science from Politics: Regulation and the Distortion of Scientific Research* (Cambridge: Cambridge University Press, 2006).

THE PRECAUTIONARY PRINCIPLE IN THE EU

Origins

The introduction of a precautionary approach to risk regulation in Europe dates from the 1970s, when the concept of *Vorsorgeprinzip* emerged in Germany. Commonly interpreted as "precaution," or "foresight," though the term also implies "good husbandry" or "best practice," it represented an important innovation in German regulatory policy. As applied to German pollution control law, "the *Vorsorgeprinzip* stands for the premise that various adverse impacts of industrial air emissions justify regulatory interventions geared at their control, even if the link between exposure to specific pollutants and causation or particular diseases remains uncertain."[47] As a 1984 German government report on air quality noted a decade later, "[precaution] means acting when conclusive evidence ascertained by science is not yet available."[48] The concept was subsequently invoked by German authorities to justify technology-based standards designed to reduce sulfur emissions from coal-burning power plants in order to protect the deterioration of German forests (a phenomenon known as *Waldsterben* in German) from acid rain—even though there was as yet no scientific consensus about the causes of forest deterioration.

The 1990 Ministerial Declaration on the North Sea, signed by each of the countries bordering that body of water—most of which were EU member states—represents the first introduction of the precautionary principle into international law and also constitutes one of its strongest formulations. It explicitly urged signatory governments to "apply the precautionary principle, that is to take action to avoid potentially damaging impacts of [toxic] substances . . . even when there is no scientific evidence to prove a causal link between emissions and effects."[49]

A number of other European countries subsequently adopted various versions of the precautionary principle and thanks to pressures from Europeans, it was included in the Rio Declaration on Environment and Development in 1992.[50] Principle 15 states: "In order to protect the environment, the precautionary approach shall be widely applied by

[47] Noga Morag-Levine, *Chasing the Wind: Regulating Air Pollution in the Common Law State* (Princeton, NJ: Princeton University Press, 2003), 11.

[48] Ibid., 55.

[49] Cited in E. Soule, "Assessing the Precautionary Principle," *Public Affairs Quarterly* 14, no. 3 (2000): 318.

[50] For the adoption of the Precautionary Principle by European countries, see Nicholas de Sadeleer, ed., *Implementing the Precautionary Principle: Approaches from the Nordic Countries, EU, and the USA* (Sterling, VA: Earthscan, 2007).

States according to their capacities. Where there are threats of serious or irreversible damage, lack of full scientific certainty shall not be used as a reason for postponing cost-effect measures to prevent environmental degradation."

Adoption by the EU

The principle was officially introduced into EU environmental policy by the Treaty on European Union (the Maastricht Treaty), which amended the Treaty of the European Community). It was approved in 1992 and went into effect the following year. Article 130r(2) states: "[EU] policy on the environment . . . should be based on the precautionary principle and on the principles that preventive action should be taken, that environmental damage should, as a priority be rectified."[51] The European Court of Justice subsequently broadened its scope from environmental protection to include human, animal, and plant health in its decision on the BSE case.[52]

Its legal codification in an EU treaty provoked considerable controversy, including from the American government, which officially criticized both its vagueness and its potential as a justification for protectionist policies. The EU Committee of the American Chamber of Commerce expressed "grave concern" that its application could lead to a politicization of science."[53] It urged the EU to instead follow the example of the United States and make risk assessment the "cornerstone on which fundamental science decisions were based." In a full-page advertisement in the European newspaper, *European Voice*, Pfizer, a major producer of beef hormones whose use had earlier been banned by the EU on precautionary grounds, stated:

> However vaguely it is defined in official documents, everyone knows that the precautionary principle entails—a cautious approach to change. . . . Allowing the precautionary principle to dominate decision-making in Europe could suppress the very forces of economic and technical innovation that make the current world possible, and deprive the EU of necessary investment and jobs. That is why . . . excessive caution may be the biggest risk of all.[54]

[51] Andrew Jordan, "The Precautionary Principle in the European Union," in *Reinterpreting the Precautionary Principle*, 148. Following further amendments, this became Article 174, and is now Article 191.2 of the "Lisbon" Treaty that currently governs the EU.

[52] For this and other early ECJ cases that applied the precautionary principle to food safety risks, see Alberto Alemanno, *Trade in Food: Regulatory and Judicial Approaches in the EC and the WTO* (London: Cameron, 2007), 111–18.

[53] Quoted in Jordan, "The Precautionary Principle," 158.

[54] Quoted in ibid., 154.

For its part, the EU also found itself under pressure to address the implications of the 1997 decision of the World Trade Organization's (WTO's) appellate body in the *hormones* case (discussed in chapter 3). The dispute panel ruled that the EU was obligated to produce risk assessments capable of "reasonably supporting" its claim that imports of beef produced with hormones endangered human health, which it had not done. The EU thus needed to find a way to (re)formulate its risk regulations in terms that would make them more consistent with its WTO treaty obligations. It also wanted to reassure its trading partners, most notably the United States, that the application of the precautionary principle would not be abused for protectionist purposes.

Another important factor prompting the Commission to address how the precautionary principle should be implemented arose from the actions of member states, many of whom were using it to challenge EU regulatory policies that they viewed as insufficiently protective of the health and safety of their citizens. For example, France invoked the principle to justify its continued unwillingness to end its ban on British beef following the BSE crisis, notwithstanding the official judgment of the Commission that British beef was now as "safe" as French beef. These and other national regulations based on the precautionary principle threatened the authority of the European Commission as well as the integrity of a single market.[55] Thus it became important for the Commission to "rein in" what it considered the abuse of the precautionary principle by member states, while at the same time defining what role it should or would play in shaping both national and European EU risk regulations.

In 2000, after considerable delay, the European Commission issued a comprehensive policy guideline that sought to clarify the conditions under which the precautionary principle would be applied.[56] The importance of this communication was underscored by the fact that it was issued by the entire Commission, rather than DG Environment. The Commission essentially sought to strike a middle ground between business groups who wanted preventive measures to be adopted only after a risk assessment had clearly identified both the extent and limits of existing scientific knowledge, and environmental groups who believed the precautionary principle should be applied not only in the case of uncertainty, but also in the case of ignorance, which the European Environmental

---

[55] For this and other examples of the tension between the Commission and the application of the precautionary principle by member states, see David Vogel, "The Politics of Risk Regulation in Europe and the U.S.," in *The Yearbook of American Environmental Law*, vol. 3, ed. H. Somsen (Oxford: Oxford University Press, 2003), 27–31.

[56] "Communication from the Commission on the Precautionary Principle" (February 2, 2000). See also Jordan, "The Precautionary Principle in the European Union," 143–62.

Bureau defined as "that which is not known; this also includes that which we are not aware that we don't know."[57]

The Commission stated that the acceptable trigger points for precautionary intervention should involve cases of "potential" risk, which it understood as falling somewhere between "actual" and "hypothetical" risks. The principle should be invoked when "potentially dangerous effects deriving from a phenomenon, product, or process" have been identified, and a "scientific evaluation of the risk, which because of the insufficiency of the data, their inclusive or imprecise nature, makes it impossible to determine with sufficient certainty the risk in question." As more data became available, regulations initially based on the precautionary principle would be reassessed.

While the Commission noted "the absence of scientific proof of the existence of a cause-effect relationship . . . should not be used to justify inaction," it also emphasized that "every decision must be preceded by an examination of available scientific data," since without some kind of scientific risk assessment there is no way of identifying which "potentially dangerous effects" should be addressed. It then added that precautionary regulations must also be consistent with the proportionality principle, a key principle of European law which states that a regulation should be the least trade restrictive in order to achieve its policy objectives. Finally, the Commission stated that risk management decisions "can and should incorporate a much broader range of considerations, including an examination of the costs and benefits of both action and inaction as well as the level of risk the public considers appropriate."

The Commission's document, which was subsequently endorsed by the European Council of Ministers and the European Parliament, was ambiguous. On one hand, it emphasized the role of scientific evaluation and application of generally accepted principles of risk management, including the need for risk assessment and the application of the proportionality principle. But on the other, it also included the "level of risk the public considers appropriate" as a legitimate decision-making criterion. Significantly left undefined was who should determine public acceptability, how "potentially dangerous effects" are to be identified, what level of scientific evidence makes a risk "potential," how much "scientific uncertainty" is required before a provisional regulation is adopted, and what level of "scientific certainty" is necessary to revise it. Whether or not these ambiguities or contradictions are inherent in the precautionary principle itself, as many of its critics have contended, the Commission's document

[57] Quoted in Veerle Heyvaert, "Guidance Without Constraint: Assessing the Impact of the Precautionary Principle on the European Community's Chemicals Policy," in *The Yearbook of European Environmental Law*, vol. 6 (Oxford: Oxford University Press, 2006), 32.

provided the European Union with sufficient flexibility to decide when and how it would actually be implemented—a point that was underlined by the Commission's characterization of the precautionary principle as a tool of risk *management*.[58]

IMPLEMENTING THE PRECAUTIONARY PRINCIPLE

The division of labor between scientific advisory bodies—which include the EU's various regulatory agencies as well as an extensive network of scientific advisory bodies from the member states—and those who actually make European regulatory policies, namely the Commission, the Council of Ministers, and the European Parliament, is critical to understanding how the precautionary principle is applied in the EU. The responsibility of the former is to offer scientific advice to the EU's decision-making bodies. While both scientists and policy makers are encouraged to exchange information at each stage of the regulatory process, it is the latter who are responsible for deciding which risk management decisions to adopt since "in the end, the decision is always a political one."[59] As an influential memo from the European Commission put it, "it is not up to individual scientists to decide on the acceptable level of risk imposed on the society as a whole." Rather, making such a judgment and deciding what "other legitimate factors" should also go into it is the responsibility of policy-makers."[60] Accordingly, it is "for decision-makers and ultimately the courts to flesh out the [precautionary] principle."[61]

The precautionary principle has played an important role in shaping the European approach to risk regulation. Its explicit inclusion in the Maastricht Treaty "marked a new, and more self-confident stage in the evolution of the EU's environmental performance," one which indicated that the EU was no longer willing to let "the USA set the pace when it came to developing and implementing environmental standards" and which implicitly challenged the increased American reliance on risk assessments as a guide to risk management decisions.[62]

---

[58] For a detailed criticism of the Commission's statement, see Giandomenico Majone, "What Price Safety? The Precautionary Principle and its Policy Implications," *JCMS* 40, no. 1 (2002): 89–109; Natalie McNelis, "EU Communication on the Precautionary Principle," *Journal of International Economic Law* (2000): 545–51; Jim Dratwa, "Taking Risks with the Precautionary Principle: Food (and the Environment) for Thought at the European Commission, " *Journal of Environmental Policy & Planning* 4 (2002): 197–213.

[59] Dratwa, "The Precautionary Principle," 9.

[60] Comments from the European Commission Services to the Codex Secretariat.

[61] Quoted in Heyvaert, "Guidance Without Constraint," 33.

[62] Jordan, "The Precautionary Principle in the European Union," 149.

Since the Commission's 2000 communication, references to the precautionary principle have been included in almost every major European policy document on health or environmental regulation. It has been referenced in scores of resolutions adopted by the European Parliament. The EU has also actively sought to make it into an international legal norm, pressuring for its incorporation into international environmental treaties as well as international trade law.

Many of the EU's regulations that were more stringent and comprehensive than those of the United States described in this book have been either explicitly or indirectly based on it, including some which were adopted before it became an official part of European law. These include the EU's hormone ban, its refusal to authorize rBST, its restrictions on antibiotics in animal feed, its restrictive policies toward GMOs, its ban on phthalates in children's products, its restrictions on chemicals in cosmetics, and most significantly, REACH, which explicitly incorporates the principle in Article 1.3. The White Paper on which the latter regulation was based explicitly noted the danger of *not* adopting regulatory restrictions until conclusive scientific data became available, adding that "whenever scientific evidence is available, but, there is still uncertainty, decision-making must be based on precaution."[63]

The Role of European Courts

Its importance in European law is also reflected in frequent references to the joint decisions of the European Court of Justice and the Court of First Instance. The 2002 *Alpharma* judgment confirmed the status of the precautionary principle as a "central plank in EU policy-making," while the subsequent *Artegodan* judgment made it into a "general principle" of European law. Generally speaking, European courts have given European institutions' broad discretion in deciding how and when to apply it. For example, as discussed in chapter 3, in a series of high-profile actions taken between 1998 and 2002, the Council voted to withdraw marketing authorizations for a range of antibiotics in animal feed, notwithstanding the lack of risk assessments that clearly connected their use to an identified health threat. In deciding against Pfizer, the European courts ruled:

> Community institutions were not required, for the purpose of taking preventing action, to wait for the risk to become a reality and for adverse effects to materialize. . . . If the Community institutions were unable to take any preventive measures until such research is completed, the precautionary principle, the

[63] Heyvaert, "Guidance Without Constraint," 51.

aim of which is to prevent any such adverse effects, would be rendered devoid of purpose.[64]

It then essentially reversed the burden of proof, holding that since Pfizer had been unable to prove conclusively that there was no link between its animal antibiotics and the development of antibiotic resistance in humans, the Council's ban was justified. According to Veerle Heyvaert:

> On specific cases where precautionary action might be advisable . . . the Council, the Commission, and the Courts endorse quite a strong version of precaution, which does not require a completed substance-based risk assessment, and does not depend on agreement by designated scientific expert committees before precautionary intervention can be undertaken.[65]

She adds: "Acceptable trigger points for precautionary intervention are set at a low threshold."

Transatlantic differences in judicial review are thus an important factor underlying many of the differences in the risk regulations adopted in Europe and the United States. However, European courts have generally subjected national regulations to more demanding standards, and these are similar to those applied by courts in the United States to the decisions made by American regulatory agencies. In fact, the holding of the European court in the *French BSE* case was essentially similar to that of the American Supreme Court in the *Benzene* case; both courts struck down risk regulations on the grounds that the risks from which they were trying to protect the public were not "significant." European courts have generally insisted on stronger scientific evidence to justify national risk regulations because such regulations threaten the single market.[66] In effect, European law privileges the role of European institutions to make regulations based on the precautionary principle.

Yet at the same time, as this book has also demonstrated, not all EU risk regulations have been shaped by the precautionary principle.[67] For example, the EU's drug approval policies have been unaffected by it.

---

[64] Quoted in Ragnar Lofstedt, "The Swing of the Regulatory Pendulum in Europe: From Precautionary Principle to Regulatory Impact Analysis," *Journal of Risk and Uncertainty* 28, no. 3 (2004): 248.

[65] Heyvaert, "Guidance Without Constraint," 35.

[66] For relevant cases, some of which have upheld more stringent national risk regulations and others which have struck them down, see Alemanno, *Trade in Food*, 325–28, and Alberto Alemanno, "The Shaping of Risk Regulation by Community Courts," *Jean Monnet Working Paper* 18/08, http://ssm.com/abstract=1325770.

[67] For examples of its lack of influence on some European chemical regulations, see N. Eckley and Henrick Selin, "All Talk, Little Action: Precaution and European Chemicals Regulation," *Journal of European Public Policy* 11 (2004): 78–105, though it is important to note that their examples pre-date the passage of REACH.

What its status in European law has done is to give policy makers at the European level broad discretion in deciding how and when to apply it—including the ability to decide when to ignore it, when to defer to scientific risk assessments, when to adopt more stringent regulations than those recommended by its scientific advisory bodies. This discretion was confirmed in the 2010 *Gowan* case in which the ECJ delivered its most important judgment on European risk regulation since *Pfizer*.[68] In upholding the Commission's ban on a pesticide, the court stated that the Commission must be allowed wide discretion in assessing risks in order to maintain a high level of protection of the environment, and human and animal health.

CHALLENGES TO PRECAUTION

The application of the precautionary principle, the public risk perceptions underlying it, and the risk regulations that have been influenced by it, have been strongly criticized in Europe. For example, Frank Furedi argues that much European risk regulation is based on a "culture of fear."[69] According to Bill Durodie, "we should be wary of creating a culture of unnecessary fear. . . . Rather than embracing the opportunities latent with uncertainty as did previous generations, today we appear to reject them and highlight the risks." Echoing Aaron Wildavsky and Mary Douglas, he argues, "What really may have changed is not so much the scale of problems we face, but rather the outlook with which society perceives its difficulties, both real and imagined."[70] Ragner Loftstedt writes that regulators who employ it "may be highly biased and put forward impossible environmental and public health criteria which industry will never be able to meet . . . leading to . . . irrationality and emotionalism."[71]

Significantly, the same year that it approved the Commission's Communication on the Precautionary Principle, the European Council of Ministers launched a "Better Regulation" initiative in the framework of

[68]Case C-77/09. Gowan had challenged the legality of a Directive restricting the use of the pesticide fanarimol on the grounds that its restrictions were not justified by the scientific studies that informed the EU's decision-making processes. The court affirmed the legality of the Directive.

[69]Frank Furedi, *Culture of Fear: Risk-Taking and the Morality of Low Expectation* (London: Cassell, 1997).

[70]Bill Durodie, "The True Cost of Precautionary Chemicals Regulation," *Risk Analysis* 23, no. 2 (2003): 396. For a detailed criticism of a wide range of European regulatory policies, see Christopher Booker and Richard North, *Scared to Death From BSE to Global Warming: Why Scares Are Costing Us the Earth* (London: Continuum, 2007).

[71]Ragnar Lofstedt, "The Precautionary Principle: Risk, Regulation and Politics," *Process Safety and Environmental Protection* 81, no. 1 (January 2003): 38.

the Lisbon agenda. Its purpose was to help the EU achieve its goal of becoming the "most competitive and dynamic knowledge based economy in the world."[72] The EU's "Better Regulation" program, which explicitly draws on American policy approaches, requires that impact analyses be conducted for all legal instruments, including regulations, directives, and decisions as well as nonbinding legislative proposals such as communications and White Papers.[73]

In 2006, the Commission established an EU Impact Assessment Board (IAB) located in the office of the Secretariat-General, in order to oversee the quality of the impact assessments by the Directorates-General. It has also strengthened its administrative capacity to conduct risk assessments and to give them a more prominent role in its risk management decisions. These efforts took on a renewed sense of urgency following the economic and financial crisis of 2008, as the Commission sought to promote European economic growth by reducing its regulatory burdens on business, especially for small and medium enterprises. However, unlike the Office of Information and Regulatory Affairs (OIRA) which is located in the Executive Office of the President, the IAB has no veto power over the impact assessments submitted to it, though it can suggest that they be revised. Nor can it legally prevent any DG from proposing a regulation.

One of the most important objectives of "Better Regulation" has been to simplify, reduce, and streamline European regulations by targeting many that were regarded as unduly costly, administratively burdensome, too complex—and often unpopular. The scope of the EU's "Better Regulation" initiatives extends far beyond consumer and environmental risk regulations, and indeed, few of the regulatory "reforms" issued under it

---

[72] Quoted in Robert Hahn and Robert Litan, "Counting Regulatory Benefits and Costs: Lessons for the U.S. and Europe," *Journal of International Economic Law* 8, no. 2 (2005): 493.

[73] For descriptions and analyses of of the EU's Better Regulation initiative, including comparisons with administrative regulatory review in the United States, see Jonathan Wiener, "Better Regulation Europe," in *Current Legal Problems 2006*, vol. 59, ed. Joane Holder and Colm O'Cinneide (Oxford: Oxford University Press, 2007), 447–518; Ragnar Lofstedt, "The 'Plauteau-ing' of the European Better Regulation Agenda: An Analysis of Activities Carried Out by the Barasso Commission," *Journal of Risk Research* 10, no. 4 (June 2007): 423–47; and Jonathan Wiener and Alberto Alemanno, "Comparing Regulatory Oversight Bodies across the Atlantic: The Office of Information and Regulatory Affairs in the U.S. and the Impact Assessment Board in the EU," in *Comparative Environmental Law*, ed. Susan Rose-Ackerman and Peter Lindseth (London: Edward Elgar, 2010), 309–35. Although the annual reviews of the Commission document its overall economic benefits and the considerable number of EU laws it has reduced or revised, neither these reviews nor the above studies describe any specific risk management decisions that the EU's "Better Regulation" initiatives and impact assessment requirements have affected, though in the case of REACH, they were used by the Commission to estimate the costs of compliance with it.

have addressed risk regulations. However, the Commission's guidelines, which require that regulatory impact assessments be assessed across three dimensions, namely economic, environmental, and social (which includes health) obviously can and do apply to health, safety, and environmental regulations.

But like the Commission's 2000 White Paper, the policy impact of the IAB's impact assessment guidelines remain ambiguous as they do not specify the relative weight or importance that should be accorded to each of these dimensions. This has important policy consequences since an impact assessment that emphasizes economic impacts may lead to rather different regulatory policies than one that emphasizes its environmental or social ones.

While both "Better Regulation" and the Barasso Commission have sought to slow down the growth of European regulation, the precautionary principle continues to influence European regulatory policies. For example, in 2009, the EU enacted an important new pesticide directive based on it: it instructed the member states to address the "potential" health and environmental damage caused by pesticides, and the Commission immediately banned twenty-two active chemicals found in pesticides. (It was one of these pesticides that the plaintiff unsuccessfully challenged in *Gowan*.) The Commission also issued a precautionary ban on the chemical BPA in 2010, which was not subject to a regulatory impact assessment.

THE PRECAUTIONARY PRINCIPLE IN COMPARATIVE PERSPECTIVE

While there are scores of definitions of the precautionary principle, in essence, it enables, encourages, or requires policy makers to "err on the side of caution" by adopting relatively stringent regulations—even if the available scientific evidence of the risks posed by a particular business practice or product to public health, safety, or environmental quality are unclear, inconclusive, ambiguous, or uncertain. By not requiring substantial or conclusive scientific proof of harm, it enables policy makers to impose regulations on the basis of a potential or reasonable likelihood of harm, especially when there is a possibility that the harms stemming from a failure to regulate may prove serious or irreversible.

One of its primary purposes is to reduce the ability of policy makers to use scientific uncertainty as a justification for avoiding or delaying the imposition of more stringent protective regulations. In essence, the precautionary principle decreases the burden of scientific certainty of harm necessary to impose additional restrictions and increases the level of scientific certainty of safety required to approve new products and production methods. It is premised on the assumption that too many risk regulations have been under-protective.

The extent to which scientific knowledge or risk assessments provide sufficient information to enable policy makers to rely on them in making decisions that adequately protect public health, safety, and environmental quality represents a critical difference between recent European and American approaches to risk management. "During the last decade, U.S. environmental law has increasingly stressed risk assessment and cost-benefit analysis . . . both of which presume that we have sufficient knowledge of measure risk and calculate the appropriate responses."[74]

Sheila Jasanoff writes, "risk is actuarial in spirit . . . When used in environmental decision-making, risk retains the connotation of something that can be clearly defined and quantified, hence managed."[75] But such confidence in science's ability to assess, measure, and predict health, safety, and environmental risks is precisely what the precautionary principle challenges.[76] If a reliance on risk assessments assumes that the ability of scientific knowledge to understand and predict the risks we face has increased, then the precautionary principle is based on a rather different assumption, namely that it is precisely *uncertainty*—that which we do not know—that has increased, and that moreover the dangers that we do not yet adequately understand or know about are likely to be more serious than those about which we already know.[77]

In 2002, the EU's European Environmental Agency published a revealing collection of essays that critically reviewed fourteen European risk management decisions. This report represents a direct counterpoint to the policy reviews published by the EPA between 1987 and 1990. While the latter studies documented numerous shortcomings of American regulatory policy stemming from insufficient reliance on risk assessments, *The Precautionary Principle in the 20th Century: Late Lessons from Early Warnings*, as its subtitle makes clear, drew precisely the opposite policy conclusion.

---

[74] Bodansky, "The Precautionary Principle in U.S. Environmental Law," 205.

[75] Sheila Jasanoff, "Technological Risk and Cultures of Rationality," in *Incorporating Science, Economics, and Sociology in Developing Sanitary and Phytosanitary Standards in International Trade* (National Research Council, Washington DC: National Academies Press, 2000), 72.

[76] See Oliver Goddard, "Social Decision-Making Under Conditions of Scientific Controversy, Expertise and the Precautionary Principle," in *Integrating Scientific Expertise into Regulatory Decision-Making: National Traditions and European Institutions*, ed. Christian Jeorges, Karl-Heinz Ladeur, and Ellen Vos (Baden Baden: Nomos Verlagsgellschaft, 1997), 65.

[77] For an extended discussion of these issues, see Tobias Arnoldussen, "Precautionary Logic and a Policy of Moderation," *Erasmus Law Review* 2, issue 2 (November 2009): 259–85.

A central lesson of this book concerns the importance of recognizing and fully understanding the nature and limitations of our knowledge. What is often referred to as "uncertainty" actually hides important technical distinctions. All the activities in these case studies were subjected to some form of (formal or informal) assessments of risk. What remained neglected, however, was the virtual certainty that there would be factors that remained outside the scope of risk assessment. This is the domain of ignorance—the source of inevitable surprises or unpredicted effects.[78]

It then added that "a key element in a precautionary approach to regulation involves a greater willingness to acknowledge the possibility of surprise."

The influence of the precautionary principle in Europe is also related to an important difference across the Atlantic regarding the "perception" that our environmental problems have worsened in recent years and we are now "*more* vulnerable today in the face of technological catastrophe."[79] If, as cultural theory suggests,

> Those who regard the environment as inherently robust and capable of withstanding sustained human impact (i.e. individualists) will tend to be less precautionary than those who regard human impact on nature as unpredictable and potentially calamitous (i.e. egalitarian-hierarchists), . . . [then] in cultural theoretical terms, the U.S. [has moved] . . . much close to the former, where the EU now conforms more to the predictions of the latter.[80]

In short, part of what changed on both sides of the Atlantic is "the outlook with which society perceives its difficulties, both real and imagined."[81]

A critical difference between recent European and American approaches to risk regulation has to do with the role that public opinion or public preferences should play in shaping regulatory policies. An influential criticism of American regulatory policy, made, for example, in the EPA reports as well as by Breyer, Wildavksy, and Sunstein, is that an important reason for the shortcomings of many American regulatory policies is that policy makers were *too* influenced by public fears and anxieties. Hence

---

[78] Poul Harremos, ed., *The Precautionary Principle in the 20th Century: Late Lessons from early Warnings* (London: Earthscan, 2002), 187.

[79] Emphasis added; Arnoldussen, "Precautionary Logic," 267.

[80] Jordan, "The Precautionary Principle in the European Union," 155. See also Aaron Wildavsky and Karl Dake, "Theories of Risk Perception: Who Fears What and Why," in *Risk and Modern Society*, ed. Ragnar Lofstedt and Lynn Frewer (London: Earthscan, 1998), 101–14. For a critical assessment of this explanation, see Barbara Adam, Ulrich Beck, and Joost Van Loon, eds., *The Risk Society and Beyond: Critical Issues for Social Theory* (London: Sage Publications, 2000).

[81] Durodie, "The True Cost," 392.

they emphasize the importance of insulating policymaking from public pressures by rooting them more firmly on cost-benefit analyses and risk assessments.

But the precautionary principle approaches the role of public preferences in shaping risk management decisions differently: it endorses the view that they *should* be accorded a legitimate policy role—a point made explicit in the European Commission's White Paper and then reinforced in the Council of Minister's adoption of it. In fact, the precautionary principle is most likely to be invoked as a response to public fears, concerns, or, in some cases, values. "Precautionary measures . . . are most likely to be applied when public opinion is instinctively or knowledgeably risk-averse."[82] For example, in the case of genetically modified foods, German Foreign Minister Joschka Fisher informed the United States: "Europeans do not want genetically modified food—period. It does not matter what research shows; they just do not want it and that has to be respected."[83]

In sum, while critics of stringent American regulatory policies have often argued that many of its shortcomings stem from it often being *too* responsive to public pressures, for the EU an important strategy for strengthening the legitimacy of its regulatory institutions and to protect the single market has been to make them *more* responsive to strongly or widely held public preferences.

CONCLUSION

This chapter explores the political and legal dimensions of the third component of my explanatory framework, namely how policy makers assess and manage risks. It describes and explains the policy changes that facilitated the adoption of more risk-averse regulations in Europe and impeded their adoption in the United States. This analysis overlaps and compliments the one presented in the preceding chapter. Thus the influence of the precautionary principle in Europe reflects both increased public pressures for more risk stringent regulations and the greater willingness of policy makers to respond to them, while the increased reliance on regulatory risk assessments in the United States is linked to a decline in public and political support for further expansion of risk regulation.

---

[82] Andrew Jordan and Timothy O'Riordan, "The Precautionary Principle in UK Environmental Law and Policy," in *UK Environmental Policy in the 1990s*, ed. Tim Gray (London: Macmillan, 1995), 61.

[83] J. A. Moore, "More than A Food Fight," *Issues in Science and Technology* 17, no. 4 (Summer 2001): 37.

CHAPTER NINE

Broader Implications

THIS CHAPTER EXPLORES SOME of the broader implications of this study, specifically its contributions to our understanding of the dynamics of policy convergence and divergence, the relationship between political institutions and policy styles, and the public perception of risks. I conclude by suggesting the implications of my explanatory framework for the future of consumer and environmental risk regulation in both the United States and the European Union.

THE DYNAMICS OF POLICY CONVERGENCE AND TRADING UP

The extensive literature on policy convergence addresses two issues: the extent of policy convergence and direction of policy convergence. Several studies have identified a number of mechanisms that promote policy convergence.[1] First, countries may adopt similar policies because they face similar problems. Second, countries' policies may converge because they are pressured to do so by a country or a group of countries that are more economically or politically powerful. Third, national policies may converge because countries have agreed to be bound by international treaties. Fourth, countries may mutually adjust their policies to those of other countries as a response to global economic integration. Finally, policy convergence may occur because of the international communication or policy learning that takes place in transnational networks of policy

---

[1] See, for example, Katharina Holzinger and Christoph Knill, "Causes and Conditions of Cross-national Policy Convergence," *Journal of European Public Policy* 12, no. 5 (October 2005): 775–96; Christoph Knill, "Introduction: Cross-national Policy Convergence: Concepts, Approaches and Explanatory Factors," *Journal of European Public Policy* 12, no. 5 (October 2005): 764–74; Andrea Lenschow, Duncan Leifferink, and Sietske Veenman, "When the Birds Sing. A Framework for Analyzing Domestic Factors behind Policy Convergence," *Journal of European Public Policy* 12, no. 5 (October 2005): 797–816; and Stephan Heichel, Jessica Pape, and Thomas Sommerer, "Is There Convergence in Convergence Research? An Overview of Empirical Studies on Policy Convergence," *Journal of European Public Policy* 12, no. 5 (October 2005): 817–40. See also David Lazar, "Regulatory Interdependence and International Governance," *Journal of European Public Policy* 8, no. 3 (2001): 474–92, which compares three ways in which regulatory policies may be made interdependent, namely competition, coordination, and policy learning.

experts, epistemic communities, nongovernment organizations, or firms. These mechanisms can often complement or reinforce one another.

A second body of literature addresses the impact of convergence on the direction of public policy. Much of this literature focuses on the impact of increased economic integration and global competition on the stringency of environmental regulation. Some studies argue that increased international competition is likely to either make governments weaken their environmental standards—"the race to the bottom" thesis—or make them reluctant to strengthen them—the "regulatory chill" thesis.[2] Other scholars have challenged these conclusions, demonstrating that increased economic interdependency may also lead to upward policy convergence or "trading up."[3] A "race to the top" typically occurs when a country is dependent on exports to a larger "greener" market. This in turn makes it in the interests of export-oriented producers to support national regulations similar to those of its important export market. These firms can then also benefit from economies of scale by producing the same products for both their home and export markets. Moreover, more stringent domestic standards may also serve to disadvantage their domestically oriented competitors. This dynamic of policy convergence has been labeled the "California effect," in recognition of the role of California's large "green" market in promoting the strengthening of both federal and European environmental standards, most notably for automotive emissions.[4]

Both the responses of the EU to many of the more stringent regulations adopted by the United States between around 1960 and 1990 and the responses of many other countries to the more stringent European regulations adopted after around 1990 are consistent with the major findings of the literatures on both policy convergence and trading up. The United States between 1960 and about 1990 and the EU since about 1990 each

---

[2]See, for example, D. Rodrik, *Has Globalization Gone Too Far?* (Washington, DC: Institute for International Economics, 1997), and L. Zarsky, "Stuck in the Mud? Nation States, Globalization and the Environment," in *The Earthscan Reader on International Trade and Sustainable Development*, ed. K. Gallagher and J. Werksman (London: Earthscan, 2002), 19–44.

[3]See, for example, David Vogel, *Trading Up; Consumer and Environmental Regulation in a Global Economy* (Cambridge, MA: Harvard University Press, 1995); A. Rugman and A. Verbeke, "Corporate Strategies and Environmental Regulation: An Organizing Framework," *Strategic Management Journal* 19 (4), (1998): 363–75; Aseem Prakash and M. Potoski, "Racing to the Bottom? Trade, Environmental Governance and ISO 14001," *American Journal of Political Science* 50, no. 2 (2006): 350–64; and Thomas Bernauer and Ladina Cadiff, "In Whose Interest? Pressure Group Politics, Economic Competition and Environmental Regulation," *Journal of Public Policy* 24, no. 1 (January–April 2004): 96–226.

[4]For an empirical test of this example of the California effect, see Richard Perkins and Eric Neumayer, "Does the 'California effect' Operate across Borders? Trading and Investing-up in Automobile Emission Standards," unpublished paper (June 2010).

played important roles in promoting *both* increased global policy convergence *and* stronger national and international risk regulations.

Moreover, the fact that both the United States and the EU have adopted a wide range of risk-averse and comprehensive consumer and environmental regulations—many of which were or are the world's most stringent—suggests that powerful political and economic states, or in the case of the EU, a group of states, enjoy substantial discretion in responding to domestic pressures for more stringent consumer and environmental regulations. At least for the United States between 1960 and 1990 and the EU since about 1990, the pressures of global competition have not prevented them from imposing significant burdens on domestic firms in order to improve health, safety, and environmental quality.

The decisions of a number of American states to adopt risk regulations more stringent than those of the federal government as well as those of many other states, also suggests that sub-national governments are also not necessarily engaged in a regulatory "race to the bottom" or "stuck at the bottom." On the contrary, this book has documented an important interstate "California effect": several American states have chosen to adopt regulatory standards similar to those of California. Likewise, in Europe, some member states have enacted more stringent and economically burdensome risk regulations than other member states. Accordingly, even within the highly integrated American and European "single markets," some "local" governments evidently are both willing and able to strengthen their consumer and environmental risk regulations.

The Dynamics of Regulatory Divergence

But while the patterns of transatlantic policymaking through 1990 do roughly conform to the theories of both policy convergence and trading up, this is not the case after 1990. The extent of economic integration and interdependence between the EU and the United States has continued to increase. Because of the creation of a single market within the EU and the subsequent expansion of the EU to Central and Eastern Europe, the size of the EU's internal market is now considerably larger than that of the United States. Moreover, both sides of the Atlantic arguably continue to face many similar health, safety, and environmental risks, and there is extensive transatlantic communication among policy makers, business firms, scientists, and political activists. Equally important, their economies have become increasingly integrated through both trade and investment. One or more of these factors should have led American regulatory policies to become *more* similar to those of the EU.

But regulatory convergence, diffusion, and emulation have primarily crossed the Atlantic in only one direction: from the United States to

Europe. Since 1990, the federal government has adopted few of the EU's more stringent and comprehensive risk regulations. Nor has it agreed to be bound by several of the international environmental treaties initiated or backed by the EU. Thus, contrary to the predictions of theories of both global policy convergence and trading up, since around 1990 transatlantic policy divergence has *increased* for many important health, safety, and environmental risk regulations. The dominant pattern of American regulatory policies since around 1990 reveals important limitations of the impact of increased global regulatory interdependence in promoting regulatory convergence. We need to add another important variable to explain when regulatory coordination or cooperation occurs.[5] To understand the sources of increased transatlantic policy *divergence* since around 1990, we need to turn to the role of domestic economics and politics.

The Role of Business Preferences

One important reason why the United States has adopted very few European risk regulations has to do with the preferences of American-based firms. Clearly, American firms with substantial investments in or which export to Europe have been affected by the strengthening of European risk regulations; they have often been forced to change what products they produce or how they produce them in order to retain access to the EU's large internal market. According to the logic of the "California effect," which views the role of global markets as regulatory "transmission belts," these firms should then support federal regulations that would bring American requirements into closer coordination with European ones, especially as many European regulations have been adopted by other countries with whom the United States trades extensively or where American firms have substantial investments. But they have not. Why?

In the case of European agricultural production policies for growth hormones for cattle and cows, genetically modified (GM) varieties, and antibiotics in animal feed, the costs of bringing American business practices in line with European ones are too substantial.[6] Each of these pro-

---

[5]For an analysis of the different strategies governments may pursue in response to "regulatory turbulence," i.e., the adoption of more stringent standards by an important trading partner, see Noah Sachs, "Jumping the Pond: Transnational Law and the Future of Chemical Regulation," *Vanderbilt Law Review* 62, no. 6 (November 2009): 1817–69. See

[6]For a description and explanation of patterns of policy convergence and divergence between the EU and the United States that parallels my analysis, see Sebastiaan Princen, "Trading Up in the Transatlantic Relationship," *Journal of Public Policy* 24.1 (2004): 127–44. Princen specifically contrasts the differing responses of the United States to the EU's data protection directive and its ban on hormone-treated beef. He explains why trading up

duction methods has become critical to the way food is produced in the United States; the benefits of bringing them into closer alignment with those of the EU in order to lower the costs of transatlantic commerce have been outweighed by the considerable costs of doing so. Accordingly, American agricultural producers have adopted two strategies in response to more stringent European agricultural processing regulations.

First, in the cases of the EU's restrictions on growth hormones for cattle and the introduction of genetically modified varieties, each of which have restricted or eliminated American agricultural exports to Europe, they successfully pressured the United States to challenge Europe's more stringent regulations as illegal non-tariff trade barriers under the rules of the World Trade Organization. They have attempted to use international trade law to bring about greater policy convergence by pressuring the EU to adopt regulations similar to those of the United States—essentially pursuing a strategy of "negative harmonization."[7]

Second, American agricultural producers have changed some of their production practices in order to retain access to European and other markets. For example, they have produced hormone-free beef for export to Europe, planted GM varieties that have been approved for use in Europe and, in the case of wheat, they have not planted GM seeds. However, these represent relatively modest adjustments; many agricultural products produced in the United States cannot be exported to the EU, or to other countries that have adopted similar regulations.

The EU's restrictions on greenhouse gas emissions are primarily production rather than product regulations. Accordingly, they do not adversely affect American exports to the EU and thus American-based firms face no incentives to have the United States adopt the Kyoto Protocol. Moreover, because the Protocol raises the costs of doing business in Europe, it actually advantages producers in the United States. Even though American firms in Europe are forced to comply with different regulations than they face in their home market, there is no reason for them to support the domestic adoption of more costly European standards.

In the case of REACH, American chemical firms responded to the European Commission's regulatory proposal by waging a vigorous, though largely unsuccessful, effort to derail it. Because the divergence of American and European chemical regulations is now substantial, REACH clearly

---

occurred in the former case but not the latter due to the greater costs of policy adjustment by the United States. But his analysis can also be extended to other cases of transatlantic policy divergence. For a similar analysis of the importance of adjustment costs, see Daniel Drezner, *All Politics Is Global: Explaining International Regulatory Regimes* (Princeton, NJ: Princeton University Press, 2007): 45–51.

[7] David Wirth, "The EU's New Impact on U.S. Environmental Regulation," *Fletcher Foreign World Affairs* (Summer 2007): 95.

imposes additional burdens on American-based corporations. But in contrast to the EU's adoption of the Sixth Amendment, which brought European regulations into closer alignment with 1976 Toxic Substances Control Act (TSCA) in order to facilitate transatlantic trade in chemicals, the American chemical industry has not backed a new American chemical regulation modeled on REACH. The explanation for the differences in these responses to stronger chemical regulations on the other side of the Atlantic is straightforward: the costs of bringing American chemical regulations into alignment with REACH are much more substantial than European firms faced in bringing their chemical regulations into closer alignment with TSCA. It thus makes economic sense for American chemical firms to comply with REACH for their production in or exports to Europe, but to continue to produce and market chemicals that comply with TSCA in the United States.

To the extent that many global electronic and cosmetics companies based in the United States have chosen to comply with European regulations for many of their products sold in the United States as well as globally, these firms might well have an incentive to support similar federal regulations—especially as these might then disadvantage their domestically oriented competitors. But their compliance with European standards has been selective rather than comprehensive. Thus, the lack of comparable American federal standards for hazardous substances in electrical and electronic products and various chemicals in cosmetics, such as phthalates, provides these firms with a degree of flexibility they would lack if the United States adopted restrictions similar to those of the EU. It has enabled them to selectively and gradually reformulate their global products, which means that in some cases the products they sell in the United States continue to differ from those they sell in Europe and in some other countries.

In sum, an important reason why American-based firms have not supported federal regulations that would "trade up" to or converge onto European ones is that it has not been in their interests to do so: the benefits of policy convergence have been outweighed by its costs. This suggests that the adjustment costs of having a country's domestic regulations converge on the stricter standards of a major trading partner are a critical factor in explaining when policy convergence and/or trading up is or is not likely to occur. It also helps explain why the Transatlantic Economic Council, which was established to lower the considerable costs to transatlantic commerce of divergent European and American regulations, has had such limited success in improving regulatory cooperation for several of the health, safety, and environmental risk regulations described in this book. The EU is unwilling to weaken risk regulations which enjoy substantial public or political support in response to pressures from the

United States, while American producers do not have sufficient financial incentives to support changes in American regulations to bring them into closer alignment with those of the EU.

The Broader Political Context

But this is only part of the explanation for the divergence in the risk regulations adopted by the United States and the EU. For business preferences do not automatically translate into public policy. As many of the case studies of more stringent European regulations discussed in this study reveal, many European regulations were strongly opposed by business firms and business associations on both sides of the Atlantic, yet they were still enacted. Accordingly, we need to not only understand American business preferences, but to explain why they have been so influential.

Each of the factors I have identified to explain why the U.S. federal government has adopted fewer more stringent risk regulations since 1990 has served to strengthen the political influence of business firms opposed to more stringent consumer and environmental risk regulations. First, the degree of public support for more stringent protective regulations has declined, thus reducing the pressure on policy makers to challenge business interests by enacting them. Second, the national electoral strength of Republicans, along with increased partisan polarization, has made it much more difficult for regulatory policies to be adopted when important segments of business are opposed, especially through legislation. Third, the increased scrutiny of the scientific basis and cost-effectiveness of proposed regulatory agency rules by the courts, Congress, and the Executive Office of the President has often constrained the ability of regulatory agencies to adopt more stringent risk regulations. These three developments have not only strengthened the political influence of business, but some business firms and associations have also played a role in promoting them.

The political context in Europe has been different. During the 1980s, European consumer and environmental activists strongly and effectively pressured the EU member states and the EU to adopt several risk regulations similar to those of the United States. In the case of automotive emissions standards, the interests of European environmentalists and German car exporters to the United States converged; both supported strengthening European standards to bring them into closer alignment with American ones. Accordingly, American consumer and environmental organizations could have played a similar role after around 1990. In fact, many such organizations have lobbied for the enactment of risk regulations similar to those adopted in Europe. For example, they have supported American ratification of the Kyoto Protocol, restrictions on the use of antibiotics in animal feed, the labeling of genetically modified ingredients, and the adoption of chemical safety regulations modeled on REACH.

But, in marked contrast to the increased ability of European activists to help strengthen European risk regulations, since the early 1990s the political impact of American consumer and environmental lobbies on federal regulatory policies has declined. They have become less effective in mobilizing public opinion to challenge business political preferences. Americans and Europeans may well face similar health, safety, and environmental risks, but the public perception and political salience of many of these risks has differed across the Atlantic, as has the willingness of policy makers to respond to them. In sharp contrast to the EU since 1990 and the United States before 1990, the federal government has adopted relatively few risk regulations that have been strongly opposed by or would disadvantage important elements of the business community. In this area of public policy, as in some other areas, the political position of business in the United States has been both strong and relatively stable since around 1990.[8]

In sum, business preferences are not by themselves sufficient to explain why few federal regulations have "traded up" to match those of the EU and why many European and American regulations remain divergent. The relative political weakness of pro-regulation political constituencies at the national level has also been critical. Had the latter been stronger, segments of the business community, especially those firms that have changed their practices to maintain access to the EU or that have voluntarily adopted European standards in response to domestic consumer or political pressures, might well have entered into alliances with consumer and environmental organizations to support public policies that brought American regulations into closer alignment with European ones. But "Baptist–bootlegger " alliances require, at a minimum, politically influential Baptists. However, the former, namely environmental and consumer lobbies, have not been sufficiently powerful at the federal level to make it in the interests of "bootleggers," namely business firms, to enter into alliances with them.

[8] For changes in the relative power of business and public interest lobbies in the United States between 1960 and the late 1980s, see David Vogel, *Fluctuating Fortunes: The Political Power of Business in America* (New York: Basic Books, 1989). For an extensive discussion of the role of business in affecting environmental policy, which however does not explore changes in its political influence over time, see Michael Kraft and Sheldon Kamieniecki, eds., *Business and Environmental Policy: Corporate Interests in the American Political System* (Cambridge, MA: MIT Press, 2007). For a broader analysis of the increased influence of business in Washington, which they date from the late 1970s, see Jacob Hacker and Paul Pierson, *Winner-Take-All Politics* (New York: Simon & Schuster, 2010).

A similar logic holds for the lack of support of American firms for new international environmental treaties. As Elizabeth DeSombre writes,

> The regulations that the U.S. decides to push forward internationally are those for which there is a coalition of environmentalists and industry actors . . . who benefit from increasing the number of actors bound by the regulations. . . . For industry actors, internationalization avoids a situation in which they suffer a competitive disadvantage relative to their foreign competitors who do not otherwise have to bear a costly environmental regulation.[9]

But since the early 1990s, thanks to the political weakness of American "Baptists," the United States has approved few environmental regulations that are stricter than those of its trading partners. This in turn has weakened the incentive for firms to support international treaties that would also bind their competitors, including those in Europe. Hence the lack of American business support for American ratification of the Kyoto Protocol, the Basel Convention on hazardous waste exports, and the Convention on Biodiversity, each of which would impose more stringent standards than does American domestic law.

Other Forms of Trading Up

At the same time, however, as this book has repeatedly shown, European regulatory policies *have* affected American public policies. But they have done so primarily at the state rather than the federal level. The role of many state governments in "importing" a wide range of European risk regulations to the United States is an important development. It means that, at least for the United States, we need to broaden our understanding of the dynamics of both international regulatory convergence and "trading up."

Historically, American states have typically been regulatory laggards, rarely strengthening their health, safety, or environmental standards in the absence of federal requirements that they do so.[10] This explains why, during the 1960s and 1970s, the environmental and consumer movements placed a high priority on shifting the locus of regulatory policymaking from the states to Washington. But more recently, the failure of the federal government to strengthen a wide range of risk regulations has created a policy vacuum which many American states have attempted to fill. The fact that since around 1990 many states have adopted *more*

---

[9]Elizabeth DeSombre, *Domestic Sources of International Environmental Policy: Industry, Environmentalists, and U.S. Power* (Cambridge, MA: MIT Press, 2000): 245.

[10]See, for example, Peter Swire, "The Race to Laxity and the Race to Undesirability: Explaining Failures in Competition Among Jurisdictions in Environmental Law," *Yale Law & Policy Review* 14 (1996): 67–110.

stringent risk regulations than the federal government represents an important reversal of an historical trend and requires us to rethink our understanding of the policy impact of American regulatory federalism.[11]

Transatlantic regulatory convergence has also taken place in the United States through market mechanisms. As this study has repeatedly shown, many of the same firms that have opposed the enactment of more stringent regulations on both sides of the Atlantic have voluntarily complied with European standards for many of their products sold in the United States. While much of the literature on global corporate social responsibility has focused on the role of global firms in "exporting" Western standards to developing countries, this book reveals that the private diffusion of more stringent standards can also take place among firms in *developed* economies.

Many global firms, as well as some domestic agricultural producers, have chosen to produce or sell products in the United States that conform to or approximate European regulatory standards. They have thus adopted many policies and practices that are more stringent than those required by most states as well as the federal government. Public pressures, as well as the economic interests of global firms in producing many of their products according to similar standards, have brought a de facto convergence between some important European risk regulations and some American business practices.

Finally, it is possible that the strengthening of many risk regulations by American states, product labels which allow American consumers to purchase food products, often at a price premium, produced according to more stringent European regulatory standards, and the commitments of many global brands, such as cosmetics and electronics firms, to comply with some or all European product safety and environmental requirements, may have played a role in weakening or diffusing public pressures for the adoption of more stringent risk regulations by the federal government. In any event, any analysis of the transatlantic dynamics of "trading up" and the global diffusion of regulatory standards must also incorporate the policies of state governments and practices of business firms.

INSTITUTIONS AND POLICY STYLES

An important finding of this study is that in important ways the EU and the United States have, since 1990, "traded places" with respect to

---

[11] For such an important analysis of this development in one critical area of environmental regulation, see Barry Rabe, ed., *Greenhouse Governance: Addressing Climate Change in America* (Washington, DC: Brookings Institution Press, 2010).

regulatory styles. This means that the contrasts between American and European styles of consumer and environmental regulation described in many academic studies written during the 1980s no longer hold. Many of the features that formerly characterized the "American" style of risk regulation, namely its adversarial relationship with business, multiple venues for affecting public policy, substantial opportunities for participation by non-business constituencies, and responsiveness to risk-averse public pressures, have become *more* characteristic of how consumer and environmental regulation is made in the EU and *less* characteristic of how it is made in the United States.

In an essay published in 1990 entitled "American Exceptionalism and the Political Economy of Risk," Sheila Jasanoff writes that "the U.S. process for making risk decisions impressed all observers as costly, confrontational, litigious, formal and unusually open to participation," while in Europe, "policy decisions about risk, remained, as before, the preserve of experienced bureaucrats and their established advisory networks."[12] Her depiction of the contrasts between the making of risk regulations in Europe and the United States is echoed in other comparative studies of consumer and environmental regulation in Europe and the United States published during the 1980s, including my own.[13]

But since around 1990, rather than continuing to be made by "experienced bureaucrats and their established policy networks," risk regulations in Europe have become more "costly, confrontational, formal" and "unusually open to participation." Stephen Breyer's "vicious circle," a term he coined to describe how the "alarm bells" rung by activists often pressured American policy makers to adopt highly stringent risk regulations, more accurately characterizes the way many European risk regulations have recently been made than it does the American regulatory policy process after 1990.[14] What John Dwyer characterized as "the pathology of symbolic legislation," namely the legislative enactment of highly ambitious and often impracticable policy goals in response to strong public fears about "particularly dreaded health threats," better describes many of the regulations and directives approved by the

---

[12] Sheila Jasanoff, "American Exceptionalism and the Political Acknowledgement of Risk," in *Risk*, ed. Edward Burger (Ann Arbor: University of Michigan Press, 1993), 63, 66.

[13] See, for example, David Vogel, *National Styles of Regulation: Environmental Policy in Great Britain and the United States* (Ithaca, NY: Cornell University Press 1986); Ronald Brickman, Sheila Jasanoff, and Thomas Ilgen, *Chemical Regulation and Cancer: A Cross-National Study of Policy and Politics* (Ithaca, NY: Cornell University, Program on Science, Technology and Society, 1982); Lennart Lundqvist, *The Hare and the Tortoise: Clean Air Policies in the United States and Sweden* (Ann Arbor: University of Michigan Press, 1980).

[14] Stephen Breyer, *Breaking the Vicious Circle: Toward Effective Risk Regulations* (Cambridge, MA: Harvard University Press, 1993).

EU since around 1990 than it does the pattern of recent federal risk legislation.[15]

These developments suggest that the American "style" of making consumer and environmental regulation was not as deeply rooted in American political institutions or American political culture as many scholars had assumed. Rather, it turns out to have been historically contingent: it emerged during a particular period of American political development as a response to a distinctive set of factors—many of which have since changed. By the same token, the new institutions of the EU have created a regulatory policy style that differs in many important ways from the approach to regulatory policymaking that was deeply rooted in the political institutions of many of the European countries that now belong to the EU. It is more legalistic, transparent, and contentious, less corporatist and more pluralist, provides multiple points of access to the policy process by non-government organizations and, notwithstanding all that has been written about the EU's democratic deficit, has often provided more opportunities than many national governments for non-business constituencies to participate in the policy process.[16]

The typical regulatory "policy style" of the United States after about 1990 reveals that the development of the new institutional and legal regime for making consumer and environmental regulations at the federal level which emerged during the early 1970s was a necessary but *not* a sufficient condition for the "American adversarial style" of risk regulation.[17] Those institutional features persist: regulatory policy is still made in multiple, overlapping, and potentially conflicting venues. American citizens can participate in the rule-making procedures of administrative agencies, challenge regulatory rule-making in the federal courts, and participate in congressional reviews of agency policies as well as in the legislative process. But the way federal regulatory policy is actually made has changed significantly; since around 1990, *these same institutions and policy procedures have produced very different policy outcomes.*

---

[15] John Dwyer, "The Pathology of Symbolic Legislation," *Ecological Law Quarterly* 17 (1990): 233; see also John Mendeloff, "Does Overregulation Cause Underregulation?" *Regulation* (September/October 1981): 47–62.

[16] For a detailed description of changes in European law prompted by the growing regulatory authority of the EU which complements my analysis, see R. Dan Kelemen, *Eurolegalism: The Rise of Adversarial Legalism in the EU* (Cambridge, MA: Harvard University Press, 2011).

[17] For an analysis of the still important differences in legal systems in the United States and Europe which extends beyond the policy areas explored in this book, see Robert Kagan, "Globalization and Legal Change: The 'Americanization' of European Law," *Regulation & Governance* (2007): 99–120. See also Robert Kagan, *Adversarial Legalism: The American Way of Law* (Cambridge, MA: Harvard University Press, 2001).

Paradoxically, the formal structures of policymaking in the United States and the EU have become *more* similar: the governance of the EU, most notably its quasi-federal structure, its bicameral legislature (the Council of Ministers and the European Parliament), extensive judicial review (the European Court of Justice), and its separation of powers and checks and balances among the Commission, the Council, and the European Parliament, and the European Court of Justice more closely resembles the United States than it does any European country.[18] But the regulatory policies produced by these more similar structures have significantly diverged.

This analysis also has an important implication for our understanding of regulatory politics and policies in the EU. For it reveals that while the institutions of the EU may represent a necessary condition for the emergence of a new European style of risk regulation, they are *not* a sufficient condition. For, just as occurred in the United States, the way the EU goes about making risk regulations could also change, if, for example, consumer and environmental pressure groups were to become much less influential or a powerful group of member states changed their regulatory policy preferences. In which case the EU's governance structure that has emerged since the late 1980s would persist, but its approach to making risk regulations would not.

THE HISTORICAL CONTEXT OF RISK PERCEPTIONS

A consistent finding of studies of health, safety, and consumer and environmental risks is that there is typically little or no relationship between the public's risk perceptions and those of "experts." For example, citizens are more likely to worry about risks that are unfamiliar, involuntary, that disproportionately affect children, affect future generations, are man-made, poorly understood, and whose harms are catastrophic.[19] This means that in some cases the public worries excessively about some risks and in other cases worries too little about others.

These insights, however, are of limited use in explaining why citizens on both sides of the Atlantic have worried about identical risks differently. Thus they cannot explain, for example, why during the 1970s, Americans worried more about the risks of Alar, lead in petrol/gasoline, and ozone

[18] For a comparative analysis of the constitutional governance of the EU with that of the United States, see *Comparative Federalism: The European Union and the United States in Comparative Perspective*, ed. Anard Menon and Martin Schain (Oxford: Oxford University Press, 2006).

[19] Howard Margolis, *Dealing with Risk: Why the Public and the Experts Disagree on Environmental Issues* (Chicago: University of Chicago Press 1966), 28.

depletion than did Europeans. Nor do they explain why Europeans subsequently worried more about the risks of genetically modified varieties, global climate change, and chemical safety than many Americans. These insights fail to account for the fact that following the thalidomide disaster, the risks posed by the approval of unsafe pharmaceuticals became much more politically influential in the United States than in Europe—even though many more Europeans were adversely affected by this drug.

However, this book does support the broader claim made in many studies of risk management that there is no necessary relationship between the public's risk perceptions and the actual risks they face.[20] Consider, for example, the dramatic changes in the American public's concern about environmental quality, both in the United States and globally, between the mid-1980s and the mid-1990s. During the second half of the 1980s and continuing through around 1990, the level and intensity of public concern about environmental threats and risks increased substantially. Then, beginning in the early 1990s, it suddenly declined.

Yet it would be hard to identify any objective measure, let alone measures, of either domestic or global environmental quality that showed a marked deterioration during the second half of the 1980s and an equally significant improvement beginning in the early 1990s. Nonetheless, both sets of perceptions had important policy impacts: the former contributed to the last wave of legislative environmental expansion, while the latter has played a role in reducing public pressures for more environmental regulation.

In Europe, the BSE, or mad cow, crisis and other food safety policy failures had a far-reaching and long-term impact on the European public's risk perceptions. They not only helped make many Europeans more risk-averse toward genetically modified agricultural varieties, but they also increased public concern about the health, safety, and environmental risks of chemicals—even though the latter two risks were unrelated to food safety. Europe's food safety crisis thus had a broad and sustained impact over multiple policy domains.

These observations point to the importance of an additional factor that affects the public's risk perceptions—one whose importance underlies a central thesis of this book. This is the critical role played by timing, or *when* a particular risk emerges. The public typically does not view risks in isolation; rather, it links them to other risks about which it has heard, its broader appraisal of health, safety, and environmental conditions, and its assessment of how well the government can be trusted to protect them. *When a particular risk emerges matters: identical or similar risks may be perceived differently depending on the broader political context.*

---

[20] See Paul Slovic, ed., *The Feeling of Risk: New Perspectives on Risk Perception* (London: Earthscan, 2010).

A focus on the historical contingency of public risk perceptions raises a number of intriguing counterfactuals. For example, suppose that the risks of citizens dying from BSE in Europe and the United States were reversed. Would Americans then have become more opposed to and Europeans less worried about the introduction of genetically modified varieties? Or what if the risks of genetically modified organisms had become highly salient in the United States during the early 1970s or the second half of the 1980s rather than after 2000? Might this have affected the American public's perceptions of the risks and benefits of this new agricultural technology?

What if the risks of hazardous substances in electronic and electrical waste had emerged in the United States during the mid- and late 1970s, when the health hazards posed by chemicals and toxic waste dumps were highly politically salient? Might the public then have pressured for regulations similar to those subsequently adopted by the EU? What if the thalidomide disaster had emerged in Europe during the 1990s? Might it then have affected public attitudes toward the EU's harmonization of its drug approval policies? These questions emphasize the historical context of the public's risk perceptions—and the policies that flow from them.

THE FUTURE OF RISK REGULATION

What are the implications of my analysis for the future of consumer and environmental risk regulation in the United States and the EU? A key finding of this book is that past patterns of regulatory policymaking do not predict future ones. If this study had been written around 1990, it is highly unlikely that its author would have predicted that the politics of risk regulation in *both* the United States and Europe would subsequently change so significantly. On the contrary, such a scholar would have had every reason to assume broad policy continuity on both sides of the Atlantic. Thus, he or she presumably would have predicted that the United States would continue to adopt a broad array of highly risk-averse and at times precautionary regulations in response to periodic public pressures and that these regulations would be supported by Democrats as well as by some Republicans. Likewise, the stringency of European risk regulations would have remained weaker than those of the United States because of the lack of strong public support for highly risk-averse regulations and the inability of the member states to reach agreement about whether or how much health, safety, and environmental regulations should be strengthened. But, in fact, a significant policy discontinuity *did* take place on both sides of the Atlantic—one that has now persisted for more than two decades.

What would it take for another important policy discontinuity to take place? I have identified three broad and often interrelated factors that affect the likelihood that a political regime will or will not choose to adopt a broad array of relatively stringent risk regulations. They are the intensity of public pressures for more risk-averse regulations, the political preferences of influential policy makers, and the policy criteria used to assess and manage risks. Accordingly, each would have to change on either or both sides of the Atlantic.

In the case of the United States, "alarm bells" would need to ring more loudly and be listened to by more people, regulatory officials would need to be both able and willing to make more risk management decisions on precautionary grounds, and influential national policy makers would need to become more supportive of more stringent risk regulations. The latter would require increased bipartisan support for expanding the scope and strengthening the stringency of risk regulations. In the case of the EU, public support for more risk-averse or precautionary regulations would need to weaken, impact assessments would need to subject risk regulations to more rigorous scientific and economic scrutiny—and these assessments would become subject to careful judicial review—and the support for more stringent regulations by the Commission, influential member states, and the European Parliament would need to decline. The latter might well be associated with a sharper division in the regulatory policy preferences of the EU's member states, similar to those that prevailed in Europe before around 1990—perhaps triggered either by a broader political and ideological backlash against more stringent risk regulations such as occurred in the United States.

The absence of any or all of these changes does not, of course, preclude the adoption of *some* more stringent regulations by the United States or their non-adoption by the EU or additional examples of policy convergence. My causal factors explain and predict broad trends in public policies toward health, safety, and environmental risks caused by business, but they do not preclude some deviations from it—as have occurred in both the United States and Europe during the last five decades. Even if the rate at which the EU enacts more stringent regulations declines—as periodically took place in the United States between 1960 and 1990—to the extent that new regulations adopted by the EU diverge from those of the United States, my analysis predicts that the former are likely to be more stringent than the latter. In sum, barring a significant change in the factors that have shaped the relative stringency of risk regulations on both sides of the Atlantic since around 1990, the transatlantic divergence in the stringency of risk regulations that I have described in this book is likely to persist.

Index